# DIGITAL IDENTITIES

# DIGITAL IDENTITIES
## Creating and Communicating the Online Self

**ROB COVER**
School of Social Sciences
The University of Western Australia
Crawley, WA, Australia

ELSEVIER

Amsterdam • Boston • Heidelberg • London
New York • Oxford • Paris • San Diego
San Francisco • Singapore • Sydney • Tokyo
Academic Press is an imprint of Elsevier

Academic Press is an imprint of Elsevier
125, London Wall, EC2Y 5AS, UK
525 B Street, Suite 1800, San Diego, CA 92101-4495, USA
225 Wyman Street, Waltham, MA 02451, USA
The Boulevard, Langford Lane, Kidlington, Oxford OX5 1GB, UK

**Notices**
Knowledge and best practice in this field are constantly changing. As new research and experience
broaden our understanding, changes in research methods, professional practices, or medical treatment
may become necessary.

Practitioners and researchers must always rely on their own experience and knowledge in evaluating
and using any information, methods, compounds, or experiments described herein. In using such
information or methods they should be mindful of their own safety and the safety of others, including
parties for whom they have a professional responsibility.

To the fullest extent of the law, neither the Publisher nor the authors, contributors, or editors, assume
any liability for any injury and/or damage to persons or property as a matter of products liability,
negligence or otherwise, or from any use or operation of any methods, products, instructions, or ideas
contained in the material herein.

**British Library Cataloguing-in-Publication Data**
A catalogue record for this book is available from the British Library

**Library of Congress Cataloging-in-Publication Data**
A catalog record for this book is available from the Library of Congress

ISBN: 978-0-12-420083-8

For information on all Academic Press publications
visit our website at http://store.elsevier.com/

Publisher: Nikki Levy
Acquisition Editor: Emily Ekle
Editorial Project Manager: Timothy Bennett
Production Project Manager: Chris Wortley
Designer: Mark Rogers

Typeset by Thomson Digital

Printed and bound in the United States of America

Working together
to grow libraries in
developing countries

www.elsevier.com • www.bookaid.org

# CONTENTS

# ACKNOWLEDGMENTS

Parts of Chapter 1 were previously published in an earlier version in "Performing and undoing identity online: social networking, identity theories, and the incompatibility of online profiles and friendship regimes, *Convergence*, *18*(2), 177–193, 2012." Parts of Chapter 3 were previously published in an earlier version in "Audience inter/active: interactive media, narrative control & reconceiving audience history, *New Media & Society*, *8*(1), 213–232, 2006."

The author would like to extend his appreciation to Emily Ekle at Elsevier for suggesting this book and encouraging its development, to Timothy Bennett and Chris Wortley for managing its production, and particularly to Dr. Kyra Clarke at The University of Western Australia for her superb editorial support. Thank you also to Professor Anjali Gera Roy and the staff and students of the Indian Institute of Technology, Kharagpur, for providing a productive environment for work on this book.

*Digital Identities* is dedicated to my many undergraduate, honors, and PhD students at The University of Western Australia with whom I have had the great benefit of fruitful exchanges and shared ideas on how we live, who we are and who we might be in terms of digital belonging.

# INTRODUCTION: UBIQUITOUS DIGITAL NETWORKS, IDENTITY, AND THE SELF

## 1 UBIQUITOUS DIGITALITY: BEYOND THE REAL/VIRTUAL DISTINCTION

In the everyday experience of the affluent West, the tools and technologies of digital communication surround us to the extent that they are no longer noticeable, remarkable, or distinct from other forms of communication, such as face-to-face or traditional analog and print media. In some respects, the tools of digital connectivity literally encircle us as we move through space across day and night: from the desktop computer to the laptop, the tablet to the smartphone, the connected fitness device or smartwatch to the radio frequency identification device (RFID) trackable card, the networked car to the online fridge, the wifi access points in the office to the use of high-quality mobile and cellular data connectivity in the street, we are surrounded, connected, always online, and making use of these connective devices as part of all our many everyday interactions, engagements, desires, and routines. This fact is what makes them banal and mundane (Baumann, 2003, p. 65), which is not to say that they are uninteresting or unexciting, but that this digital connectivity is as commonplace today as the likelihood of finding a television in the family home, or running hot water in the everyday apartment. They have slipped so much into everyday experiences that they are only noticeable and remarkable on the rare occasions they fail, in much the same way as we might become aware of our hot-water systems on the morning in which a rare breakdown of the service results in us having to take a cold shower. Indeed, today digital connectivity is so commonplace that we might already have been alerted to a failure of hot water through an online alert or a warning email long before we begin to try the taps in the bathroom.

This digital "Internet of everything" that, in its everyday familiarity and sense of naturalness as a dominant form of communication, disappears into the background of our everyday space has substantial implications for how we create, conduct, articulate, and perform our identities in everyday life. The fact that digital communication is no longer that which we do at one moment or in one space or with one device that we then put aside to have a conversation with another person in a face-to-face context has an enormous impact on how we do our relationships, subjectivities, and produce ourselves. We do not put those devices aside and, even when we do, our conversations, relationships, and our everyday "being" are still strongly in-fluenced by the communications and media access we experience.

We talk of identities being "online" and that very idea has shifted con-siderably over the past few years. In the 1990s and 2000s, it was possible to think about identity as something one did, performed, engaged with, or represented differently online from offline, as if an online identity was somewhat fake, virtual, unreal and then we had our real, embodied selves. Today, however, identity is always online. We are, in some ways, always per-forming ourselves online because even when we are nowhere near a digital communication device (which is now extremely rare), we leave traces all over the Internet, social-networking pages, blogs, Twitter, and other sites that are actively contributing to elements of our identity. If I wish to get to know you, I may look up your social-networking profiles, whether they are professional or personal. And I am not necessarily getting a sense of "who you are" surreptitiously, secretly, privately, but may well be sharing that experience with you, in front of you, together. In that context, we are always online, and our identities are "always on." Identity and its online rep-resentation is therefore not something we switch off, move away from, or otherwise demarcate from the everyday practices of selfhood.

I would like to use this introduction to walk through some of the key concepts related to identity in a digital era, particularly using the example of the selfie image to help make sense of some of the implications for sub-jectivity and selfhood an interactive, networked, technological environment has for us and our futures. One very important fact about identity in a digital environment that needs to be addressed is the move from a practice in which subjects make use of online communication separate from other aspects of their life to one in which digital media infiltrate and network with all aspects of our everyday. While there are many on the planet who do not have this kind of access to digital technology, I am interested here in the implications for those in the affluent West, the urban worlds of constant connectivity, and the environments in which mobility and technological access to the Internet occurs while on the move. This shift to ubiquitous digitality is the central idea discussed in this book, and I work through it from a number of different angles.

## 2 IDENTITY AND PERFORMATIVITY

Identity or subjectivity are, in basic terms, ways of conceptualizing the self in the context of representations, self-representation, demarcations of iden-tity categories, linkages between self and behavioral attributes, and ways of approaching and understanding "being" in our everyday lives. There are many different ways of understanding and theorizing identity, and there is a very rich, complex history of philosophies and approaches relating to some of the key questions addressed in cultural and artistic expressions of the past and present: Who am I? Who are we? I use the term identity in this book to refer primarily to the self-perception of being, which also is known as subjectivity and selfhood. Identity is comprised of identifications with particular categories or demarcations that are given in language, media, and culture – I often refer to these as the "coordinates" of identity that, along with memory and experience, come to make up the contemporary subject. Such coordinates might include the common denotations of identity categories such as gender, race, ethnicity, class demarcations, and sexuality, alongside nationality, citizenship, schooling background, socioeconomic status, educational experience, and career, all of which to varying degrees in varying contexts add to the personal and individual experience to make up the figure of the *I,* the subject, the self. Subjects are invited to identify both actively and passively with categories and frameworks of identity and selfhood and, today, those categories are given in media and digital media, and played out through our practices in relation to communication and digital participation.

In very pedestrian ways, there is a tendency to speak of identity in what is sometimes referred to as "essentialist" terms – the idea that our identities (or major facets of them) emerge from the inside, and are fixed over time, innate. Genetic theories of identity that attribute, say, criminal behavior to the identity category "criminal" and see it as caused by one's genetic heritage (Pilnick, 2002, pp. 38, 39) is an example; likewise many contemporary perceptions of nonheterosexual identity through very simplistic "born that way" notions are examples of essentialism. Some psychological approaches to identity assume that our sense of self and our subjectivities emerge through a "nurtured" way of being that is formed in early childhood by relationships with parents that have had an impact on our psyches. Although these approaches continue to be dominant in much public discourse, such theories are, since the twentieth century, in contrast to what are sometimes referred to as "constructionist" approaches which, broadly speaking, understand identity as formed through cultural and social forces that change over time and are produced in the unfolding of history. For example, some racial identities (and the very concepts of race) change over time, such that in past eras, particular racialized groups were considered "more human" than others. Likewise, the idea of an intersex identity that differs from cisgendered masculine/feminine norms is only possible in the current cultural and historical frameworks that make possible a more nuanced approach to gender. From a constructionist perspective, it is important therefore to think about the role of media and digital communication as a contemporary, historically derived, and culturally significant formation that governs how our identities are constituted and formed, and the very meanings of identity, subjectivity, and selfhood today. For example, in a constructionist framework, we need to take account of the fact that our contemporary culture of communication is increasingly dominated by visual representation and the flow and exchange of high-quality visual images (Giroux, 2004, p. 789), circulating not through text, which increasingly becomes a communication form for the cultural elite, but through mass-mediated communication such as television, film, music, online engagement, and music video (Lessig, 2008, p. 68). In that sense, how we produce and figure our identities, the information we encounter that helps construct and constitute our identities, and the norms, categories, and elements of culture with which we identify are more readily circulated to us through image than through written text. This, of course, is broadly unproblematic and not a judgment or a denouncement of the visual culture in which we live – merely an observation that some of the frameworks that govern how we do identities in contemporary society have changed and, in a constructionist perspective, how we as a culture and as a people change along with them. Important here is that identity is best conceived of as a project in which we are actively engaged, a process of moving toward some sense of identity with no necessary arrival at some fixed sense of selfhood (Barker, 1999, p. 3). In that context, the trajectory of identity is one which is both helped along and disrupted by the ever-changing presence of identity information in both traditional and digital media and communication.

Historian, philosopher, and theorist of subjectivity, power, thought, idea, and knowledge, Michel Foucault, noted that identity, subjectivity, or the self is not a substance or thing, but a form (Foucault, 1988, p. 10), constituted in the discourses or languages that represent and make available the ideas around selfhood. Foucault's work powerfully overturned the idea of the liberal subject as being free, self-contained, and rational. The early liberal subject of modernity was presupposed in liberal discourses, then, as that of a self-governing, natural person, able to make rational choices, act upon them, and thereby "influence intentionally the way the world goes" (Benn, 1982, pp. 4, 5). John Locke and Laslett (1988), the former being a liberal philosopher, attributed natural rights to this subject as a free and equal individual capable of consent to be governed (pp. 337–338, 428). For Locke and later liberals such as John Stuart Mill, the concept of the self-contained, self-present individual subject was characterized as autonomous and self-governing, constituted through nature, and with a natural right to liberty because, at heart, the subject was able to make rational choices by virtue of being a human subject. The free individual has thus come to be seen in contemporary society as "the apogee of all modern desires and possibilities" (Walker, 1999, p. x). Alongside the powerful work of psychoanalysis emerging with Freud and Lacan, as well as Marx's decentering of the liberal subject in favor of identities that are, in part, produced through ideologies and false consciousness, Foucault's approach has opened the possibility for thinking about identity and subjectivity as constituted in and through the power/knowledge network of discourse as it speaks the subject into its subjectivity. While such views are not necessarily how we ordinarily perceive ourselves and others – and, of course, we do not necessarily engage in such self-reflective thought in our everyday lives at all times – the decentered, constructed, and sometimes fragmentary subject has come to be important in theoretical accounts of contemporary life and contemporary culture. Fredric Jameson (1985) was correct to point out that in a postliberal or postmodern culture not only should we think of the individual bourgeois subject as a thing of the past, but we ought to understand the constructed nature of subjectivity so that we can see that the figure of self *"never* really existed in the first place; there have never been autonomous subjects of that type" (p. 115). For Jameson, the autonomous subject has been a "cultural mystification that sought to persuade people that they "had" individual subjectivity and possessed this unique personal identity" (p. 115). However, despite such theoretical decentering of the subject, contemporary culture and our everyday practices of identity regularly persist in relying on the notion of a fixed, natural subjectivity or identity. The question this leaves is why is the illusion of identity so convincing? What are the forces of contemporary media and digital communication that build, produce, and maintain notions of subjectivity that, on the one hand, are so readily decentered and, on the other, allow the liberal notion of subjectivity to endure?

One of the very important and highly influential theoretical approaches to identity that I rely on heavily in this book helps to answer that question. Gender theorist and philosopher Judith Butler has written extensively on the identity as "performative." In her earlier works such as *Gender Trouble* (1990) and *Bodies That Matter* (1993), Butler rejected some of the inherent foundationalisms and residual normalizations that persist in liberal, essentialist approaches as well as some brands of constructionist modeling of identity.

She found that the constructionist approach in which identity is overlain on a foundation (the body) emphasized too greatly the linear power of culture to exhaustively produce the subject. Likewise, essentialist approaches rely on an idea of an inner foundational identity that is ultimately unknowable, since there is no prediscursive "I" that drives our identities. Instead, she turned in her work to show that the very structure of signification and how language gives and produces meaning opens the possibility of understanding identity as constituted in the reiterative performances of selfhood that produce, retroactively, the illusion of an inner identity core (Butler, 1990, p. 143). We perform our identities – never consciously or voluntaristically – "in accord" with cultural demands for recognizable, unified, and coherent norms of identity as a tendency that responds to the broad cultural demands for intelligible selves necessary for social participation and belonging. Importantly, then, Butler opens the way for thinking about how language and discourse are encountered through media and digital media, and how performances can be more than just how we comport our bodies, conform to gender norms, speak in ways relevant to our cultural or class backgrounds, hold attitudes intelligible and in relation to our affiliations and kinships to confirm and continue the coherence of our identities. Rather, we also perform those identities in how we articulate ourselves online, whether that be through designing and maintaining a social-networking profile, contributing to discussions on a blog, editing and distributing a self-image or selfie, or selectively encountering information on Wikipedia, among many other forms of "identity work" undertaken knowingly or surreptitiously online. In light of the above points, there is no longer any real sense of offline and online in a world of ubiquitous digital media and digitization. How we perform our selfhood in the context of digital media is also no longer separable from how we perform in other spaces where our digital devices may be less readily at hand or less important in the communication we are presently undertaking. I take up and expand upon these queries related to how identity can be understood as performative in the context of our digital-dominated environment in the chapters that follow. Part of the task at hand is to bring Butler's theories of performativity into close articulation and alignment with the new and emerging practices of digital media use, such as interactive engagement with cocreativity of texts, the fast-paced social networking of identity relationalities, the vastly new ease of access to information including at times highly obscure discourses, and the frameworks through which we record, surveil, and archive our sense of subjectivity in online sites and situations.

# 3 SELFIES: INTERPELLATION AND SPECTACLE IN A PRODUCTIVE WORLD

Before getting into greater detail regarding how we can understand our performative selves as produced in the context of social networking and other digital practices, I would like to spend a little time here thinking about the very important and very recent digital practice of the shared selfie, particularly as a way of introducing what will follow in this book. The new custom of taking self-images by turning our cameras onto ourselves along with the backgrounds against which we might be depicted and sharing these online serve as technologies of selfhood that are built on high levels of critical self-awareness (Tiidenberg, 2014). The selfie is, in many ways, emblematic of the questions opened up about selfhood, identity, and digital communication, and it is useful to ponder, albeit briefly, how what little we know about selfies today provides a framework for some of the shifts in how identity is being performed in digital contexts. Butler went to considerable lengths in her book *Bodies That Matter* (1993) to demonstrate that identity performativity is not an individual act but "is always a reiteration of a norm or set of norms" (p. 12). That is, a subject does not express or articulate an inner truth, but cites, repeats, and mimes the norms, attributes, and codes of coherent behavior that fabricate the idea there is an inner essence (Butler, 1990, p. 136). In this context, the figure of the selfie is important in that it may at one level be seen as an act of proclaiming a particular identity but, at the level of performativity, is about shoring up the coherence and ongoingness of the performance of that identity.

I will use here a relatively mundane example: a male selfie taker who has, either deliberately or unthinkingly, taken a self-image that includes some sporting equipment in the background in a way that expresses masculine identity attributes in terms of cultural assumptions, norms, and stereotypes of masculine behavior. The selfie that, here, might be distributed across the user's social networks is not a declaration of masculine identity, nor is it a moment of becoming masculine. Rather, it is one element in the complex chain of performances and articulations that are required of subjects to produce a coherent, ongoing, linear pattern of masculine identity over time. It is the necessary "work" of doing identity in order to fulfill the cultural demands for coherence, intelligibility, and recognizability (Cover, 2004a). In that context, the selfie has drawn on a stereotype of masculinity that links the identity (masculine) with a set of attributes (enjoys sport, proficient at sport), because stereotypes are, while problematic and often demeaning, also a very efficient "byte" of quick and recognizable communication

(Cover, 2004b). Digital, networked media actively invite subjects to perform this work because it is an efficient way of articulating and therefore shoring up an identity performance (although, as I discuss in Chapter 1, social networking's complexity can also be that which brings down the coherence of an identity performance over time). As a tool of convenience, digital computing power and networked distribution of images is as inviting as, in the context of the drudge work of laundry, choosing the high-powered washing machine over the act of washing by hand in a tub – like identity performance, the washing needs to be done regardless, but the appealing activity is the one which requires the least labor.

In responding to the need by articulating oneself through digital communication in forms such as the selfie, subjects are simultaneously interpellated into the identity positions and categories interpretable in such image and spectacle. The metaphor of interpellation, used by French theorist Louis Althusser and built upon by both Foucault and Butler, describes the way a subject is subjectified by language and institutional power – here we must take into account the double-play of subject as sovereign over one's own identity and subject as subordinate, in the form of, say, British subject. For Althusser (1971), subjects are made subject in both senses through interpellation, using the metaphor of the policeman who subjectifies the subject into suspicion or the identity position of criminal with the hail "Hey, you there!" (pp. 162, 163). In terms of our masculine example, we might say that ideology hails the subject who has been coded man, demanding that the performance of masculinity be coherent with that manliness, and inviting the subject to conform by finding attributes, representations, and self-depictions that ensure masculinity – sporting goods will certainly do the trick, although sporting goods are not necessarily always linked to masculinity in all discourses. All subjects are produced as concrete subjects through ideology's work in categorization, even if we must understand that production of the subject as partial (Butler, 1999, p. 164) and even if we must acknowledge that all subjects are constituted through multiple, competing, and conflicting processes (Butler, 1993, p. 116). Subjects proceed from interpellation by practicing the rituals of recognition (Althusser, 1971, pp. 161, 162) and perform that constitution or reconstitution in ways that stabilize, albeit awkwardly, over time (Butler, 1991, p. 18). By turning to the hail, the subject comes to be recognized and recognizes herself or himself as a subject within the context of the ideology at play. Interpellation may, of course, fail at any time, given the possibility of misrecognizing to whom it is addressed (Butler, 1997, p. 95), indicating that there must be an acceptance of the hail by the subject in the moment of interpellation, which may or may not be a conscious, voluntarist act.

This process of interpellation makes a certain amount of sense in terms of how identity is acquired and built in ways that are not within our own control or agency. But it does also depend very much on understanding the process within a narrow, outdated, and linear communication format of sender (the metaphorical policeman in Althusser's account), message (the hail, accusation, interpellation, or categorization), and recipient (the subject who is subjectified). Of course, all communication is more complex than this, and the very act of communication has its own forms of subjectification – into identity position of audience, for example. However, in an age of user-generated content, where nonprofessionals are actively summoned to engage with media processes by contributing to media practices as producer–consumers or what have come to be referred to as prosumers (Bruns, 2008), such processes of interpellation are somewhat further complexified. In this context, the subject is produced through responding to the invitation to participate in the act of interpellation, not merely confirming identities through the taking and distribution of selfies, but through articulating that interpellation, self-managing the process on behalf of, through, and within discourse. In saying this, I am pointing to the fact that the "work" of identity *is* work, and sometimes performing a coherent identity is *hard work* (e.g., the masculine subject who must avoid slippage in that masculine identity by ensuring that any nonmasculine behavior is explainable, otherwise risking coherence – e.g., ensuring that a particularly feminine brand of cosmetic does not appear in his selfie). Work, yes, but there is also a pleasure in being made subjects and engaging in practices of identity. Roland Barthes' (1975) trope of the "pleasure of the text" is markedly useful here. When the question of interpellation through a text arises, it is, for Barthes, about the text's pleasure: "what the text says, through the particularity of its name, is the ubiquity of pleasure, the atopia of bliss" (pp. 58, 59). Subjects engage in identity work through the simultaneous reception and production of texts of the self, such as selfies, because there is a pleasure in the performativity of conformable identities. Identities are produced through, and serve, power relations, and such productive forces as interpellation, performativity, authorship, recognition, and subjectivization are not repressive but incite, induce, and seduce (Deleuze, 1988, p. 7), whereby subjects recognize themselves within sometimes narrow and sometimes constraining categories of identity and all the attributes and performances that make them coherent because "turning toward the voice of the law is a sign of a certain desire to be beheld by and perhaps also to behold the face of authority" (Butler, 1997, p. 112). In the era of the selfie, of course, the face of authority is hidden further, obscured by the face of the self in the selfie itself.

## 4  ABOUT DIGITAL IDENTITIES

Selfies are interesting here as an example of a way in which the ubiquity of digital communication, media, and technologies have an impact on how we think about, perform, articulate, and engage in identity practices as social norms, issues that are addressed throughout this book. Selfies are regularly distributed through social networking, a topic I discuss in Chapter 1 as a site through which identities are both articulated purposefully and wilfully through our contribution of profile information, self-selected image uploads, and participation in conversations, but are also put in question by the persistent engagement in conversation, "likes" (or failures to like) and replies, responses, and taggings from friends, family, and others, complexifying and changing how identity is represented in such a site. Selfies, then, become part of the regime of articulating selfhood through selectivity, but they are not without critique, since they are subject to friends' criticisms, liking, additional tagging, and further sharing in ways that are not necessarily within our control as authors or users.

Additionally, selfies operate as performative of identity in the context of both older and newer media. That is, the factors which make selfies recognizable as selfies include traditions of amateur photography (Lister, 2013, p. 7), but they also are the product of certain ruptures in cultural practices and attitudes toward photography, image, representation, and selfhood, particularly in the context of understanding how we capture, caption, and share representations of life in ways which place us under increased scrutiny by one another (Gabriel, 2014, p. 104). This includes the shift from analog production of the occasional self-portrait to the digital capabilities for taking, testing, choosing, and deleting digital images by the thousands, as well as the capabilities afforded by newer, portable, lightweight mobile devices that ensure the "capturability" of self-images as long as one has not forgotten one's phone (as well as providing the easy capacity to turn around the device to take one's own image). Such cultural practices in relation to selfies emerge in sometimes unexpected ways, indicating that uses and gratifications of devices that have been designed for other purposes are made complex and result in surprises that emerge from desires to produce representations of the self to be shared online. In Chapter 2 of this book I address some of the theoretical "mechanics" of understanding the performativity of identity in the context of a fast-changing digital media technological environment, and among those mechanisms is the encroachment of a neoliberal commodification of digital activities. In this respect, we might consider some of the ways in which the development and marketing of certain devices such as the selfie stick operate both as a response to the emerging cultural popularity of selfies as an everyday activity, but also serve to normativize the activity as that which is inseparable from the production of selves as commodities through self-representation. At the same time, this is not to suggest that the production of selfies is wholly subsumed by capitalist interest — there is also an element of critique, albeit one which is not necessarily separable from consumption. For example, Ellen DeGeneres' group selfie with other celebrities at the 2014 Academy Awards became one of the most retweeted images of recent years. But it also served as a form of popular criticism — something comedians often do well — that turned around celebrity culture from that which is always "gazed at" to that which, under certain conditions, sets the limits and productivities of gazing through a particular formation of the self-gaze. This is not, of course, to suggest that such gazing does not further "sell" those celebrities who trade on notoriety and the circulation of their image, but it does open up some interesting ways for thinking about how selfies might radicalize the relationship between image and commodity.

I would also like to refer to Chapter 3 of this book, which engages with questions related to interactivity and participation. There, I draw on some of my older work (e.g., Cover, 2006) to reiterate the important point that the participatory nature of contemporary digital media is not a new "invention" that drastically changed how we communicate, but can be understood as the fruition of some deeply held desires, cultural demands, and attachments to participating in and sharing processes of authorship and creativity. Here, too, the selfie stands as a good example of that kind of participation in creativity, in which photography and experimentation with image, lighting, portraiture, and distribution are not necessarily any longer in the hands of professionals, but are activities that people actively flocked to and engaged with as part of everyday culture. This is to say that, if there were not a deeply held cultural attachment or desire for participation already at play, there would not have been such a phenomenal take-up of the activity. This is an important conceptualization of the relationship between digital participation and cultural practices of identity, because it is a valuable response to those who actively bemoan digital activities that seem new, novel, or inno-vative, usually with the claim that the activity has somehow "wrecked" soci-ety or past ways of doing things (Blaine, 2013). It is also a way of opening up new processes of thinking about digital practices as not necessarily being all that new but, even when they are new or unexpected, as being the product of history rather than the product of some notion of an invention alien to culture or conspiratorially created in some Silicon Valley laboratories.

In Chapter 4, I address a number of issues about the relationship between the body, identity, and digital cultures. I am interested particularly in moving beyond the idea that there is any kind of distinction between "real life" as the site of embodied and face-to-face communication, and "virtual" which is usually represented as disembodied, anonymous, a site of identity experimen-tation, and something one engages with when physically solitary at a desk-top computer. Such views are remarkably outdated, as I argue many times throughout this book. Digital communication is omnipresent for those who are fortunate enough to be characterized through the processes, cultures, and economies of the affluent West, and this means that how we make use of digital technologies is no longer something which is separable from our everyday, embodied, and corporeal subjectivities. This is not to suggest that networked digital communication is not used surreptitiously, nor to say that no one at all is online using false identities on the Internet. Rather, it is to say that the practices related to the use of digital communication are a lot less ex-perimental, but are also a great deal more important for how we think about and do our identity practices. Once again, the figure of the selfie is character-istic of some of the concerns addressed in that chapter, particularly in terms of the ways in which the selfie captures an image of the body for distribution among online viewers, the way in which it encourages practices of producing the best possible, most disciplined, and fittest bodies for the scrutiny of oth-ers (Kwon & Kwon, 2015, p. 302) while also being both the product of and encouraging shaming practices in relation to bodies deemed not fit enough (Tiidenberg, 2014). I argue in Chapter 4 that bodies and digital spaces can be characterized as being in a process of moving ever closer to the seam that differentiates the two but, unlike the interesting although ultimately fruit-less accounts of cyberpunk uploading of "minds" online that leave behind a wasted and unnecessary body, there is no actual crossing. Bodies are not simply left behind when one engages with digital media but are an integral, well-emphasized element of that activity, whether it is through the holding of the mobile device that is taking the selfie, playing a game, or engaging in debates and discussions online about the selfies we might just have taken and uploaded. The body must not be forgotten when we talk about digital media as if they are no longer relevant, for it is more relevant now that we connect our devices to them in such close proximity – fitbits, smartwatches, held mobiles, Bluetooth headsets, and so on. Our bodies are, following Butler (2003), materialized, given meaning, borders and boundaries only in the context of how they are performed and in the terms of the discursive norms that both precede and surround us. In this case, that also includes the practices and normativities produced and emerging with digital media cultures.

In Chapters 5 and 6, I discuss some of the ways in which digital media connect us across space, particularly in terms of the discourses of globalization that expose us to different bodies and identities and cultural practices as well as make available and share our own practices and experiences across long distances in instantaneous ways. There is nothing particularly new in terms of thinking about communication as that which makes faster and faster connections over longer and longer distances (Meyrowitz, 1997). However, it is important to develop new ways of thinking about what that mutual exposure on a global scale does for how we perform and produce our identities creatively and, particularly, in relation to others who may be visually, practically, and ritualistically marked by radical difference, or may surprise us by not being different at all, or may not necessarily be online and accessing digital media as a result of an economic, skills-based, and infrastructural digital divide. If a global identity is to emerge as one which is ethical, nonviolent, and mutually beneficial through the great affordances of peaceful and positive communication, then, we might think about some of the things the selfie – as a produced, curated, and distributed performance of the self – might do for the establishment or dissolution of norms of visual appearance and the ways in which these have been connected in the past with the valuation of human subjectivity. In Chapter 6, I address some of the possible ways of thinking about this, in the context of connectivities that move from notions of bounded communities to ideas related to networked relationalities, social relationships, and affiliations – new forms of kinship that occur through mobility, movement, and ubiquitous connectivity. I do this by drawing on early 1990s' ideas of mobile communication as represented among the technological early adopter group of lesbian, gay, bisexual, and transgender (LGBT) communities in the United Kingdom. Here, too, selfies might be considered as indicative of the mobility of the body and therefore the movement of identity through and across space, particularly in terms of the geolocational tagging of images that serve as "proof" we move around the world and across space both corporeally and digitally.

In Chapter 7, I take up another of the older issues related to criticisms of digital cultures of communication – the idea of digital addiction through the problematic claim that the technologies of the Internet, mobile phones, and digital gaming are inherently productive of compulsive behaviors. While there are those who compulsively use digital technologies in the same way as there are those who compulsively wash their hands, it is important to pay attention to some theoretical conceptualizations in order to point out that the technology is no more the cause of digital addiction than running water and bathroom fittings are the cause of compulsive self-cleaning behaviors. The idea that the world has been swept up by a digital addiction is one that typically assumes there is still a distinction between the "real world" and "digital communication" (to return again to this important point). In Chapter 7, I again argue that this not the case, rather digital and mobile forms of communication and intensive participation online have become part of that everyday real world in ways which are not as harmful as alarmists seem to think. The idea that people are running around addicted to taking selfies and then sharing self-images online is a problematic one. I do not address selfies in Chapter 7, but it is useful to see that such accusations ignore the fact that while there might be changes in our everyday practices in regard to images related to ourselves, the fact that people are doing this regularly and often is not necessarily something which we can equate with the addictive power of chemical drugs, despite the attempt of many to do so.

In the final, conclusive chapter of this book, I return to questions related to space, surveillance, and digital archiving, particularly in the context of the ways in which the convergence of all three provide certain kinds of frameworks for making identities normative and intelligible. Google Earth and Google Maps are important digital activities that have quickly become an important part of everyday life, although they are often invoked as examples of fears of surveillance. I address some of these fears in Chapter 8, pointing out that the more interesting element is the way in which these are implicated in reorientations of space that, effectively, change how we do identities in relation to space. At the same time, archives are an important element of our digital activities and such surveillance is implicated in the establishment of digital media as a kind of archive of the entire world. Here, too, selfies are illustrative of the way in which subjectivity is produced in the context of that which we record, distribute, and which remains at risk of online permanency. This is not something to bemoan, but opens up a number of ways in which we might begin to think about the ethics of our digital communication, and explore the opportunities and constraints in regard to the production of more ethical identities in digital media contexts.

By invoking the figurative concept of the selfie in describing the contents of the theoretical engagements with digital cultures and identities that I discuss in this book, I am not only illustrating the importance to identity and selfhood of digital media, but I am making an invitation – in reading these chapters, one might like to think about the self-practices and self-images produced through digital media engagement. How we perform ourselves, our identities, our subjectivities in new and older ways, how there are continuities and ruptures in our practices of selfhood since digital media really became part of our everyday lives, and how we might both conform to and breach norms and disciplines of identity over time through our use of digital media, are important things to ask ourselves in order to become more ethical in our relationalities and social engagement if those are, now, to be governed by our online practices. While I would not suggest that I necessarily learned new, wonderful things about myself while thinking about the material of digital communication in each of these chapters, I did learn that, more than ever, the practices of performing a coherent, ethical, and engaged identity are relational with others and produced in the context of others in ways which only become obvious when we start to critique, understand, and embrace digitality as part of our everyday cultural practices and our everyday lives.

# CHAPTER 1

# Understanding Identity Online: Social Networking

If we are to investigate the available ways of understanding identity in the context of online communication and digital media cultures, then there is enormous value in paying attention to how identity can be seen to be "performed" in one of the most popular, contemporary online platforms and practices – social networking. In an always connected and cloud driven communication environment, identities are performed, articulated, represented, and negotiated in relation with those who are not necessarily physically present in our everyday lives but also with those we engage with in the "networked social." Founded in 2004 and available for use by anyone aged 13 years and above, Facebook has over 1.3 billion active users as of June 2014. The largest social network by virtue of active users, Facebook represents approximately 18% of the world's population. Facebook is rivaled only by social networks that originate in China and, despite common predictions in early 2010 of its eventual downfall in favor of newer sites, its name is increasingly synonymous with online activity – more so even than Twitter. Facebook has come to stand for the notion of representation of identity and selfhood online as much as for communication among potentially distant friends. By its very name, Facebook points to the interface between the corporeal and the digital, a site through which identity is both expressed and acquired: the face (traditionally the site that betrays or hides facets of identity but that is the point of corporeality through which we routinely make relational contact with each other) is replaced by the more complex array of what we post, how we read posts, how we post about each other, and how we interact through varying, complex degrees of friendship and affiliation online.

Social networking sites have been investigated and discussed by researchers, journalists, and public commentators. Much of the time the range of uses, tools, functions, or gratifications of social networking sites are overlooked giving them the appearance of having a singular, unified activity or sole "purpose". A site for sharing personal experiences among friends or sometimes strangers (Ellison, Steinfeld, & Lampe, 2007, p. 1143); as a site for the articulation of one's identity-based interests through the construction of

*Digital Identities.*
http://dx.doi.org/10.1016/B978-0-12-420083-8.00001-8

1

taste statements which act as identifications with objects and with other people (Liu, 2008, p. 253); as a site for relationship maintenance (Hoadley, Xu, Lee, & Rosson, 2010, p. 52) and connecting unfamiliar people with one another (Hoadley et al., 2010, p. 53); as a networked space for the expression or representation of preexisting and salient aspects of users' identities for others to view, interpret, and engage with (boyd, 2008b); as a space for young people to engage with each other outside of the physical world's constraints and parental surveillance (boyd, 2008b, p. 18); as a site for the expression and/or self-regulation of narcissistic personalities (Buffardi & Campbell, 2008); and prioritizing the idea that being friended and linking to friends whether close friends, acquaintances, or strangers as "one of the (if not *the*) main activities of Facebook" (Tong, Van Der Heide, Langwell, & Walther, 2008, p. 531). These are all ostensible reasons for the use of social networking – conscious, self-aware purposes articulated by different users in varied contexts.

However, an alternative approach to understanding social networking and identity is to take into account some of the ways in which social networking activities, as digital media use *par excellence*, are performative acts of identity which actively constitute the user. This requires us to make use of some of the most powerful, albeit complex, theories of identity performativity circulating in poststructuralist writing, particularly the work on gender performativity by Judith Butler. A Butlerian approach to identity as performative helps us to understand how identities and practices of using online communication in everyday life are interwoven and cocreative, rather than to take the more simple approach of assuming that we have a fixed identity which we express and represent (perhaps truthfully, perhaps fraudulently) through our activities online. We can therefore draw together poststructuralist, antiessentialist theories of subjectivity and identity with prior work on social networking to do two things: (1) expand the critical frameworks by which social networking can be contextualized within the broader cultural practices of identity and selfhood; (2) further destabilize the problematic dichotomy of a "real identity" in an offline capacity and a "virtual identity" represented in digital, networked communication. Additionally, by exploring social networking through Butler's theories of identity performativity, it is possible to show that social networking activities and behaviors are both a means by which subjectivity can be performed and stabilized and, simultaneously, made more complex and conflicting. This comes from the fact that social networking is not a singular activity but a set of interrelated – sometimes incompatible – interactivities which include identity performances through profile management, friending, liking fan pages, tagging, being tagged, updating statuses, and having responses given by others to one's own status updates. That is, an *array* of activities requiring the users to "work" to perform a coherent, intelligible selfhood extending across all these online activities in addition to offline behaviors.

Working from a poststructuralist, antifoundationalist perspective that draws on Foucault, Lacan, and Derrida, Butler's theory of performativity is based on the idea that identity and subjectivity is an ongoing process of becoming, rather than an ontological state of being, whereby becoming is a sequence of acts, that retroactively constitutes identity (Salih, 2002, p. 46; Butler, 1990). That is, identity formation occurs "in accord" with culturally given discourses, structures, and practices which, once stabilized for the subject come to feel like common sense, and by which any actions, performances, or behaviors of the subject appear to emanate from that identity rather than constituting it. The self or "I" is made up of a matrix of pregiven identity categories, experiences, and labels (Butler, 1990, p. 40) that, through repetition, lend to the illusion of an inner identity core (Butler, 1993, p. 12). Where Butler's theories provide an important perspective for the study of social networking and identity construction is in extending the very idea of performance from the bodily, the experiential, and the affective into the field of online acts; in other words, online social networking behavior is just as much a performance as any other "real life" act, and equally constitutes a sense of self and identity. That is, online behavior should not be understood as an activity separate from those more ostensibly embodied performances of identity categories.

Working Butler's theory of identity performativity alongside existing discussions of social networking, I argue that the online performance of subjectivity is articulated in at least two, sometimes competing ways: (1) modifying your own profile (boyd, 2008a, p. 122) by: (a) developing the profile through choosing particular categories of common identity coordinates or demarcations as well as stating categories of taste and providing and deciding on particular information that, in the act of deciding, is in itself a performance of identity, that is, age, gender, relationship status, indicators of sexual orientation/identity, and making biographical statements; (b) ongoing activities such as status updates, uploading and captioning photos, sending messages, rewriting biographical statements, and other forms of updating, refining, and manipulating one's profile; (2) identifying in a relational sense with various friends and networks through adding and accepting adds – and, of course, updating, changing, and making new additions or deletions to your friends list. Both of these are performances of self-identity which, in Butler's formulation of subjectivity, retroactively constitute identity, just as offline performances of selfhood do. Separately, these two social networking activities are acts of identity performance; however, the extent to which these two areas of social networking operate together toward a coherent, unified self needs to be explored. Lewis and West (2009) have indicated that while social networking sites require "both the presentation of self and a process of "friending" … there is a degree of incompatibility between these imperatives" (p. 1224). Since identifications are, as Butler (1993) noted, "multiple and contestatory" (p. 99), and the subject is produced at the "cost of its own complexity" (Hall, 2004, p. 127), a stronger understanding of the use of social networking in the construction of intelligible and coherent identities can be explored by thinking through the ways in which the complexity and multiplicity of social networking friendship activities, comments, discussions, tagging, etc., work both to build and undo narratives of selfhood. Concentrating on Facebook as the most common example of social networking, this chapter will begin by giving a theoretical account as to how Butler's performativity can be utilized to understand the contemporary cultural role of social networking in relation to how identities are constituted, played out, transformed, and stabilized online. The first section of this chapter will argue that profile management can be understood as an act of identity performance, while the second will explore some initial approaches to understanding how the relationality of friendship lists provide a somewhat different framework for the performance of identity. In the final section, I analyze some of the ways in which these two areas of identity performativity – profiles and friending – produce gaps and rifts in the coherence of an identity narrative, creating "extra work" for identity self-management. Ultimately, this chapter intends to provide a few directions for continued theorization and analysis of identity and subjectivity in an online context, and the ways of approaching, in greater complexity, the relationship between Web 2.0 interactive environments and contemporary shifts in how selfhood and identity are constructed and played out.

## 1 APPROACHING IDENTITY

Before we can investigate the usefulness of a Butlerian account of identity performativity for understanding how our selves are constituted and played out, in part through online activities, it is useful to think about other approaches to identity and whether or not they have value for understanding the complexity of selfhood in online frameworks and digital cultures. Modern identity emerged in Western Europe and Great Britain during the fifteenth and sixteenth centuries, culminating in the humanist figure of the free and autonomous individual in the eighteenth century Age of Enlightenment. Humanist notions of subjectivity, provide the conceptualization of the subject as having unquestioned certainty, truth, and presence. Central to the contemporary, everyday, and "common sense" understanding of identity and selfhood is René Descartes' (1596–1650) fifteenth century notion of *cogito ergo sum* ("I think, therefore I am"), which operates as a first principle for the idea of an "I" as a conscious and reasoning individual in which thought or "mind" is given preference over corporeality and bodily sensations. Significant to western thinking on identity, this notion of the autonomous, coherent, unified self was extended and solidified by numerous writers and thinkers, including John Locke (1632–1704) who posited the liberal and free individual; Jean-Jacques Rousseau (1712–1778) who argued for a human individuality grounded in nature; and Immanuel Kant (1724–1804) who equated selfhood and consciousness.

However, although the notion of the unitary, autonomous, coherent, and essentialist subject remains commonsensical, everyday understanding of identity, theories, and philosophies emerging throughout the twentieth century have questioned this notion of identity and rejected the idea of subjectivity as a self-contained being. Several competing theoretical positions led to the decentering or rejection of the humanist subject in poststructuralist theory. Marxism refuses recognition of the subject as a "conscious" subject, attributing it a "false consciousness" in a capitalist socioeconomic system. The structuralist–Marxist critique of subjectivity undertaken by Louis Althusser (1971) questions the integrity of the universal subject by showing it to be bound by its interpellation through institutions and ideology. In Sigmund Freud's psychoanalytic critique, the discovery of the unconscious fragments the subject at the point of its consciousness, and suggests that one's identity is bound by one's desires. Jacques Lacan (1977), extending Freud's theory through structuralist semiotics, makes clear that desire and subjectivity are inseparable: there cannot be a subject without a concept of desire – in coming in to language in the Symbolic, identity is separated from the unconscious. Other, thereby resulting in a subject that is always described as "split." For Lacan, desire is constituted by lack, as a result of the inability to reacquire the preoedipal and premirror stage *jouissance*, hence the subject (always unsuccessfully) seeks fulfilment by trajecting desire toward the *objet petit a* (an object of desire), be it a sexual object, a "personal goal," or otherwise – a desire that can never be satiated. Thus, the psychoanalytic approach posits a subject which is always "in process."

From the 1960s and 1970s, the Enlightenment humanist notion of subjective identity was put further in question by theories of social, cultural, and discursive constructionism in which the subject is not born or the result of nature, but produced within the environment, language, and sociality. Both building upon and rejecting the dominant psychoanalytic critique of identity, this antisubjective structuralist and poststructuralist criticism has become the prevailing understanding of a critical and cultural theory of identity, although it has by no means resulted in a wholesale rejection of the Enlightenment figure of the subject in contemporary everyday and pedestrian thinking about identity. Significant among constructionist approaches to identity is the work of Michel Foucault (1926–1984) who posits identity not as an "effect" of power, disciplinarity, and biopolitics, which includes processes and techniques of surveillance and normalization. Foucault's theory of subjectivity as a *form* constituted in and by discourse approaches a poststructuralist position – and contributes heavily to it. For Foucault, the subject is inculcated by, and through the deployment of power-relations, normalized variously in accord with regimentary, disciplinary, and biopolitical discourses. The humanist subject of Descartes as self-existent, coherent, and consciously active is rejected by the Foucauldian position in favor of the disciplining of bodies made "docile" (Foucault, 1977) and conforming. Three modes of objectification of identity in Foucault's work can be identified: the first is dividing practices, such as the isolation of "the mad" in asylums. Second is the Foucauldian concept of "scientific classification" arising from modes of inquiry given the discursive status of science. In the context of Web 2.0 digital media environments, we might similarly refer to this as profile categorization or "naming"; a discursive practice which in Foucauldian analyses of identity plays a pivotal role in the inculcation of the subject as subject. Finally, there is "subjectification," the processes "of self-formation in which the person is active" albeit with conformative regimes. Biopolitics is a technology of power that both analyzes and constructs not the individual subject but whole populations as subjective through a range of techniques from statistical measurement to health promotion to immigration controls; its governance mechanics are generally, but not always, located within the administration of the nation state. Emerging slightly later than discipline in the second-half of the eighteenth century as part of the further developments of governance for larger states, biopolitics can be a useful tool for understanding the relationship between online environments and identity in that the use of digital communication tools results in the capacity for large-scale data collection on the level of whole populations, thus, producing certain forms of identity which are normalized not along the disciplinary normal/abnormal distinction but in terms of distance from a norm along a distribution curve of normativities (Foucault, 2007).

Building on the work of Foucault (although at times deploying Lacanian psychoanalysis), Judith Butler projects one of the most useful, poststructuralist theorizations of identity by suggesting that the subject is constituted by repetitive performances in terms of the structure of signification that produces retroactively the illusion of an inner subjective core (Butler, 1990). Identity/subjectivity becomes a normative ideal rather than a descriptive feature of experience, and is the resultant effect of regimentary discursive practices. The subject, then, is performatively constituted by the very "expressions" that, from a humanist position, have been considered the essential subject's subsequent conscious actions. As Butler notes, "performativity is not a singular, deliberate, and self-conscious act, but a reiterative and citational practice in which discourse produces identity as its effect in a form which stabilizes through repetition over time, but remains always at risk of showing itself up by the constitutive failure of genuine repetition. For Butler, discourse remains the key to subjectivity, but her extension of Foucault's thesis provides a less universalized account of subjectivity. Butler has taken great pains to point out that her theorization of performative identity does not suggest a conscious performance with all the agency that would be accorded in a humanist account (Butler, 1993).

Butler's theoretical account of the performativity of identity puts both liberal–humanist essentialism and postmodern radical constructionism into question in favor of a Foucault-driven antifoundationalist view of identity. The essentialist/constructionist debates are best delineated by Butler (1993), who points out the ways in which both sides have missed the point of deconstruction by refusing "the constitutive force of exclusion, erasure, violent foreclosure, abjection and its disruptive return within the very terms of discursive legitimacy" (p. 8). While the essentialist position, for Butler, is both Cartesian and phallogocentric, constructionism leaves a residual essential subject on which cultural construction (sometimes referred to as "socialization") overlays ideological concepts and gets them "wrong." She also identifies an overly radical constructivist position which dislodges not only the essential subject but makes a claim to the constructive composition of all objects. She argues (1993) that this position understands culture as exhaustively constituting identity, ultimately creating and determining it in its naming that which it names, or, rather, it is that kind of transitive referring which names and inaugurates at once. Her answer to these two positions is to dislodge both the fixity and foundationalism of essentialist views and the determinism of the radical constructivist position in favor of performativity as establishing the subject as effect and, more specifically, viewing the subject as a process that stabilizes to produce the effect of fixity over time.

## 2  WEB 1.0 AND ONLINE FLUIDITY

In the early days of the Internet, which were marked by slow communication speeds and therefore involved activities that centered on text, still images, a decreased capacity for immediacy, and access predominantly through nonmobile desktop computers, a number of approaches to online identity worked to produce a notion of cyberculture that was deemed separate from the "real" of the "real world." This produced the idea that there were different "modes" of identity, a real, corporeal, and embodied social experience and a separate, new, and playful identity that was experienced by "jacking in" to the Internet, usually depicted as occurring privately and engaging with distant others online. Early approaches were therefore quite narrow in their definition or were sometimes highly utopian via the notion that playful fluidity in the realm of cyberculture opened new ways of thinking about identity that would change how we culturally produce, articulate, and represent identity categories and norms, particularly around gender, sexuality, and race. Mark Dery (1992), for example, focused on the subversive and oppositional forms of identity that emerged in early Web 1.0 Internet use, while Howard Rheingold (1993) presented an idealistic conception of harmonious, online virtual communities. Despite the substantial shift from Web 1.0 text-based personal hyperlinked webpages toward Web 2.0 social networking – characterized by participation, audio/video sharing, interactive remixing, and upfront, nonanonymous engagement – older theories of online identity presenting the notion of the digital self as theatrical and, sometimes, fraudulent, have continued to frame much public discourse on subjectivity in online contexts.

One such example is the concept of the fluid self, marked and produced in online play in text-based, Web 1.0 chatrooms. Discussing such a self, cyber theorist Sherry Turkle (1999) contended that theories of identity that frame the self as largely decentered, such as Mark Poster's (2006) approach to anonymous speech on the Internet as being without limits, gender, religion, ethnic, or national requirements, face a constant disjuncture between concepts of unitary identity as an illusion and, on the other hand, lived experience in which the unitary self is popularly felt to be the most basic reality. The Internet, particularly in the form of early Web 1.0, text based chat rooms, offered technological objects to think with that allowed postmodern understandings of identity as multiple, and always decentered, to be explored by facilitating experiential understandings of the illusion of a unitary self (Turkle, 1997). In the often anonymous environments of text based, virtual reality, multiuser domains (MUDs and MOOs) one could invest in and construct oneself in a simulated environment understood to be free of embodied territorial constraints. In effect, one could challenge the idea of unitary identity through the willful experimentation with identity categories. Turkle (1999) introduced the well known example of a user known as Case: a male industrial designer who maintains a "Jimmy Stewart versus Katharine Hepburn dichotomy" of online personae to exemplify a notion of identity as distributed and heterogeneous, facilitated by text based online forums. For Case, presenting himself as a feminine "Katharine Hepburn ideal" online allowed an externalization of an aspect of himself that he would be unable to fully explore in "real life" masculine embodiment.

From today's perspective, examples of identity play such as Turkle's are not only highly outdated in the context of the broader use of online communication for visual representation of the self, but can be understood to be problematic for two reasons. First, they maintain the real world/virtual world dichotomy that is pervasive in much of the cyberculture and mainstream discourse of online communication and social networks. The dualism of the human and machine boundary is far less discernibly established and may be more usefully described in terms of a series of performances across a sociotechnical network wherein the "interface" consists of a multiplicity of aligned and dynamic encounters between different configurations, including as persons and machines. Examples of identity play and identity fluidity through the utilization of online sites, such as Turkle's exploration of Case, rely on acts self-stereotyping in order to maintain online personae. While not explicitly explored, Case's use of film icon stereotypes highlights the theatricality of his online personae, which falls short of the performative approach to identity espoused by Butler. Although celebrated as examples of identity fluidity, these online performances are thus theatrical and maintain the consistency and coherence of offline embodied identity, rather than being a genuine challenge to prevailing everyday concepts of unitary and essentialist identity.

Resulting from the increased materiality afforded to multiple and divergent identity category expressions online, it is understandable that early cyberculture theorists postulated a future where the unbridled expansion of identity categories might lead to a utopian world wherein "identity" could be extricated from foundationalist principles. What the success of a social network like Facebook might suggest, is that all of the identity "choices" presented online necessitate a mediatory tool if one is to readily articulate a coherent and intelligible self and present a picture of selfhood for the scrutiny of a plurality of gazes. However, despite the shift from early anonymous text based communication, Turkle's early work remains helpful in framing the possibility for some technologies to impact "older, centralized ways" of considering identity. Within Turkle's framework, objects anchor experience and memories. So while her example of Case's online personae is problematic, it is nevertheless helpful in highlighting how objects contribute to identity construction.

## 3 PROFILES AND PERFORMATIVITY

Many current approaches to understanding the relationship between Web 2.0 environments (characterized by YouTube, Wikis, and – most particularly – social networking sites such as MySpace and Facebook) are grounded in the notion that social network use emanated from a coherent *a priori* self (e.g., Donath & boyd, 2004; Liu, 2008; Livingstone & Brake, 2010), despite the powerful arguments put forward within poststructuralist theory that "show up" the possibility of a genuinely coherent, intelligible, and unified self (Cover, 2012b). Although, from a Foucauldian, Butlerian, and poststructuralist perspective, all performance of identity is relational in that it requires the citation of discursive categories of identity, is performed for recognizability, and operates within constructed "truth regimes," the relationality of Web 2.0 digital media and communication environments further implicates identity within a network of others in which mutual surveillance can be understood as the key to identity articulation in an online environment – a surveillance in which online users are always from the beginning complicit. Identifications and categorizations online thus function to assert individuality and often involve a process of stereotyping that allows group members easily to distinguish self, others, and group members (Buckingham, 2008).

Much of the early current literature on social networks describes the conscious, willful use of an online technology like Facebook. This position is coterminous with early cyberculture work that maintains the "real life" versus "virtual self" dichotomy and, effectively, the reification of a "real" identity out of which the "virtual self" could be voluntarily created. However, several more effective and theoretically grounded approaches to understanding the relationship between social networking and identity build on the work of Erving Goffman (1959). Goffman's dramaturgical analysis of identity performance offers a convenient framework for the analysis of identity expression only. Social networks, situated in the broader cultural practices of individualism, self-narration, and interconnectivity, offer many parallels to Goffman's work. Goffman points to the self-conscious presentation of selfhood in different contexts as well as the symptomatic elements of performance – that is, what people "give" and what they "give off." An individual, for Goffman, performs identity through both of the forms of intentional and unintentional expression. In the context of social networking and other online forms of relationality, Goffman's approach to the performative expression of selfhood points to the ways in which the online acts of typing, updating, uploading photos and videos, and other activities serve as both intentional and unintentional forms of expression to varying degrees depending on intent and context.

Beyond the anthrosociological work of Goffman that makes available the notion of front-end and back-end performances of selfhood, poststructuralist and feminist theory since the 1990s has contributed to a broader understanding of subjectivity as contingent, multiple, and fluid, operating variously through historical, cultural, and narrativized structures and frameworks. This is a substantial and critical shift from the more traditional, Enlightenment perception of identity as emanating from an inner essence, and represented through behavior and communication. While it is a critical standpoint, it is also evidenced in the cultural frameworks through which subjects are beginning to articulate concepts of identity in digital frameworks through which social relationality, through "always connected" digital belonging, becomes increasingly normative. Judith Butler's work on performativity has been particularly important in expanding the ways in which such behavior, communication, articulation, and activity can be understood as constituting – rather than merely representing – identity and selfhood. Although Butler's work is complex and wide-ranging, there are four nodes of her theories of performative identity which are significant in the study of online, interactive behaviors and experiences. These are best summarized as follows. (1) Extending the work of both Nietzsche and Foucault, there is no core, essential self from which behaviors and actions – both offline and online – emerge, only a set of performances that retroactively produce an illusion of an inner identity core: the actor behind the acts is really only ever an effect of those performances (Butler, 1993, p. 12). (2) The self is performed by the citation and repetition of discursively given norms, categories, stereotypes, labels, and expressions: in the context of social networking, such discursively given language is always mediated by interactive relationships, including available lists of profile categories ranging from a user's gender and relationship status to choices around favorite films and other taste categories, plus many other complex articulations, posts, interpretations, searches, and what appear ostensibly as choices. (3) Selves are constituted in discourse but can be reconstituted or reconfigured differently if encountering different, new, imaginative discursive arrangements (Butler, 1991, p. 18): these include new categories or alternative names and norms of identity encountered online – for example, the decision to add or "like" a fan page on, say, animal rights which might reconstitute a coordinate of that user's identity as vegetarian. (4) While never complete or without flaw, the process of performing identity occurs within a narrative of coherence over time, motivated by a cultural demand or imperative that we are coherent, intelligible, and recognizable to others in order to allow social participation and belonging (Butler, 1997, p. 27). In other words, a sense of self is forged across an array of identity categories or "coordinates" (Cover, 2004a) – which include common axes of discrimination such as gender, ethnicity, ability, and age but might also be comprised of spurious experiences that are less easily categorizable and less well demarcated in an identity/difference dichotomy – and that these are articulated through an ongoing process of "shoring up" or "answering" any anomalies between those coordinates to present a coherent, recognizable, and intelligible self.

Performativity, then, is identity produced through the citation of culturally given identity categories or norms in a reiterative process, and occurs across both offline and online actions – in this theoretical framework it would be a mistake to think of social networking behavior, for example, as being only a disembodied representation or biographical statement or set of conscious and voluntary choices. Such performance which, in the context of social networking, might be "liking" a fan page, adding a friend, or choosing a gender category are not merely voluntary, self-conscious decisions but acts which at a deeper level of analysis can be seen to construct the identity or self perception of making those decisions. Contemporary western culture compels such acts of identity in the demand that one articulate oneself as a rational, reasonable, coherent, and recognizable self (Woodward, 2002, p. 89), despite poststructuralist theory "showing up" the impossibility of a genuinely coherent, intelligible, and unified self (Butler, 1997, p. 99; Jameson, 1985). Social networking sites, and particularly their profile management function, can thus be understood as one tool or mechanism for attempting to be effective in articulating a coherent and recognizable self, much as diaries, journals, conversations, or other communicative acts have been. As the work of self-coherence becomes ever more difficult, the time spent in profile maintenance, which may be as complex as profile revision or as simple as making a status update or adding an image caption, pays off as the (never quite) coherent and intelligible profile continues to perform the self over time.

Aspects of social networking sites such as Facebook can thus be said to be the tools *par excellence* by which to perform as a coherent subject. As Helen Kennedy (2006) pointed out about webpages generally, they are a media form which is never entirely finished, just as identity composition is a continuous process – both are constantly "under construction" (p. 869). A user exploiting Facebook for performing identity in a never ending process toward coherence and intelligibility is, effectively, doing what we do when we have a conversation, perhaps in a café with a friend and speak of ourselves, desires, experiences, recent actions, and tastes. Within a disciplinary society of surveillance (Foucault, 1977), we police each other's subjecthood for coherence, often in line with stereotypes and easily recognizable "norms" and narratives: one subject's taste for classical music, but punk outfits, demands an explanation for consistency, intelligibility, and uniformity in order to belong and maintain participation in social. Within cultural frameworks that posit the stereotype that gay men are particular about interior décor (an old but persistent stereotype), one's queer identity but household messiness is seen as noncomplementary or outside the restrictive norm or stereotype demanding explanation. Two conflicting political views must be smoothed over as in conversational language: "But you said earlier…" demanding the work of bringing the performance, articulations, expressions, back into coherence and stabilizing once again the projection of identity.

On social networking sites such as Facebook, the tools for producing and articulating oneself in coherent and unified intelligibility are effectively supplied in the profile management interface, providing a discursive framework used to give performative acts of identity consistency and coherence. The profile basics can be said to include: gender, birth date, gender of sexual/romantic interest, relationship status (and who), a biographical statement, political views, religious views, a short written biography, a profile photograph or image, a favorite quotation, education and work, and likes and interests. Notably, sites such as Facebook have responded to the ever increasing idea of microcategorizations of identity by expanding the possibilities for how one represents oneself – the expansion of multiple gender categories being one such notable example, whereby gender can be expressed by choosing one from a vast range of gender descriptors beyond the more common and violently limiting male/female descriptors.

For Sonia Livingstone (2008), whether those choices are limited or expansive, such choices are always acts of biographization of the self, in which users "select a more or less complex represent of themselves" (p. 403). To view this in a framework of performativity, the establishment and maintenance of a profile is not a representation or biography but instead a series of performative acts which constitute the self and stabilize it over time as the effect of those choices. Written, selected, and revised, this is a performance which requires carefully chosen responses that present an intelligible self with integrity, unification, and recognizable coherence. An inconsistency (say, conservative political views that rub awkwardly against the act of "liking" an antiwar fan page) can be explained and made intelligible, cohering together through perhaps a lengthy biographical entry on the Facebook Info Page. A straight man's status of relationship with another man can be indicated or recognized as an act of irony or humor, leaving the identity of heterosexuality intact (depending on the reader's digital–cultural literacy or knowledge of the person). The important element here in understanding social networking as a site for an intelligible identity performance is that different users will exploit these tools in different ways and to varying degrees, and that at no stage is this necessarily a conscious, voluntary moment of identity construction but just as reiterative, hidden, and disavowed as a masculine way of walking performs, stabilizes, and is consistent with a male identity, or choices around household furnishing performs and coheres with, say, a middle-class income bracket, affiliation, or identification. These are never complete, but always and forever remain a process – persistent maintenance of the self and constant maintenance of the profile.

Subjectivity as an effect within an interactive digital environment occurs not through an external act of "naming" but in "taking" the name or category or label as if one were interpellated by it simultaneously, as if it were simply a choice for a convenient representation. None of these forms of performativity online operate as freefloating decisions but, in line with a theory of performativity are constituted by the available, provided categorizations in line with the available discourses of selfhood. An obvious but significant example being that gender configurations in contemporary society are expected to conform to available cultural categories (masculine/ feminine and various emerging, sometimes controversial alternatives) but, in performing these online through an enunciative act on a social networking profile, one is required to declare a category on the assumption that this is a fixed and relatively unchangeable necessary facet of selfhood. This forecloses on the broad range of alternative possibilities that might emerge in languages not yet utilized or terms not yet categorizable or, indeed, by articulating nonwestern androgynies which cannot be expressed through either a dichotomy or even a singular concept label. As Ian Buchanan (2007) put it in discussing the cultural, linguistic, and discursive options available to us around gender identity, "you can choose to be man, woman, or transgendered, but you cannot choose to be nongendered." The categories available in making profile choices in social networking sites provide, indeed, the same limitations – if not stricter ones – as the discourses available to us. In Butler's (1990) terms, like discourse, these are "constitutive categories that seek to keep gender in its place by posturing as the foundational illusions of identity" (pp. 33–34).

Although not wholly constrictive given the range of counter options for performing otherwise (e.g., the biography text-box or ongoing status updates), the provided categories on social networking sites offer a notion of freedom to "choose" that which is endemic to neoliberalist thinking and digital technology's either/or framework (Lazzarato, 2004, 2009). Yet they risk for some users the violence of a normative truth regime that excludes alternative, postmodern, poststructuralist ways of reconfiguring identity, self-complexity, or doing subjectivity otherwise (Butler, 1993, p. 53). In other words, while culture might demand identity coherence in accord with a culturally recognized discourse, the social networking tools of subject performance provide limited scope for playing out an identity in accord with anything but the most simplistic and simplified discourses articulating only the most limited normative choices – at least around gender, age, and relationship status as three areas of demarcated and heavily politicized identity coordinates. What is important about the profile pages of Facebook is that the information, often provided as an initiation into social networking (boyd, 2008a, p. 128) and subsequently updated as the "narrative" of our performed identities, might change, shift, or stabilize over time, in response to the cultural demand for coherence. Social networking sites provide the tools for smoothing over the inconsistencies into an intelligible, recognizable presentation of selfhood. This is not the site of the chatroom experiment of Turkle's (1995) pre-Web 2.0 understanding of Internet identities, but is coterminous with an offline sense of self, masquerading as a biography and representation but just as constitutive of self-identities.

Social networking sites can therefore be understood as sites through which identity categories are most effectively performed. Most social networks are built around individual user profiles, even though these are always produced and utilized in relation to others. The first step for the creation of any given profile is to engage in a form filling process; a process that now occurs countless times over one's lifetime. As Butler notes, the repeated act of "naming" identity categories is an institutionalized form of regimentation that produces and circulates normativities by requiring the construction of an identity in accord with dominant discursive arrangements like heteronormativity and naturalized principles of sexual difference. As initial profile creation frequently involves submitting gender and age, and often includes sexual preference, nationality, and relationship status, it can be viewed a set of acts that are repeated over time to produce a mythical reality.

## 4  IDENTITY, FRIENDSHIP, AND THE NETWORK

Although not wholly disconnected from profile management, the act of friending and relating to others through social networking on Facebook is a separate set of performances of identity expression. This second "field" of online performance focuses on the social or relational, producing conformity through interactive identification with others: friends, acquaintances, strangers, persons known only online, coworkers, employees, students and teachers, parents, and family – all typically presented under the problematically simple label of "friends." Online relationality is developed through (1) the creation and maintenance of friends lists through the reciprocal adding and accepting of friends (Lewis & West, 2009, p. 1210) and (2) engaging with those friends to varying degrees through interactive communication such as updating, commenting, responding, and tagging (Green, 2008, p. 7). Both are performative acts of identification articulated through frameworks of relationality and belonging; specific activities which produce, constitute, and stabilize the self. Friendship, kinship, and other relationships are significant elements in the performance of identity (Lewis & West, 2009, p. 1210) and within this theoretical approach it can be argued that the act of coherent and intelligible identity performances are not only to maintain norms for social participation but are done in the context of those in our circle of friends who – often unwittingly but within disciplinary society – surveil. Those who will engage with the narrative of my performance, those who will look for coherence, and those who will recognize my self as a subject do so on behalf of power formations of normalization. This is something that occurs within a construction not just of identity norms, categories, and names as given discursively, but within a matrix of identification and belonging.

Much writing on social networking and identity draws on the early work of Erving Goffman (1959), Erik Erikson (1968), and the slightly more recent accounts of subject formation presented by Anthony Giddens (1991). For these writers, a notion of performance is utilized to place the process of identity maintenance, and the overcoming of identity crises through re-flexive behavior in relation to the presentation of the self, among a group or the public in sociality. In some recent work on how users present themselves through social networking on LiveJournal, Hodkinson (2007) points out that friending is about an individualized set of choices as to how one inter-acts and customizes the self within shifting personal priorities rather than within fixed and ongoing group structures (p. 646). Following Donath and boyd (2004), Liu points out that a user's friends' connections are an expres-sion of identity and "the public display of friend connections constitutes a social milieu that contextualizes one's identity" (Liu, 2008, p. 254). They are, for Liu, "willful acts of context creation" (p. 254) that aim to produce group identifications through solidarity between a user's tastes and a social group's taste norm (pp. 261–262). This perspective is notable for the way in which it places identity within the context of surveillance through spectatorship and interaction with others within a social network. Liu sees this as a self-conscious act by which performers are reflectively aware of the impres-sions fostered within the network of friends. However, the relationality of social networking can be understood as a nonostensible activity taken up unwittingly by users as part of the "biographical 'narratives' that will ex-plain themselves to themselves, and hence sustain a coherent and consistent identity" (Buckingham, 2008, p. 9). In line with Butler's more nuanced ap-proach to performativity, we can thus argue that the performances of iden-tity which may appear to be wilful and reflexive are acts which constitute the narrative of selfhood, retroactively establishing the subject who speaks – or in this case, speaks the self through status updates and interactions with friends or speaks the self through the performative acts of friending. The performative interaction and relationality with others online comes in two forms: (1) friending and friend list maintenance and (2) synchronous and asynchronous communication between those "friends," both of which I will outline below.

*Friending.* To understand the identity implications of the act of friending we need to explore the way in which the performance of subjecthood operates in the context of online social networks: that is, by asking what this "friendship" might actually come to be. There is some emerging work which looks the ways in which friends are categorized variously by the user via new mechanisms that allow certain information to remain private from certain groups (Diaz, 2008); others have explored some of the ways in which friendship online is understood as a weak form of relationality with others as opposed to social contact in a fully embodied, offline sense (Ellison et al., 2007, p. 1146; Baym, Zhang, Kunkel, Ledbetter, & Lin, 2007, p. 737; Tong et al., 2008, p. 537); and still others have suggested that social networking sites' singular conceptual category of friend (regardless of various privacy distinctions on Facebook) is a flattening out of the complex relationships and multiple categories of friendship, kinship, and acquaintanceship experienced in offline spaces (Lewis & West, 2009, p. 1211). We can advance these important points by noting that the act of friending – of adding a friend, whether that be an acquaintance, a stranger, an old friend, or some other category of relationship, is an act of identity performance in and of itself. But that act is channeled through a concept of identification – of acknowledging and thereby producing and stabilizing some relationship and some sense of like (whether that be liking in the sense of fondness or being akin to another, noting that Facebook frequently uses the signifier like as a means of response to friends' comments and the terminology for joining a group fan page). Choosing to add a friend may well be a voluntary act of seeking information or gaining access to another's profile; in Butler's performativity framework it is what that act "says" about a user that retrospectively makes it a factor of identity performance.

In the case of Facebook, one thus forms an identification with another through the performative act of adding a friend or liking a group, and this responds to the very gray set of distinctions between identifying with another in relation; possessing another as a friend on a list, and possessing a particular "friend count" (Tong et al., 2008, p. 545). Given that friending on Facebook, as on several other social networking platforms, is also an action which allows access to one's profile of "managed" self-information, prior postings, photographs, and other artifacts (Tufekci, 2008, p. 23), the act is a sort of double performative – it is an identification that is simultaneously an articulation of the history of identifications given through that profile, a simultaneous act of relationality and of speaking the self. None of this is to suggest that there is some flattening out of all persons on a friendship list, as if a group has come together through sameness. Rather, identifications can be constituted in difference and distinction (Butler, 1995, p. 441). For a singular user, what can occur is a set of identifications that are marked by varying gradations and fragmentations of identification, of sameness and difference, of closeness and distance, and of other categorizations which may not be stated obviously through Facebook's friends lists. The act of adding – and, by corollary, the decision not to add – friends is thus an act of performance that constitutes the self through a complex array of claims to relationality and sociality.

*Networked communication.* As for the second form of performativity through friendship and relationality, identifications are stabilized through commentary, updates, discussions, communication, and interactivity. The performativity of relationships and belonging in social networking is, in other words, not limited to (1) owning a list of friends and/or (2) being on another's list of friends, but on maintaining flows of communication through the multifarious vectors of friendship and relationality on social networking sites. These are by no means the only ways in which relational communication flows: social networkers today utilize a multiplicity of communication platforms both offline and online, through synchronous and asynchronous means, and across more than one social networking site. Communication and comments are not always necessarily simply updates on one's actual status, thoughts and feelings, or responses to others' comments, etc., that can be read by or are intended for a wider audience. Rather, they can work within various sets of connotations and significations that may be understood by, for example, the friends of the user: common experiences, shared amusements, in-jokes among a close inner circle (Lewis & West, 2009, p. 1222), or "seemingly random statements that only their recipients could truly appreciate" (Walker, Krehbiel, & Knoyer, 2009, p. 686), are among the codes of speech of insider remarks and asides that formulate and perform certain types of belonging in the space of the social networking site.

Perhaps the best way of understanding the interface between belonging and identification through social networking sites is in line with Manuel Castells' network morphology that characterizes contemporary sociality across political, economic, labor, and technological environments (Castells, 2000). It is no surprise that the relationality of social networking fits with Castell's description of the network (despite predating the uptake of Facebook and, slightly before that, MySpace), given social networking sites are, of course, the culmination of its logic. As far as the logic that directs social networking sites goes, Castells suggests that relationality occurs along the lines of an increasing complexity of interaction (Castells, 2000, pp. 70–71) which is witnessed in the multiplicity of communicatory engagements across a social networking site from the perspective of a single user (and, indeed, also in offline situations). For example, a user makes a status update that is able to be seen by all or some on a friends list who have access to that profile's wall. One friend can begin a commentary that surreptitiously questions how that update fits within the user's recognizable identity: "But you said last week that you preferred…" demanding an explanation. The complexity occurs not because the borders of a community are being policed through surveillance and the imperative to confess for normalization, coherence, and recognition, but because the original status update is open to a multiplicity of "activated meanings" within a complex set of discursive reading formations (Bennett, 1983, p. 218). For different friends, this will depend not on where they are located within a network morphology, but on how they are located. Friends lists are not a flattened group of individuals but identify with users variously, through multiple typologies: family/ friend/acquaintance, extent of experience with the user, shared identity experiences, and production and maintenance of online and offline knowledge. Of course, each user's typology of friends and how they operate on the network of relationality will differ (perhaps rapidly) over time, and will include how other meanings and identifications are produced in other ways across the network – such as how that user commented on a photograph on the friend's sister's partner's site. In other words, complexity is found in the variances in knowledge around a user and the considerable variety of networkers, but is managed through the technological paradigm of a social networking site. Simultaneous complex and easy belonging becomes not a thing but a momentary intersection between different dimensions of identification, which is managed, but always persistently in flux. Online relationality, identification, mutuality, and performance, are constituted by a structural logic of "nodes and hubs" (Castells, 2000, p. 443). Within Facebook, as well as other social networking sites, friends become placed in an amorphous nodes, hubs, and points framework, allowing us to see a releveling of relationalities such that from the perspective of all users there are multiple network formations at play.

Relationality may thus depend on a number of social factors, but how it is expressed online conforms to this newer logic of the network that shifts from one formation to another depending on different contexts, times of day, topics of conversation, issues arising, and so on. Thus, the framework of identifications which occur across the network in its very instability, amorphousness, and flux are multiple, and this aligns with Butler's point that identifications are always multiple and occurring all the time, therefore never driven by a singular identification or rule (Butler, 1990, p. 67). The degree to which social networking friendship constitutes one's subjectivity is, of course, variable and must never be considered out of the context of the full, complex array of relationships, spaces, places, and experiences occurring across everyday life – that is, not just the Web 2.0 world of online communication and interactivity. What social networking has enabled, however, is a shift in the logic of identification and belonging from spatial, kinship, and community patterns into an everincreasing cycle of complexity in which belonging continues to be the primary aim of performing identities toward intelligibility and coherence, but whereby the notion of belonging is defined differently now through the network of flows. Ultimately, this makes subjectivity more complex: the logic of social networking postmodernizes subjecthood in a way different from the late capitalist postmodernization of identity through consumption (Jameson, 1985). While some might bemoan the simpler, more stable frameworks that belong to Enlightenment's demands for coherence, this somewhat rival logic opens up new possibilities for, at the very least, alternative ways of being a subject.

## 5  IDENTITY, MULTIPLICITIES, AND UNDOING

While profile maintenance and online friendship/relationality are both sets of performative acts which in Butler's framework of performativity constitutes narratives of selfhood, while evaluating their effectiveness as tools for the coherent and intelligible performance of identity there emerges a critical argument that these two facets of social networking compete with each other and risk the undoing of identity narratives and coherence. That is, while they both provide a useful and effective means by which to articulate self-identity, in ways that aim to fulfill the cultural demand for intelligible selfhood, viewed together they open either the possibility of revealing the basic incoherence and multiplicity of identity or adding to the task of "identity work." It is important to remark here on some of the ways in which the use of Facebook generates an inconsistency is in the performance of a coherent identity. This incompatibility of the two activities might best be figured as one of the gaps in citation, reiteration, and repetition of which Butler (1990) has demonstrated "shows up" the persistent instability of coherent identity (p. 145). In fact, it may only be by taking the risk of showing an identity's incoherence that identification with others – the networking with, for, and by friends in various formations – can occur. The profile, as I have been arguing, is the site of a reiterative performance or practice of identity that, carefully constructed, works as part of an overall narrative and a strategy toward the coherent performance of a unified identity/subjectivity, answering the Enlightenment imperatives for intelligibility and recognition in order to participate socially and achieve belonging within a disciplinary society of norms. While sites such as Facebook and other social networking formations provide a convenient tool for the construction and clarification of selfhood online (and one that is capable of being utilized as an archive for offline performances for others and self), they also present the greatest risk to narrative coherence through the specifically digital and asynchronous forms of friending and friendship communication and interactivity. This occurs in three identifiable ways: (1) through the capacity of social networking walls and commentary spaces by which a friend is invited to surveil, identify, and point to a breach in identity coherence most easily; (2) through the possibility of disruption by being able to point to the specific moments in the record of identity narrative represented by wall posts and status updates and in contrast with other parts of the social networking site such as photographs; and (3) by the fact that the narrative of the self is not entirely "managed" by the user (in the same way as, say, a diary maintained over time has been), meaning his or her performance of coherent selfhood is persistently countered by the comments about that person and – particularly – the possibly unwanted tagging of the user in photographs that may be unwanted, not in his or her possession, and not under his or her control (except to keep tabs on this regularly and remove tags where possible).

## 5.1 Commentaries

The fact that participants in the social networking nodes and hubs of relationality are in a position to surveil each profile, creates the possibility for the undoing of identity coherence, noting the point that this is not necessarily a negative thing, but something which creates difficulties in fulfilling the continuing Enlightenment imperative of intelligible, reasonable, and recognizable subjectivity. This is akin to the "café conversation" mentioned earlier. In the act of conversing about oneself, one may be called upon by a friend to clarify any perceived incoherence in identity, frequently seen as a lack of "integrity": "But yesterday, you said that you were a vegetarian…" or "but I had no idea you'd slept with women, so are you bisexual or what…?", and so on. The call from the friend to clarify in terms of a known, recognizable, and perhaps normative narrative is undertaken on behalf of contemporary culture's imperative for coherence. This might easily be resolved by an explanation that reweaves the life story, the narrative of identity. The response restores one to recognizability, even though it may be a recognition or rethinking of the self: "Yes, I am vegetarian, I had a moment of weakness", "sometimes I do eat fish", "I've always found both genders attractive", or "it was something I was doing in college – everybody was." But once this "conversation" and the demand for confession, clarity, and coherence shifts to the Facebook wall we have a markedly different scenario which more effectively undoes identity coherence and selfhood than a fleeting verbal remark: a textual comment, a request written on the wall is no longer simply a spoken demand for a recognizable identity narrative but is on the one hand a call that is made in a semipublic environment and on the other a call that persists over time.

The fact that the conversational policing of identity occurs through wall and photo/video commentary responses provides what might otherwise have been a spoken request the cultural perception of authority that comes with written/produced text (Foucault & Bouchard, 1977, p. 128; Biriotti & Miller, 1993, pp. 2–6, 12). At the same time, however, it should be remembered that this is not a one-sided form of conversing whereby an author–user is interrogated by a reader–feedback–friend. Rather, this goes both ways, for the request for a clarification, a comment, a caption, etc., made by a friend is also his or her act of subject performance, an articulation constitutive of the self within the nodes and hubs arrangement of the network morphology of online identification. The multiple directions of the flow of such performative commentary and conversation is an interactivity which, for Mark Andrejevic (2002), has an element of the confessional culture that stems from a contemporary desire for subjection to "a discursive regime of self-disclosure" (p. 234). For some time now, media scholars have noted the ways in which confession of the self has been remade as entertainment, across television shows such as *Sex and the City* to reality television to the talkback show epitomized by *Oprah* (Attwood, 2006, p. 84). However, the Facebook Wall can be characterized as confession of the self, remade as friendship and relationality, indeed there have been suggestions that earlier homepages and other interactive sites of biography are the culmination of a confessional society (Kennedy, 2006, p. 870).

Where disciplinary surveillance itself shifts into a network morphology, its efficacy is no longer in the possibility of being watched, as Foucault puts it using the metaphor of the Panopticon (Foucault, 1977), but in the certainty of that surveillance operating within the network flows of relationality. Friends are no longer thus those who might surveil and normalize; rather, their relative placement as nodes and hubs, in an interactive flow of question and answer, constitutes their performativity as Facebook friends within a framework of regularization and normalization. In that sense, Facebook friendship is the disciplinary regime of confession *par excellence*. However, due to the multiplicity of flows that contrast with the centralization of the Panopticon metaphor, we see not its effect as normalization, rather multiple attempts to normalize from multiple angles that can come with diverse "conversations" from different friends, about different updates, across different formulations of private and public speech, and alongside different activations of meaning – the user and his or her narrative of recognizable identity risk being forcibly fragmented or, at the very least, requiring even greater "identity work" to perform, retain, and stabilize coherence and intelligibility.

## 5.2  Disrupting the Past – the Archive

Confession in the face of the other is, as Sally Munt (2002) has pointed out, a technique of the self which renders the subject "visible and plausible to itself, and to others" through a reiteration which gains the force of a plot and involves a persistent and retrospective reordering (p. 19). But what happens to that retrospective remembering and reconfiguring when the momentary articulations of an identity performance, and the many conversations and regimentary instances of surveillance and confession, are laid out across a social networking wall as a written history? What Brett St. Louis (2009), following Stuart Hall, has referred to as narratives which account "for peoples' arrival at the present through a past that is imaginatively reconstructed and dramatized" (p. 565) and Buckingham (2008) points to as part of the "project of selfhood" in which biographical narratives articulated over time, are both useful in pointing to the ways in which the narrative of performative selfhood, that is developed by the user through profile management, is put asunder by friendship wall discussions, additions, commentary, and tagging that acts as an archive. That is, the memorialization of the past is not as easily refigured, reordered, and reremembered when an order, a history, and a set of collective memories are laid out as an archive. An autobiography or a reflective construction of a user's online profile involves a memorialization of a past which never existed but which retrospectively narrates and justifies the current moment of identity coherence in order to lend the illusion of an ongoing fixity of selfhood across time (Mendelson & Papacharissi, 2011). However, an archive of the past is precisely that which opens up the possibility of incoherence by having documented the past identity configurations at various moments.

For Castells (2000), the network captures within its domain "most cultural expressions, in all their diversity" (p. 403), and it is in the powerful tools of a Web 2.0 digital environment that data and articulations from different points in subjective time are brought together. This, again, will be in the form of status updates, commentaries, feedback, conversations, images, and videos which flow across the network but are gathered together on a single page as a documentation of every shift in identity. I can look at my friend's wall and read a biography which is presented in reverse order, hitting the "older posts" button to take me further and further back. While my friend's profile presents a coherent and constructed narrative, a biography and set of educational and employment posts, a list of various tastes, combined with my knowledge of his or her other activities and experiences, there is a clear and discernible narrative available to me. This profile may have been revised a dozen times, but when read as a profile there is no necessary reason to tease out its constructedness. But reading the wall posts, commentary, and friends' views along with the updates on when friends were added and so on, I can see a documentary record of momentary snapshots of a fragmentary self that has not been shaped into performance masquerading as a representation of intelligible selfhood. My friend's recognition as a coherent subject is at risk. What is important to note, however, is that online commentary can be, to use Vikki Bell's (1999) phrase, "the constitutive moments and modes of identity" (p. 7). For performativity to "work," those constitutive moments must be smoothed over, disavowed, forgotten, or rememorialized into something else. It is precisely this that the documentary record of these moments does not allow, instead making visible the fact that any subject may have had a multitude of those moments corresponding to shifts in identity.

## 5.3 Tagging

Tagging of images and other artifacts has sometimes been a slightly controversial element of Facebook, given that it allows a user to link the name of another user to a photograph which the tagged person may not have seen, been aware of, or authorized. Tagging is very much the epitome of an interactive, participatory Web 2.0 culture of communication (Walther, Van Der Heide, Kim, Westermanand, & Tong, 2008, p. 30). Tags create identificatory links, giving an association or a connection between a user and a set of behaviors that may be discerned in a photograph – which is not to deny the multiplicity of meanings that can be interpreted, read, or activated by view-ers of that image. To tag a photograph on Facebook, a user uploads it to an album, selects the tagging tool, selects a face or other body part (or anything else really) in the image, and either chooses a person's name from their list of network contacts (friends) or types any other name or tag. Now, there is nothing particularly new about being able to make this kind of association in an online capacity. One could establish a website and caption or other-wise tag people's names to images which, again, they may not have seen or authorized for distribution. What is significantly different in the case of Facebook is that once tagged, an alert will appear on a user's wall, fed to the newsfeed seen by all other people in that person's network. This, of course, is part of the increasing capacity of digital environments to organize data and online artifacts in ways which are more easily accessible through classi-fying, filtering, and tagging, even though it replicates older conceptual issues around the relationship between image and word (Prada, 2009). An image of a user may be captioned, but for anyone searching for those images, with-out digital tagging they would be difficult to find, similar to, for example, a handwritten caption in an analog, physical album in grandmother's attic. This element of rationality has caused concern and panic around the pri-vacy and control of information over the past couple of years in the popular press. There have been concerns about the ways in which tagged nontextual items become increasingly searchable online (Hearn, 2010a), which, given how different in tone and context an image or video can be from text, may have an impact not just on how one is represented but on how one per-ceives oneself – particularly if the tagged image or video comes back as a surprise. According to recent reports, several European countries' regulators, including those in Switzerland and Germany, are currently investigating the practice of posting photos, videos, and other information about people on sites such as Facebook and tagging them without their consent as be-ing a breach of privacy laws (Privacy Battle, 2010). It might be argued that privacy concerns are not only about control of ostensible information but about the management of identity performance, and preventing the presen-tation of the self from spiraling out uncontrollably across networking sites and over time.

An example of the ways in which tagging acts to disrupt or undo the coherent narrative of an identity performance is as follows: a recent news report has addressed issues of jealousy that might occur when one's current partner is tagged in photographs by – and with – an expartner (Who's that girl, 2009), clearly addressing the distinction between an older model of analog photographs and the social practices around the removal or hiding of photographs that present past relationships. Where acts of coupledom are central to identity practices in contemporary culture (Cover, 2010), an unwanted, unintended reemergence of a past relationship can create, preserve, and archive additional layers of relational identifications for that user, and indicates an incompatibility with the invited profile statement naming the current partner. This might, of course, be further complexified should the gender of the past partner be different from the current one, opening fragmentations for some networked friends in the sexual orientation of the profiled user. From the perspective of the user who has utilized Facebook's profile function and wall in the construction of a performance of coherent identity which has, by necessity, involved disavowing past experiences, the undoing of identity is initiated by an encounter with the past. Not a memorialized past – rewritten in one's memory or narrative through the framework of an identity present, but an archaeological artifact that might grate against the currency of one's identity performance, both online and offline. In other words, tagging not only takes identity out of the myth that it is represented, articulated, commanded, and controlled by the subject through profiles and performances, but acts as a reminder that the network framework commandeers and potentially thwarts the performativity of an intelligible selfhood.

In advancing our understanding of the relationship between social networking (and other online activities) and the performance of identity within contemporary cultural norms, structures, and frameworks, it is important to bear in mind that social networking uses, activities, changes, updates, and account management are not only conscious representations and choices made for access, but simultaneously activities or performances which construct identity and selfhood. What is significant here is that rather than thinking of social networking as singular activities, the ways in which sites social networking through Facebook have developed through the growth of applications, user-uptake and favored user activities has provided us with a multiplicity of activities and communicative forms which, as I have been arguing in relation to (1) profiles and (2) friendship networking, are not always mutually compatible with the project of subject performance. This theoretical account is one among several ways in which we can approach social networking and identity; additional empirical work will reveal other understandings of this significant tool of everyday identity.

# CHAPTER 2

# Performativity, Communication, and Selfhood

In the previous chapter, I introduced a number of key concepts related to how we can think about identity in an online, digital context by drawing on Judith Butler's work on identity performativity to explore the increasingly ubiquitous use of social networking and complex representation of identity in contemporary online contexts. There, I worked through some of the increasingly outdated approaches to identity as well as some increasingly irrelevant notions of online selfhood that belong to Web 1.0 text-based experimental worlds of online engagement to demonstrate that Butler's approach to the performativity of selfhood is one of the strongest – albeit, one of the most complex – theorizations of subjectivity most suitable to today's online environment. In this chapter, I would like to extend that analysis further and think about identity performativity in the context of media forms and use. In the context of the historical movement toward a media-saturated and global communication environment, I explore the different arrangements for approaching the role of media and communication in terms of their influence on the identification and representation of resources taken up for different ways of doing and performing identity.

There are three aspects necessary to cover here in order to make sense of the ways in which digital, networked activity and identity, subjectivity, and selfhood are intertwined in a contemporary era. First, it is necessary to delve deeper into the relationship between the media itself since it is that which "makes available" the very discourses through which identities are made intelligible and cited in performative articulations of selfhood. Second, we then need to question this media–identity couplet further by asking how access and the audience operate to produce particular readings of those identity categories – in other words, to interrogate how subjects read from identity positions when identities are only understood from highly subjective interpretations of what is given in a media context. Third, we must put this complex circularity to task by asking how the self is fashioned through broader cultural frameworks of subjectivity. For example, an environment in which we are, at one level, compelled to produce and articulate identities in line with Enlightenment perspectives of coherent, unified, and narrowly

*Digital Identities.*
http://dx.doi.org/10.1016/B978-0-12-420083-8.00002-X

categorizable and recognizable notions of selfhood and, on another level, framed through postmodern approaches that articulate the self as always being available to be produced through notions of agency and consumption. Only by exploring these matters can we begin to make sense of how identity is produced in the context of digital interactivity, in the über-mediated world of participatory engagement through remixing, borrowing, playing with textuality, communicating at speed, and generally engaging in ways which are, on the one hand culturally "new," while on the other, are fast becoming ubiquitous for those on the "right side" of any framing of the digital divide.

In thinking about the implications of the broad role of the multifaceted saturation of everyday life by media and digital communication in the context of how identities are recognized, made intelligible, and performed, it is important to note that we are never talking about a standard singular practice of using media and digital textuality. Communication is of many sorts (Urry, 2007, p. 158), and these are accessed in everyday ways from the face-to-face conversation to those that might be said to fall in the "traditional" category such as letters, books, radio, television entertainment, television news, and music. In addition, there are those forms which fall under what we, as recently as a decade ago, termed "new media" and which may now be termed "digital communication": email, text messages, mobile telephone calls, skype calls, video conferencing, social networking, YouTube remixes, and dating app messages conveyed through both mobile and fixed sites such as Tinder or Grindr, to name a few. John Urry makes the valid point that the dichotomies of "real/unreal, face to face/life on the screen, immobile/mobile, community/virtual and presence/absence" are no longer helpful (pp. 180–181). I agree completely, and would suggest that there is no longer any real point in assuming that some people prefer traditional media while, say, younger persons are engaging in identity practices in online contexts. Indeed, as an example, it is no longer valuable to assume that one has a particular reading practice in watching the news on television and recognizing oneself or one's identity category in news stories without this being markedly influenced by the practices of utilizing digital media in non-news contexts (and when one sits in front of the television with a tablet device in hand and the hand of one's partner in the other, this influence across the networked fabric of traditional and digital and corporeal occurs simultaneously). "New media" is now so ubiquitous and, as David Buckingham (2008) has pointed out, its everyday use is so banal (p. 14) that we are in a good position to investigate its utilization as a resource for identity formation and for providing the codes that make identity performativity coherent through older theories of traditional media. It is thus possible to attend to all media through an acknowledgment and awareness that there are new and emerging practices of how we "do" identity that are in alignment with the emergence of new digital practices of "doing media."

For Butler (1990), to be "constituted" as a subject with a particular set of identities and attributes means "to be compelled to cite or repeat or mime" the signifier itself that is made available in discourse (p. 220) and, today, through the media processes of distribution, audience engagement, interpretation, and authorization. The persistent impossibility of any true repetition makes a genuinely coherent, fixed, and ongoing identity a myth – this is despite the fact that we can never escape the social requirement to repeat a discursively and media-given identity (Butler, 1990, p. 148; Campbell & Harbord, 1999, p. 231) – we cover that failure over with performances that lend the illusion that all acts stem from an inner identity core in order to maintain intelligibility for social participation and social belonging. Citation, however, is more complex than merely reading and "taking on" that discursively given and mediated identity signifier, category, or name and repeating it as coherently as we can. For Butler (1993), while a subject can produce an effect in discourse by articulating the self,

> there is first a discourse which precedes and enables that "I" and forms in language the constraining trajectory of its will. Thus there is no "I" who stands behind discourse and executes its volition or will through discourse. On the contrary, the 'I' only comes into being through being called, named, interpellated (to use the Althusserian term), and this discursive constitution takes place prior to the 'I'. … the discursive condition of social recognition precedes and conditions the formation of the subject: recognition is not conferred on a subject, but forms that subject. Further, the impossibility of a full recognition, that is, of ever fully inhabiting the name by which one's social identity is inaugurated and mobilized, implies the instability and incompleteness of subject-formation. The 'I' is thus a citation of the place of the 'I' in speech, where that place has a certain priority and anonymity with respect to the life it animates: it is the historically revisable possibility of a name that precedes and exceeds me, but without which I cannot speak" (pp. 225–226).

In this key paragraph from the essay "Critically Queer" in *Bodies That Matter* (Butler, 1993), the key element of her thesis of performativity being spelled out to indicate the instabilities of citation – that a subject has his or her identity interpellated unwillingly through forms of recognition that are conferred by being emplaced as a social being within language. We can expand on this to suggest that one is emplaced with discourse that is mediated and engaged with predominantly through media forces and conditions that depend, first, on the ways in which the categories of identity given in mediated discourses are read, interpreted, and understood, second, in the ways that media formations make some discourses available while obscuring, hiding, or marginalizing other discourses, and third, through the complex circularity of citations of identity that, themselves, need to be recognized from standpoints of identity. In other words, media and digitally conditioned discourse precedes the subject and constitutes identity. However, this is not a wholesale, simplistic linear pattern of text reading–interpretation–selfhood.

In this chapter I work through each of these three conditions that expand Butler's approach to account for media and mediation as key forms through which discourse is engaged in contemporary society, beginning – somewhat at the end of the traditional concept of the communication process – with audiencehood, moving to interrogate some of the ways in which media is responsible for the kinds of identity produced by certain dominant and nondominant discourses of subjectivity, and then briefly pointing to some of the instabilities of citation by invoking a concept of recognition that is also a recognition or rethinking of the self. I would like to end with some thoughts on media's relationship with identity norms and concepts of normativity and the ways in which media texts are, often in nonvoluntary capacities, taken up as pedagogical resources for identity formation. An important caveat here is that we are dealing mostly with media in its twentieth century forms – film, television, broadcast – and some of the ways in which such models of communication continue in online, digital formats. I leave questions of interactivity and cocreativity of discourse for the next chapter, as they are key to considering how we can go forward to understand the conditions of identity in the twenty-first century media mode of digital belonging.

## 1 IDENTITY IN A MEDIA-SATURATED CONTEMPORARY WORLD

Discussions of the relationship between identity/subjectivity and media forms have, to date, been somewhat limited to a set of fairly discrete disciplinary categories, each working with particular sets of theories of subjectivity as well as theories of media production, dissemination, and spectatorship. Many of these are popular in the public sphere, in both journalistic and opinion-writing discourses, particularly for their simplicity and for the ease by which we can "blame the media," "blame the Internet," "blame computer games," or "blame mobile telephony" for all the ills of the world. Yet media scholars and theorists have often pointed to the need to embrace more complex ways of thinking about the role of media and digital communication and the influence it has on people which, in the case of the topic at hand, includes the influence on identity. What I would like to demonstrate in this section is that there are a number of ways in which both twentieth century and twenty-first century media forms are implicated in constituting particular kinds of identity, ways of knowing identity, and mechanisms by which we learn to perform identities. However, it is not as simple as making the claim that we are "influenced" or blindly led into narrow ways of thinking about ourselves in identity terms or that our identities are exhaustively constructed by our media, spectatorial, online, and interactive communication practices. I will discuss relatively briefly here five different theoretical approaches that present ways of thinking about the relationship between media/communication, behavior, and identity: (1) effects theories, (2) psychoanalytic Screen Theory, (3) early cultural studies approaches and Stuart Hall's encoding/decoding approach to audience interpretation, (4) poststructuralist approaches to the active production of meaning through discursive formations, and (5) neoliberalism's role in framing audience normativities, acknowledging the push and pull between Enlightenment rationality and postmodern, consumer-driven fluidity as competing forms of contemporary identity production.

## 1.1 Media Effects, Imitation, and Identification

Media effects models continue to dominate public discourse and certain brands of psychological study of media and digital communication, often resulting in a narrow, linear understanding of media that assumes all audiences, readers, and users are actively "duped" into performing types of self and behavior that are presented to us in limited ways, without accounting for the complexity of reading practices, capacity to interpret, ability to be active in making identifications, and recognitions with a text or any element of agency of the self. Media effects models are often related to discussions about violent television and video games, and to online pornography, whereby exposure to the first is seen to produce violent personalities and violent behaviors, while exposure to the second is generally and in some public discourse presumed to produce men who will rape (identity: rapist) or women who behave sexually in particular ways (identity: submissive; or, sometimes, identity: slut).

Based on an oversimplified linear understanding of communication, media effects theories include various ways of understanding media processes from the perspective that changes in belief and behavior occur through subjection to mass media forms (Shannon & Weaver, 1949). While media stories can indeed influence the behavior of others, the ways in which that influence occurs is complex and always contingent (Curran, 2002, p. 158). Emerging from predominantly North American communications research in the 1940s, 1950s, and 1960s, effects theories are based on a linear understanding of communication; that is, messages sent and received in a particularly "unmediated" fashion and in which the message or meaning itself is understood as relatively unproblematic (Shannon & Weaver, 1949). Looking for a purely "scientific" model of influence, those who worked on and developed the effects approach ignored the role of interpretation, more complex understandings of reception, and diverse meanings or textual polysemy. Effects theories suggest that behavioral and belief changes occur through persuasion, propaganda, manipulation, and – to use a term less widely deployed today – brainwashing. Such theories, particularly the "hypodermic syringe" model in which the media message is seen to get "under the skin" of the viewer/reader and the "blame-it-on-the-TV" motif, continue to ground most understandings of media as effective for audience conduct, notions of copycat behavior, and particularly the fears that suicide representation leads directly and unproblematically to imitation by vulnerable and receptive readers or viewers. As media theorist James Curran has argued, "The conviction … that the media are important agencies of influence is broadly correct. However, the ways in which the media exert influence are complex and contingent" (p. 158). To put this another way, we might say that while there is influence through the dominant role media practices play in everyday and working life, the ways in which that influence occurs is complex. A range of factors may be seen to influence the role of media practices, including (1) the matrix of different media and communication tools accessed, used, deployed, and engaged with in sometimes cross-influential or conflicting ways; (2) the increasing ubiquity of access to sources of information in which an answer (whether right, wrong, or indifferent) to any question can be found very quickly, in contrast to earlier times in which patience, imagination, or forgetting were the dominant ways in which questions and answers about ourselves, others, and the world were dealt with; (3) the speed of change of information, where new information about ourselves, others, political arrangements, social engagements, and the world are open to quick shifts across many platforms from the 24-h news cycle to the persistent updating on Twitter. That is, while there are effects of engagement with media and digital communication, the model of effects is vastly different from that articulated within early effects theory or its deployment in pedestrian and journalistic writing on moral panics and scandals.

For many media and communication studies scholars today, effects approaches are seen to be limited because they confine themselves to immediate and observable changes in human behavior that leave the formal structures of media output untheorized, while isolating the import of media from economic, cultural, and identity-based processes (Moores, 1993, p. 5). Borrowing from literary studies, criticism, and sociolinguistics, cultural studies slammed the effects approach by arguing that this empiricist-based field of study left processes of reception both undertheorized and oversimplified. Media and cultural theorist David Gauntlett (1998), for example, has pointed to a number of conceptual problems with an effects approach. Gauntlett considers not only the linearity of the media experience it actively assumes in its conception of effect, but the lack of empirical evidence that media viewing of violent films and television creates the identity of a "violent offender," the ways in which it individualizes the viewer or media spectator away from the "group" or "community" aspects of how we think about ourselves as members of diverse audiences, its tendency to focus on subjects who are seen to defy a conservative status quo, and its reliance on an assumption that the scholar who identifies media "problems" (violence, pornography, etc.) is superior to the audience member who is seen to lack the critical capabilities of similarly making judgments and criticism or viewing texts in a critical way. Certainly, media effects approaches throughout the twentieth century – and in moral panic reportage today – are wholly disinterested in any positive effects of exposure to media and mediated communication, despite all the powerful work on the pedagogical relationship younger persons have with media, for example, *Sesame Street*.

An example of the media effects model's problems in the context of identity might relate to the common perception that media depictions of suicide position other subjects to commit suicide – that is, to be identifiably a suicide victim, ideator, or attempter. This is a topic I have been looking at in depth for some time in the context of queer youth suicidality. The notion that the dissemination of a "suicide logic" or script that "creates" the identity of the queer youth suicide victim is wholly related to the circulation of such suicide stories can be found in the media and in well-meaning online activist settings such as the advocacy site *It Gets Better* (Cover, 2012a). Imitative or copycat suicides have a checkered history in suicide literature, with Emile Durkheim exploring how the suicides of others in close geographic proximity can impact on one's consciousness and imagination refiguring the self in a collective state that is neither a copy nor a model but a giving over of individuality to the imagined collectivity of a suicidal group (Durkheim, 1952, pp. 125–126). Published originally in 1897, Durkheim's analysis significantly predates the media saturation of contemporary public life and the kind of celebrity culture that is implicated in ideas of the media-constituted imitation of suicides of high-profile figures such as singers Kurt Cobain or Michael Hutchence (Jaworski, 2008). The New Zealand Ministry of Health (2000), as an example, views the research as providing evidence that there is an increased risk of "copycat" suicides or suicide "contagion" resulting from the effect the media and public communication may have on influencing a vulnerable person "struggling with apparently insurmountable personal, interpersonal, or family problems." Warwick Blood and Jane Pirkis have investigated some of the reasons why a heightened rate of suicides might occur after media depiction, arguing that in general terms there is some evidence of a causal link between depictions of nonfictional suicides and subsequent attempts and limited evidence in the case of fictional depictions of suicide, but acknowledge that there are several questions for further research and a need to develop a more complex theoretical framework for understanding how imitation suicides can be discussed and recognized (Blood & Pirkis, 2001, p. 167). The distinction between fiction and news in establishing the conditions for media imitation is, of course, substantial in demonstrating that "effect" is neither ubiquitous nor determining, but depends on multiple factors ranging from how much importance is placed on the media form (e.g., the extent to which the reader identifies with the form as a pedagogical source) and how much that form evokes an identification (e.g., the extent to which the reader finds similarities with those regularly depicted in that form).

The idea that media depictions lead to a particular way of being or behaving as a suicide victim, and that they thereby generate an ongoing spate of further suicides, is therefore regularly taken to be simplistic, but involves caution – media recipients actively identify meanings based on existing knowledge, the environment, and available discourses (Bennett, 1983) as I will argue in more detail below, but some are positioned to make identifications that can be "read" as pedagogical. In the case of suicide imitation, then, it is important not to assume that media depictions or news stories about suicide directly cause subsequent suicides of vulnerable persons because those persons see themselves as vulnerable, identify with the suicide reported, and therefore adopt an identity category and concomitant behavior "as suicidal"; rather, if there is any relationship – as Blood and Pirkis have argued – it is more complex than a linear effects model can show. This is not to argue that media forms are not implicated in the dissemination of discourses that relate particular, subjective forms of media reading practices and digital media use to suicide. But suicide is not simply an imitation of what was seen on TV as viewed by vulnerable or "at risk" individuals cata- lytically causing suicide ideation and imitation of suicide effect or method. Indeed, Durkheim's sociological work on suicide a century ago attempted to negate the idea that suicide is produced through imitation of others (Durkheim, 1952, pp. 131–132; Simpson, 1952, p. 13). While it was possible to show suicides in geographic clusters, bunched suicide attempts had much more to do with regional and local social conditions and the individuals' relative integration within a local sociality than imitation. Durkheim ad- dressed the question of imitation and imagination in the identity of suicide, with the following instructive statement:

> A number of men in assembling are similarly affected by the same occurrence and receive this at least partial unanimity by the identical signs through which each individual feeling is expressed ... Each one imperfectly imagines the state of those about him. Images expressing the various manifestations emanating, with their different shades, from all parts of the crowd, are formed in the minds of all. Nothing to be called imitation has thus far occurred; there have been merely perceptible im- pressions, then sensations wholly adventitial with those produced in us by external bodies ... Once aroused in my consciousness, these various representations com- bine with one another and with my own feeling. A new state is thus formed, less my own that its predecessor, less tainted with individuality and more and more freed, by a series of repeated elaborations analogous to the foregoing, from all excessive particularity ... One should say creation rather than imitation, since this com- bination of forces results in something new. This is indeed the only procedure by which the mind has the power of creation ... Actually, there are here neither models nor copies. There is a penetration, a fusion of a number of states within another, dis- tinct from them: that is the collective state" (1952, pp. 125–126, emphasis added).

Durkheim's analysis here, while predating broadcast, electronic, and inter- active media forms and the cultures in which media engagement is practiced today, presents a cogent argument for thinking beyond imitation. The act of copying or the effect of influence is not, as he points out, imitative but creative – the subject forges a particularly different form of suicide ideation suited to that subject rather than following a model. As an early work on suicide it thus makes the initial argument that imitation is not only a facile conception of the ways in which suicides occur, but is an impossibility since true imitation is unattainable. This certainly puts in question the typical fear that the media reportage of a celebrity suicide is likely to produce ongoing, further suicides among his fans and followers. Durkheim's emphasis on creation provides a useful tool for rethinking imitation in terms of identification. That is, the reading subject who has been subjected to media representations of suicidal vulnerable persons does not fall prey to a power of suggestion that influences an imitation of those suicide images, but may in some circumstances be positioned to make an identification with those represented, perhaps fictional, persons and coming to see their actions, behaviors, desires, and ideations as natural to the identity so acquired and so performed.

Put into the context of how media might be understood to be associated with the inculcation of particular kinds of identity, subjectivity, and selfhood, what is suggested here is that forms of identification are implicated in creating (rather than copying) identity and behavior among those who access media depictions and representations, whether in online or traditional media settings. By identification, I am not referring to the idea that an individual truly recognizes himself or herself as being of a particular category of individual – a particular identity – and thereby goes on to behave in accordance. Identification and imitation of role models are not the same thing. Identification is not a realization that one is the same as the represented figure and should thus act as that figure acts or solve problems as that figure would do. Rather, identification is an ongoing process by which one acquires the signifiers, names, labels, attitudes, and codes of behavior that make a performative selfhood coherent and intelligible in order to participate socially and belong in a contemporary society – a task which is perhaps increasingly difficult in a postmodern, media-saturated culture that conveys not only the appeal of the consumer-based multiplicity of identity but presents persistent conflicting images and what is sometimes referred to as "information overload" as experienced everyday. In that sense, identification is not with an image of an individual, whereby a reader has recognized himself or herself as similar and thereby imitates that subject, internalizing the depiction into the self that results from media spectatorship or online engagement. Instead, it is an identification with a node of (collective) cultural knowledge – a discursive "byte" of information linking subjectivity and behavioral attributes – one sees oneself as part of a community whereby certain recognized and recognizable actions, solutions, styles, attitudes, and behaviors become plausible.

## 1.2  Psychoanalysis, Screen Theory, and the Gaze

While media effects approaches continued to dominate public and, sometimes, reactionary discourses in relation to media, digital communication, new technologies, and youth or generational media utilization practices (such as mobile telephony and the cultures that emerge alongside their use), more complex theories of the relationship between identity and visual media emerged in the latter half of the twentieth century relying on continental European philosophies and theorizations of language in relation to the psyche from a perspective not of effect but of a deeper identification. What came to be called Screen Theory, for example, is one such idea which takes a Lacanian psychoanalytic approach to subjecthood by assuming that all textuality is interpretable from the perspective of the psyche and, therefore, the best texts through which to understand both the self and selfhood as well as through which to explore the meaning of identity are complex, avant-garde texts.

Screen Theory emerged within the pages of the British journal *Screen*, and brought together the brand of Marxism most associated with Louis Althusser and his concept of interpellation and the brand of Freudian psychoanalysis most associated with Jacques Lacan. The main tenet of Screen Theory centers on the way in which the identity of the audience is inscribed in the text in a way which works similarly to Althusser's approach to ideological state apparatuses that, likewise, hail, call upon, and thereby performatively produce the figure of the subject. Louis Althusser's terminology of political subjectivity notes that this subject is constituted not just as the speaking "subject" but the subject in political "subjection" who is given a category or identity through language and institutional power. This latter form of subjection occurs in the inaugurating moment of the metaphorical "turn" to the hail (Althusser, 1971, pp. 128, 160–168). The individual subject does not preexist the discourses which call for the subject to recognize himself or herself in the text and in the codes by which a performativity of subjectivity is culturally intelligible. For Althusser, ideological state apparatuses and ideologies more generally can be understood through the metaphor of the policeman who – in ideological terms – calls upon the subject with a "Hey, you there!"; the subject "turns" to this hail and in the act of turning is subjectified, becoming both a subject and subject to the domination of the policeman. The subject, effectively, turns in guilt and regardless of his or her innocence is subjectivated as criminal under the surveillance and categorization of the policeman. Although Butler has shown that the "hail" is open to refusal (Butler, 1997, pp. 95–96) thereby undoing the determinism of the Althusserian model, terminology of the "turn" as response to the "hailing" of the text remains an immensely useful way of thinking about the inauguration of subjectivity through the entry into a particular set of discourses. We might extend this by noting the ways in which the hail is less likely to be refused, thereby explaining why particular subjects and identities are really quite "common" when there is no logical reason why they necessarily should be so – for example, why the identity of the "bully victim" who performs identity in a particular way does so, other than the "force" of ideology that has induced a particular subject position through the "turn" toward the hail of the bully. In the context of media formations, then, the policeman comes to be replaced with the on-screen text which hails the subject by demanding a particular kind of recognition (of the self) on the screen, producing identification. The act of identifying represents, in a Screen Theory framework, the "turn" toward the ideology that subjectifies, positions, and produces the subject.

Practitioners of Screen Theory largely explored those films which appeared disruptive to the hegemonic construction of language and subjectivity in order to examine and theorize the ways in which these might be seen to produce more complex, interesting, avant-garde, or revolutionary psyches (Moores, 1993, pp. 12–15); in other words, texts which might be understood to refuse the "hail" of ideology and bring about the revolutionary subject. The process of identification that is assumed in Screen Theory is best described by communication theorist Martin Allor (1995):

> Within this approach, the audience member becomes the spectator within the text, filling subject positions within particular discursive practices. In the moment of 'high' Screen Theory, the textual forms of dominant media systems (e.g., the classical continuity editing system) were related to psychoanalytic accounts of the construction of ways of seeing and forms of investment (fetishism, scopophilia). In focusing on the processes of subject formation, film theory displaced the problem of audience activity and effects (and questions of social formation) onto the level of discourse. The spectator was a construction of the text/in the text (p. 545).

In this context, then, Screen Theory came to be seen as that which allowed the scholarly investigation of audiences to move beyond the concern that an effect theory was substantially difficult to prove, and established the audience as individualized dupes of the communication process on the one hand and, on the other, the regular and common liberal presumption of audience members being actively able to choose the extent to which they were influenced by a text. In identity terms, *Screen* encouraged the field to embrace more complex ways of thinking about how identity is formed beyond the dichotomy of (1) it being formed as a wholesale effect of media that is followed unthinkingly, and (2) the audience having preestablished, individual identities that they brought with them to the act of media viewing and that remained unchanged unless they took it upon themselves to change their sense of selfhood.

One useful element that emerged from Screen Theory and, particularly, the work of Screen Theorist Laura Mulvey centers on the identity attribute or factor of gender in the context of on-screen positioning in relation to the gaze. As media theorist Barbara Creed (2003, p. 126) notes, much film theory has continued to be heavily influenced by the work of Laura Mulvey who, building on psychoanalytic and other approaches to the screen, identified a primordial psychological desire for pleasurable looking and developed the concept of the gendered gaze, particularly that of the male gaze: "a world ordered by sexual imbalance, pleasure in looking has been split between active/male and passive/female. The determining male gaze projects its fantasy on to the female figure, which is styled accordingly" (Mulvey, 1999, p. 837). In this analysis, both the subject's viewing practices and the gender of the subjects are available to be understood as produced in the scopophilic pleasures of audiencehood, whereby the screen positions both man and woman into particular roles and attributes (active and passive) and thereby into particular identity expectations. However, while such positioning has value in opening the possibility of thinking beyond the traditional film/television spectatorship model and moving us toward a more profound critique of audiencehood by asking how this might be thought through the figure of the online, digital communication user on, say, YouTube who is simultaneously gazing into the screen and out from it – a point I will come to in later chapters – the efficacy of the underlying theoretical framework here is limited by its determinism. That is, while Screen Theory represented a complex and, perhaps, appealing framework through which to understand the processes by which identities are formed in the context of media (visual and otherwise), it exhausted its potential for two reasons: first, the fact that it is broadly built on a notion of textual determinism (Moores, 1993, pp. 5–6) that leaves no room for agency, interpretation, alternative reading practices, resistance, or diverse audience membership. Rather, any possibility for breaching dominant ideological perspectives is disavowed and, instead, it is by exposure to the avant-garde text that an alternative or resistant subject can be produced. All power is in the hands of authorship. Second, it is problematic by virtue of the failure to account for the potential of popular culture texts – the only films and (in today's terms) sites or online practices that would be of value are those that are identifiable by a scholar as being disruptive and avant-garde. The theory thus fails wholly to understand the diversity of popular culture, the nuances that might be found in the everyday or commercial text, or the fact that even simple texts might leave open the possibility of a greater capacity for the audience to interpret variedly (Eco, 1979) or in more sophisticated, critical ways.

## 1.3 Encoding/Decoding

The shortcomings of Screen Theory in explaining the relationship between media, communication, and identity opened the pathway in the 1970s and 1980s for the emergence of cultural studies models making sense of that relationship from the perspectives of sociality, culture, practice, and every-dayness, while not disavowing the centrality of complex semiotic construction of texts and communication forms. The cultural studies approach shifts, at least marginally, the power of the audience over the authorial control of the text and its meanings. The early 1970s cultural studies approaches brought together the ethnographic interest in the real, lived experience of people that came from writers such as E.P. Thompson and Richard Hoggart, and the structuralist and later poststructuralist emphasis on understanding the discursive structuration of texts as cultural that came from the search for post-Marxist theories and continental European philosophy from Althusser and Antonio Gramsci (Hall, 1980). Stuart Hall's encoding/decoding thesis built on these two poles or paradigms by presenting a model that focused on the ideological production of textuality and the ideological position of the audience who experience the text partly on their own terms – the new model made way for a conception of the possibility (at least) that an audience will "decode" a text in ways not foreseen during the ideological encoding of the text at its moment of production and distribution (Hall, 1993). Hall allows for the possibility that the act of reading a text can result in an ideological decoding that occurs along negotiated or oppositional lines, although he does concede that decoding along dominant "preferred" lines is the more likely. Hall's encoding/decoding thesis articulates a sender–message–receiver process of media dissemination that articulates all messages as being encoded within a particular, authorial and authorized ideology, transmitted, and decoded according to the reader's ideological perspective. The theory sectionalizes audiences into those who accepted a preferred reading of the text in line with its codes of production, a negotiated reading in which elements of the text were accepted and read in line with the producers' meaning but with some elements found to be unacceptable, and an oppositional or resistant stance involving the detotalization of the text, recontextualizing it according to resistant codes (1993). In identity terms, then, this theory makes possible the point that in the encounter with media and online discourses, a subject comes to perform a particular kind of identity in the context of intelligibilities made available by the ideological framing of the text as well as the ideological framing of the subject who reads it. This might be a website which depicts a particular ethnicity as generally submissive; a reader recognizes himself or herself in that text and accepts the preferred reading that this is how he or she should behave, therefore performing that perspective and, retrospectively establishing themselves as that identity subject. In a negotiated reading, in which the reader accepts – ideologically speaking – certain global factors but not necessarily those which are local, the identity attributes depicted are accepted as "truthful" but seen not to apply to them or their nearest kin and peers. Finally, in an oppositional perspective, the reader might be seen in general terms reject the depiction as ideologically driven, critique this perspective and "refuse" it, articulating instead an alternative identity that might be driven by other ideologies made available previously.

A particular emphasis has been placed in late twentieth century cultural studies analyses on the possibility of resistant or oppositional readings in a trajectory which stems from Hall's (1993) encoding/decoding toward a celebrationist account of readerly resistance that is most readily found in John Fiske's work of the late 1980s (Fiske, 1989). It is important in the context of understanding digital identities to ask how resistance can be figured in terms of the analysis of textual subjectification and identification, particularly given the ways in which online communication and engagement are often figured in public sphere discourse through concepts of diversity, alternative textuality, and opposition to "traditional" norms. Fiske's major contribution to audience analysis has been his expansion of the notion of resistant reading. Drawing largely on the theories of Michel de Certeau, Fiske follows Hall's encoding–decoding method but takes it a step further to suggest the high potential for oppositional or resistant readings. He seemingly ignores the "middle-ground category" posited by Hall; that of "negotiated" readings for a dichotomous system of preferred/oppositional readings. Seeing western society as "intransigently diverse", he argues that diversity is maintained by popular and cultural forces in the face of strategic patriarchal capitalist homogenizations (p. 29). For Fiske (1989):

> What a text 'utters' determines, limits, and influences the links that can be made between it and its readers, but it cannot make them or control them. Only readers can do that. For a text to be popular it must 'utter' what its readers wish to say, and just allow those readers to participate in their choice of its utterances (for texts must offer multiple utterances) as they construct and discover its points of pertinence in their social situation (pp. 145–146).

What Fiske misses is that such "resistances" are momentary acts that ignore the continued readerships or the multiplicity of the reasons for reading. This is particularly the case in community and alternative media where publications and narrowcast websites are popular because of their targeting of, and distribution among, a "niche" community. Momentary resistances can instead be understood as fallacies, "distractions," or "entertainments" that allow people to "forget" the position from which they read. By assuming the audience will always make readings which are resistant, Fiske problematically excludes the possibility that a momentary reading may not, in fact, alter the attitudes of a reader to social conditions nor resist the performative effect of a discursive interpellation. A resistant reading to a one-off article or, say, an online blog post on a particular topic does not necessarily change or affect the reading of the discourse in terms of the positionality of the reader. Rather, temporality needs to be factored in here to account for the fact that it is not a matter of a resistant reader with a single, ongoing, fixed and timeless identity, but a reader or digital media user who engages with the text to different degrees, in different ways, from the perspective of different facets or attributes of identity at different times and on different days. In other words, to look toward the multiplicity of the subject rather than the subject who is produced once or who remains forever fixed in that particular subjectivity.

## 1.4  Active Production, Postmodern Approaches

Although not always dominant in communication and media analysis, the most productive approaches to understanding the role of audiences in engaged relation with texts involves seeing them not as media dupes, as psychically constructed by the text, as preferred or resistant readers but as subjects who actively make meaning from the engagement with the text in the context of the available knowledge, discourses, and frameworks through which the text can have meaning for them. This does not mean readers that read as individuals, but as subjects who generate meanings, effect, and impact in relation also to other readers, other texts, other discourses, and other experiences. In the interaction between text and reader, other discourses are always in operation besides those of the particular text in focus (Moores, 1993, p. 16). The discourses through which a reader, user, or audience member generates meaning through the media process depends on the subject's particular placing within other practices – cultural, educational, and institutional – thus predicating reading as interdiscursive. What is "read" in the text in a seemingly voluntaristic way – its content, its politics – is only one element of a reading or spectatorial or interactive practice among several in operation. By reading and rejecting, say, the stereotyping or the positing of bourgeois lifestyle encodements in a contemporary men's magazine, the discourses of identity that are being sought or confirmed by the reader (not necessarily voluntarily) become obscured but are, nevertheless, efficiently communicated.

This possibility of any text performatively effecting the "naming" or the categorization, and thereby inaugurating a subjectivity in process, is reinforced when recent reception theory is considered, and particularly the poststructuralist analysis of reading, meaning, and discursive reading formations developed by Tony Bennett. Bennett critiques the position that is best represented by Stuart Hall's highly influential encoding/decoding understanding of reception, whereby a text is encoded by its author and decoded by audiences variously, according to dominant hegemonic, negotiated, or oppositional codes (Hall, 1993, pp. 100–103), each of which is dependent on the ideological positioning of the audience member or group. Bennett (1983) positions the text such that it never itself possessed a "meaning" to be interpreted correctly or incorrectly:

> Meaning is a transitive phenomena. It is not a thing which texts can have but is something that can only be produced, and always differently, within the reading formations that regulate the encounter between texts and readers (p. 218).

For Bennett, it is the "reading formation" which governs the reception, "the set of intersecting discourses which productively activate a given body of texts and the relations between them in a specific way" (p. 216). This poststructuralist theory of reception makes possible the idea that any text, utterance, or discourse can be read for its "naming" potential, it can be embraced for the way in which its meaning (for the reader or for the subject) inaugurates a subjectivity. Thus, while a particular film, book, pamphlet, photograph, or other formation that can be named a text might have no intention of providing an explanatory logic that relegates certain subjects (in formation) into certain categories, the underlying discourse can have such a performative effect that it initiates the process of a specific, particular subjective positioning. The codes that will make a subjective performativity intelligible are activated in the process of reading.

The extent to which a reader activates a particular meaning in a text in relation to the codes and signifiers of identity and selfhood is, then, variable as that extensiveness too depends on the reading formations and the discourses available to that reader or communication user. That is, all textual production – whether on the printed page or produced interactively and digitally on-screen – is read only in the context of the broad, complex, and variable network of other available texts, utterances, speech, flows, and materialities. Such "prior" texts and intelligibilities differ for different people and in some part that relies on experience and age – so it is of course possible to argue that the younger the reader the fewer the discourses through which to activate broad meanings and the reduced capacity to read or make meanings in a critical framework (this is not by any means guaranteed).

## 1.5  Consumption: Neoliberal Positioning of Audiencehood

If audiences are active in making meaning, then, we need to consider what is the framework through which meanings about identity are made within the contemporary, twentieth century positioning of both audiences and citizens as "consumers." While audience engagement has moved beyond simple consumption into what is sometimes labeled the interactive prosumer – which I will discuss in the next chapter – the practice of engagement that is built on media, communication experience, and the experience of selfhood as a commodity provides a specificity to the use of media as a resource for subject formation and the performance of selfhood. All contemporary media and communication forms that are accessed or utilized today are, I argue, located in the middle space between an Enlightenment, modernist demand that its readers and users adopt, perform, articulate, and maintain a coherent, intelligible, and recognizable identity on the one hand, and, on the other, self-manage the production of identity through the fluid, changeable, and manipulable self-fashioning that comes with contemporary neoliberal consumer practices. Less rigorous accounts of postmodern culture and identity celebrate the communication practices and, particularly, Internet subjectivities as examples of fragmentary identities, the very evidence of the postmodern. I would suggest instead that the practice of producing identities in the context of media use and, as discussed in the previous chapter, digital communication and online social networking, is marked by both continuities and ruptures from practices of the past. In other words, there is nothing particularly new about producing identities "in accord" with discursively given categories and frameworks, nor is the drive to produce coherent, intelligible and socially recognizable selves new. Rather, these are built within post-1750s Enlightenment era demands for coherent, unified, and intelligible identities. What is new in this context and – indeed – sometimes less stable, fast changing, and producing social anxieties over how we do "identity work" is the overdetermined role of media and digital communication in making available vast amounts of conflicting information on identities, identity categories, on what it is that constitutes a coherent self, and on the production of identities as forms of consumption. This is postmodern. The distinction produces a fragmentation or what I refer to as a push and pull between contemporary and Enlightenment practices that are both implicated in the multiple frames that constitute identity practices today – sometimes these are in conflict in what Fredric Jameson (1985) identifies as a form of schizophrenic disjuncture; at other times such complexities are glossed over as we get along with everyday life. In other words, what I am suggesting here is that fragmentation is not a distinctly postmodern experience, but that a (sometimes productive, particularly theoretically so) identifiable taste for fragmentation (of bounds, borders labels, meanings, etc.) and a compulsion to embrace it in some contexts has become a significant element of western cultural production, and thereby goes on to influence the ways in which we (both in the language of theory and in the unspoken enactment of the everyday; if the two should indeed be separated) think about subjecthood.

I like referring to this as a push-and-pull scenario, a push from postmodernist culture, a pull from Enlightenment's compulsion toward the articulation of coherence and singularity and intelligibility. This is not necessarily always the best metaphor, because to some extent it implies two distinct cultures between which "we" are torn. Obviously the relationship in terms of identity is more complex than this, but at this stage it seems secure enough to say that an imperative to articulate coherent, intelligible, and recognizable subjectivities (performative, Foucauldian confessional) extends from the continuation of Enlightenment institutions of reason, truth, and humanity, and that this framework for "doing identity" remains at least partly in force despite various shifts toward the (postmodern) neoliberal economization of identity.

The fluidity of consumption as the means by which performance of selfhood is made in late contemporary capitalist cultures (Papacharissi, 2011, p. 304; Jameson, 1985) occurs in the context of the global triumphalism of enterprise and the support it receives from contemporary nation states, together in the context of norms that are given in media and through the practice of understanding media sometimes as consumed rather than as that with which one engages. The role of the neoliberal state with regard to the market is to resist intervention in order to allow the free, *laissez-faire* conditions of exchange while, at the same time, providing a set of mechanisms to support this at the biopolitical level of the population that enable all "activities to be measured and assessed" (Foucault, 2008, pp. 12–24). Through surveillance, marketing, and representation, media plays a central role in this normativization and measurement. This, then, is not to say that the biopolitical power mechanisms of the state are defunct within neoliberalism and allow nothing but the free play of exchange. Rather, in line with the way in which state governance operates, the practices of media production, circulation, and consumption serve to encourage, foster, and promote neoliberalism's particular regime of truth such that it subsumes ways of thinking in all other fields aside from the economic – this includes ways of thinking about the self, subjectivity, and identity. It "involves generalizing it throughout the social body and including the whole of the social system not usually conducted through or sanctioned by monetary exchanges (p. 243)." Every social and identity activity falls under the framework of an economic rationality, from motherhood (pp. 243–244) to the governance of the self (p. 286). Within this framework the *homo oeconomicus* or "economic man" is produced. This is not, for Foucault, the classical economic man who is understood to be a partner in exchange. Rather, this is a neoliberal remodeling of the subject as that which manages itself within the bounds of the biopolitical and the economic as an investment:

> Homo oeconomicus *is an entrepreneur, an entrepreneur of himself. This is true to the extent that, in practice, the stake in all neo-liberal analyses is the replacement every time of* homo oeconomicus *as partner of exchange with a* homo oeconomicus *as entrepreneur of himself, being for himself his own capital, being for himself his own producer, being for himself the source of [his] earnings (p. 226).*

The economic man is produced, or rather reproduced differently, in neoliberalism through the application of economic analyses to all domains of behavior and conduct, particularly those around which biopolitical measurement and population assessment can occur at the level of the population (pp. 267–268). Economic man is thus a production or construct of a symbolic system and set of axioms, rules, and reasonings related to the self that conforms to economic principles of exchange in all forms of self-behavior.

Foucault's turn to the economization of subjectivity in *Birth of Biopolitics* (Foucault, 2008), although sometimes understood as a divergence from his study of biopolitics (2004) and biopolitical security (2007), is highly significant, then, in figuring the ways in which media consumption operates in the production and constitution of contemporary subjectivity. Although on the one hand the normativization of subjectivity, as communicated and made available through media practices, produces subjects that are required to conform to particular ranges of norms, whereby exact conformity found in institutional disciplinarity and produced through mechanisms of surveillance, policing, and rehabilitation to produce docile bodies is overwritten, on a population wide scale with the more pragmatic conformability to ranges and curves of normativities, the economization of subjecthood results in the further self-management of identity through the self-supervision of risk. Risk, here, is not only financial risk, but the risk of distancing from the norms that are represented in media, including journalism, film, and television representation, the circulation of stereotypes (Cover, 2004b), the magazine quiz on, for example, relationship practices, the online survey, the facebook circulated marketing questionnaire, the comparisons and contrasts with friends and peers in a social network setting and so on. As a force which seeks to extract profit from all human activity in a way which is subjugating and brutal, yet excites fantasies about the available good life of property ownership, "bourgeois self-fashioning," commodity fetishism, and ranges of normalcies (Butler & Athanasiou, 2013, pp. 30–31) it is active in the production of new forms of identities that appear or masquerade as liveable but, of course, are built on making other lives unliveable. Media and the circulation of digital information are absolutely central to the project of new neoliberal identities, as we witness in the absolute subjugation of communication (Lazzarato, 2004, p. 189) to practices of encouraging consumption between radio, television, and print advertising and the enticement to "like" products on social networking cites and thereby participate not only in the act of advertising but in building our own identities. This occurs not only by consuming and purchasing the necessary commodities that shore up and make our identities momentarily intelligible, but also in affiliating ourselves with acts of potential consumption, thereby participating in the media work of looking ahead (not necessarily "thinking ahead") as to what our identities might be.

As Butler has suggested, the fragmentation or questioning of identity categories is not to be understood as a postmodern victory over the Enlightenment, a removal of the shackles under which we have articulated ourselves from within Enlightenment modernist culture – there is no return to the premodern in the postmodern, and the mistake is to conflate the two (Butler, 1999). Nor is it possible to call for a nostalgic return to the Enlightenment simplicity of categories or reason over consumption and neoliberalism, much as either of these past figurations sometimes seem desirable. Rather, the way forward is to see the juxtaposition in the multiplicity of approaches itself as a framework for the decentering of Enlightenment codes of reason in favor not of postmodern identity practices built exclusively on the neoliberal, late capitalist practices of consumption of identity attributes and characteristics, but instead as a potential opening of the field of identity for critique. And all that can be said is that, at this stage, there is a potentially productive, potentially dangerous push and pull between the compulsion and imperative toward coherence, and the compulsion toward fragmentation, play, ephemerality, theatrics, identity "pastiche," and the "work" of identity performance that is now found when negotiating between coherence and reiteration of identity codes that are flashed before us on screens, clothing, bill boards, and in the sheer multiplicity of identity. Being better, more critical, and critiquing readers of media and users of digital communication is the pedagogical means by which we can move beyond some of the political and ethical downfalls of contemporary pushes and pulls between coherence and irrational consumption.

With regards to thinking about how audience members engage with media and digital communication in order to produce the self, we can say that no media text has a direct influence or effect on the subject in a deterministic way – no one is exposed to a text that depicts womanhood and then goes on to be woman. Wholesale diverse resistance is not an available possibility either. Subjects do not come to a media text, a website, a Facebook post or an Instagram image as a blank slate, but as subjects who also engage with other media and who have previously experienced media, mediated language, and discourse that informs that reading. But this is not to say that subjects come to the media as fully formed selves with clear, coherent, and fixed identities. Just as language does not represent a preexisting set of identities but, rather, is active in constituting those identities, so too does the media, digital, or interactive textuality constitute the subject. If we take identity to always be performative, then all identity is a process (Barker, 1999, p. 8) and subjects come to do identity ever so slightly differently in part through engagement with mediated discourse that is, itself, read diversely and actively and sometimes critically. What that means, then, in attempting to understand how identity is produced through media and digital communication engagement is that we need to turn now to ask what processes are specific to media and digital communication in making available and unavailable sets of ideas to be taken up and used as resources for identity formation, regardless of the extent to which those resources will have their meanings activated in broader contexts. That is, to turn from the audiencehood in order to allow us to think about distribution and dissemination and what role that has in the constitution of identity, self, and subject.

## 2 ACCESSING IDENTITY INFORMATION: AVAILABLE AND UNAVAILABLE DISCOURSES

I have been arguing above that the relationship between media and identity is multiple and mutually constitutive, that it involves a diverse range of practices in terms of the utilization of media, is implicated in the production of normativities in complex ways that articulate the need for both coherence and neoliberal consumption of the "commodities" of identity attributes, and is broadly far more complex than is accounted for in older theories of media effects or psyches produced in relation to the identificatory practices on-screen. Identity is produced in complex ways and the more recent complex theorizations such as those which understand all meaning to be productively activated and those which account for the broader social (and neoliberal) frameworks that govern contemporary reading practices are implicated in how we produce and articulate identity in media-dominated and digitally saturated communication environments. As Butler (1990) has demonstrated in her antifoundationalist, poststructuralist theorizations of gender subjectivity, identity can be thought of as being performative in such a way that it is not that we are and then go on to express that being through a set of attributes, but that the very articulations, behaviors, and performances of identity stand in for – and obscure – the fact that there never was an inner identity core, or self, directing us:

> The foundationalist reasoning of identity politics tends to assume that an identity must first be in place in order for political interests to be elaborated and, subsequently, political action to be taken. My argument is that there need not be a 'doer behind the deed,' but that the 'doer' is variably constructed in and through the deed. This is not a return to an existential theory of the self as constituted through its acts, for the existential theory maintains a prediscursive structure for both the self and its acts. It is precisely the discursively variable construction of each in and through the other that has interested me here (p. 142).

Performative selfhood means that all identity is performed "in accord" with discursive norms (categories, signifiers, names, stereotypes, and intelligibilities) that predate the performance, although those norms are always read variably. In performing toward an aim of unified, coherent, and recognizable identities we lend ourselves the illusion of having an inner identity core, essence, or substance (Butler, 1990, p. 136). Such performances are repetitive and come to stabilize over time, although they are always open to reconstitution in the encounter with new discourses (Butler, 1991). It is the "in accord" that should interest us most if discussing identity performativity in the context of media and digital communication, because it implies a need to investigate thoroughly the ways in which discourses that convey identity information (acting as kinds of "resources" for building, stabilizing, and confirming the performances of selfhood) are "made available" through communication and distribution practices in a mediated world. As Manuel Castells (2000) put it neatly, "Cultures are made up of communication processes … It is through the polysemic character of our discourses that the complexity and even contradictory quality of messages of the human mind manifest themselves" (p. 403). For the human mind, then, when we do identity we do this only ever in the context of relational communication, remembering that all communication is constitutive (of identity) and not merely reflective (of identity) (Giroux, 1999, p. 2) – there is no identity that occurs outside of the exchange of information, which means there are no identities that occur outside of communication practices, including dominant ones such as visual media and digital communication.

The fact that discourses utilized in constructing, recognition, and making sense of identity performances are, in very diverse ways, made available means we must attend to some of the different ways of approaching, thinking about, theorizing and understanding the conditions of availability. What is it, then, to understand discourses as available and unavailable? What media relationships and dissemination practices constitute availability and unavailability? Is censorship still a useful category or do we – today – need to think about unavailabilities that might occur in the vast plethora of information, in which certain texts, sites, and discourses can become "lost" in the array of material available in today's environment of "information overload" (Nicholls, 2011, p. 5)? While earlier we were examining some of the practices of audiencehood and spectatorship as ways of understanding the communication/identity relationship, and while in the next chapter we explore some of the new ways of understanding authorship in the context of interactivity, cocreativity, and the figure of the media prosumer who is both author and audience simultaneously, here we are thinking about some of the important aspects of communication related to dissemination and distribution as a novel way of "coming at" the identity question. I will work through agenda setting and gatekeeping to consider whether or not these remain effective and efficient ways of thinking about availability before discussing some of the ways in which we can frame systems of "available and unavailable" discourses.

## 2.1  Agenda Setting

There is a plethora of alternative media online aside from newspapers and broadcast radio and television, and the ways in which people generally communicate include doing so through a "matrix" formation of multiple forms that are not distinguishable but arise as part of a proliferation of alternative media forms, whether through traditional dissemination channels or digital channels accessed online and on mobile devices (Deuze, 2006). However, certain media forms, including papers and news programs, continue to play a role in setting agendas for public discussion, sometimes by "deciding" which topics will have dominance, at other times thereby making particular discourses – including ways of understanding selfhood and otherness – more available than others. What is important, however, is that in everyday practice it is not always possible to think critically about the extent to which public discourse is dominated by internal, external, institutional, and normative practices of decision making that make some ways of thinking available and others less available or marginalized. That is, because we are so used to seeing media texts in our everyday life (from billboards to screens to pop-up advertisements) and to taking part in the processes of communication (from telephone calls to tweeting to a news program on television) we have become situated so that the social production of meaning through the media is invisibilized (Turner, 1993). This is not, of course, to suggest that those processes are deliberate editorial decisions, and we certainly want to avoid conspiratorial discourses that suggest there is a particular agenda for global corporate media (although they do clearly uphold particular ways of thinking about formal politics and the economy as we have seen in the 2010s climate change solution debates); media itself is not wholly deterministic and it does not actively seek power to produce norms at all times, sometimes producing ways of thinking and ways of being and doing identity that it has no control over. For example, where transgender identities have become not only increasingly tolerable but deemed accepted within particular frameworks over the past few years, much of the credit for this can go to the way in which a range of television media have depicted transgender as an issue. In many cases, the way in which it frames transgender identity is, precisely, as an issue – an abnormality, an exception. Yet, unwittingly, the circulation of images, ideas, and debates it produces has changed the political, social, and cultural landscape such that transgender identity can, increasingly, be seen as a legitimate identity position and an acceptable way for people to view and live their own gendered realities. That is to say that while there are particular agendas at play in the decisions of the kinds of information that will be available and how it is framed and conditioned for distribution, agendas are not, themselves, monolithic, but play a particular role in constituting how identity information is articulated and, thereby, how it is cited in the performance of selfhood.

Agenda-setting theory emerged in the 1970s in order to answer questions about the sense that news media may not be able to tell people how to think, but can and does play a role in controlling what people think about (Boyce, 2007, p. 203). For the Glasgow Media Group proponents of this theory, the concerns over media power relate to the extent to which key items left "off the agenda," such as critiques of normative class demarcations, allow norms circulating in mass media to become "accepted wisdom" (Philo, 1995, p. 177). According to Nicholas Garnham (1995), much of the concern in the scholarship of agenda-setting deals with the notion that journalists, as unelected officials of the fourth estate, and sometimes their employers, "decide the agenda of what is relevant" (p. 248). We can, however, widen the perspective here to think about the broader, more complex ways in which public sphere discourse makes certain ideas available while subordinating, submerging, or invisibilizing other ideas related to identity. Part of this has to be thought of in the context of the "mass" of "mass media" broadcasts as a distribution platform that maintains an ongoing dominance over public sphere discourse. David Buchbinder (1997) suggests that mass forms of media are a formation that remain "particularly powerful, because popular" (pp. 25–26). That is, by the popular appeal generated, and the fact that they can command attention and ongoing discussion, certain media forms (which may be a news channel at one particular time, or a popular reality television show or even LOL cat images distributed on social networking), relegate other media forms, for example, alternative sites for very specific audiences aimed at the very margins of public discourse. Mass media orders society's discourses by "structuring the thresholds of thought, knowledge, and communication" (McCoy, 1993, p. 141). The role of news media, television, and film in discursive selectivity and agenda setting is a result of their scale and pervasiveness and forms of ownership (Turner, 1993, pp. 232–233; McCoy, 1993, p. 146; Philo, 1995, p. 176). An example of this includes the ways in which mass media forms perpetuate "coupledom" as the "natural" way of conducting relationships, marriages, and the upbringing of children (Cover, 2010). This is despite the many available sites online and the many alternative romantic affiliations that depict more complex, interesting, innovative relationship models that might have more appeal (threesomes, open relationships, no relationships, celibate coupledom, and many others). In other words, there are many ways we could begin to identify with other than husbands, wives or coupled partners. Yet even the challenge to contemporary coupledom that alternative (and increasingly mainstream) media depictions of nonheterosexuality and LGBT cultures make (to conservative norms of coupledom) retain the dominant "assumed" figure of the couple. This is an example of agenda setting that we might understand as being unwitting because it is normative. A major network television series on, say, the US Presidency, is not going to depict the President in a mutual five-way relationship between himself and four other partners of multiple gender categories. This is not because it might be absurd, but because it will not be considered to fall within the realm of normativity. Yet we might find such a story about such a scenario in some online setting, a book, a marginal underground film or in a quiet public debate on a blog. What this means for identity is that, in terms of how we structure and make sense of our identities in the context of relationships and trajectories for relationships throughout the course of our lives, the capacity to consider alternative relationships such as polygamy, multiplicity, or other complex and nonnormative ways of "doing" romantic relationality are not necessary available to us because public agendas keep such discourses relegated to the margins. This is not to say that they can never emerge – indeed, sometimes radical ideas emerge when a conservative perspective is pushed so hard that it inadvertently draws attention to the appeal of alternative ideas – conscious, voluntary, and political attempts to produce a narrow set of identity and relationality practices can sometimes produce more complex, interesting, alternative, and radical ways of doing and performing selfhood – if the cultural conditions are right. However, the near monolithic dominance of coupledom – regardless of the genders involved – as the acceptable global way in which to "do" relational, sexual, and romantic selfhood is an effect of mass media, despite the possibilities afforded by online communication that can depict a broader range of selfhood.

## 2.2  Search Engines: Availability, Accessibility, and Popularity

Once we begin thinking from the perspective of digital media and communication environments, the conceptual framework through which information, material, resources, ideas, and meanings are "made available" needs to shift from one in which we ask questions about corporate, community, and publisher agenda setting and gatekeeping, toward thinking about how one accesses material online. In an online environment in which the search engine plays one of the most significant roles for users accessing new information, it is important to bear in mind that making information available depends wholly not on the idea that information is horizontally free and accessible, but that it is hierarchicalized by search results. A user may well be happy to work through thousands or tens of thousands of websites that have been returned in, say, a Google search. However, the reality for most is that they will be accessed by the selection of a handful of early hits that have been hierarchically produced and presented – few people engaging with online information will have the time and patience to undertake a genuinely exhaustive reading of all the available material. In the context of information that makes new material about identities intelligible, and thereby exposes a subject to discourses which may reconstitute that subject within previously unencountered frames of subjectivity and selfhood, it is the information that is most accessible (ordered in the first handful) and thereby more likely to be popular that is most commonly accessed. Although the algorithms used to rank pages in any search are often elusive (as they carry their own intellectual property), it is broadly understood that certain factors make a site more likely to appear toward the top of the results. Aside from those that are actively sponsored and paid for (at this time appearing above result #1 in a search on Google, separate but not always distinguishable, much as paid-for informercials can resemble documentaries or paid-for advertorials can resemble news columns in print publications), pages are ranked to some extent on the basis of their extant popularity, making "ways of thinking" that are already broadly available, *more* available, rather than promoting alternative and new ideas.

> PageRank tends to reinforce the mechanism of preferential attachment. Preferential attachment occurs in large part because those authors who create hyperlinks are assumed to locate the authoritative pages by surfing the web. Much of the browsing and searching process now occurs within search engines, but since PageRank posits a 'model surfer' within the PageRank algorithm, it tends to recreate and enforce the process of preferential attachment … PageRank and related esteem-enhancing search algorithms clearly increase the current imbalance, calcifying existing networks of popularity (Halavais, 2009, pp. 67–68).

Rather than the Internet being a site of great democratic gathering of information, then, online communication and information exchange is in some ways as tightly controlled as television – at least in the context of the differences between broadcasting certain information at popular viewing times in contrast with information that is broadcast at three o'clock in the morning.

Search engines, as Alexander Halavais has argued, play a central role in contemporary culture, a role of categorizing and organizing information in a way that has come to seem trustworthy through its appearance, look, and feel of being nothing more than a functional tool – but it may not neces-sarily be as "innocent" as we genuinely believe when we conduct a search (pp. 1–2). Manipulation, or "optimization" of search results by some orga-nizations, industries, and institutions, can be used to gain greater attention than a rival, and has become a skill, a profession, and increasingly an industry itself. That is, those with access to particular techniques and knowledge on how search engines work are able to make certain that the information that they provide has a far greater likelihood of being viewed than the informa-tion of others, and that makes for a conservative, controlled, and potentially untrustworthy environment, in much the same way as an advertiser with greater financial resources is able to capture attention in a broadcast setting.

In the vastness of online information, with over one billion websites, (http://www.Internetlivestats.com/), search engines are absolutely central to the activity of finding information and providing a taxonomic framework for access. While I do not wish to overemphasize comparisons with earlier media and communication frameworks – because such comparisons tend to be overreaching and oversimplify the complexity of new communication technologies and the practices and desires that foster their development – this can be said to be not entirely different from the absolute centrality of the library catalogue systems which, in a large physical library space, are central to finding specific information and, even when one wishes to browse, play an organizational role in directing people toward particular parts of a library (history versus natural sciences) and specific shelves. Much as library cata-loguing in combination with the physical environment of the library (dis-tance from the center or the door) can make some information more avail-able that other information, the search engine's hierarchicalization through often indiscernible ratings and organizations produces results in a way which makes some information more available than other information as well.

While it is true that the Internet appears to be flat, diverse, and free as a result of the ease by which we can publish material online (Halavais, 2009, p. 59), the reality is that information is gathered in peaks and troughs around the extent to which it is able to gather attention. So by virtue of the fact that audiences are users who actively need to search to access information pub-lished or made available online, the resources for identity formation found on the Internet can broadly be conceived of as "narrowcast" rather than "broadcast." Narrowcast information can, at best, serve niche audiences – usefully serving the needs of target groups, often deliberately in public rela-tions and promotional campaigns (Glik, Prelip, Myerson, & Eikers, 2008, p. 94). At the same time this means that information that is unpopular or which does not appeal to broader audiences, while failing simultaneously to compete with large corporate online dominance, does not have the reach of online spectacle that tends to mirror broadcast. Writing about the narrowcast formation of cable in a multicable media environment (which, in several ways, is an earlier precursor to online information gluts; more so than broadcast television models), Beretta Smith-Shomade (2004) notes that not only does narrowcast serve niche audiences (p. 73) but can do so in ways that are discriminatory against those who are actively oppressed by hierarchical identity thinking:

> Narrowcasting appears in many aspects, a way to keep the marginal as marginal. It encourages a center – a space where the really important demographics reside. Within this space, those who know how to behave, assimilate, and look live. Unfortunately, this space also harbors those who produce, distribute, exhibit, manage, and control (p. 78).

For Smith-Shomade, then, the world of online information is not a world of free exchange of diverse ideas, but a tightly controlled environment in which the figure of the "prosumer" making ever-new dialogue is mythical. The fact that online communication is built on narrowcast models produces control over the flow of communicative space in a way which both breaks down private/public distinctions and reinforces them (Tufekci, 2008, p. 22) in ways which make certain discourses official and leave others belonging to the realm of the domestic – another hierarchy that reduces the capacity for democratic exchange and, thereby, reduces the capacity for social cohesion (Powers, 2005, pp. 122–123).

In a cultural framework in which use of the Internet has tended to produce an unquestioning acceptance of search engine ranking (Brabazon, 2007, p. 42), the capacity of users to desire to search beyond the knowable, the popular, and the accepted is reduced. More importantly, so too is the capacity to be critical of the frameworks through which information related to how we do, think, and engage with identity is presented. Ethical relations are produced through a critical understanding of the complexity of identity, how subjects are constituted, and through a reflexive approach to performing those identities. Critiquing the frames that make some subjects appear worthy and others less so is the means by which subjects become recognizable and therefore worthy of a response and responsibility. As Butler (2009) puts it:

> When those frames that govern the relative and differential recognizability of lives come apart, as part of the very mechanism of their circulation – it becomes possible

*to apprehend something about what or who is living but has not been generally 'recognised' as a life (p. 12).*

If the accessibility to diverse information and the ability to critically reflect on that information is necessary in producing the conditions for socially inclusive identities – a question to which I will return in later chapters – then it is not through the contemporary organization of information online dominated by search engines that we will find responsibility and critical relationality. This is not, of course, to say that emergent knowledge does not surprise us, indeed, in many cases marginal and alternative forms of thinking can be distributed widely when they "go viral" online. The very use of digital media can produce critical engagements with knowledge. That, of course, is different from the perspectives in which we think about the Internet as a repository of existing and new information organized only by seeking through authorized search engines.

## 2.3 Available and Unavailable Discourses

While mass media and its very processes of distribution establish agendas that communicate particular frameworks of normativities, and while other kinds of norms can be produced in digital communication through the near monolithic power of the search engine, it is necessary finally to ask how discourses can be understood as a "available and unavailable" in ways which operate to regulate and regiment identity. In other words, if all identity is performative, and if performativity requires the citation of the signifier that is made available as a "prior" in language, and if that language is not always free but mediated, then, to what extent can we – or should we – be thinking about the regime of available/unavailable as regulatory? Additionally, how is it possible to think that when we always have to acknowledge that "the media" is not a single entity but part of a dialogic process – even noninteractive and broadcast media – that builds narratives over time through ongoing myths, histories, and formations that shape our perceptions of the world and do so in ways which are diverse rather than all encompassing (Poynting, Noble, Tabar, & Collins, 2004, pp. 13–14)?

Following Foucault, one of the most important approaches to understanding selfhood and society in contemporary scholarship involves understanding how ideas and knowledge circulate through discourse. Discourse establishes certain kinds of truth statements that come to seem real and meaningful (Foucault, 2004, p. 25). Discursive formations and practices are best understood as "the ensemble of heterogeneous dispositifs for making statements. They function and produce statements in different ways – for example, … media constructs opinions, and experts make informed judgements" (Lazzarato, 2009, p. 112). When it comes to subjectivities, this is not about the representation of a falsehood about identity characteristics (such as through stereotyping) while subjugating the actual and real truth about identity. Rather it is about making identity seem to follow certain disciplinary rules by following one discursive framework or practice over another and thereby establishing normativities: "The discourse of disciplines is about a rule: not a juridical rule derived from sovereignty, but a discourse about natural rule, or in other words a norm" (Foucault, 2004, p. 38). When a discourse is made available and an alternative set of truth statements is made unavailable, the field of legitimate reason is produced through the conditioning and limiting of certain kinds of rationality (Butler, 2009, p. 790). That is, by the domination of one discourse while others remain unknown or unknowable to particular kinds of audiences or digital media users, the dominant discourse allows variation of identity (e.g., male/female biological gender identities but also transgenderism) while obscuring alternative perspectives (such as understanding gender on a continuum that accounts for all possibilities without a dividing distinction).

In understanding the constitutive role of media distribution in making discourses, texts, concepts, and ideas about identity available and unavailable, the distinction between broadcast and narrowcast remains pertinent and significant, even today. Broadcast, as I have been describing it, continues to dominate because it is popular and "received" by very large numbers. An alternative framework for being or doing sexual and romantic intimacy, such as a polyamorous relationship of multiple persons and configurations uncovered in an online narrowcast blog, might be highly meaningful to some people, but that number will be small by the very nature of narrowcast (although it is never guaranteed that it will not, of course, go "viral" and come to replicate the same kinds of popularity of broadcast, widespread, public discussion). Narrowcasting is a concept that emerges through social marketing public relations that assumes targeted, small group populations of "interested" audiences (Glik et al., 2008, p. 94). Narrowcast information might, at times, be assumed to be toward an audience of like-minded readers, for example, a blogger writing about alternatives to romantic coupledom might assume that all his or her readers are also identifiably polyamorous. This does not necessarily change communication in the way that might occur if it were a broader, more conservative broadcast audience (Luders, 2008, p. 689). At the same time, however, the target audience is not necessarily "contained"; the information is not necessarily controlled for a specific small group of people, and how that information seeps and circulates to reimagine an agenda for thinking about and discussing relationships is not controllable. However, how it is read may well depend on how broadcast media texts and the agendas at play have operated – a new reader may come to view and understand this alternative not as an acceptable or tolerable new way in which think about romantic and sexual selfhood but as a set of crackpot ideas, because it is so completely different from the kinds of norms of coupledom that have circulated for such a long time in more dominant broadcast television and film.

When it comes to the formation of identity where media makes available a set of resources for the intelligible, articulate performance of recognizable selves in order to fulfil that ongoing cultural demand that we perform ourselves as coherent and unified, the kinds of agendas established and circulated – whether knowingly or unwittingly, through more deliberate editorial or through the emergence of new ideas outside media control – can be understood as regulatory. For Butler (2005), the performative self is produced as an effect not just of language, discourse, and cultural significations but of regulation and regulatory ideals. Regulatory ideals are truth regimes (p. 30) that establish norms, exclusions, categories, and identities. Through processes of subjection and regulation, subjects are produced and required to perform, behave, and desire by maintaining and exploiting the cultural demand for "continuity, visibility, and place" (Butler, 1997, p. 29). That is, it requires the subject to respond and "fit" within regulatory norms in order to fulfil the condition of existence through performing as a "recognizable social being" (p. 27). Within her concerns over what constitutes recognizable, Butler notes that certain juxtapositions of identity make some not only unrecognizable but impermissible and illegitimate. Here, she is thinking about the ways in which certain broad "values" (such as a pro-Americanism in the years just after the September 11 attacks) result in mainstream media enterprises refusing to publish alternative ideas "because to voice them is to risk hystericization and censorship" (Butler, 2004, p. 2), that is, to risk presenting something which cannot be recognized as legitimate. Here, regimentation becomes exclusion, whereby an identity that is linked to an antiestablishment political framework is actively invisibilized or pathologized. For Butler, however, regulation through regimentation of discourse and constitution of identity are not always the same thing, but are a "dual operation of power" that function sometimes together to produce identities, but that risk the failure of regimentation through the constitutive force of alternative media depictions that frame, articulate, and produce identities and particular ways of doing subjectivity that cannot always be known in advance.

I do not want to suggest that what is made unavailable discursively through particular media processes, decisions, cultures, and practices is necessarily always something which is discursively "censored" and can therefore be found if one is able to release a text from censorship, to dig online for it, or to stumble upon alternative ways of speaking and thinking about a topic. Rather, some of what is left unavailable in media and public sphere discourse is actively felt by subjects in ways that sometimes indicate a sense of fragmentation, multiplicity, and incoherence in identity. All subjects, as Butler (1993) has argued, are multiply constituted (pp. 116–117) and this can include manners of constitution that are not discursively available or translatable into public discourse but are submerged in corporeal, embodied, and felt contexts of everyday selfhood. So what is unavailable is not necessarily that which can only be found on the thousandth page of an extensive online search. Rather, although all discourse extends beyond formal language, it is in the languages of the body, the gait, the sound, and others, that are not easily translatable into either text or machine code for digital distribution (e.g., smell), that can be constitutive of alternative identities yet remain broadly unavailable due to the very fact that it is not a discourse with which one critically engages. In spite of this, it is important to remember that it is a complex range of processes and experiences that make some discourses more available, more acceptable, and more easily read than others, and the circumstances through which those are read for the (usually unwitting) purpose of identity formation as a resource through which the signifier that is cited in performativity is accessible and intelligible, depend on the kinds of readings available to subjects, the kinds of frameworks a subject is able to deploy, and the critical capacities of the subject in regard to that frame and the nuances through which subjects read. This is why we now need to turn back to reading practices in the context of performative subject formation to answer the question as to how a reader can read a category, signifier, or norm that is discursively available in media or digital communication when the meanings are only activated in the context of the subject's subjectivity.

## 3  MEDIATING THE SELF IN A CIRCULAR WORLD – CITATIONALITY AND READING FORMATIONS

Before we can understand what it means for our identities to be formulated through interactive engagement with textuality and communication in Web 2.0 and Web 3.0 frameworks of networking and "always online" cloud-based connectivity, it is necessary to think through some of the potential approaches to media and textual reception. That is, if media and communication today are the key formations that "frame" categories of identity and make ways of performing selfhood and subjectivity intelligible, coherent, and recognizable, how do we in fact come to interpret and make sense of those media texts? Additionally, how has this been done at the simpler level of texts with which we do not necessarily actively participate as cocreators of the text, merely as coproducers of meaning (as we do with any text, whether a novel or a menu)? That is, how do subjects who performatively articulate self-identity by citing the media given signifier, receive mainstream mass culture? Is it possible to suggest a coherent way of understanding the presumed message of identity-based reiterative citation on-screen? Is the signifier to be cited recognized and, if so, from what discursive positioning does that recognition occur?

Citation is part of the key practice as to how identity works in Butler's framework. Discourse always precedes the formation of the "I" (Butler, 1993, p. 225) and that discourse has a history which also precedes and "conditions its contemporary uses" (p. 227) – at the same time, as I have been arguing, discourse is conditioned in the present, and by present circumstances, through a range of media processes from interpretation to dissemination to engagement marked by contemporary practices of communication and digital media use. Identity, here, is to be understood as the compulsion to reiterate "a norm or set of norms" which "conceals or dissimulates the conventions of which it is a repetition" (p. 12). We cite the signifier, category, name, and attributes of identity as they are presented, in mediated ways, in discourse and go on to perform these. So, for example, the ways in which sexual identity (lesbian, gay, straight, bisexual, or otherwise) is produced as a named identity with its attribute that make its repetition and performance coherent and recognizable (which can include sexual and romantic practice, but also other attributes or signifiers of that identity) begins with an encounter with the discursively conditioned and mediated discourses of sexuality – there are both dominant and nondominant discourses at play here and the dominant is typically one which assumes that sexual identities are innate, fixed, and generally aligned with the dichotomy of straight/queer. Here, there is thus an assumed subject, usually teenage, who "encounters" that compulsive discourse and in the moment of the encounter is required to adopt or add new codes of performance, reconstituting subjectivity and self-awareness as a straight or queer subject. This of course leaves open the possibility that one may be reconstituted differently at different times: the avowed heterosexual who suddenly becomes a lesbian at the age of 53 and comes to stabilize as one with the retrospective "sense" that she always was lesbian, for example. It is important to acknowledge that the moment of encounter with discourses of sexuality does not result in a reconstitution that is immediate and permanent, but stabilizes like all identities over a longer period (p. 9). One does not begin as a lesbian and recognize oneself in the discursively given text, given that such recognition relies on being able to have already known being a lesbian before one can suddenly recognize oneself as a lesbian. Without wishing to be obtuse, the linear media process is too simplistic to account for the performativity of identity, as the complexity of reception, understanding, and meaning are at stake.

As I discussed above, recent theories of reception have suggested there is no content-definable effect or influence of media examples on any given audience. Instead, they suggest that meanings are reconstructed to such an extent by audience members that we are unable to analyze potential effects or potential responses to a media production (Allor, 1995, p. 551). Bennett (1983) takes meaning as something that can only be produced in its reception, and suggests that Hall's three-tiered decoding relies unnecessarily on the notion that texts have meaning that can be interpreted. Bennett is critical of the cultural studies media analysts' method of first determining the meaning of the text (their receptive meaning), going on to examine how audiences interpret those meanings variantly. Bennett's theory provides the important concept of "reading formation" as the discursive position from which a reader provides a text with its meaning. If meaning is something that is totally divorced from the media–given text that acts as an identity resource, and if meaning is only productively activated in the act of reading from the subjective position of the discursive reading formation of the reader, then we need to account for what it is that makes identities recognizable. In other words, for example, if one were only to recognize and understand and interpret the identity "European" from the perspective of a reading formation in which one activates that meaning, then how is it possible for me to cite, repeat, and mime that identity in order to produce it in a recognizable way? What this means for us, then, is that understanding and recognizing the signifier, identity category, name, or stylization given in the media text depends on the intertextual fabric of discursivity and the persistent circulation of information in order to begin to recognize oneself.

Making identifications with the category, signifier, or name of an identity in a communication or media formation therefore depends on the capacity not only of audiences to recognize a depiction (say, a stereotype or a narrative of selfhood) as an identity and thereby identify with it, but to fabricate that identification through a sense of recognition. Rather than relying on an unproblematized concept of recognition, I am interested in how this recognition can in fact be a sort of recognition or rethinking of the self that occurs in an encounter with a media representation and that operates under the guise of identification. I derive the trope "recognition as re-cognition" from Alexander García Düttmann (1997). In exploring the political notion of lesbian/gay and AIDS-related "representation" in German politics, Düttmann uses this play on words in order to question the iterability of cognition and the conception of a movement's call for legislative recognition. He suggests that it is only in the elimination of the process of recognizing that one might deploy a group unity that genuinely bridges the difference between heterogeneous acts (p. 31). In the process of performing subjective identity and selfhood in contemporary western culture, it is through various practices of communication and reception that subjectivity is rethought or reconfigured as a particular kind of subjectivity or identity. This occurs through the "encounter" with dominant discourses of subjectivity that inaugurate identity performativity. The process of reading particular media forms contributes to the reconfiguration and stabilization of identity, much as media images are utilized as a "resource" for the codes that make performativity of that identity coherent and recognizable. Where, at first, understandings of subjectivity are rethought or recognized, that recognition comes to be felt and remembered as recognition, a sense that one always was this or that identity, a sense that one always had an inner identity core along the lines of that discursively given category or signifier (Butler, 1990, p. 143). In encountering discourses of subjecthood, the subject who recognizes himself or herself in the text is impelled to perform actions, behaviors, and attitudes culturally recognizable to others in order to participate socially and to belong: the imperative to perform identity as a coherent, intelligible, and recognizable being. In the encounter with new and previously unencountered discourses, the subject is not so much produced in that singular moment – for citation and performativity are not singular acts – but comes to be reconstituted through a rethinking of the self that masquerades as a recognition. In that sense, one's interpretation or activation of meaning about that identity is possible only retrospectively. The media and communication process here is not one of temporal linearity from text to distribution to audience but can be understood retroactively in reverse.

# 4 CONCLUSIONS: MEDIA, NORMATIVITY, AND PEDAGOGY

If we ask about the relationship between contemporary media, the ways in which it circulates norms, and how these might operate in a complex reception framework as broadly pedagogical, then we need to keep bearing in mind that there are three distinct but highly intertwined aspects that need to be put into question within the context of any investigation of the relationship between the production of contemporary, performative identities and the role of media in making particular intelligibilities of identity available. That is, in trying to make sense of the connection between subjectivity/selfhood and media reception in the contemporary period we must consider the following. (1) The location of a culture of identity not under the dictates of the Enlightenment brand of modernity or in a wholesale notion of postmodernity as fragmentation, but in a culture that produces a push and pull between unified individuality and consumerist fluidity and postmodern fragmentation. (2) The location of the performative signifier not in the stereotyped categories given in discursive formations but in the interstices between the category of "group" and the category of self, revealing a multiplicity of identity signifiers available for reception, interpretation, evaluation, and performance; what might be thought of as the culturally given "coordinates" of a performative identity along the lines of common axes of discrimination and demarcation (gender, ethnicity, race, ability, class, and sexuality) as well as experience (personal, memorial, group, and affiliational). (3) Modern and postmodern understandings of play and performance as the means through which identity is not only understood to be expressed but as the activities which retroactively constitute and stabilize identity and selfhood. Subjectivity is always produced through the social order that organizes and makes intelligible our experiences (Eribon, 2004, p. 5). Today, the social order that is organizing experience and making the very ideas of identity sensible, intelligible, and available as resources for the self-construction, performativity, and self-management of identity is – broadly – media and communication. This media is one which changes and is in flux, it is one which involves complex patterns of reading, matrices of corelative information across different platforms, ever-increasing numbers of channels from traditional to digital, and practices in which some identity material is subordinated while other is foregrounded through both conscious and nonconscious decisions, ranges of normativities, and the cultural conditions that make certain ideas "more popular" than others.

However, the experience of becoming particular identities through media "regulation" will be different for some than for others. For those who will — for whatever reason — not "fit" or be able to perform coherently within the dominant identity regime, there is the consequential risk that imperils:

> ... the very possibility of being recognized by others, since to question the norms of recognition that govern what I might be, to ask what they leave out, what they might be compelled to accommodate, is, in relation to the present regime, to risk unrecognizability as a subject or at least to become an occasion for posing the questions of who one is (or can be) and whether or not one is recognizable (Butler, 2005, p. 23).

If there are, indeed, pedagogical questions on the extent to which traditional and digital media, popular culture, and cocreative texts operate as resources for educating oneself in the intelligibilities of identity and subjectivity, those can be critiqued through a framework that takes into account the relationship between the multiplicity of audiences for a subject making use of media and digital communication as a resource for the formation of identity. For Henry Giroux (1999), a cultural approach to pedagogy begins with the foundational point that culture is constitutive rather than reflexive in that it shapes the larger forces of pedagogy and identity (p. 2). Thus, Giroux suggests that media and digital communication become not only tools for learning but sites of pedagogy itself as part of the "whole range of new cultural forms within media culture that have become the primary educational forces in advanced industrial societies" (p. 4). In that context, making use of media critically has value in encouraging "young people and adults to engage popular, media, and mass culture seriously as objects of social analysis and to learn how to read them critically through specific strategies of understanding, engagement, and transformation" (pp. 4–5). Like audiences, literacy for Giroux is multiple and plural rather than fixed in singularity, and thereby requires that users become not only literate, but literate in the forms through which such multiplicities of engagement are produced. Within this framework of pedagogy, both traditional and networked, digital media have multiple roles — they act as (1) tools of pedagogy in a regimentary environment in which the cultural demand that we learn to perform our identities in ways which are coherent and recognizable is key to social participation and belonging; (2) the site of pedagogy in which users engage not only with other users and audiences and other subjects but with the multiplicity of audiences, interpretative frames, and manifold utterances that present a range of discursive approaches to understanding the everyday and the professional forms of communicative engagement in order to perform identity in relational contexts; and (3) as a form of pedagogy itself that is located within a number of different and sometimes competing media models of identity, including both those that uphold and those that put into question Enlightenment models of the coherent and unified subject.

What is learned in the pedagogy of media includes the skills and tools for plotting the extent of one's social participation and belonging through understanding our own identities in the context of frameworks of normativity as biopolitical norms, to use Foucault's terminology. In the context of the production of identity through media-given information utilized pedagogically as a resource, biopolitical formations (which emerge as technological frameworks of power deployed by governance) are implicated not only in how we cite the signifier from media and communicative texts in order to perform coherently, but how we go on to maintain that coherence through repetitions of intelligibility. Biopolitics is significant here, because it is about power formations that produce and materialize identities as bodily, including in ways that are felt to emerge from within the body. In Foucault's analysis, biopolitics is not "disciplinary" in the sense that it does not work with individuals or corporeal bodies in practical terms through surveillance, training, and other actions that produce norms. Rather, it works with ranges at the level of whole populations, in this case we might say the mass audiences of massively distributed and broadly disseminated textuality, whether through broadcast or narrowcast forms of communication. As Foucault (2004) noted, in biopolitical formulations:

> … regulatory mechanisms must be established to establish an equilibrium, maintain an average, establish a sort of homeostasis, and compensate for variations within this general population and its aleatory field. In a word, security mechanisms have to be installed around the random element inherent in a population of living beings so as to optimize a state of life. Like disciplinary mechanisms, these mechanisms are designed to maximize and extract forces, but they work in very different ways. Unlike disciplines, they no longer train individuals by working at the level of the body itself. There is absolutely no question relating to an individual body, in the way that discipline does. It is therefore not a matter of taking the individual at the level of individuality but, on the contrary, of using overall mechanisms and acting in such a way as to achieve overall states of equilibration or regularity (p. 246).

Here, as Judith Revel (2009) has pointed out, Foucault is attempting to develop an understanding as to how it is possible to live in relation to others in a manner in which differences between the self and the other "are neither reified, objectified, reduced to the least common denominator (such as a contrived universalization, or a reduction to sameness), or what one must rely upon to have access to the other" (p. 48). The means by which subjectivity is produced in correlation with the biopolitical, then, is by the establishment not of norms through a normal/abnormal distinction as might be found in disciplinary institutions that exclude the latter or regulate the latter into becoming the docile former. Rather, it is through normativities which are produced as ranges that subjects come to be emplaced.

Where disciplinary power mechanisms distinguish between the normal and the abnormal, the regulatory functions of biopolitical power technologies plot the normal and the abnormal along "different curves of normality" whereby certain distributions are considered to be "more normal than the others, or at any rate more favorable than the others" (Foucault, 2007, p. 63). For Foucault, biopolitical discourses do not have a dichotomy of the normal and the abnormal, but

> a plotting of the normal and the abnormal, of different curves of normality, and the operation of normalization consists in establishing an interplay between these different distributions of normality and [in] acting to bring the most unfavorable in line with the more favorable. So we have here something that starts from the normal and makes use of certain distributions considered to be, if you like, more normal than the others, or at any rate more favorable than the others. These distributions will serve as the norm. The norm is an interplay of differential normalities. The normal comes first and the norm is deduced from it, or the norm is fixed and plays its operational role on the basis of this study of normalities. So, I would say that what is involved here is no longer normation, but rather normalization in the strict sense (p. 63).

To perform a coherent identity, then, is to be active in that process of plotting where one lies on the distributional curve through self-surveillance and self-checking, and the curve that one accesses is typically that given in media formations today. This is the question that is seen most ostensibly in magazines that provide normative advice or present quizzes in which one finds out if one's behaviors are more or less normal than others. It is also the form in which identity is given, broadly speaking, in the reception of certain texts through viewing in a comparative mode – for example, in the spectatorship of a reality television show in which one views the behavior of others, recognizes those behaviors, recognizes or reconstitutes the self and goes on to ask how different one might be or how similar one might be to that character or performer. Or it might be the mode of reading when one searches for health information relative to ageing online: to see if such aches and pains are more or less normal for one's age group with which one has made an identification. What this means for subjectivity and identity is that in some contexts, including the contemporary neoliberal formations of governance and society, the strictures of, say, national identities do not map to a normal/abnormal set of mutually exclusive categories such as national subject and foreigner or immigrant other. Rather, it is a matter of distribution and distance from the norm and all performativity is actively conditioned by the compulsion to plot, check, analyze, and understand where one's identity lies on that normative distribution. National identity, for example, is discursively performed as normative, while nonnormative identities are deemed so due to being framed as a minority statistic within a population which might include certain immigrant community groups living with the field of the nation. These are by nature not identities of opposition but of distance from the normative along a curve. This set of distributions and curve of normativities, then, produces certain discourses of regulation by which identities can be performed. So, rather than the performative national identity being produced over time and repetition through being fully and only disciplined into particular docile ways of being that are coherent and recognizable, the range of those which can be recognized as (at least) tolerable and certainly as intelligible as part of the relationality of population − as part of the curve of normativities that is figured through statistical analysis and dissemination of the biopolitical knowledge of the population − produces the curve of possibilities and limitations for the performance of a subjectivity that can "fit" within a broad grouping such as that of a mass audience.

# CHAPTER 3

# Interactivity, Digital Media, and the Text

Although the concept of interactivity is sometimes used to discuss the ways in which people engage and communicate relationally and affectively in a face-to-face (F2F) environment, the term is more popular today as a way of describing contemporary online communication, even though that communication is often characterized as only mimicking F2F interaction. The term was something of a buzz-word in the early to mid-2000s (Cover, 2006), being used to describe all digital communication generally, as a "selling point" of digital commodities and technologies such as any network-enabled desktop computer. The term was drawn upon as an intellectual concept describing some forms of networking in organizational communication environments and social settings. Sometimes the term is simply used to describe what we talk about today as "digital" (technologically based communication and media engagement that involves capacities for users to do more than read text, but, to select, gather information, provide further feedback, or participate in the creation of user-generated information and other texts). While the word digital is, indeed, useful as an umbrella term, I am particularly interested in foregrounding some of the ways in which the notion of interactivity points us to the need to think beyond online communication as simply communication that is facilitated through online networks and more toward the implications of digital communication and emergent digital cultures for thinking about authorship, cocreativity or coparticipation in the production of texts, remixes, and mashups that produce new texts and new ideas, and the changing nature, role, and function of audiences. In other words, the concept of interactivity provides new and useful ways of understanding how selves are produced not merely through the complex performativity that results from forms of citation of discursively given and mediated concepts of subjectivity, identity, and selfhood but also that those very mediated texts are – today – engaged with interactively, such that subjects are not only performers but cocreators of the textuality that makes particular kinds of identities intelligible, recognizable, and coherent in social perspectives.

*Digital Identities.*
http://dx.doi.org/10.1016/B978-0-12-420083-8.00003-1

The interactive and digital nature of computer-mediated communication results in several new tensions in the author–text–audience relationship, predominantly through blurring the line between author and audience, and eroding older technological, policy, and conventional models for the "control" of the text, its narrative sequencing, and its distribution. Many authors, media producers, content creators, government officials, experts, medical and psychological practitioners, and teachers continue to operate in the dominant paradigm of intellectual property that is deemed to be the way in which texts – including popular culture and those texts that serve either deliberately or unwittingly as resources for identity formation – are controlled, stabilized, and made permanent and fixed. Such texts are seen to disavow and not invite participants to contribute, change, alter, rearrange, remix, or otherwise interactively cocreate. It can also be said, however, that interactivity describes not merely participation and a desire to engage creatively with the texts that describe ourselves to ourselves and thereby establish norms and frameworks of identity, but also portrays a particular kind of struggle against the authorial and authorized control of texts. One way in which I have been characterizing this struggle is through another kind of sociocultural push-and-pull relationship in which interactivity opposes itself to the political and social protection of the text that is enacted through all legal (copyright), social (respect for authors), and technological (digital control) protections. Audiences continue to fight back with ever new disregard for copyright regimes (e.g., peer-to-peer distribution and torrenting of texts), with new frameworks of understanding authorship (e.g., through the concept of the prosumer or, increasingly, through a breaking down of the professional and the amateur in terms of contributions to the public sphere) and technological innovations (e.g., new hacks that release technological limitations of texts thereby opening them up to manipulation, redistribution, and control not by the "author" or the "authorized" or the "authorities" but by participants themselves). In developing theories around interactive media, it is important to look not only at how this contestation is new, but how the development of interactive technologies can be seen as a new field of engagement in a much older struggle around the concepts of author, text, and audience. At the same time, however, I do not characterize this struggle as new and as a complete break from the Enlightenment past of author–text–audience arrangements, for it is instead characterized by both ruptures and continuities. Some of those continuities can, I argue, be described as very old cultural desires and demands to participate cocreatively in the narratives, texts, and ideas that give meaning to our identities, ourselves, and our lives. At some level, we might describe human life as being characterized by creativity and that includes participating – whether voluntarily or unwittingly – in the creation and recreation of stories about ourselves and our societies that have been, effectively, "released" by the affordances of digital media.

I am interested here mostly in forms of interactivity in which the text or its content is affected, resequenced, altered, customized, or renarrated in the interactive process of audiencehood. This is the sort of interactivity in which content is affected not only at the "nodal point" at which it becomes textual – a set of points that includes broadcast or release time or other forms of digital dissemination – but also, and particularly, the point at which a text leaves the hands or immediate, real-time control of an author or content creator and becomes available to alteration in some way by a reader or content user. Such interactivity, I am arguing, has resulted in new tensions in the author–text–audience relationship, predominantly by blurring the distinction between the author and audience. These tensions sometimes result in that struggle for control over the authorial "purity" or "authenticity" of the text through intellectual property management or digital programming protections or limited, channeled, or "permitted" forms of interactivity; they also result in attempts by audiences and users to "fight" these new controls through the development of programming tools that unlock digital codes, attempt to resequence textual narratives, or permit other forms of customizing the text beyond authorial intent.

A digital environment promoting interactivity has fostered a greater capacity and a greater interest of audiences to change, alter, and manipulate a text or a textual narrative, to seek coparticipation in authorship, and to thus redefine the traditional author–text–audience relationship. I argue here that in light of both new developments in interactivity as found in the increasing popularity of new media forms such as electronic gaming, and the "backlash" development of new technologies, software, and legal methods that actively seek to prevent alteration and redistribution of texts, the historical and contemporary conception of the author–text–audience affinity can be characterized as a tactical war of contention for control over the text. This is a struggle set across a number of different contexts, media forms, sites and author/audience capacities. I would like to begin with a discussion of some of the new elements that have emerged in a digital media environment today, particularly in the framework of Web 2.0 interactivity and Web 3.0 interconnectedness before unpacking some of the ideas and concepts around interactivity and what the concept does for the author–text–audience relationship.

I will then go into a little more detail about the push-and-pull relationship that marks the struggle for control over the text (authorial purity versus interactive cocreativity) and some of the technological struggles between major software development companies and hackers that, likewise, mark the contemporary "era of interactivity." Before returning to the implications an interactive and online world has for identity (including how cocreativity and shifts in the character of citation change performativity in online contexts) I will present a short discussion of how interactivity can be figured as both opening and closing off the field of popular and public engagement with ideas.

## 1  DIGITAL MEDIA ENVIRONMENTS AND IDENTITY TODAY

Users, creators, producers, readers, and social beings who make use of digital media also thereby forge identities in contexts that implicate digital networks. As I discussed in Chapter 1, we have moved on from the text-based world of the mid-1990s Internet that framed ideas of online subjectivity through fluidity, play, pretence, and theatrics in chatrooms and the like to one which is vastly more visual, emphasizes the use of digital communication for the presentation of "actual" selves, and in which we engage cocreatively with texts. Today, such engagement includes producing a conversational blog, remixing film texts into a music video for pleasure, politics, or the creation of some other kind of meaning, contributing to knowledge by providing and arranging photographic images for a Wikipedia page, or updating peers on daily activities in social networking. Understanding how we engage with digital media needs to account for this shift, which is sometimes characterized as a shift from Web 1.0 to Web 2.0 and onward toward the über-connectivity of Web 3.0. Web 2.0 generally refers to the idea there is a "second generation" of web development and design that aims to facilitate user communication, to secure information sharing, to enhance interoperability between sites and platforms, and to emphasize collaboration and user participation on the World Wide Web. Web 2.0 concepts have been implicated in the development and evolution of web-based communities and new applications such as social-networking sites (e.g., Facebook and MySpace), video-sharing sites (e.g., YouTube), wikis (e.g., Wikipedia), and blogs. Web 2.0 has multiple definitions, although the key to understanding the definition is to (1) differentiate it from what was retrospectively called "Web 1.0" and (2) to understand the Internet and the World Wide Web as a platform for cocreation rather than a space in which content developers "put up" material that is consumed by readers/users (Walther et al., 2011, p. 26). In technological and access terms, Web 1.0 is linked with dial-up use, whereas Web 2.0 is seen to depend on broadband (ADSL and cable) speeds.

Web 1.0 is also a term applied retrospectively to the initial World Wide Web environment and may be used to describe a series of activities before the advent of technological advancements and their more widespread use around 2001 that enabled increased broadband capability for the sharing of large digital image and video files, new platforms (i.e., social networking sites such as Facebook and video uploading sites such as YouTube), and evidence of new uses such as self-conscious interactivity, cocreation, remixing, and user-generated content development (e.g., for Wikipedia). Web 1.0 is best described as a dual-platform that, on the one hand, provided capacity for chat that operated through textual engagement in the style of telephone party lines and mimicking one-to-one phone calls and letters (e.g., email and chatrooms) and, on the other hand, a distribution network making available textual information in static webpages that might be thought of as magazines, newspapers, and books with images made available on a screen. Hypertextual links were the chief new characteristic of this latter component, allowing navigation between different pages in sometimes rhizomatic formations that facilitated "surfing" quickly through pathways that appealed to the user rather than a linear, page-by-page approach to text. While this framework seems limited today, it naturally had enormous influence on how we think, behave, create, respond, and interact in communicative terms, and led to new ways of thinking about communication and media engagement.

Media theorist Terry Flew described the shift from Web 1.0 to Web 2.0, suggesting it characterized a "move from personal websites to blogs and blog site aggregation, from publishing to participation, from web content as the outcome of large upfront investment to an ongoing and interactive process, and from content management systems to links based on tagging" (Flew, 2008, p. 19). That is, in a Web 1.0 environment, users retrieved information whereas in a Web 2.0 environment, site architecture is more frequently built around the idea of users as participants. A number of changes and developments – both culturally and in terms of use technique – are discernible through this distinction. For example, digital skills in development, content creation, film production, and writing are no longer the sole province of professional/trained web designers and media practitioners, rather the skills are dispersed among "ordinary" users and become commonplace (e.g., the skills needed to create and/or remix and upload digital content). Computer-related activities shift from being understood as the domain of the "nerdy hobbyist" to an everyday pursuit that allows a continued uptake of digital skills and content-creation activities and, indeed, a broad desire to engage in such settings and interactions.

The term Web 3.0, however, has emerged as a way to describe further developments beyond interactivity and widespread cocreative engagement as part of an ongoing digital revolution. Web 3.0 is sometimes used to refer to new frameworks for thinking about the building of software applications away from broad-purpose programs such as Microsoft Word to customizable applications that are developed for very specific activities – something the small-sized mobile and the development environment of Google for its Android platform has facilitated. At other times, Web 3.0 is described as centering on connective intelligence in relation to powerful search engines that customize search results in a way that we might ordinarily experience from a personal assistant – preempting our needs. Still other ways of thinking about this new post-2010s generation of web use is built on ubiquitous connection, for example, being "always connected" and "always available," experiencing seamless connection between desktop, laptop, tablet, and mobile phone devices – a formation we see in the example of browsers that keep open tabs and recorded bookmarks regardless of which device one logs in on, and in the use of cloud storage to make available one's entire archive of material regardless of where one is in the world and the device being used. The World Wide Web Consortium (W3C) speaks of the "semantic web" as a framework for the development of standards to allow data and processing standards to be shared across an ever-greater number of devices and digital experiences. Sometimes referred to within concepts of Web 3.0, is the increasing connection of other nontraditional computing devices within networked frameworks – intelligent lighting that is linked to home and office wi-fi connections, allowing increased flexibility, customizability, and control at a distance, as well as the recording of useful data and the making available of this data for a range of purposes. All of these have an impact on how we think about identity, because the connections we make using tools of identity formation and performance – such as the on-screen social networking site – are reframed through our very personal and sometimes corporeal connectivity across an even broader range of devices from our Internet-connected washing machine that can start its cycle when we are at a distance, to the fitness wearable technological device that tracks our calorie depletion, our rates of exercise, and bodily health information, producing new ways of thinking about ourselves as embodied beings in relation to the technologies we use.

This historical progression of the interactive nature of connective, networked digital media is framed by a pronounced mix of continuities and progressions as well as novelties and ruptures. However, the most important element indicated by the developments and changes is that the older models of fluid identity produced through chatroom play, shifting gender pronouns, and the pretence of anonymous online identity no longer seem to have any bearing. That is, the idea that one of the primary activities of online use is to invent new personas or to recreate one's own identity through experimentation (McMillan & Morrison, 2006, p. 79) is no longer at play. In fact, what is so remarkable about online use is that such identity questions have become, in Web 2.0 frameworks, hidden, ordinary, mundane, and banal, meaning that identity creativity is framed even more so by the process of use than by deliberate acts. Online, interactive behavior is not articulated through anonymity (Kennedy, 2006, p. 860) but, instead, through the far more boring and therefore far more powerful articulation of one's actual name in a more genuinely connected articulation of self that operates across online and nonnetworked everyday activities. Online engagement can, of course, involve conscious and deliberate falsehoods and identity fraud – for example, one can establish a social networking profile that is purely fictional (although this is increasingly difficult in a Facebook setting), exaggerate, test out, or play with ideas and behaviors. The real versus digital distinction that marked such concepts of fluidity is no longer workable in an always-connected mobile-media and cocreative environment (Urry, 2007, pp. 180–181). The era in which apparently large numbers of men performed a kind of online drag by pretending in chatrooms to be women, undoubtedly for a range of reasons (Creed, 2003, p. 126) is over, although this has not meant a return to the idea that, say, gender is always bodily fixed to biology. Rather, that historical moment informs the broader notion that all identity is like such online play, so that we can indeed be "real" about who we are in articulating ourselves in an online setting while acknowledging culturally that identity is performed, performative, and playful. This means that in the contexts of today's Web 2.0 and Web 3.0 frameworks of digital interactivity, fluidity of identity is notably different, more nuanced, and recognizably more complex, rather than being seen as something one plays with online in a virtual setting before returning to one's embodied real life.

It is partly through the increased capacity for networks to carry high-definition video and still images that the possibility of anonymous performance online has become a disavowed activity on many sites (with, perhaps, the notable exceptions of cyberbullying activities and political trolling).

Additionally, the capabilities afforded by device connectivity – such as the ability to upload images directly from a digital camera, or more recently to upload directly from a camera-enabled smartphone, reframes the Web 2.0 and Web 3.0 interactive environment of the Internet as a space that emphasizes the representation of the embodied, corporeal "real" of social, physical space in online settings rather than chat-based pretence and no-name contributions. This is important in reframing how identity is formulated in a visually interactive environment. While much Screen Theory of the 1970s, as I mentioned in Chapter 2, perceived identity as formulated through the spectatorial gaze that positioned audience members to identify with particular perspectives and frames given on the film screen, the fact is that today the gaze on a site such as YouTube is fragmented (by the sheer volume of videos available to watch, from repetitions and fragments of professionally produced material from the past and present, to people's own blogs, to remixes, new music, and so on), embedded within the capacity for persistent addition and reframing of meaning (by the comments, notes, numbers of hits, etc.) and recombined with the self as actor not spectator (by the capability to easily and seamlessly record oneself on the simple camera built into most digital communication devices today and with almost no production experience, produce and upload a video in which one's own face is that which gazes back at the viewer). YouTube's primary affordance is its useability (Burgess & Green, 2009, p. 64) and this is a powerful shift in how we are able to think about the relationship between the self as a spectator engaged in a media world and the self as a creator of media content that can be made available to potentially huge crowds. Who we are as digital selves is something that needs to be thought through the frameworks, nuances, and complexities of interactivity as a theory of digital relationality, as a popular taste for engagement, as a marketing term, and as an element in the history of human communication.

## 2 THE NATURE OF INTERACTIVITY

Interactivity is a key element of contemporary digital media and communication and an important communicative formation to investigate if we are to better understand the relationship between identity and digital media. In thinking about how we might describe the "nature" of interactivity it is important to remember that at one level, the Internet is still relatively new and therefore to some extent interesting to us by virtue of having still uncertain outcomes; at another level the Internet is increasingly ubiquitous and underlying of all contemporary communication given the centrality of digital networks in everyday engagement for the majority of the western world; at still another level, given the ways in which digital interactivity is sometimes characterized to mimic F2F communication, it is marked by much older forms as well as a very basic desire to communicate and engage socially by humans as social subjects who perform that engagement through a broad, complex range of methods of communication. Although interactivity has been difficult to define, and is frequently used so broadly that it loses its significatory value, the sort of interactivity that impacts most on the author–text–audience relationship and that allows us to expand our understanding of communication is that which cultivates some element of user control over narrative content in a media or new media text. In the context of emerging theories of interactivity, this is an admittedly broad conception, but it is one articulated not as determined by technology, programming, production, and authorial "permission" to alter the text, but constituted within culture as a means or desire to coparticipate in the textuality of the text, in its narrative, in the course or temporality of its flow, or in its structuration. That is, some level of engagement with the text in the act of reading or usage that substantially and self-consciously shapes the text or the experience of its reception. The problem with theories of interactivity is the extent to which they can be located between seeing that which is technologically or authorially determined, and how much activity is required on the receiver's part to shape reception. While interactivity often entails a built-in capacity to transform, shape, or customize the text in accord with an author's wishes, it spurs on and sometimes encourages a desire to transform the text in ways that are out of the hands of an author and in accord with the individual wishes of an audience member or user. Digital media environments promote convenient and comfortable ways of altering a text: to coparticipate, resequence, or interactively transform a printed book would require literally cutting and pasting pages, whereas the opportunity to cut and paste in order to resequence or substantially transform a digital text has become not only easier, but a matter of contention.

Interactivity can be thought of both as indefinable and as something to be contained. Spiro Kiousis (2002) argues that there should be no alarm expressed at the indefinability of interactivity: "as long as we all accept that the term implies some degree of receiver feedback and is usually linked to new technologies, why should there be a problem?" (p. 357). In the broadest of definitions, receiver feedback might constitute the changing of television channels or the use of a pause button on a DVD player or selecting a song on an iPod – the exercising of user choice is not, however, necessarily interactive.

Other writers have presented more narrow understandings of interactivity. Lelia Green (2002), for example, suggests that interactivity implies the capacity of a communication medium to be altered by, or have its products altered by, the actions of a user or audience, as well as suggesting a technology that requires input from a user to work effectively (p. xx). This definition would cover such products or texts as electronic games, but the extent to which this form of interactivity depends on the technology is more complex – a flash movie might utilize its digitality to build in a feature allowing user selection or reordering of scenes, but at the same time a user can interactively engage with a DVD disc to select a numerically nonsequential order of film chapters – the key question here is one of diverse useability in which different levels of user interest and effort intersect to create a sense of the extent to which a text, medium, or channel is interactive (ironically, it is sometimes framed as a case of the less bodily, corporeal effort the user needs to go to, to affect such an interactive action, the more interactive it is or feels). While the latter is not often a built-in feature of a film, and while the technology does not specifically direct this sort of choice, it does involve receiver feedback and considerable engagement with a digitally manipulable text.

Sally McMillan provides a categorical typology of interactivity definitions, some aspects of which have a good fit with the kinds of cocreative engagement I am discussing in this chapter. Drawing on the work of Bordewijk and van Kaam (1986), she delineates the concept of interactivity into a typology of four intersecting levels or uses: (1) *Allocution*, in which interactive engagement is minimal, and is set within the context of a single, central broadcaster and multiple receivers on the periphery. This would ordinarily include most mass media forms such as television, as well as real-time events like a lecture or a play (McMillan, 2002, p. 273). (2) *Consultation*, which occurs in the use of a database, such as a CD-ROM or a World Wide Web site, where a user actively searches for preprovided information (p. 273). Feedback is clearly minimal in this case, and although some recording of access patterns might be a feature of the site or database, it does not necessarily alter the content, the narrative, or individual subtexts or sections of information requested. (3) *Registration*, which does record access patterns, and as with many forms of digital surveillance, accumulates information from the periphery for use in a central registry (p. 273). Although McMillan's example of registrational interactivity is the Internet "cookie," which tracks and customizes content of Internet sites visited by the user. (4) *Conversational* interactivity, for McMillan, occurs when individuals interact directly with each other, mimicking F2F contact through computer-mediated communications technologies (p. 273), a form that locates the "text," as it were, predominantly in real-time rather than in a prior recorded format. Problematically, none of these definitions account for media forms such as the digital multimedia clip or the electronic game in which the user or player has considerable control over the text and its narrative. In such cases, the computer or computerized device keeps constant track of inputs from the user and alters the narrative accordingly and over time. The narrative flow of a video game will be dependent not only on authorial or programming structure, but on both user inputs and via a random number generator for diverse gameplay. Such an interactive text falls outside the definitions of interactivity given in McMillan's account.

Both Green and McMillan's definitions invoke the structure and arrangement of the technology or the medium as the central criterion of what it is that counts as interactivity. Although neither are technological determinists, the spectre of digital technology haunts these definitions, tending to locate interactivity too securely within digital paradigms, recent media, and those texts that are self-consciously built around interactive engagement. However, it need not be the case that interactivity must be linked with the structure or purpose of a technology or medium. As Rafaeli and Sudweeks (1997) put it:

> … *interactivity is not a characteristic of the medium. It is a process-related construct about communication. It is the extent to which messages in a sequence relate to each other, and especially the extent to which later messages recount the relatedness of earlier messages.*

That is, there is no set of logical reasons to suggest that interactivity, even as it forms a central feature of recent computer-mediated communications, is a technologically driven concept or determined wholly by technological development. Rather, what Rafaeli and Sudweeks do is shift the focus of interactivity from the technology to the form of communication and restore the figure of the audience member, user, or receiver by acknowledging the relationality of communication processes. Likewise Denis McQuail (1997) reinstates the question of the audience member, user, or receiver as a human subject in a communication process:

> … *this would seem to run counter to the general trend of media history, restoring a human scale and individuality to mediated social communication, restoring the balance of power of the receiver at the periphery as against the dominant centralized sender. But it also increases the individuation of use and fragmentation of the mass audience. It is also still unclear how far the audience wants to be interactive (p. 10).*

Following the cultural materialist models of Raymond Williams (1990), the concept of interactivity need not be understood as the "making available" of a newly invented technological tool, but the extension to media technologies of a culturally constituted desire for communication that is located in the lived expressions of culture (1981, p. 10, 1990). Counter to McQuail's assertion that it is unclear just how interactive an audience member or digital media user may wish to be, it is becoming increasingly the case that the "uptake" of interactive forms of media entertainment – particularly the digital game, but also new forms of Web 2.0 online engagement such as wikis, image sharing, and cross platform – is not only significant, but is driven by popular cultural demand. That is, users desire to participate in the textuality of the text, to engage in its narrative, to resequence texts on their own terms, and to find new and imaginative ways to do so even when the text does not specifically encourage choice, engagement, or activity. Such a perspective on interactivity is to see the audience as active and aware participants in the media process, and not as the cultural dupes of marketing techniques or authorial intent.

I am characterizing this desire here as one that emerges and reemerges in various periods, sites, alongside various new technologies, and which, since the advent of the concept of the "author" has frequently been juxtaposed against questions of authorial control over the creation of both recorded and performed content. The aesthetics and architectures of ancient theatre, the rise of audience theories of interpretation and productive activation of meanings, and the attempts to engage in redistribution of media texts from reselling of books to the dubbing of audio tapes are just a few among the many instances in which we see this desire emerge prior to the digital interactive technologies that facilitate it best. It is my argument here that the rise of interactivity as a form of audience participation is by no means the latest trend in media history, nor something that disrupts a prior synergy between author–text–audience, but a strongly held and culturally based desire to participate in the creation and transformation of the text that has effectively been denied by previous technologies of media production and distribution. I would suggest that it is no longer all that "unclear how far the audience wants to be interactive" depending on what it is we characterize as media texts, particularly if we take into account the popularity of multimedia and electronic gaming as media forms.

Important work *Culture Jamming* by Mark Dery (1993) described the tactics of a new grassroots resistance to textual control, simplification, and the power of an information industry that manufactures consent through the maintenance of control over textual interpretation. For Dery, this re-sistance took the form of media hacking, informational warfare, terror art, and the guerrilla semiotics of work that sought to point out the significatory foundations of existing mass-media texts. This conception of an emerging, diametric war between media creators/industries and audience participa-tion and interpretation is something I want to consider here in light of both the past history of the audience in its *longue duree,* and the ways in which emerging forms of interactivity that empower audiences over text and nar-rative – as found in both lip-service gestures to interactive television and new digital media formats such as the macromedia flash file – extend Dery's forms of audience resistance by putting the author–text–audience relation-ship of textual control into question. This is not to equate audience interac-tive participation with audience resistance, nor to suggest that participation is a self-conscious form of resistance. Rather, the concept of interactivity allows us to see a manner of cultural resistance against prevailing human-ist notions of the author–text–audience relationship, and as resistances that have emerged historically rather than just technologically. Although I accept the mimicry of real-time F2F computer-mediated communication as one formulation of interactivity (among many), I am interested in examining here predominantly the interactive forms and texts that, across a variety of mediums, allow control over the narrative – the digital game being the most obvious example although online interactive fiction, digital image manipul-ation (photoshopping), and remixing of digital videos being other forms in which we witness high levels of such interactivity. The point here is that this form of digital interactivity is the culmination of a much older and ongoing contestation over control of a text as if a text were a finished, unified, and coherent whole at the time at which it has been disseminated.

## 3  INTERACTIVITY AND THE AUTHOR–TEXT–AUDIENCE RELATIONSHIP – SYNERGY AND STRUGGLE

In the early 2000s, CNN.com had a television advertisement that con-trasted broadcast with online communication – the advertisement's tag was to point out that "the average computer has 101 keys" while, for the cable news company: "We say, you only need three – CNN." Although making a particular play between the physical interface device for standard Internet access and the brand name, it is considerably representative of the ways in which interactivity is both enabled and stemmed in popular discours-es around new media, authorship, texts, and audiences. The keyboard, the extension of the traditional typewriter with all the creative connotations that go with it, is the interface device of content creation *par excellence*. The implication of CNN's reduction to needing only three keys is that news and information creation is, and should be, in the hands of a media industry and its authors, journalists, or content creators. Mass news media purporting to represent "the people" (as the mass, the reader, the audience) are, of course, not quite as independent from capital or state (Hardt & Negri, 2000, pp. 311–312), and do indeed stand to lose the network power of "voice" and the gatekeeping power of "making discourse (un)available" the greater the interactivity over the text that is granted to an audience. The struggle between author and audience, characterized as a struggle between corporate media industries and consumer users, is well illustrated in the juxtaposition of the undertone in CNN's advertisement against not only online visual, textual, and moving image news (increasingly produced through cross-media news companies) but also independent online writing ranging from indymedia-style radical reframing of current affairs and the forms of engagement with contemporary society that emerge from citizen journalism, blogging, vlogging, and other online opinion representation. Indeed, dominant as a political alternative to mainstream news in the early 2000s, indymedia.com's motto was, "Everyone's a journalist."

The very idea of the author as the central authority of a work is, as Foucault and Bouchard (1977) pointed out, one which is regulated within culture, and the concept of which is available for critique (p. 123). The operations of the name and role of the author as a rule for the quality and power of a work is an historical one, and one which continues both to change as well as be defended – questions over, for example, intellectual property illustrate the two poles of authorship in which, on the one hand, a work can be disputed as having needed the protections that accord its "ownership" to an author, and on the other as defending a set of rights asserted by an author not to have that work altered or distributed outside of his or her control (or, more properly, the rights of the industry owner to whom the author, as a semifoundational law in this case, signs over his or her rights to that control). Foucault and Bouchard adeptly demonstrated the ways in which the author is not only historical, but that conception of it is one that is threatened at various times and in various forms:

> The 'author-function' is tied to the legal and institutional systems that circumscribe, determine, and articulate the realm of discourses; it does not operate in a uniform manner in all discourses, at all times, and in any given culture; it is not defined by the spontaneous attribution of a text to its creator, but through a series of precise

*and complex procedures; it does not refer, purely and simply, to an actual individual insofar as it simultaneously gives rise to a variety of egos and to a series of subjective positions that individuals of any class may come to occupy (pp. 130–131).*

The argument here, then, would be that the rise of media technologies that encourage interactivity with the text, combined with the ways in which the pleasure of engagement with the text is sold under the signifier of interactivity, puts into question the functionality of authorship and opens the possibility for a variety of mediums no longer predicated on the name of the author: "We can easily imagine a culture where discourses would circulate without any need for an author. Discourses, whatever their status, form, or value, and regardless of our manner of handling them, would unfold in a pervasive anonymity" (Foucault & Bouchard, 1977, p. 138). The Internet in general could be considered the site at which the author's name disappears as a plethora of anonymous sites, commentaries, knowledges, and textualities emerge amidst an environment predicated on its interactivity and exchangeability, although in the sometimes push toward a recorporatization of the Internet as it functions as a public sphere, the role of the author and the emphasis on author verification are restored in the tide toward recentralization of the medium (Ess, 1994; Dahlberg, 2001; Papacharissi, 2002). The continuation of the mythos of the author into the digital age is one which is now to be located in what Manuel Castells (1997) refers to as a pluralization of sources of authority (p. 303), which includes the audience exercising consumer choice in the weakest definition of interactive feedback, and in the strongest a full interactive engagement with the text beyond the requirements installed by an author or form creator. This system witnesses a continuing backlash as other persons, sources, and institutions attempt to centralize the authorial voice as the only source of speaking–writing–saying power.

Textuality itself, then, becomes something that is put into question. Such a critique of the coherence of a text depends not on the question of audience interactivity over content, but on the concerns of cultural studies and critical theory that have argued for the incoherence of the text as that which is located in a network of intertextuality (e.g., Barthes, 1975, 1977) in which it is necessary to account for the form, the frame, the absent, and the instability of context (Derrida, 1978, 1988). Nevertheless, the text persists as a unified, coherent, and fixed whole – particularly as a recorded work – within the popular imaginary. As interactive engagement and participation reemerge as features of audience desire and behavior, that textual coherence is further interrogated, such that we witness questions over the textuality of, say, electronic games whereby there remains a pointed and fruitful undecidability between the game as text or play (Berger, 2002, pp. 11–12; Pearce, 2002). I would argue that even as the text becomes more amorphous the "location" of the text becomes increasingly difficult to place, particularly when it is digital and networked rather than carrying the "aura" of the physical and the individual (Benjamin & Arndt, 1992).

What occurs once interactivity is deemed to make available an aspect of participation within text creation or the ability to alter, transform, or redistribute a text has been considered on the one hand as the empowerment of audience (McMillan, 2002, pp. 279, 285), and on the other the dissolution of the traditional concept of audiencehood (Brooker & Jermyn, 2003, p. 333; Webster, 1998, p. 190). Definitions of audience are of course diverse and contested, but by necessity have been subject to various forms of categorization, particularly where such categorizations occur in ways that give the power of the audience to interpret, act, transform, or redistribute different valencies. In her canonical work *Desperately Seeking the Audience* Ien Ang (1991), for example, categorizes the audience across two paradigms as on the one hand a public and, on the other, a market. Ang's distinction is also of significance in demonstrating the gap between the audience desire for participation, and the authorial desire for textual control (p. 29). However, Ang's dualist system is open to a reinterpretation in terms of the rise of interactive engagement: for Ang, the audience-as-public paradigm locates the audience in a transmission model of communication, viewing the audience as that which requests and, under paternalistic systems, requires information and meaning. This view of the audience is of a mass group of "receivers" within a system of more or less ordered transference of meaning (p. 29). The desire for narrative interactivity under such a view would be seen to be a disruption of this order of transference, and would dissolve the centrist model on which transmissional systems are based. The audience as a market notion, however, raises the question of transfers of meaning. Indeed material from which to make meaning in an "active audience" conception is given only a secondary level of importance, after the primary business of providing goods and services to potential customers, aroused in order to maintain their interest (p. 29).

We might view the interactive audience – where such interactivity involves participation in the transformation or cocreation of the text – as a new category to describe both an ancient form and its reemergence alongside digital media technologies. In his *Communication as Culture*, James Carey (1988) identifies two views of communication practices from a culturalist perspective taking into account the role of the audience – the transmission view and the ritual view. The transmission view is the standard, pedestrian account of communication as it occurs in line with, say, Shannon's sender-message-receiver (SMR) communication model, and is defined by key terms such as "imparting," "sending," "transmitting," and "giving information to others." Messages are transmitted and distributed across space for the control of distance and of people (p. 14). The ritual view, on the other hand, likens communication to acts of "sharing," "association," "fellowship," and "possession of a common faith." He suggests it is more ancient than the concept of transmission, and is not directed toward the extension of messages in space, but toward the maintenance of society across time (p. 18). Although neither of these perspectives on the role of the audience (as receiver; as fellowship) entirely precludes interactivity, it remains that the transmission model is lodged in a sense of the primacy of authorship, whilst the ritual understanding model sees communication as participatory, but ultimately for the organization and management of the people around a set of authored texts – a view not different from a Foucauldian governmentality approach. It is my suggestion here that the audience, being interactive, constitutes a third position, one which is dominant but has been obscured by the twentieth century prevalence of recordable media. It is this third position or view that works to blur the distinction between author, text, and audience by suggesting that such a distinction is a false one which by cultural signification or by technological availability, has attempted to shore up the idea of the author as one of authority over the text and has simultaneously attempted to assert the unity, coherence, and completion of the text. The interactive position is one which is located in the push and pull struggle between author–industry and audience–user over the right and ability to access and utilize the text in ways more than just scavenging through interpretation and the readings of alternative or marginal meanings.

Certainly audience members and those who would ordinarily be defined by media industries as content receivers or content users are aware of the push-and-pull relationship between authorial/narrative control and audience interactivity. Edward Downes and Sally McMillan (2000) interviewed a number of users on the impacts of computer-mediated interactive communication, finding responses categorizable across the three areas of the revolutionary potential of interactivity, the general consequences to media consumption, and an uncertainty over the future of media use. What is interesting about the interview extracts used by the authors is the location of questions of interactivity within the semantics of threat, empowerment, opposition to media industries, and communications control. As one respondent put it, interactivity "threatens whole industries, threatens whole professions" (p. 164). Another found that the ability to access and utilize knowledge was in general empowering, and located this empowerment in controller/user and corporate/media citizen dyads: "Because I have a voice now. I think the threat is to existing institutions and the old ways of doing things" (p. 164). Although it appears their respondents valued the concept of a threat to authorship diversely, others seemed to speak more in terms of wresting control from the author (p. 170), and in creating a territory or space as a sense of "place" within new computer-mediated environments (p. 166).

This notion of online environments as having separate kinds of spaces in which authorship is done differently is, perhaps, a moot point today in a digital network in which such diversity of material is available. One of the key questions, then, becomes not a matter of whether traditional institutional controls, content creators, news producers, etc. can or will exist alongside the entry of newer startups and individuals writing, but the extent to which a democratically feasible mix of alternatives is available and how they will be accessed in a search engine regime that can seemingly give preference to larger corporate distribution networks. This is highly significant for how we do identity, given that an interactive environment that preferences the potential of interactivity can make available new, democratically creative and potentially radical formations of identity that are right now unknowable but may have value either to individuals or socially beyond that.

## 4 PUSH AND PULL: AUDIENCE INTERACTIVITY IN HISTORY

Interactive engagement versus authorial control can be witnessed across a wide array of mediums, both ancient and contemporary, and in some ways we might argue that if identity is always performative in a manner that involves the citation of categories of identity given in discourse prior to the self, then one aspect of how identity is done has always depended on the kinds of controls, struggles, dominances, and alternatives over the communication of discourse. While it is not possible to encompass every instance of new communication mediums across the broad history of communication, interactivity, and engagement, there is some value in tracing aspects and examples of this push-and-pull juxtaposition between authorial control and interactive dissent across a longer period drawing briefly on the evolution of media forms from theater as a real-time events through to recorded analog media forms such as cinema and television toward the Internet and electronic gaming as contemporary popular forms of interactive engagement.

One way in which we can broach the question of authorial/authorized/authority control versus interactive, cocreative, and participatory engagement is through noting that the contemporary, late twentieth century form of live, real-time theater is one which in its dominant, middle-class mode returns to an even earlier form in the presentation of the sacred. In the theater, any attempt to interfere or involve oneself from the audience is to cross a line; the penetration of the sacred space that, to use Julia Kristeva's (1982) term, would be an act of abject behavior, disrupting both the social and the ritualistic processes of language and the emplacement of selves as coherent selves which, in this particular scenario, is the self as the intelligible, coherent, and perhaps "sane" audience member. To speak during a play is not merely to disrupt the audience and actors, and not merely to draw attention to the self in a way that might afford the label of "insane," but to disrupt the theatrical work as a finished work, put it into question, destabilize the finality and exact reproducibility of the play. Thus, where the very architectural aesthetics of the Greek amphitheater that sponsors interactive engagement with the text/play is contrasted against the Victorian stage is in the restriction of the audience members from exercising an explicit ability to control or interrupt the unfolding, real-time text. Under the Victorian model, cinema is viewed as the theater performance *par excellence*, because it is restricted by a screen operating as an impenetrable seam and by the lapse in time that halts any possibility of destabilization of the text as a finished text (although censorship commissions, cinema management, equipment problems, and other factors might come to be seen to interfere with the finished, authored work, and such disturbances are usually treated in contemporary culture with some irritation for the very same reasons). For Williams (1997), it is highly reductive to treat the cinema as a noninteractive form of theater, but it is a comparison that is often made, and one which views the mechanical technologies of the twentieth century as impersonal compared with earlier forms of communication:

> Where the theatre presented actors, the cinema presents the photographs of actors. Where the meeting presented a man speaking, the wireless presents a voice, or television a voice and a photograph. Points of this kind are relevant, but need to be carefully made. It is not relevant to contrast an evening spent watching television with an evening spent in conversation, although this is often done. There is, I believe, no form of social activity which the use of these techniques has replaced (p. 21).

It is in the fact that forms of theater as interactive have been replaced neither by cinema nor by the sacred "textuality" of the theater that attests to the push-and-pull struggle between an audience desire to participate and an authorial desire to maintain a controlled textual coherence and impenetrability. Space has always been made for more interactive, innovative, and radical forms of theatre, particularly in texts we would ordinarily call avant-garde, and while they continue to be marginal they are open to being viewed as small niches of resistance to mass media's closure of interactive forms. Cinema and television with their impenetrable screens involve, to some extent, new forms of conversation that utilize new mediums alongside existing ones, although in this case there are some obvious limitations to the extent to which one engages with the narrative of the text and the range of meanings that can be made available, interpreted, or inferred.

The basis on which we traditionally differentiate the theater as a communication text from the scripted or printed book, the cinema, the television, the radio, and the html Internet website is that for the greater part the latter make available a text that is recorded as opposed to one disseminated in "real time" or, if it is to be in real time such as the television "live coverage" news, for example, it is distributed through a one-way, noninteractive system, and thereby not available for interruption, interference, or transformation in any form. Even in the case of a live, real-time event, the audience is disempowered from a creative and transformative role by the simple fact of distance: broadcast mass media, as Meadows (1994) suggests, effectively separates media program makers and audiences (p. 133). Various developments do, of course, allow greater user control, and we can figure the development and the utilization of these as a part of a struggle against authorial and industrial control over the text – the pull from the audience. In the case of television, the advent of the video recorder not only released the text from the broadcast imperatives of time (Cubitt, 1991, p. 42), but allowed a user to watch at various speeds, forward through segments of little interest, rewatch the entire text a second or third time and, for the more advanced, utilize two video recorders to reorder sequences or sections of the text (Jenkins, 1992b, p. 212; Penley, 1997, p. 114; Jenkins, 2003), thereby allowing an early form of narrative interactivity that provided control over the text and the narrative.

There is nothing new in this point, other than to suggest that should we look for causal factors in the rise and popularity of interactive entertainment, it would always be wise to avoid a technological determinist approach and to view this emergence as one activated from within culture.

As Williams (1990) attests, making sense of media technologies depends on understanding them as located within culture and within an interpretation of their development that restores intention to the process of development:

> The technology would be seen, that is to say, as being looked for and developed with certain purposes and practices already in mind … [T]hese purposes and practices would be seen as direct: as known social needs, purposes and practices to which the technology is not marginal but central (p. 13).

That is, no media technology is alien to culture, impacting on it and changing it, but actively emerges from within culture. Interactive technologies, like other developments, are not the brainchild of a crazed inventor working in a laboratory or a basement that then have appeal and are taken on popularly; instead, for Williams, they are actively sought in order to address a popular problem, a need, a cultural desire or demand – otherwise the huge research and development funding required and the investment in infrastructure would not have occurred. Indeed, this point becomes obvious when we bear in mind the ways in which imaginative and even sometimes quite mundane science fiction from earlier years, foreground such technologies as part of "future" everyday life – *Star Trek's* communicator from the 1960s series that is today's mobile phone; *Star Trek's* touchscreen pads that are today's iPads and tablets, and the wearable technology from the 1980s and 1990s series. This is just one example of how the very ideas of technologies are actively part of cultural representation, understanding that if a technology was truly alien and therefore truly changing cultural processes of communication, it would be unthinkable even in the most speculative of science fiction. That is not to say that technologies do not have unforeseen uses and gratifications that come from particularly innovative uses, only that they should not be seen as being the source of change. Whether that is a change to cultural and communication practices or a change in how we think about ourselves, those changes are always emergent from within cultural processes, and communication technologies form part of those processes.

Bearing this in mind, it can be suggested that one way in which we can view the historical development of various media technologies is from a perspective which understands their emergence as driven by a cultural – that is, popular – demand for the democratization of control over the text. This is a demand to take it out of the hands of authors, to allow not only the recording and rerecording of the text and some ability to distribute it independently, but to resequence the text, reorder it, change its quality, and so on, in accord with the imaginative requirements and gratifications of the audience user. It is, of course, digital media and mobile communication that are then to be understood as the culmination of this cultural desire in that they allow the greatest ease of textual manipulation, copying, and distribution across a network. What such technologies do is effectively restore to the audience their capacity to participate in the same ways in which a contemporary culture views ancient Greek theater and communicative forms as being driven by active and creative participation over transmission.

## 5  REALITY TV, MIXED MEDIUMS, AND OPEN/CLOSED TEXTUALITIES

The popular phenomenon of reality TV that emerged in the early 2000s makes an interesting gesture toward interactivity in that audiences become participants through cross-media platforms in the direction of narratives. This has, in some ways, provided a benchmark point for how audiences can be understood to operate as "users" who labor to engage in textual cocreative endeavors (Banks & Humphreys, 2008). For example, internationally recognizable reality television shows such as *Big Brother* or *Survivor* operate by making use of various media networking and convergences in order to indicate the potential for interactivity that skirts around the unidirectional mode of the standard television broadcast. Audience members are positioned to "play" with the real-world narrative by voting characters out of the show (among other interactive "gimmicks") thereby permitting an engagement with the hyperreality of reality TV that serves ultimately to make its real highly simulacral and spectatorially driven. With an entertainment phenomenon crossing television broadcasts, Internet updates and feedback forums, telephone and cellphone voting, and most recently SMS text messaging (bidirectional), the interactive potential of a television show is provided through alternative means, rather than waiting until various forms of interactive television can be developed in a format decentralized enough to allow participatory engagement through the one medium (Kim & Sawhney, 2002). They explicitly market interactivity as both the promise and the premise of the reality TV experience, suggesting that "viewers/consumers will have a greater ability to participate in the production process" (Andrejevic, 2002, p. 260).

  If, as Michael Meadows (1994) put it, electronic mass media "effectively separate media program-makers and audiences with little chance for interaction" (p. 133), then it is important to see the ways in which various media industries are making use of this separation not merely to maintain authorial control, but to utilize forms of "lip service" interactivity that encourage the pretence of interactive engagement with the text. Indeed, the capacity to provide an audience with the sense that collective voting has changed the composition of the household and thereby altered the composition of the narrative as it proceeds temporally, is a form of interactivity, and it is one that obscures the authorial control in the provision, selection, and ordering of segments from the household footage as the major vector through which the narrative travels in combination with the "nodal" commentary provided by the program's various host(s). Other television programs have attempted to do the same with fictional series such that narratives are determined by audience interactivities with the plot in ways that permit sometimes quite a pertinent and complex engagement with narratives, characterizations, character development, and story formation (Nguyen, 2002). Such interactive engagement with the plot is by no means a purely lip-service gesture – rather, it deals with considerable character development and provides a strong sense that the audience member has a level of interactive participation in the creation and future of the plot which, unlike the reality TV programs such as *Big Brother* with its emphasis on randomness, is presented as a programmatic plot.

Whether or not, such a choice-based interactivity arrangement allows a genuine sense of creativity, is a different matter. To put such an arrangement in terms of Umberto Eco's (1979) open/closed texts categorizations, the open text that deliberately gives an audience more than one possible interpretation is, in fact, less open to creative interpretation than the closed text which, for Eco, is variably and diversely interpretable along individual and imaginative trajectories. An open text calls for the active cooperation of its reader, "but also wants this reader to make a series of interpretive choices which even though not infinite are, however, more than one" (p. 4). The closed text, on the other hand, which we might consider as being any televisual text deliberately and explicitly designed for transference through a unidirectional system, is actually open to a greater number of "aberrant" decodings by nonaverage readers, since such texts have, as a minimum requirement, a sociologically "average" reader in mind. This thinking would suggest that the open text, such as those in which an audience can make particular decisions, such as vote whether a television character in a fictional series will have a relationship with this person or that person, would in fact direct its audiences to any of the three possible interactive plot lines and thereby foreclose on thinking through the possibilities for cocreation that might occur along other lines, whereas the closed text, perhaps a very standard episode of a very standard television series, would be more likely open to a broader array of interpretations and cocreative possibilities – if only the interactive potential was afforded through the technology to allow such cocreative participation to its fullest extent. Nevertheless, the gesture toward interactivity here does indeed appear to be one made to the audience, but only as a tactical, if nonconscious, movement from the perspective of advantaging the media industry and its position of authorial control.

As Andrejevic (2002, p. 256) argues, the promise of interactivity from a media industry's perspective is one which is given within the realm of profit rearing, and certainly in the case of reality TV the added costs of providing an interactive component is offset by effectively offloading the dial-up, Internet access and other component costs of interactive engagement to the consumers themselves (Mougayar, 1998, p. 170). Dallas Smythe (1995) points out the ways in which the labor of audiences is bought by advertisers, enforcing the work to "create the demand for advertised goods which is the purpose of monopoly-capitalist advertisers" (p. 222). The labor of the audience is their "attention" or "potential attention" sold on to the advertiser, and the act of laboring is the learning of "appropriate" spending practices. Smythe believes audience members may resist this "work" but that "the advertiser's expectations are realized sufficiently that the results perpetuate the system of demand management" (p. 222). What occurs in the gesture toward interactivity is that audiences experience a novel means by which audience maximization is intended (Ang, 1991, p. 27), although it should be pointed out that audience maximization is not always to be collapsed with a profit motive. It is the illusion of participation that is powerful and compelling to audiences in general (Schultz, 1994, pp. 108–109).

Under this analysis it is suggested that an industry maintaining a certain form of authorial control over a cross-genre drama/gameshow media experience is presenting its own tactic by which to allow a gesture toward interactivity, without actually forfeiting ground in the challenge over narrative control. Of course, the extent to which audiences and individual audience members find such a form of interactivity compelling over a longer period remains to be seen, and it may indeed be the case that the reader of the "closed" text will find compelling new ways in which to engage and participate interactively in reconfiguration, transformation, and cocreation of the text.

## 6 DIGITAL RIGHTS MANAGEMENT AND FLASHES: DIGITAL WARS AND INTERACTIVE STRUGGLES

The push-and-pull relationship between content creators and interactive audiences is witnessed perhaps most strongly in certain kinds of digital media that fall under copyright and intellectual property concerns, particularly around digital rights management regimes that attempt to work across complex national/international legal frameworks and technologies that actively seek to prevent users from making changes, adjustment, reutilizations or redistributions of texts (all of which we would consider to be interactive here today). Admittedly, there are many everyday, practical purposes for an author to maintain a certain form of control over the text produced – for example, many professionals, educators, and enterprises will distribute information in a PDF format in order to prevent the material from being accidentally or deliberately altered, thereby preserving not only content but the look and feel of the text and its layout. This would be in contrast to the distribution of a text in a word document, which, depending on the settings and standards of the device and the program used to open the document would be persistently at risk of accidentally or purposefully appearing differently, and could easily be copied for utilization in other ways and in other texts. At the same time, moving visuals played on a site such as YouTube are generally well protected from manipulation and download, whereas other platforms for video distribution such as Vimeo are more open to being purposefully set for download (and thereby for future alterations or other uses of the file), while still other platforms are barely protected from this at all or are not set up in a way which indicates anyone should be bothered how it is utilized and who has copies of the file. There are some obvious reasons in the case of the latter example as to why some organizations' platforms are set up this way – maintaining the need for users to go directly to that platform exposes the user to the labor of reading advertisements which is the form of profit derived by that organization for making the platform available. This is about control and the ways in which new digital forms of distribution have allowed easy alteration and utilization of a document, to interactively engage with the text, such that practical forms of control are occasionally warranted. The ethics of doing so are, nevertheless, complex. This does, however, illustrate the ways in which the push and pull of author versus (intended) audience control over the text is heightened dramatically in a digital environment.

An interesting example is seen in the shift of much Internet content from hypertext markup language formats to the more professional production of .swf and .flv files through programs like Adobe Flash (formerly Macromedia Flash) in what were for a time in the early 2000s accessed through professional learning in the field of "multimedia," a term less popular today. Although this marked an overall and perhaps temporary "professionalization" among the general user demographic who were fast developing skills in the creative tools used initially in digital industry environments, the programming at the time was often about shutting down the potential accessibility of content and content components; that is, preventing content alteration – including that of an end user with only one of several hundred thousand digital copies on a home computer – and stopping individual parts of a textual product, such as photographs or sections of text, being copied, individualized, cut and pasted into other texts, or stored individually and independently of the rest of the content. In the completion of a Flash text and its conversion to its final locked format, the possibilities for an audience user or recipient to engage interactively in active reconfiguration, transformation, and utilization of the text are shut down (Probets, n.d.). By locking down the code or preventing its copying or printing – an inbuilt feature of the Flash program in its form at the time (Rey, 2002, p. 334) – the author–producer was able to maintain control over the text and its narrative, no matter how hypertextual that narrative might prove to be. Indeed, any interactivity built into the text would be choice based and via the options presented by the author–producer, much as Eco's "open" text described above, thereby relegating the extent of interactivity to the conditions set by the content creator. This is the push.

The pull from the audience in the continuing desire to have participation and interactivity – that is, the capacity to change, alter, or utilize a document on one's own terms – came in the form of the development and proliferation in the early 2000s of what were sometimes collectively known as either swifty or swiffer programs (named after the Flash extension .swf). One such swiffer program was defined as follows:

> Swiffer is a surprisingly useful MSDOS routine that easily creates an HTML file for any SWF document and automatically puts both it and the new HTML file in the Active Sync 'My Documents' folder. All you do is drop the SWF file on the desktop Swiffer icon, give the HTML a name when prompted, sync, then use Pocket File Explore to find the HTML file and then execute it (http://members.cox.net/nnsydev/#FlashBrowser).

Other, similarly amateur programs were able to remove protection tags from an .swf file, unlock the code to be edited, reconfigured, or utilized otherwise, and a Swiff Extractor program allowed the extraction of JPEG files from the previously protected .swf format. The development of tools by which to regain a certain level of control over an authored, distributed text, that is, to copy aspects or to rearrange, are all part of what I describe as the "pull" from the audience in the struggle for textual and narrative control, actively and deliberately seeking a means by which to make files and documents open to manipulation and alternative, unintended uses, almost always for creative purposes.

Clearly the push back response from the media and computing industries is the development of ever more complex forms of control, one
example being the development of Digital Rights Management (DRM) programming (alongside legal provisions), giving media conglomerates greater
control over the ways in which their content is viewed by consumers.
As Nathan Cochrane (2002) put it, "Microsoft has unveiled its vision for
the future digital media landscape and it's a world where content creators
are king." Part of the process of developing DRM programming was to
force the makers of media players to ensure their software was not used to
view suspect media streams – a process not dissimilar from the DVD Copy
Control Association that is used by Hollywood for dealing with DVD makers.
The addition here is to utilize networking to request a license key from a
copyright clearing house, which will be reissued each time a player begins
a particular track, file, or document. As Cochrane notes:

> It enables finely tuned licensing terms and conditions, such as limited 24-hour play,
> a set number of plays over a given time, or an outright purchase license that lets the
> viewer watch the video or listen to music whenever they want. It will also be used
> to bind content to a specific PC, so that it cannot be redistributed around a house
> or played on a different device … The idea is 'to keep honest users honest', … by
> greatly restricting the ability of consumers to dictate how the media they consume
> is used.

The rhetoric here makes clear the ways in which a particular form of
struggle between author and audience or creator and consumer is ongoing
in the planning and development stages of new technological evolution and
growth. The critical response has been to articulate a fear over the abolition
of consumer rights to such forms as timeshifted video recording and "fair
use" for the purposes of education and criticism. How much it matters may
be a moot point, with users always innovatively developing new and more
effective workarounds in order to make texts available again. The networked
nature of digital communication allows, of course, the alternatives and workarounds to be knowable broadly through viral communication, making these
not only popular but a threat again to such authorial/authorized/authority
control.

## 7  INTERACTIVE IDENTITY

In the context of the forms of cocreative interactivity I have been describing here as a key element of the contemporary Web 2.0 and Web 3.0
digital communication and media environment, we might ask what digital

communication does for thinking about identity as that which is performatively inculcated within media and communication regimes. I would like to return to some of the questions that are opened up in thinking about digital interactivity as both "open" and "closed" participation in cocreative engagement by asking how narrative changes the ways in which the signifiers, categories, intelligibilities, and notions of identity are communicated and accessed. Arguably, subjects are more active in engaging with narrative as cocreators of both meaning and text.

If identity is a citation of the identity that precedes and exceeds our selves in discourse (Butler, 1993, pp. 225–226), and if, as I discussed in the previous chapter, that discourse is made available today only through forms of mediation, then in an increasingly online world in which user participants are also active cocreators, what does it mean that the citation is of a category, signifier, name, or intelligibility that is not only conditioned by communication technologies, but is one to which we contribute actively? In a traditional media setting, for example, a subject may "encounter" a sense of national identity that comes to be meaningful for that subject in a television narrative, for example, in an ongoing series such as *24,* in which a representation of national identity is depicted to have particular (perhaps stereotypical) attributes, ways of thinking, ways of speaking, and forms of attitude. Should that subject recognize (in a recognition or rethinking of the self) themselves and thereby be reconstituted under that identity category or banner or name, then they will be culturally impelled to cite not only that identity but the concomitant attributes that help to give the performance intelligibility and recognizability within the social field. That is one way in which we can understand identity being produced, altered, and performed in the context of traditional media forms, although obviously factors of surveillance through user generation of content (Andrejevic, 2011, p. 83), social participation, relationality, and the range of other "coordinates" of identity that form the multifaceted self are at play.

However, we now have to account not only for audience interpretation or activation of meanings in the spectatorship of a television series but the interactive environment in which participation in the creation of the text itself becomes normative. Here, identity is produced at the same time as one helps to "write" that identity. This might occur in, for example, remix textuality. There has been a proliferation of remixed (audiovisual) texts such as fan music videos, slash video, mashups, and digital stories utilizing and combining both existing and new visual and audio material on sites such as YouTube, opening important new ways of thinking of media engagement as predicated on interactive and cocreative formations. Remixed texts can be understood as a new and transformative form of user engagement with media that, despite industry copyright concerns, does not compete with existing texts but makes use of them as "found material" in order to produce an ostensibly intertextual experience (Lessig, 2008, pp. 11–12). For Lawrence Lessig, remix is a form of creativity that puts in question the separation between reader and writer and, instead, emphasizes the participatory form in which read–write creativity (or cocreativity) becomes the normative standard of high-level engagement with extant texts through both selection and arrangement (p. 56). Remix culture, Lessig suggests, makes use of digital technologies that have been developed for other purposes and practices and delivers forms of collage, complexity, and cocreativity directed toward a broader audience.

The role played by YouTube as a sharing site that makes available the massive number of remixed texts is testament to the form's significance as an interactive, intertextual creation or cocreation. As Burgess and Green (2009, pp. 4, 5) have argued, consumer cocreation is fundamental to YouTube's mission and role in the distribution of texts, and the site can be considered more than just a sideline distribution site for either existing texts or private video logs, but as a mainstream component in a broader media matrix in which the experience of textual audiencehood is recoded as participatory engagement with prior texts in order both to reflect on those texts and to produce new ones in a cocreative capacity. This is not to suggest that YouTube is not complicit in copyright regimes that actively seek to restrict participatory and cocreative artistic practice in favor of older models of textual ownership and control over distribution (Cover, 2006). Its digital capacity to police remixed texts that have been marked by corporate copyright holders as unavailable for further use or manipulation has been a substantial development on the side of traditional copyright in the push-and-pull struggle between free cocreativity and limiting regimes (Cover, 2004c), although this does not altogether stem the production of the remix as a substantial experience of artistic practice and of user participatory engagement with media matrices.

A user might, say, take a number of scenes from the television series *24*, resequence them into a new order, juxtaposed and aligned, and place them against a 3 min audio track of Madonna singing "Justify my Love." Let us say that in this example the clips from *24* were neither ostensibly nor unconsciously meaningful to the reader. However, in the act of remixing them and hearing them "speak" back against Madonna's unrelated lyrics, new meanings emerge. This is not simply the productive activation of meaning in the act of reading and interpreting a text, but the active production of new textualities that come to have meanings for identity, creating new, unexpected, and unanticipated categories, significations, and attributes for a set of identities which the reader recognizes (and thereby is actively reconstituted as a new kind of self). While reconstitutive transformations are theorized within Butler's work on performativity from the perspective of the encounter with new discourses that may have been previously unavailable to the subject (Butler, 1991), in this context those new discourses are produced by the subject, allowing wholly new configurations of identity possibilities available for citation and reconfiguration of selfhood (which is not to say that they were built from a perspective outside discourse, for that is always impossible, but that they may emerge from the margins of the barely thinkable, new emergences that are unexpected). This is thinking about the relationship between interactivity and identity performativity for the individual. However, if we put this into the much broader schema of thinking about the proliferation of remix interactivity as a form of media engagement (and the vast availability of the outcome of such interactivities) for a broader audience/user basis, then these new emergences have the capacity to refigure and reconstitute the frames of recognizable performativity on a wide scale, changing both the discourses available for citation as well as the very form in which citation is undertaken as a central part of performativity and maintenance of the coherence of the self.

In the previous chapter, I took the concept of identity performativity to task in order to put it into the perspective of a broad contemporary media and communication framework which involves limitations and possibilities for making textual information on which identities have inaugural intelligibilities as well as a number of processes for thinking about interpretation as part of audiencehood and spectatorship. In this chapter, I have sought to further this critique by accounting for the remaining component in a traditional media process model – authorship – that, today, is reconfigured by interactive engagement. If interactivity is not only the current "taste" in media and communication engagement but, as I have discussed, a long sought after element of human social engagement with textuality and narrative that, in digital media, finds its fruition, then the argument emerges that identity produced through active participation and cocreation of its meanings is, in some ways, an opening of the field of subjectivity itself. This is not a wholesale destruction of normativity, which, of course, through a number of shared factors and social processes remains at the core of the demand for identity. I address these normative practices from a number of different perspectives in later chapters, returning to corporeality in the context of digital media in Chapter 4; the meanings for identity produced within concepts of space, place, and time in the context of globalization in Chapter 5; mobility in Chapter 6; the implications for identity that emerge from the potentially addictive taste for digital interactivity in Chapter 7; and the visualizations of the globe in terms of surveillance, space, archives, and digital normativities in Chapter 8.

# CHAPTER 4

# Bodies, Identity, and Digital Corporeality

The notion that the digital experience is somehow disembodied, a concept from Web 1.0, and continues to dominate many of the available ways in which we understand digital media use. Relying on a very problematic distinction of "mind" from "body" in the framework of mind/body dualism by René Descartes (1968), this early perception of the Internet was one grounded in the idea that once a subject was online the body was left behind, with early cyberculture figures sometimes referring to the body as merely "the meat" while an imagined astral projection of the subject's mind traveled, surfed, or associated through a conception of cyberspace. In this early frame, when the user or subject dialed up to the Internet, they were "jacking in," connected in a way that perceived the mind as being suddenly activated while the body was made redundant, further exacerbating the perception of a mind/body dualist subjectivity. In the contemporary experience of the digital communication environment, however, the body is not only shown to be very much not the redundant meat and not a separate, unnecessary part of the subject connected to the Internet. Rather, it is powerfully present and highly active, whether in online gaming, digital communication, narrowcast in Skype, photographed and uploaded, wearing digital technologies of connectivity, touching, holding, and embracing mobile telephone devices and smartphones that have shifted from the pocket to being always "at hand" to, most recently, always "in hand," or engaging in the production, consumption, interaction, or performance of online pornography and sexual activity. Indeed, views of digital communication that assume a disembodied subjectivity at play tend to ignore the very recent contemporary reality of the Internet: that it is now ubiquitous and unavoidable, and that includes in our embodied experiences everyday for much of the day. In that sense, we do not jack-in and jack-out as if making an occasional visit.

Bodies provide an important frame for study in the conceptualization of digital technologies and identities. While the sexualization of communication is often central to public articulations of digitality in terms of sexual risk and sexual pleasure (Lumby, Green, & Hartley, 2009), there has been an ongoing fascination for the relationship between bodies and technologies

*Digital Identities.*
http://dx.doi.org/10.1016/B978-0-12-420083-8.00004-3

103

in philosophy since – at least – the work of Heidegger. According to Simon Cooper (2002), some of the early Web 1.0 focus on the "question" of the role of the body in terms of technology drew unwittingly from Heidegger's framing of the ways in which bodies were, in the context of technologies, reduced to mere objects, potentially losing the conceptualization of the subject as a mortal one by virtue of disavowing the limitations of nature (pp. 36–38). Technologies lack a reciprocity that is found in other bodies, yet ironically for Heidegger, by increasing the polarity between subject and object; the object itself appears to disappear (p. 37), allowing for it to collapse into the subject in a way which foreshadows the 1990s obsession with the figure of the cyborg as a merging of flesh and technology and, as problematically, the cyberphilosophical claims of the possibility of losing the body altogether in favor of technology enhanced minds that exist alone in a spatialized concept of the interactive network.

Theorization of the body–technology relationship is also influenced by the work of Foucault who, in providing an account of the ways in which disciplinarity as a technology of power operates to produce subjectivities, makes very clear that power centers on the figure of the body. This helps to overcome the philosophic notion of the mind/body dualism that dominated critical thinking and continues to dominate many public, journalistic, and pedestrian perspectives on subjectivity. For Foucault (2004), while sovereignty had its own relationship with the body – bodies as under the control, command, ownership, or responsibility of the figure of the king – discipline, sovereignty's replacement, encouraged the development of institutionalized forms of power that produced not just ideas about the body but bodies themselves in new ways:

> ... an important phenomenon occurred in the seventeenth and eighteenth centuries: the appearance—one should say the invention—of a new mechanism of power which had very specific procedures, completely new instruments, and very different equipment. It was, I believe, absolutely incompatible with relations of sovereignty. This new mechanism of power applies primarily to bodies and what they do rather than to the land and what it produces. It was a mechanism of power that made it possible to extract time and labor, rather than commodities and wealth, from bodies (pp. 35–36).

Bodies come to be understood as the site at which (disciplinary and biopolitical) power is enacted. When the body comes to be understood as able to be produced – and produced differentially – through discipline, we can see the ways in which bodies are malleable and adaptable, through technological production of identities, is at stake (Miller, 2011, p. 209). Within this thinking, technologies of communication, entertainment, workplace labor, and everyday social and economic participation (such as social networking, electronic banking, and eBay) can be understood as being developed and made available for the instrumental production of bodies that are docile, which does not of course mean sleepily immoveable, but as conforming to particular sets of norms, frames of being, and devotion to activities related to labor and consumption for the benefit of neoliberal, socioeconomic goals. Disciplinary technologies here include surveillance (which incorporates activities of self-surveillance, such as the filling out of forms and surveys online, or making use of wearable technologies such as iPhone adapted pedometers to measure fitness and capability) and the communication of discursive textualities that provide information, technical comparisons, and frameworks for producing bodies within particular normativities. This is not to suggest, however, that all technologies are used in disciplinary endeavors; rather, technologies are sometimes, unwittingly and otherwise, taken up in ways which resist discipline and the disciplining of bodies. For example, technologies that enable obesity or failures of fitness, and forms of digital communication that, on the one hand, produce certain efficiencies while, on the other hand, reduce the longer term efficiency of the body, such as using email in the workplace rather than walking up the corridor to pass on a message.

I would like to take up the question of the body from a number of different angles in this chapter in order to think beyond the Web 1.0 cyborgian and mind/body dualist accounts of the body as sedentary and nonparticipatory to query how the body–technology relationship travels across the shifts in modes of digital interactivity. In Web 2.0 the body was more readily represented through visual images, moving footage, face to face digital and networked communication, and advances in gaming that provide capacities for highly embodied gaming activities both alone and in groups. In Web 3.0's networking of things, objects, and technologies, wearable technologies have emerged in ways which bring the body and digital communication closer together and have the potential to rearrange further the constitutive conditions of identity in the context of new ways of articulating, recording, measuring, and engaging with our corporeal selves and corporeal others. I would like to begin with some initial analyses of how we define the body in technological and digital frameworks, and demonstrate the fruitlessness of arguments about digital media that figures identities as postcorporeal. In the second section, I will move to some of the questions opened by bodies of difference and distinctiveness in the context of representation, including how online representations of image, gender, and race can, in online contexts, reinforce stereotypes which themselves participate in the constitution of subjectivity by fixing knowledge around what it is that we recognize as a coherent category, label, or selfhood. In addition, in that section of the book, I would also like to make some points about how representations of identities as avatars work on-screen, and consider some of the perspectives of representation in terms of interactive, digital gaming. In the third section, I present an argument that helps us to reconsider some of the ways in which the relationship between bodies and technology can be understood today, particularly in the context of wearable technologies and what I refer to as the "seam" between self and screen (or between self and digital information that also incorporates sound and knowledge) as something we approach but, despite concepts of immersion, never cross. Before ending with an account of the ways in which bodies are, in Butler's framework, given intelligibility and, indeed, materiality through discourse and, here, through techniques of technological use, I would like to explore some of the ways in which the body is understood in contemporary society as a "project" to be managed (for fitness, health, longevity, beauty, and self-gratification). In this case, we might think about contemporary digital communication and interactive networking as a particular kind of assemblage between body and machine, without necessarily becoming cyborg. Rather than being understood as the posthuman merger, this assemblage is, instead, over determinedly human by serving as the most efficient development for managing the project of human corporeal selfhood.

## 1  DEFINING THE BODY

The way the body is understood in critical theory, cultural studies, social psychology, and the social sciences changed during the 1990s, differing from the common public and pedestrian views on the body as a machine controlled by the mind and soul of the subject. What has been referred to as the "corporeal turn" has informed so much scholarship since the mid-1990s by investigating how Western philosophy and culture had been premised on a profound separation or disregard of the role of the body in lived experience and thought (Grosz, 1994, p. 5). Subsequent to this scholarship, it has been important to understand that the body is not simply a biological machine or a neutral or natural object separate from culture, language, and social discourse. Rather, it is absolutely and dynamically tied up with culture and cultural practices. That is, the body is actively produced through cultural forces, formations, and discourses that serve to define bodies, present them as subjective, organize them in separation from each other, and build understandings of bodies as bounded at the skin, as being made abject when penetrated by foreign instruments (Kristeva, 1982), and as being felt to be served by the objects and tools in the environment around our bodies.

The more common, contemporary conception of the body as whole, unified, natural, and fixed is, however, limited by being a linear conception. According to Alphonso Lingis (1994), we perceive of our bodies as "constant" and "stable" (p. 155). If subjectivity is dependent on reiterative performativity, then a linear performance of the "constant" and "static" body is constant and disguises the fact of reiterative performance. In other words, it is not that reiterative performativity is a series of independent "acts" as such, but that in the perceived linear and stable conception of the body, it is an ongoing reiteration in continuity and linear temporality. This is not to suggest that there is no possibility of undermining subjectivity. In pointing out the necessity of repetitive citation, Butler (1997) makes clear the ultimate impossibility of consolidation of the dissociated unity of the subject (p. 93). The linear constancy of the body is mythical, an illusion that is itself dependent on repetitive performativity for its very materialization as constant. Nevertheless, in its linear presentation in contemporary western society, it certainly makes it more difficult to undermine the notion of fixed and essential bodily subjects.

Many contemporary, everyday perspectives problematically rely on the idea of the body as an *a priori* given: real, material, and self-contained. From a cultural theory and poststructuralist perspective, however, a body is not to be understood as "real" and "material" but as produced through cultural and historical formations. Following Grosz (1994), we can take the body to be constituted and produced within frameworks of social, cultural, and psychic representation, discourse, and language (pp. x–xi) that, for us, includes mediated and digitally communicated discourses of embodiment and corporeal normativity. According to Grosz, "bodies must take the social order as their productive nucleus. Part of their own "nature" is an organic or ontological "incompleteness" or lack of finality, an amenability to social completion, social ordering, and organization" (p. xi). Grosz (1995) presents the body as a complex formulation of matter, psyche, and the social:

> By 'body' I understand a concrete, material, animate organization of flesh, organs, nerves, and skeletal structure, which are given a unity, cohesiveness, and form through the psychical and social inscription of the body's surface. This body is, so to speak, organically, biologically 'incomplete'; it is indeterminate, amorphous, a series

*of uncoordinated potentialities that requires social triggering, ordering, and long-term 'administration'. The body becomes a human body, a body that coincides with the 'shape' and space of a psyche, a body that defines the limits of experience and subjectivity only through the intervention of the (m)other and, ultimately, the Other (the language- and rule-governed social order) (p. 104).*

While this includes a perspective drawn from psychoanalytic theory by invoking the psychical map of the body, this might as easily be assimilated to discourse by Foucault (1977a) of the inscription of discipline onto bodies that become docile (p. 138). However, like Butler (1993, pp. 4, 15), I would argue that bodies themselves are "materialized" in and through that inscription and cannot be seen as whole, unified, naturalistic, or having a knowable matter prior to that inscription or subjection.

Butler (1993) presents a framework for understanding the production of the body in her *Bodies that Matter*. There, she points out that the materiality of the body and the performativity of subjecthood are linked, primarily through the normative arrangements of "regulatory ideals," a concept she draws from Foucault. Identity performativity is not a singular or voluntary act but the repetition of a citational practice through which identity is understood as an effect of that which discourse names. If this is the case, then any sense that the body is fixed needs to account for the fact that materiality is rethought as the effect of power, producing the sense of bodily materiality, the contours of the body, and the movements of the body (p. 2). In that sense, the materiality of the body cannot be thought of as separate from the processes by which the body is materialized, whereby the latter emerge from regimentary and productive discourses, both enabling and sometimes foreclosing on other identifications of identity and subjectivity. For Butler, the idea of materialization goes beyond a notion of construction that implies an acting upon a pre-existing, passive nature too often (p. 3), that is, the notion that the body is given an identity through social forces and wears that identity. Rather, materialization allows us to rethink the very notion of the nature of the body as that which is not distinct from culture but is given intelligibilities, unification, and coherence through discourse and language. Construction is often mistaken as an act that occurs once, such as in the naming that permits a kind of "realization" that one is that identity by which they have been named, and that the body then comes to, literally, "embody" that identity. Instead, Butler proposes a return to the notion of matter, which sees it not as a natural site or a surface, "but as *a process of materialization that stabilizes over time to produce the effect of boundary, fixity, and surface we call matter*" (p. 9, original emphasis). For us, this leads to questions as to the ritual and normative practices and the regulatory norms and ideals through which particular kinds of bodies are materialized, which kinds of bodies are excluded from the full definition of the human by virtue of those norms, and in what ways the body is given intelligibility in the context of objects, tools, communicative forms, and extensions through space and time.

## 1.1 Identities without Bodies? Cyborgs?

In the context of conceptualizations of cyberspace, Kath Woodward (2002) asks if identities continue to need bodies and this is an important question in terms of the shifts from earlier frameworks of online communication that were textual and did not represent visualities of corporeal life toward the contemporary overemphasis of the body projected on-screen through both still and moving visual imagery. Woodward points to the utopian discourses that emerge in accounts of online communication and cybersex as indicating "the potential it offers for people to escape the body, especially the constraints of a body which is marked by race, age, gender and corporeal needs, such as eating and sleeping" (p. 113). Cybersex in its early accounts was often viewed as an element of activity in which unusual desires could be practiced without the need to involve or risk the body itself (Green, 2002, p. 182), although today we might wonder whether, in an era of ubiquitous computing, there is any possibility of understanding sex and sexuality as distinct from digital communication altogether. Certainly, the body is made more present in sexual encounters that occur through digital communication than in the past. The notion of the body-less self aligns with an ideal of the "projection" of the self, in that Woodward points out that subjects have always presented themselves without being physically presents by letters, telegraph, and telephone (pp. 113–114). We could add to that conceptualization of the body-less identity the presentation of the self through online textual communication (the digitally networked version of the letter), online textual real-time chat (somewhat closer to being the digitally networked version of the telegraph), online voice communication (the digitally networked version of the telephone), and, in higher bandwidth frameworks, video conferencing and other real-time visual representations (the passing over from professional production to amateur and consumer uses of video presentation technologies).

Such notions of the body-less identity build on some of the ways in which cybertheorists of the Web 1.0 era took onboard arguments considered by Sherry Turkle, some of which I've addressed in Chapter 1. There, I pointed to the ways in which certain acts of self-stereotyping allowed those using textual chatrooms to "adopt" identities that were not physically their own and that they would never express in "real life," only their "virtual life". Such online adoption of identities that are not coterminous with the representation of the body include gender play, in which a male user can perform the theatrics of womanhood online in ways which disconnect the expression of identity from the body that participates in that articulation. The notion extended not only to those who play with the identity by exploring stereotypes and self-stereotyping in chatrooms, but also to the cyber notion of the subject who might potentially "lose" the body altogether, becoming an imaginative upload living full time in an electronic network. Cyberfictional accounts of subjectivity as postcorporeal proliferated in the 1990s and early 2000s. These accounts offered some hopeful examples of the radical potential of the Internet to overcome problematic distinctions grounded in the body (e.g., in racial and gender demarcations and subordinations), and the potentiality to escape individual and universal limitations of the body (to connect to others, to move through space faster than the fastest technology, and so on). However, they are ultimately grounded in the notion of the superiority of the mind over the body. Moreover, such ideas in their limited absurdity assume it is actually possible to be a subject without a body. As Woodward (2002) has neatly put it, "Cyberspace may be disembodied but it is still 'real' bodies who press the keys and write the scripts" (p. 117). Other, similarly extreme accounts, argue that it is possible to be a subject that is partially computerized as a cyborg (which is not to say that theories of the cyborg which used to point to the role of computerized technology alongside bodies, are fruitless, only that it is indeed the "alongside" rather than the "taking over" that matters).

Rather than the pretence of the bodyless subject floating in the digital ether, or the idea of the subject who can express an identity online differently from that which is coded and constituted in representations of the body, or the notion that we all are on the way to becoming semirobotized creatures losing the primacy of the flesh, it remains that digital media and communication use in Web 2.0 and 3.0 frameworks is very much about the body. This includes, but is not limited to, representations of the self online as a visual presentation, the drawing together of bodies and digital interactivities through new relationalities that focus on the body such as wearable technologies, citations of bodily practices, and norms from online representation in the materialization of the body. Each of these, in turn, I will address in the sections below. However, it is important to point out that while the radical utopianism of early Internet and cybertheorist accounts of body-less selves is absurd in the context of the dominant uses of digital communication today, they are not entirely fruitless. For example, Donna Haraway's (1991) conceptualization of the cyborg, that melds human biological flesh with the technology of the machine, provides a conceptual framework and a theory for thinking beyond a number of dichotomies that subordinate the body and categories associated with the body. By pointing to the collapse of the distinction between bodies and machines (or human beings and machines), Haraway opens the possibility of a new way of critiquing the mind/body dualism of Descartes, in addition to helping draw attention to the fact that such dichotomies typically align with other cultural reductionisms such as masculine/feminine, heterosexual/homosexual, western/nonwestern, Christian/Muslim – and many others – which suggest the former identity category is dominated by the mind while the latter is base and focused on the corporeal. New approaches to understanding the relationship between subjectivity and the body emerge through thinking about technology, although this is of course not to suggest that the figure of the cyborg is monolithically radical, as there is enough evidence that it emerges – in both theory and science fiction – in ways which maintain traditional power relations and is arguably still located within norms of race and class as a continuation of, rather than a disjuncture from, contemporary cultural representations of identity (Woodward, 2002, p. 116). Nevertheless, the potential for critique of the culturally constituted ways in which the body is conceived, framed, interpreted, and articulated in everyday life is a central, ongoing benefit of earlier perspectives on the relationship between bodies and older perceptions of digital communication as "cyberspace."

## 2  REPRESENTING CORPOREALITY ON-SCREEN

In 1999, it was possible for many authors to argue that computer mediated communication provides a site in which participants could perform broadly different and sometimes profoundly new identities online since this was a space marked by a radical absence of gender, demeanor, style of dress as, indeed, "any aspect of social role performance, presentation of self and physical appearance are within the written text" (Wiley, 1999, pp. 134–135). While this applied to the early Web 1.0 formation of the Internet of the late 1990s, subsequent to the increases in computing speed, communication bandwidth, and the development of new network software and applications, it is unthinkable that all social roles and identities are presented in written text, absenting the body. Rather, the body is represented in very substantial ways on the Internet of today, with visual presentation of selves online, the curatorial relationship subjects have with photographs of themselves (e.g., selfies and more) in social networking practices, as images accompanying news stories, as profile photographs within sites such as LinkedIn that, increasingly, come to replace the paper based written and textual *curriculum vitae* statement, and in other online practices. In this context, I would like to make a few points about digital, interactive media as a site for the dissemination of the images of the body, and what these might mean for how we construct ideas of the body. I will concentrate here on the image as text and content and what this might mean for contemporary identity construction before turning, in the next section, to questions regarding the construction of the body in relation to technologies and practices of relating to those technologies as rituals of communication.

It is important to note the fact that diversity online remains problematic. In a social setting in which practices of discrimination such as racism, homophobia, sexism, and the marginalization of persons with disabilities center on recognition and unethical or violent responses that begin with a recognition of otherness in the body and a relegation of that body to the margins of social participation, the ways in which we view online engagement as a site for diversity must be persistently questioned in order to avoid an assumption that it is, and remains, diverse, and to avoid the wrongful idea that all persons participate and are represented equally. Rather, the Internet and other digital sites of interactive engagement tend to be dominated by a more narrow set of representations, and this is patently the result of the fact that socially dominant groups are understood to be more likely to participate in innovation while socially dominated groups are more likely to follow later (McDonald, 1999, p. 162). The critical engagement, antistereotyping, and open participation of the early Internet was not only due to the socioeconomic and educational backgrounds of those who were positioned to enjoy the early Internet (i.e., often persons connected with elite universities and technical colleges), but also because those innovations around establishing diverse participatory environments were frequently in the service of the dominant. One of the results of this is that we have a digital communicative environment in which discourses circulate, that regulate the production and materialization of bodies in ways which simultaneously demand the self-management of conformity (often in groups and categorizations) and, simultaneously, the self-management of a demand for uniqueness. Where bodies and the extent to which they sit within the competing poles of hyperconformity and hyperdistinctiveness are produced through online, digital, and interactive engagement, the corollary is that self-esteem is likewise produced differentially and thereby resilience is unevenly distributed. This matters when considering the ways in which our corporeality is not only understood as part of our identities but is at the core of the ways we act in the world, which includes acting in the communicative spaces of digital media.

## 2.1 Representing Stereotypes: Image, Movement, and Categories of Discrimination

One highly important aspect of digital media is its capacity for making available knowledges of discrimination. This might be simply offhand commentary remarks on a YouTube clip that associate the embodied image of someone of Jewish descent with particular, simplistic, false or negative ideas about money, conspiracy, or hidden wealth. It might be the way in which a right-wing, über-patriotic, or racist organization disseminates thoughtless and ignorant information about people from other countries or those who practice different religious beliefs. It might be the copious homophobic representations found online that simplify the lived, corporeal realities of gay men and lesbians. Stereotypes work through repetition in language, fixing an identity category and a set of attributes, behaviors, or beliefs (Rosello, 1998). This is typically centred on the image and representation of particular categorizations of body, which might include racialized bodies, gendered bodies, the bodies of a minority sexual orientation, or the bodies of persons with a disability. The image or idea of that particular body is fixed, highly reductively, to particular notions which, for example, might be to suggest that particular racialized groupings behave in particularly violent or ignorant ways, or that women are unlikely to catch a ball, or that all gay men are fit and toned, or that persons with disabilities hold bitter, negative attitudes. There are many such examples. In all cases, stereotypes work to bind the figure of the human by producing particular sets of borders that articulate some subjects as more patently human than others, and thereby more worthy – in ethical terms – of having a liveable life.

In an information society where sound bites and opinion dominate and judge, and in which knowledge made available digitally in the forms of information, entertainment, gossip, usergenerated commentary, and interactive contributions in all sorts of forms from text to image to moving visuals is copious and teeming, the stereotype becomes an even more important form of communication, despite the logic that might suggest stereotypes are more easily contested in an environment of free-flowing responsiveness. Stereotypes are more ubiquitous within abundant information systems and cultural practices that involve information overload for the simple reason that they communicate information, no matter how wrongfully, in very quick "bytes." By working with existing cultural knowledges and falsities that reduce an identity category to a particular set of attributes and behaviors, they circulate through images of bodies in which readers and users actively recognize that body as doing particular things or behaving in particular ways. In that sense, when one represents the figure of a lesbian through a particular image of butchness, the image is read through the stereotype as, perhaps, having a gruff voice, a surly attitude, or as being a body that performs the theatrics of man hating or some other highly problematic oversimplification of the endemic human complexity of attitude and behavior. This is not necessarily the fault of the reader – stereotypes simplify communication, something which is necessary in an environment in which communication is rich and one must make quick interpretations of information about the bodies one sees represented on a screen. Notable here is the need to understand that earlier forms of Internet use were niche uses by those who were, usually due to their socioeconomic and educational backgrounds and the fact that they had the resources and desire to engage in text based online activities, more likely to have a critical perspective on stereotypes from a subversive or radical perspective. The contemporary ubiquity of Internet use needs to account for the fact that today not all users will have had similar access to radical discourses informing how they represent themselves and others, and that there is a greater capacity for the Internet to circulate, rather than combat, negative stereotypes of racialized, gendered, and sexualized bodies (Nakamura, 2008, p. 30). This is not, of course, to suggest that such ignorance is anything but socially cultivated, nor to argue that the subversive potential of digital communication is altogether lost – only that it is just as much a site for the circulation of stereotypes as traditional media forms.

Stereotypical codes characteristically include subjective performativity of the body through particular stances, gestures, vocal intonations, glances, gazes, and looks. The body, however, does not stop at the skin. Hair, clothing, grooming, accessories, and self-presentation are as much elements of the body as are organs, skin, nerves, muscles, and flesh. This is not, of course, to suggest that we can understand a stereotype as something that is either an accusation or falsity in relation to particular kinds of bodies, nor a theatrical performance that is adopted by a subject and thus hangs on the body as stereotypical adornments. As Lingis (1994) writes:

*We conceive of our person as a subsistent constant, perceivable in the stable shapes and contours of our bodies, the recurrent verbal and behavioral patterns of our initiatives, and the recurrent diagrams of our emotions, attitudes, and posturings. It would be perceivable too in the consistent ways in which we clothe and adorn our bodies and in the stable social roles and functions in which we insert ourselves (p. 155).*

No less inscriptive than muscular exertion, says Grosz (1994), is the "habitual marking of the body by clothing, ornamentation, prosthetic devices, and makeup" (p. 144). Because there is no subject behind the choosing of such clothing and adornments, it can be said that these elements of bodily performance – in line with the cultural stereotypes – are just as much an aspect of the performativity of a subjectivity as the actions and behaviors of a particular identity understood through the narrow perspectives of stereotyping. There is a link between the visual stereotype, the performativity of the body – the subject in accord with discourses made available and easily accessible in online digital media – and the ways in which these effect and are effected by contemporary notions of subjective fixity. If stereotypes indicate a fixity of knowledge about apparently visible groups of bodies and their subsequent actions or perspectives of what particular identity categories are "like," yet are circulated and deployed discursively as tactics of racism, homophobia, and sexism (Cranny-Francis, 1995, p. 50), then they are implicated in what Butler (1993) understands as the discursive and regimentary materialization of the body and what Alphonso Lingis (1994) understands as the body's "capacities, skills and inclinations" (p. 53).

If we consider the shift in digital interactive representation from one which is grounded in text to that which, today, makes available discursive information through moving audiovisual imagery, then we need to understand the linkage between identity and attribute in stereotypes as one which is fully a representation of a relationship between the visual representation of bodies and what those bodies do. By "doing," I mean the movements, spatial relations, and gestures of the body. Here, I am not referring to the idea of a body that has already been produced in social and discursive formations and then proceeds to act, move, or desire. Instead, the very movements of the body constitute it as an explicit type of body, available for recognition as a particular kind of identity. Through the cultural force of stereotyping, a dynamic is produced such that the image, identity, and body formation will be compelled to move in specific, knowable, and recognizable ways. This relates to the element of "knowledge" that accompanies, informs, and is communicated by the stereotype, whereby it employs visuality and connotation to provide bodies and identities with attributes. For Lingis (1994):

> … bodies are sensory-motor systems that generate the excess force which makes them able to move themselves, systems that move toward objectives they perceive, that thus code their own movements. Our bodies are also substances that can be moved and that can be coded. Subjected to regulated operations of force, our bodies become subjects of capacities, skills and inclinations (p. 53).

Assigning identities to bodies through particular kinds of steroetypes, produces both pain and gratification in subjects (Lingis, 1994, p. ix) through governing particular capacities and capabilities in the context of discursive norms (Young, 1990, pp. 141–159). This is particularly so in the ways in which a stereotype operates to make that link between the imaged body and the movement (capacities, skills, and inclinations) of the body. Such stereotyping may pain or gratify, which although seemingly reductive, does imply that stereotypes may be viewed retrospectively by a subject as either positive or negative. The connection between image and body movement is likewise seen in the work of Grosz (1994), who suggests that "body image includes both the representation of the movements necessary to attain a specific goal and all the various intermediary actions required to move the body from its present position to this goal" (p. 69).

Such a link between image and body movement extends beyond the idea of an applied stereotype. It emerges through a discourse that, for Foucault (1977a), sanctions "an infinitesimal power over the body" by compelling specific "movements, gestures, attitudes and rapidity" (pp. 136–137). In the context of the analogy of physical exercise invoked by discipline, such a discourse operates to produce "docile" bodies (p. 138). "Docile" here is not meant to be taken as passive or inactive, but submissive. Working hard on the factory floor in "obedience" (p. 138) betrays as much docility as the body that fails to throw itself into rebellion against its masters. The body is not a *tabula rasa* on which is written subjectivity and identity; instead it is a complex discursivity at play that drives the production of the body as a subjectivity through which the material flesh is made coherent.

I have been suggesting here that one element of the representation of corporeality in on-screen image and moving visuals, circulates stereotypes that, then, are cited and taken onboard by subjects unwittingly as ways in which to make performativity of an identity category intelligible and recognizable to oneself and to others (Cover, 2004b). However, that is not to suggest that diversity is not present nor to say that diversity is not a founding notion of the ways in which information, entertainment, discourse, language, and interpretation are practiced in the use of digital communication and online media. Indeed, with the right kind of search, the right access to information, a critical engagement with material and textuality encountered online, and knowledges that allow for broad interpretations, there is a great deal of diverse representation of bodies available online, and it is sometimes difficult to suggest that any particular race, sex, ability, class, nationality, religion, or sexual orientation category is unrepresented. It does remain, however, that one needs to be very careful with claims to diversity and not to simply say that stereotypical representations online do not matter simply because we can point to diversity. As Sara Ahmed (2011) has pointed out, diversity claims are often a way of protecting the dominant (that is, identities of whiteness, masculinity, able-bodied, middle-classed, western nationals, Christian, and straight) by shutting down critical arguments, discussions, and accusations of racism, sexism, homophobia, and other forms of discrimination. Pointing to online discrimination is necessary as a way of undoing the false notion that digital communication is somehow free from discrimination on the basis of different bodies.

## 2.2 Real and Virtual: Digital Avatars and Gaming Bodies

The idea of immersion has regularly been used in connection with digital gaming experiences in which it is often argued that the gamer's identity extends into and beyond the screen into a conceptualization of "cyber-space," whereby the user either leaves the body behind while engaging in the imaginative, virtual world or extends the body into an amalgamation of corporeal self (real) and gaming avatar (virtual). This, again, works with the outdated notion of a real/virtual or real/digital divide. In some cases, this notion of immersion is characterized by becoming (other), or by becoming that which the user has created as an articulation on-screen. For example, Miroslaw Filiciak (2003) makes the following point in relation to gaming, bodies, and identity:

> *The process of secondary identification taking place in cinema theaters depends paradoxically on distance while in the case of games we encounter something more than just intimacy. Identification is replaced by introjection – the subject is projected inward into an "other." We do not need a complete imitation to confuse the "other" with the "self." The subject (player) and the "other" (the onscreen avatar) do not stand at the opposite sides of the mirror anymore – they become one. While using an electronic medium in which subject and object, and what is real and imagined, are not clearly separated, the player loses his identity, projecting himself inward becoming the "other," and identifies with the character in the game. During*

*the game, the player's identity ends in disintegration, and the merger of user's and*
*character's consciousness ensues (p. 91).*

This is a useful account of gameplay that describes some of the ways in which the player's identity is not necessarily to be understood as fixed while only ever performing interactive nonreal playful theatrics; rather identity is conditioned by performances that include the performance of on-screen play. However, problematic here is the persistence of the real/virtual distinction, presented through a corporeal real (the subject) and an avatar (object) that, in the act of playing are seen to unify and fuse. An alternative approach might be to view the subject/object and real/virtual distinctions here as meaningless in the first place – that is, that there is no preexisting reality in which there is a corporeal subject separated from his or her online presence that comes to merge through being introjected into one's own online representation, nor is there the possibility of a digital character having its own consciousness that merges with the consciousness of its corporeal creator/user. Such framing of the Internet user or video gamer as having an immersive experience which, by virtue of the metaphor of immersion, imagines a land–versus–sea conceptualization of the experience, that always demands the ultimate separation of the two, is highly unproductive in several ways. Among these is the way in which this concept once again restores a mind/body dualism, emphasizing the superiority of the mind over the body.

Of course, within certain practices online there are real, genuine separations between the corporeal real and the virtual activity, and we see that most commonly in the actions of subjects while playing digital games. While I do not argue that gamers leave behind a conscious sense of the body and, instead, only embody a character on the "other side of the screen," there is a clear separation of intent. Filiciak (2003) makes this point in thinking about how banal and mundane activities that, for most middle-class subjects, would be avoided in everyday life or would put enormous strain on our bodies through difficult repetitive actions are, instead, points of excitement in gaming. As he puts it:

*… the effort put into the development of a game character do[es] not necessarily*
*need to be the opposite of what happens to us in everyday life. Even worse, it often*
*happens in games that we encounter things we would not want to do every day,*
*and yet we do them. … In reality I wouldn't like to do such a monotonous thing as*
*carrying crates. Within online games there are even more examples of repetitive*
*and boring actions. While playing EverQuest, I spent long hours running around*
*the forest and looking for some creature or artefact. It would be boring in a real life,*
*but in the context of the game it was fun (p. 99).*

If we take this query to the extreme levels of games of a generation ago, we would note that the barrel hopping undertaken in Donkey Kong would be something we may be physically capable of doing in a real world, corporeal existence, but something we would never seek. Likewise, using our bodies to fight, harm, or kill others in a first-person shooter, for example, is something we would never do in our corporeal existence as social subjects, but this activity forms a particular staple of gaming narratives and interactivity. In that context, a game character as an avatar of the theatrics of selfhood presented in digital activities can be a representation of the self adopted for specific moments of pleasure in which the body's activities extend into the representation of otherness on-screen, but this relationship is, from the very beginning, underlain by a radical separation and difference between what we desire to do with our bodies and what we might do as entertainment on-screen. Performing online is, of course, one possible experience of identity performativity, which is not to suggest that there is a corporeal body that performs an identity in one way and – through a split personality framework – a separate performativity on-screen. Rather, this is to point to the fact that the adoption of a character on-screen and the actions it takes can be both consciously deliberate and a nonvoluntaristically articulation of a self, in both cases lending a sense of performative stability to the corporeal subject playing the game.

This is not to say that subjects do not form deep attachment to the interactive representations they perform in the act of gaming. Bodies can, indeed, come to feel excessive when the minute movements of a game controller shift a representation that has been actively chosen and, in some respects, feels to be a replacement for the body. This is not to suggest that the corporeality of the subject is, at times of play, a passive body – the brain chemistry, the cognitive processing (Grodal, 2003, p. 130), the adrenalin, the movement, and the engagement is always active and corporeal (perhaps just not as apparently "extensive" as a fast paced avatar shifting across the minute smaller space of the screen at inhuman speeds). I am suggesting here, however, that the two are actively linked in a way that is deeply felt, and felt in a way that is corporeal. Pierre Bourdieu (1990) argued that, in the context of social practices:"The body believes in what it plays at: it weeps if it mimes grief. What is "learned by the body" is not something that one has, like knowledge that can be brandished, but something that one is" (p. 73). In that sense, we can say that in playing a game the body comes to feel what the on-screen world insinuates imaginatively, much as the actor who remembers joy or pain in order to perform a part in a play is able to express this corporeally in a way which would convince a spectator and, importantly, convince the self – that joy or pain is really felt. We might, however, reverse and twist Bourdieu's formulation and state that what is learned by the body in acting out the theatrics of a character represented on-screen comes to feel as something that one is.

It is tempting therefore to argue that there is a performative self who articulates an identity and that the behavior on-screen is merely theatrics, much like the actor on a stage who has an identity as an actor which is not necessarily subsumed by the character she plays. However, in the context of the deeply felt connection between body, self, and on-screen character we do not need to fall into this alternative trap and consider gameplay to be little more than a pleasurable guise – it can have palpable implications for subjecthood by serving as a particular kind of interactive encounter with a representation one may have chosen or built and now serves as a form that feeds back to the body invoking affect. The separation, however, comes in the knowledge that what it is which invokes affect is the context of the game's narrative. It is no longer helpful to understand digital media as comprising a new, separate space or cyberspace behind the screen as many writers on gaming, following William Gibson's (1984) coinage of the term in his cyberpunk book *Neuromancer,* have done so (Lahti, 2003, p. 157). What, instead, is at stake is the process of narrative in the form of the game that is at a distance from the narrative through which we articulate and move our corporeal selves in everyday life. Naturally, both inform each other and they are not mutually exclusive. Rather, they are understood as having a distinctiveness – gamers are not fooled by the game, no one is hypnotized into an alternative path of thinking and the game's narrative itself sucks us in no more than did a book or television series. Indeed, all gamers play games in the full knowledge of a game's bounded separation from the everyday. The parent of ludology, Johan Huizinga (1949), made clear that all "play" must be understood as separate from the everyday, with its own boundaries of time and space: "A closed space is marked out for it, either materially or ideally, hedged off from the everyday surroundings. Inside this space the play proceeds, inside it the rules obtain" (p. 19). That is, the conceptual space of the game – which I relate here as a narrative – is consciously understood as being radically different from the narrative spatiality of everyday life; in an era of digital games, it is not that the body is left alone in a space radically separate from the space of play, but that the player is aware of the narrative's difference and yet open to the affective and, subsequently, emotional formations that produce particular responses, that is articulated corporeally.

Gaming, in that sense, may not necessarily disrupt the identity of the subject, but it informs the performativity of that self by adding experiences and perceptions that are simultaneously felt as "real" in a real bodily sense and as separated from the narrative, cultural, and social space in which that body moves and, indeed, must move as part of its biological and social existence.

## 3 BODY–TECHNOLOGY RELATIONALITIES

### 3.1 Touch-Friendly and Wearable Technologies

One remarkably important element of the relationship between bodies and technologies involves taking into account the ways in which digital communication and media tools are increasingly incorporated into uses that involve close contact with the body. The desktop computer from the 1990s onward was typically established as a device which remains under or above the desk, attached by tendrils to the parts one is permitted to touch (the keyboard, the mouse, and the joystick). The core of the device, of course, remains away from engagement and bodily touch, as is the monitor screen. Through the late 1990s, the proliferation of laptops and notebook computers brought the device and the body into closer contact, although not without controversy. Concerns that a warm laptop sitting – literally – on a man's lap might damage his reproductive potential circulated, although such concerns did not necessarily result in a reduction in their use. Rather, laptops have proliferated as a device that comes into close contact with the body, depicted in marketing images as that which is used on a couch or a bed, and as a device that is carried in satchels close to the body. With the evolution of touchscreens, this has resulted in one that is touched corporeally in many ways, from the keyboard to the screen to the properly named touchpad in place of a mouse. The residue of our corporeal lives sits across any laptop more than a few days old. In pointing to such digital media and communication technologies that are engaged with through close contact with bodies, it is important to think about how these demonstrate an historical movement of coming closer together such that these technologies become devices not only of convenient portability (by being "at hand") but also of immediate availability (by operating when "in hand"). If we envisage the cultural representation of the computer in the *longue durée* of twentieth century history, we have moved significantly from the figure of the mainframe computer that stands imposing in the corner and is touched only by men (typically) in lab coats, or the HAL 9000 computer from Arthur C. Clarke and Stanley Kubrick's *2001: A Space*

*Odyssey* which, while communicative and interactive as well as all-seeing, is only touched physically to perform major "surgery" after its malfunction. While the desktop computer is a device engaged with through the touch of the keyboard and mouse, for most users the device itself is protected from everyday hands by a secure casing. Today, we are surrounded by devices that are touched, held, travel with us, remain in-hand, or worn even when not actively in use. Although most are still encased in protective plastics, as an extreme example we might note the interesting exception of the Raspberry Pi single board uncased computer that is used to promote computer science among younger people in school – perhaps this can be understood as on par with the dissection of a small animal's body in a biology class.

A broad range of gaming devices and technologies likewise put the body into close contact with digital technologies in ways which have an effect on how embodied subjectivity is produced and how the body is materialized and given a sense of unification through contact with objects of technology and communication. Handheld games, for example, have been common entertainment pastimes since the Game & Watch phenomenon of the 1980s and the Nintendo Game Boy of the 1990s. Today, more recent versions include the playing of games on smartphones in ways which provide both entertainment and engagement with text, interactivity, and play through digitality by placing the device as a whole directly in the hand in close, regular, and ongoing contact and touch. In many cases, the "fit" between bodies and digital technologies is a deliberate result of design decisions (Benford, Bowers, Fahlén, Greenhalgh, & Snowdon, 1997, p. 93), and the emergence of such devices should never been seen to be alien and exotic but purposefully built to work with the existing perception of the body's senses, most obviously the eyes, ears, and limbs, typically the arms but also sometimes the feet. For example, while the dance pad was a particular kind of game controller for specific sorts of games based around dance, they have also been trialled as devices for typing (Dance Pad Lets Your Feet do the Typing, 2006), although they have clearly not taken off as a device of ubiquity replacing the more recognizable keyboard that developed in response to norms of dexterity through the building of the typewriter. Again, however, a move toward the placing of the device or its connectivity alongside, on, against, or held by the body indicates a pathway toward bringing the body and the digital device closer together.

Google Glass represents an interesting example of a wearable technology that closely associates digital connectivity with corporeal everyday life, but in a way that has not necessarily taken off as effectively as was imagined.

Google Glass was first announced in early 2012 as a development in progress in the Google X Lab and reported as being capable of recording what is in front of our faces while displaying information to the user on-screen based on preferences, geolocation, and need in real-time. Interestingly, they were reported as being "Terminator style," with reports often accompanied by images of Arnold Schwarzenegger in sunglasses (Olivarez-Giles, 2012) – an image which serves as the contemporary depiction of the cyborg creature who, whether for uses of good or evil, merges flesh and technology for efficiency (Ruston, 2012, p. 31). While Google Glass does not really produce the figure of the cyborg since the design is effectively a smartphone assemblage worn above the nose rather than within the skin, the metaphor importantly draws attention to the ways in which the device is seen to refigure how we do our bodies. Anxieties around the technology were present from the early days of its announcement, particularly focused on questions of privacy – the fact that it would be more difficult to know if one is recording surreptitiously, while in the case of a smartphone used to record video or take images, the gesture of holding it out is necessary and easily recognized. At the same time, discussions around the ability of users to draw information quickly, without participants in a face-to-face conversation knowing, also indicated some apprehension about the feasibility of the device in everyday use. The concerns around the proposed device as that which would bring the technology into such close proximity to the body that it had potential for surreptitious or secretive purposes were often offset by arguments that framed it as simply a tool of the body, with particular benefits for persons with disabilities (Tsukayama, 2013).

Catherine Happer (2013) has described Google Glass as a device that would "mediate between the user and reality," and this aspect of its perceived potential cultural usage is part of the presentation of anxiety around the cyborgization of the body that becomes dependent on technology. Of course, there is nothing necessarily new about a device that mediates between the corporeal everyday and the "reality" of real space around our bodies – smart phones do this the moment we use maps to help determine our location and the best ways to walk to our desired rendezvous, or when we engage in a skype conversation between two bodies on different sides of the planet. What is more startling, perhaps, about Google Glass is the fact that the screen intervenes between the eye and what the eye sees as the space around it. It is the figure of the screen that acts as a window between the eye and its surrounds rather than as a screen that displays information that is at stake here, participating in the representation of the contemporary body as – itself – "biomediated" in ways which do not necessarily understand the mediation technologies as being fully within one's control (Clough, 2008, p. 2). If "looking" is, effectively, an element of performative identity whereby it is one of the ways in which we articulate ourselves in accord with particular codes and conventions – the looks we give, the things we look at, the things we are expected to avoid seeing, how we stare or avoid staring, ways of appreciating or sizing up those around us, flirting with the eyes, communicative engagement with others through a glance – then how that sense of seeing and how we appear to be doing that seeing changes when mediated in this particular, peculiar way. The connection between the eye, sight, and the space and objects around are altered through the immediacy of that mediation in ways which can materialize our corporeal selves differently, those being ways which are too new to understand in advance.

Questions around the body and digital technology involve how they are utilized as an assemblage in connection with normative corporeality (noting that, through normativization, such connections and uses also produce exclusions, particularly for those with disabilities, for whom the relationship between the body and digital technology might be something quite different). An iPod brings music portability in such close proximity with the body that, for some, it becomes part of the material assemblage of the body through contact and presence, it is not a device that merely has a role as a tool that extends the body but comes to be felt as part of the body without necessarily joining with it, merging into it, or penetrating it. Mobile smartphones and the tablet are examples of this, bringing the body into even closer communication and connection with digital technologies. As a device of such ubiquity, it is unlike the virtual reality helmet of the equally rare Google Glass wearable computers and, instead, disappears from spectatorial view by being part of the everyday. The relationship between the mobile phone and bodies is emblematic of the shifting perception of subjectivity in terms of identity. Just like conventional landline telephones, the mobile phone is a device that has a close association with the body, being held, touched for dialing, and placed close to the face. It has been a device that has required sanitizing; as an object closely associated with the body many have a fear of using the phones of others because of the potential spread of bacterial or viral diseases. The mobile phone, of course, begins by being a portable version of the landline, with larger early phones brought into close contact not only by being carried around, but being clipped to the waist in close proximity to the body even when not in use for a voice call. The advent of the smartphone adds to this close relationship, being one that is fingered regularly even when not involved in talking to others remotely. However, cultural changes bring it into such close proximity to the human body in such regularity that it becomes part of the body. In the first episode of the third season of the HBO television series *Veep*, one of the Vice President's senior aides is distraught at the idea of having to relinquish her mobile phone into a storage bowl for a wedding ceremony. "I can still feel it, like a phantom limb" she points out. The phantom limb is figurative of the body as a psychic ideal, whereby the part that is missing is felt as if it is there, always startling when one discovers it is not (Grosz, 1994, pp. 70–73). In the same way, the mobile phone's movement in relation to the body from being a device that is always "at hand" to one that is always "in hand," and which creates anxieties when it is not being held, indicates the ways in which it is so closely associated with the body it becomes part of the psychic map of the body. This is particularly significant among children who, according to recent evidence, have felt unable to put down their mobile phones in a classroom, not because they are disobedient, but because it has become a substantial element of their identity. In this sense, as a digital technology, it is effectively part of the materialization of the body whereby it is a necessary component to the perception that one is a whole, unified, independently embodied self. Much as clothes can be understood as a technology that become part of the assemblage of bodies in public space, materializing the body such that nakedness is the sensation of clothing's absence and such an absence is a matter for anxiety (Cover, 2003), the absence of the phone from its position in-hand, with the body, and against the body is a sensation of nakedness, since it produces a sense of incompletion as a material body.

Of course, it is not only the device that is, then, part of the assemblage of corporeal subjectivity. It is also its uses, the practices that emerge around those uses, and, most importantly, the connectivity with others that is felt as absent when not available. Indeed, the missing phone causes a breakdown in the sensually felt attachment to the corporeal body, but so too does the occasion when it ceases working, when it has run out of power, when connectivity proves impossible, creating a sense of fragmentation of the material unification of the body. In the case of it being in-hand but it being ineffective in accessing communication, the body comes to be felt as a body "lost" through a temporary disconnection with sociality in conceptual space. This is similar to the way in which a subject may feel deep anxiety when lost (e.g., in the Australian bush, in the North American woods, in the Siberian snow). The separation from evidence of sociality and civilization is a palpable, common fear and this fear is replicated by the anxieties felt when this corporeal technology of relationality is available in-hand, knowable to oneself, but not able to put one into connection with others, even if that was not the intention at the time. We become, then, not only bodies fragmented and separated from our own materiality, but a body that cannot place itself into a knowable space, a body of insecurity.

## 3.2 The Concept of the Seam

The role of the corporeal body in online engagement has been, at least until the very recent past, subject to a problematic real/digital distinction that assumes a separation of the geophysical space in which the corporeal body moves and a digital space or "cyberspace" in which the subject's extended representation, interactive engagement, imagination, or even wholesale identity and selfhood move, separated from the "real world." At the same time, this establishment of a conceptual separation between the real and the virtual narrative is upheld by articulations that see it as collapsed when in the process of digital communicative or interactive engagement such as gaming or online communication, as I have described above. The separation of "spaces" leads to the notion of immersion, whereby a user, gameplayer, or web surfer is seen to reduce the "importance" of the corporeal body while being cognitively immersed in the imaginative world of the game. As Lahti (2003) has described, thinking about the relationship between text, play, and self through a concept of penetration:

> ... much of the development of video games has been driven by a desire for a corporeal immersion with technology, a will to envelop the player in technology and the environment of the game space. That development has coincided with and been supported by developments in perspective and the optical point-of-view structures of games, which have increasingly emphasized the axis of depth, luring the player into invading the world behind the computer screen (p. 159)

Certainly it is the case that technological development has fostered and been sponsored by an idea of immersion, and this crosses not only gameplay but other digital entertainment technologies. For example, in the marketing of the contemporary "home theater" suite of devices (audio, video, recording, play, connectivity), we have seen over the past 15 years a move toward an immersive environment for viewers, from larger and larger Plasma, LCD, and now LED-based television/monitor screens that, in their increasing size, draw the viewer in as if in a persistent approach toward the screen. In audio terms we have witnessed the increasing popularity of 5.1 surround sound (and sometimes now 7.1 surround sound) which, likewise, has the spectator immersed in the space of entertainment by hearing sounds as if from the center of the visual action, rather than understanding the relationship as one in which a viewer peers through a window and hears the sounds as if at the edge of that frame. In the field of desktop computers, there is an increasing closeness, likewise with larger monitors, but also the popular use in both workplaces and gaming setups of multiple monitors which partially curve around a user, lending the illusion of immersion within the space. The development of the touchscreen on laptops, now increasingly available for large size desktop monitors, again brings the user close to the screen, whether for work, entertainment, spectatorship, or play. Gaming chairs have been designed that literally surround a user, with monitors, controls all around, and foot pedals, sometimes arranged in ways which "lock in" a user much as a pilot is strapped into a military combat plane's cockpit. The virtual reality helmet is, of course, one of the points of fruition of a shift toward immersion, although the interest, popularity, and research and development endeavors on virtual reality devices have come and gone over the years, with a recent uptake in interest and reportage of new investment toward new developments (Grubb, 2014).

A more productive way of understanding the corporeal subject's relationship with digital activities avoids conceptualizing online activity as a separate space and, instead, allows us to focus on the corporeal relationship with the technologies of digital media and communication themselves. Here, I would like to introduce the notion of a "seam" that can be found at the site at which the body "rubs up" against communication technologies but at no stage can be understood as a body that is left behind while a subject's mind, in a Cartesian body/mind dualism, enters a fictional space, as if there is something behind the screen. Rather, it is the screen itself that matters here. The trend toward an increased closeness with the screen – without needing to articulate absurd ideas of crossing it – is discernible in the recent history of technological innovation I have been describing in terms of an ever-increasing closeness to a "seam" between bodies and technologies. This is a seam which cannot be crossed and it is one for which there is a productive, corporeal, and libidinal desire to rub up against, to come close, and to do so in a way which simultaneously imagines our merger with it (as cyborg, wearing it, part of it and technology as part of us). The seam highlights our radical separation as two objective spaces of the real and the virtual in which we either are bodies who manipulate an *other space* or are to be imaginary disembodied subjects who temporarily project ourselves away from the flesh and into an identity composed on the other side.

While the latter is a less common view today, given the ubiquitous normative uses of digital technologies in ways which do not ostensibly explore identity projects – and therefore are more important now in the constitution of performative selves by virtue of digitalities' everydayness – it remains that the perception of two spaces is at play. The space on the other side of the screen, however, can be figured as temporary, typically individualized, and mythical, constructed by our attempt to project ourselves toward and beyond the seam in an immersion that can never really, corporeally happen. Space is always constructed in movement – indeed, for Grosz (1995), space is constituted only in the ability to move within it:

> It is our positioning within space, both as the point of perspectival access to space, and also as an object for others in space, that gives the subject a coherent identity and an ability to manipulate things, including its own body parts, in space. However, space does not become comprehensible to the subject by its being the space of movement; rather, it becomes space through movement, and as such, it acquires specific properties from the subject's constitutive functioning in it (p. 92).

While this applies to physical space – or space that is perceived as physical – it also helps us to make sense of why we have culturally built the mythical idea of a space beyond the screen, a screen that serves as the seam that separates two spaces. Because interactivity is produced through manipulations of text, image, game character, idea, or other, in ways that require that we see these as objects and, thereby, as objects that are moved by our interaction with them, digital information comes to be understood as "locatable" within a conceptualization of space. That we are positioned not in that space but alongside it, at the seam, with tools useful to manipulate objects in that space (much as we might rake up leaves from the pool with our net on a long rod; much as we drive a car and manipulate it through streets looking through a windscreen without ever being exposed to the space, smells, or sounds of the road), we are corporeally constituted with bodies that are materialized through our positioning as coherent by virtue of, as Grosz described it above, our ability to manipulate things. Movement of things constitutes this alternative space and, in turn, we are constituted by the capacity to make those movements. This does not, of course, eradicate the seam, but makes the seam itself the site of the most important contemporary engagement with communication, culture, and selfhood.

The increasing closeness between the space in which corporeal bodies move and the space we perceive as that beyond the screen and the interface for networked communication is, then, historical, adaptable, and quickly changing. Most important here is that it is not necessarily the case that such a seam is a conceptualization that will have usefulness into the far or even near future. The Executive Chairman of Google, Eric Schmidt, has recently suggested that the Internet is disappearing. Speaking at a 2015 World Economic Forum meeting in Davos, Switzerland, he argued that the ubiquity of connected devices in everyday corporeal space – the Internet of Things – will make the idea of "going online" meaningless, as one will always already be online at all times: "There will be so many sensors, so many devices, that you won't even sense it, it will be all around you. ... It will be part of your presence all the time" (Carter, 2015). Indeed, what Schmidt is effectively pointing to is the collapse of any kind of distinction between "real space" and "virtual space" or "cyberspace." Subjects will no longer dial-in, login, jack-in, or otherwise to the Internet and then sit passively engaging in communication. Rather, we will be so immersed or, really, so close to the seam that any distinction will no longer be sensed. Perhaps, to extend the metaphor of immersion in water somewhat further, having our bodies surrounded by digital devices that are ubiquitously connected is a little like being in a very humid environment in which everything feels wet all the time, and putting one's hand into water does not have the potency of the distinction between dry and wet – only of various gradations of wetness. This does not mean, however, that we are suddenly always crossed over into water. Likewise, we do not become digitized ourselves, but our uses of digital media move in and out of various gradations as we find ourselves so utterly immersed that we do not necessarily consciously make sense of any distinction between our corporeal everyday life and our digital communication. Perhaps another metaphor is reading print: we may at times be aware that we are sitting down to read a book, but we are not necessarily paying attention to the fact that we are reading cardboard signs all around as we walk through a shopping mall. In this sense, that which was perceptible as being beyond the seam is now so close and our bodies are now so immersed in digital connectivity that it is only sensible if we consciously and critically ponder it, much the same as air or gravity.

What does this mean for the contemporary body? If we are to understand the body as materialized in the terms given by Butler (1993) as described above, then materialization occurs in the context of the "hidden" everydayness of ubiquitous digital connectivity that is unseen and unthought. Our bodies are given intelligibility and matter as bodies by virtue of the spatial, temporal movements and boundaries that come to lend the illusion of a fixed, stable, and unchanging corporeality, hiding the fact that we only have those bounds by virtue of the knowledges and practices that are at stake in how the body is perceived, used, moved, and engaged with and how it engages with others. If ubiquitous connectivity and technologies that represent a kind of seam between the space of corporeality and the space of networked communication and interactive exchange are part of the everyday experience of how bodies move, engage, and gain intelligibility, then what is changing for us now is how we do our subjectivity not simply as bodies but as bodies in persistent connectivity.

## 3.3  Bodily Practices and Technologies

A number of practices of the body in relation to digital communication technologies and the perception of the seam emerge as devices become more widespread, as children learn following adult behavior, and as new innovations in both the design of the interface and the creative uses that come about through its use, make possible new ways of engaging with technologies, new habits, and new habituses. The proliferation of devices expands the human cultural desire for touch in connection with digital spaces. This might include, for example, normative codes in relation to how desktop computer screens are touched. For standard, pretouch sensitive screens, there are particular ways of engaging with the monitor, which for some can include an aversion to dirtying or marking the screen by maintaining a physical distance from it. When a colleague makes physical contact with the screen when pointing to something on it, a user might become terse, annoyed, or politely say nothing but make a point of cleaning the screen after the colleague has left. Norms emerge as forms of etiquette, but they are also contested as well as being deeply felt and are the site of substantial attachment (hence the anger when someone touches the screen, is careless with a tablet, or leaves one's mobile precariously on the edge of the kitchen counter). For Norbert Elias (1991), the ways in which we perceive our embodiment and corporeality are related to everyday performative practices and habits, such as the wearing of clothes, behaviors related to eating, and forms of politeness and decorum in dealing with others. In that sense, relationships with technology are embodied and form a particular kind of sign system language. For Elias:

> The make-up, the social habitus of individuals, forms as it were, the soil from which grow the personal characteristics through which an individual differs from other members of his society. In this way something grows out of the common language which the individual shares with others and which is certainly a component of his social habitus – a more or less individual style, what might be called an unmistakable individual handwriting that grows out of the social script (p. 182).

Arguing that there is a language of corporeal relationality with digital technologies is not, of course, to suggest that it is singular and hegemonic. Rather, it provides ranges of norms related particularly to the relationships between subjects and devices, not dissimilar from the rules of touch that are utilized in, say, complex gender relations. For example, a man can put an arm around a friend or a sister, but usually not a stranger, unless that stranger is elderly in which case it is typically deemed acceptable under the system of the language of touch. Similarly, a person usually does not touch another subject who is in a more senior position in, say, a workplace hierarchy, although again that will be acceptable if it occurs in a moment of consoling that superior at a time of loss or distress. In some cases a substantial level of uncertainty and anxiety will occur when the language of rules of touch become markedly complex. Breaches of rules become instances for comedy, further entrenching those rules. In the same way, the device that I own can be touched by me, but to touch another person's mobile phone sitting on the table requires permission; a request for permission to use another person's desktop keyboard or mouse – "may I?" is part of the emergent cultural conditions of shared technology in relation to touch.

Cultural systems of etiquette in relation to our own and others' devices do not, of course, emerge and then remain in concrete, but develop and change over time and differ in particular contexts. For example, instances of "frape" (the untactful abbreviation for "Facebook Rape," in which a person changes another person's Facebook settings, profile, pictures, relationship status, and so on in order to cause a momentary humiliation, generally occurring when one has left a laptop open and unlocked momentarily among friends) are, contextually, comic and a scene of amusement among the group. Indeed while the victim of "frape" might indeed be annoyed at the inconvenience or the risk of being genuinely humiliated among a broader social group, cultural etiquette insists that the subject hide that annoyance and laugh off the fact that friends touched his or her device without permission. In other words, expectations, rituals, and norms in relation to touch and device can be complex, changing, context dependent, and built on a sense of play as much as the protection of one's technology, one's information, and one's relationship with digital space and self-representation.

Those rituals and norms, however, are part of the assemblage of engagement between corporeality and technology at the site of the "seam" between conceptual spaces that produces us, today, as subjects and as particular digital identities. Grosz' conceptualization of the relationship between the body and the city provides some important ideas that are useful in helping us understand our subjectivities as assemblages of body and digital technology without having to resort to the outdated notions of the cyborg or the disembodied subject. For Grosz (1995), there are two problematic models of the body and the city. In the first, the city is seen as a reflection or projection of the body in which bodies are understood mythically to predate the city and be its cause for design and construction, whereby the human subject is presented as sovereign, responsible for "all social and historical production" (Grosz, 1995, p. 105). This view tends toward a one-way relationship between bodies and cities in which the latter is its effect. If we were to replace the notion of the city here with the idea of digital technology or the older notion of a "cyberspace" in which digital activities are carried out, then this view would suggest that digital technology is always knowingly produced by subjects with agency over that space and in which digital spaces are only ever the effect of a willed creation and human creativity. This is not, of course, the case since as I have been describing, subjects are at least in part constituted by those activities in those spaces, and in ways we cannot always know in advance. This is not to say that we are digital technologies' effects either, but that the relationship is more than simply one-way, whatever the direction.

The second model of bodies and cities, to which Grosz objects, relates to the association between cities and states, and bodies and states in which the city–state has been historically understood as organized around the idea of the body, whereby a kind of "nature" of the body is seen to direct and provide a codification for other cultural artifacts – the prince as "head" of the city–state and the military as its arms, among other body parts (pp. 105–106). This model is less easily discerned in discourses of digital technology, particularly because the network formation of digital communication tends to be represented as a web rather than having a central nervous systems, a head, a brain, arms, and so on. However, within that perceptual space is the figure of the avatar which, commonly, resembles the body and in which, in conceptualizations of the disembodied subject – the corporeal self – is understood as the brain center that controls the figures on-screen moving in space. While this does not necessarily have to replicate a mind/body dualism (since it is perceptible that it is a corporeal, animate, fleshy brain that controls the extension of the body into that space in, say, gameplay) it produces a separation and a one-way direction with decisions stemming and flowing, again producing the subject as having agency in a liberal–humanist model.

In the case of bodies and cities, Grosz' solution was to view the relationship between the two as neither causal nor representational and, instead as assemblages (though not in a state of permanency):

> But bodies and cities are not causally linked. Every cause must be logically distinct from its effect. The body, however, is not distinct from the city for they are mutually defining. Like the representation model, there may be an isomorphism between the body and the city. But it is not a mirroring of nature in artifice; rather, there is a two-way linkage that could be defined as an interface. What I am suggesting is a model of the relations between bodies and cities that see them, not as megalithic total entities, but as assemblages or collections of parts, capable of crossing the thresholds between substances to form linkages, machines, provisional and often temporary sub- or micro-groupings. This model is practical, based on the productivity of bodies and cities in defining and establishing each other. It is not a holistic view, one that would stress the unity and integration of city and body, their 'ecological balance'. Rather, their interrelations involve a fundamentally disunified series of systems, a series of disparate flows, energies, events, or entities, bringing together or drawing apart their more or less temporary alignments (p. 108).

If we replace the notion of city in this long quotation with the terms related to digital communication, technologies, Internet, "cyberspace," and wearable technologies, we can see that there is a framework here for understanding bodies within concepts of the "seam" as an interface that is mutually determining of digital spaces and activities and of bodies that are materialized and given coherence in the context of the use of digital technologies. Linkages, communicative flows, collective actions, and activities over global spaces that come to resemble machines and temporary sites of group work in a disunified series of systems and flows, become not only normative in the everyday engagement of embodied subjects with others, but produce meanings in ways which mutually define bodies and technologies. Here, the "seam" again becomes the most important element in that it is the site at which we locate the conceptual and practical links, tools, techniques of wearing or manipulating technologies, techniques of working on the body and returning concepts to the body as subject, and many other activities conditioned by cultural practice, rather than agential decision.

## 4  BODY INFORMATION: THE BODY AS A PROJECT

An element of the relationship between the body and digital communication that has not yet been well explored relates to how digital technologies are used increasingly in ways that are seen to aid the subject in "bettering" the body. For Chris Shilling (2003), contemporary culture since the 1980s in the West has facilitated the concept of the body as subject to reflexive and individualized betterment by viewing the body not as static, ageing, or in engagement with its environment as assemblage, but as a "project" upon which work must be undertaken. This includes notions of dieting, the devaluation of fat on bodies, and the production of the body – today – as hard, muscular, sleek, and toned (Woodward, 2002, p. 118). In this context, the body is to be "acted upon" in order not only to produce it as an aesthetic object but also to disavow the possibility of the body as fat, lazy, undisciplined, and thereby an immoral body. This is not, of course, to suggest that such views of the "fit" body are universally held and hegemonic; there are a number of minority articulations that embrace obesity as a choice and there is a known racialization of bodies in terms of what kinds are permitted to be weightier than others, both perceptually and in practice (Walcott, Pratt, & Patel, 2003, p. 232). The substantial population health and community interest in obesity and other fitness concerns is not necessarily separable from some of the formations through which digital technologies are utilized in the context of body improvement. This is the body both subject to technologies for the purposes of betterment as a technique and as an outcome, as well as being produced and materialized as a body that incorporates technologies of fitness as assemblage.

Far removed from the alternative perspectives of the cyborg or the concepts around the approach to the seam, this is about a normative body and the normativization of the body through self-participation in disciplinary regimes. The contemporary body is, for Bryan Turner (2008), one which is instrumentalized within a dynamic that, on the one hand, seeks to enhance performance, labor capabilities, and longevity and, on the other, does so in order to produce increased pleasure through consumption and sex (p. 98). Indeed, pleasure has come to infiltrate several elements of the performativity of corporeal bodies in both space and communication (Urry, 2007, p. 48) that includes entertainment, sport, physicality, and movement. The model of masculine sporting behavior in both on-field and off-field contexts, the distinction of which often results in scandal through nonnormative behavior (Cover, 2015), can be said to be the model for the contemporary subject seeking to produce a particular kind of body through discipline in order to be, precisely, undisciplined in the search for pleasure and consumption. Traditionally, such discipline has included physical exercise activities in groups coded as forms of play, and it is helpful here to think about how sports offer particular metaphors for the competing ways in which the body is instrumentalized as a site for both pleasure and for projected advancement.

As Dunning and Waddington (2003) have argued, team based sports which took their contemporary form in nineteenth century Britain are built on two attitudinal poles, one being the extensive representation of sports participation through a puritanical and stoic perspective that emphasizes health and the naturalness of the body, the other being a Dionysian or Epicurean formation that, although both diametrically opposed to the puritanical and generally hidden within the social activities of masculine subjects, emphasizes pleasure, partying, and excess. The puritanical/stoical framework arose as part of cultural changes occurring during the sixteenth century Reformation in Europe – increasingly dominating the perception and definition of disciplining the body, typically through sport and gymnastics – and continued through to the nineteenth century. It finds its fruition in the discourses of "rational recreation" in public schools in Great Britain and the increasing social emphasis on health, consolidating in the twentieth century with the rise of physical education as a profession (p. 355). This framework produces the image of the "wholesomeness" of the subject who becomes notable for a body that reflects talent, determination, and health (Rojek, 2006, p. 685), and a rejection of passions in favor of rationality and distinction. The other framework, which Dunning and Waddington refer to as Dionysian/Epicurean, is somewhat older and refers to a culture of spontaneity, irrationality, rejection of disciplinarity, and indulgence in sensual or hedonistic pleasures. They identify a pleasure centered strain governing how the sporting behavior of bodies in on-field and off-field environments have operated historically. In the Dionysian framework, pleasure in both exercise and physical activity and the subsequent cultural rituals of sociality are the central motivators for working on the body through exercise and sport. Although the Dionysian element shifts increasingly to the submerged and frequently hidden part of sport culture throughout the twentieth century, it is through this element that boys, as subjects, are understood to be socialized into manliness, for example, not only through physical prowess but the capacity to drink large quantities of alcohol (p. 356).

In this context, it might be said that the use of online, digital communication mirrors precisely the two poles of the body (which is not to suggest, of course, that digital networks are only extensions of perspectives on how the body is used, only that there are a number of parallels that relate to pain and pleasure). Digital media provides sources of information that support the development of the body as well as particular tools and facilities that do so. Advice on weight loss as well as charts for measuring body mass index and applications for tracking calorific intake and expenditure (noting the economized terms of exchange here) are prolific. At the same time, however, digital communication is a site of pleasure, whether engaging in entertainment, interactive sociality, gaming, sexual spectatorship, or the many other activities users find pleasurable that are facilitated by online environments. Grosz (1995) points to a number of cultural changes and adaptations that have occurred in the last half-century to how we think about the body in terms of it being an objective project, separate in some respects from subjectivity but acquiescent to subjective will, requiring us to update our thinking about bodies docility:

While presenting itself as a celebration of the body and its pleasures, this fascination bears witness to a profound, if un-acknowledged and un-discussed, hatred and resentment of the body. The preferred body was one under control, pliable, amenable to the subject's will: the fit and healthy body, the tight body, the street-smart body, the body transcending itself into the infinity of cyberspace. A body more amenable, malleable, and more subordinate to mind or will than ever before. Just pick the body you want and it can be yours (for a price). Such a conception never questioned the body's status as an *object* (of reflection, intervention, training, or re-making, never even considered the possibility that the body could be understood as subject, agent, or activity. This pliable body is what Foucault and Bouchard (1977b) describes as "docile," though with an unforeseen twist: this docility no longer functions primarily by external regulation, supervision and constraint, as Foucault claimed, but is rather the consequence of endlessly more intensified self-regulation, self-management, and self-control. It is no longer a body docile with respect to power, but more a body docile to will, desire, and mind (pp. 1–2).

In light of this important analysis of the shift toward the body as a project of subjective will rather than institutional surveillance, it can be said that subjects more than ever are invited to manage their own discipline, their own self-surveillance, and their own materiality as a project for shape, movement, and adaptation. In this context, then, the tools of digital communication become not merely the site of ready access for information, but the framework through which subjects now have access to competing information (still within relatively narrow discourses of mind/body and subject/material dualisms) and to a range of tools in which to conduct the (sometimes compulsory) project of body management. The capacity not only to find scales and measurements for the normative production of selfhood, but also the compulsion to do so in order to produce the normative self is enhanced through the combination of online information made broadly available as expertise and the wearable technologies and other devices that enable measurement against those norms. This is where digital communication comes to serve as the fruition – or at least the next step – in providing the cultural conditions for the body as a project.

At one level, what occurs here is a shift of the normalization of the body from the realm of institutional discipline into that of biopolitics. Foucault (1994) defines biopolitics as:

> ... the endeavor, begun in the eighteenth century, to rationalize the problems presented to governmental practice by the phenomena characteristic of a group of living human beings constituted as a population: health, sanitation, birthrate, longevity, race. ... We are aware of the expanding place these problems have occupied since the nineteenth century, and of the political and economic issues they have constituted up to the present day (p. 73).

Biopolitics that makes population its object of analysis and governance is, for Foucault, situated within his larger questions on the emergence of biopower that transformed the classical model of power found in sovereignty (Vukov, 2003, p. 337). It is a form or "technology" of power that addresses whole populations through regulatory practices that seek to ensure an economic, cultural, and political *status quo* in order to aid the free enterprise culture of neoliberal society. As Foucault (2004) put it:

> ... like disciplinary mechanisms, these mechanisms are designed to maximize and extract forces, but they work in very different ways. Unlike disciplines, they no longer train individuals by working at the level of the body itself. ... It is therefore not a matter of taking the individual at the level of individuality but, on the contrary, of using overall mechanisms and acting in such a way as to achieve overall states of equilibration or regularity (p. 246).

Both operating alongside, and distinguishing itself from, the power formation of disciplinarity expressed through surveillance, supervision, inspections, and the production of docile bodies (Foucault, 2007, p. 4), biopolitics governs through investigation, assessment, and examination at the level of the demographic and statistical; it intervenes and regulates where necessary for equilibrium, balance, and social modification thereby producing a subject that is both in flux, flexible, and available for commodification. Biopolitics emerged in the latter half of the eighteenth century as a new technology of power distinct from disciplinarity, but not excluding it – rather, it dovetails into it and modifies it for the use of broader scale governance (Foucault, 2004, p. 242). Its main set of operations is, as Foucault notes, through the development of "a set of processes such as the ratio of births to deaths, the rate of reproduction, the fertility of a population, and so on"

(p. 243), and deals with the population as a political problem, a biological problem, and a scientific problem (p. 245). Biopolitical power is thus a framework for the governance of populations that works across a range of activities and focuses itself on the normative production of the body within a range of possibilities.

Digital media communication tools as a complex taken together are the biopolitical tools *par excellence* in that they permit and encourage engagement with ranges and scales of normativity, and provide the tools (at-hand, in-hand, and readily worn) for the persistent measurement of the body's progress. Together, this is body work that is not just a project, but which produces and materializes a body within a digital-era projection of normativity. In saying this, it is important to point out that this is not about practices of bodily inscription and shaping that would see the body as endemically an object at the will of the self, much as we might proceed with that belief in mind every time one lifts a weight or steps onto the treadmill; rather, this is about the active materialization of the body. Here, bodies are materialized not only through the available discourses that make a body intelligible – that is, in Butler's terms, to give it matter and to make it matter – but also through the cultural demands for a particular brand of bodily coherence, which is to seek pleasure for the body, often framed as a "right" of contemporary subjectivity (one which is not distributed evenly to all) and, simultaneously, through an ostensible performativity that is grounded in a diligence, self-vigilance, and self-monitoring as the means by which self-discipline is undertaken (Chaput, 2009, p. 99). We self-discipline in order to make our bodies available to greater pleasure (longevity, work, sex, and other forms of entertainment) but do so through the project work of training our bodies. This framework of biopower is infused within the knowledges of the "proper" way to care for the self by giving our bodies a materiality in the context of assemblages of corporeality and discourses/technologies of advice, expertise, and self-monitoring.

In some ways, too, it might be said that the view of the body as an eternal project that must be "jogged" daily into a standardized shape and a very high level of fitness and health is about the disavowal of the body as vulnerable – making it hard, literally. All bodies are vulnerable, as Butler (2004) has argued, although such vulnerability is differentially distributed, and vulnerability is the condition of being a social being from the very beginning of life in which our bodies are dependent on the care offered by others around us. The sense of vulnerability and the awareness of the precarity of bodies that emerges in the latter half of the twentieth century help to produce the compulsion to work on the body as a project, as a mechanism for the aversion of risk. This, among other factors, drives subjects toward the active participation in the biopolitical production of normative bodies that are docile and compliant by virtue of their fitness through the search for an inviolability as a remedy to the realities of corporeal vulnerability and precarity.

There are thus several ways in which contemporary digital communication technologies serve as tools *par excellence* for the labor of the body as a project: as a site of competing expertise, through facilitating measurement techniques including wearable technologies, and through the ways in which such technologies act as an assemblage that conceptually provides the framework for the materialization of contemporary corporeal subjectivity not as selves that are cyborgs, nor as selves that are radically disjointed from the corporeal flesh, but as bodies that are projected into a future through competing, yet mutual, poles of pleasure and training designed to reduce vulnerability. In the case of the first, digital media provides a source for expert opinion that contrasts with the "official" opinion in predigital traditional disciplinary societies of government health advice and medical community promotion of healthy living. As we know from Ulrich Beck (1992), contemporary society is marked by a breaking down of "expertise" alongside a broad proliferation of diverse knowledges (p. 131). While there is increasing – albeit varied – suspicion of official expertise in institutional settings of medicine, psychiatry, pedagogy, and governance, diverse new knowledges are distributed online that, for individuals, come to be taken onboard as expertise (Cover, 2014a). These knowledges include opinion and the experience of others. Websites, YouTube footage, social networking pages, and individual snippets of information placed online all provide resources for working on the body as a project, and this is particularly the case with advice for young men and boys regarding how to build not just toned and muscular bodies, but bodies of substantial beefiness. In some cases there are certain risks, such as those experienced by Russian–Australian bodybuilder Aziz Shavershian – known online by the moniker Zyzz – who gained a cult following of his YouTube videos detailing his bodybuilding experiences and advice, but died of a heart attack at age 22, having worked on his body unaware of a congenital health risk and also, it is understood, had been using illegal steroids (Baker, 2011). Exposure to such discourses of expertise creates uncertainties around accountability, and this complexification of advice on how to make the body less vulnerable does not always align well with representations of (masculine) inviolability.

The compulsion to seek out protections against precarity and vulnerability of our corporeal selves and identities is not, of course, forced – and by this I do not mean only that there are variants, those who, for example, seek out dangerous and risky pathways whether with health (ignoring morbid obesity or the signs and symptoms of type 2 diabetes) or with leisure activities (e.g., urban climbers who illegally climb tall city buildings without protection or equipment in order to take selfies for dedicated social networking pages or who produce YouTube videos of the climb and the terrifying precipice). Rather, I am referring to the fact that there is a gratification in contemporary cultural searches for safety and protection of the body (as a project, projection) using digital tools. Given that the alternative is that people are only driven by fear or anxiety (although these sensations may offer their own form of gratification), I believe that we can say that there is a libidinal flow and intensity that is subscribed to in the act of working on the body in order to gain a "calculable gratification" (Grosz, 1995, p. 34). This gratification is produced within a market exchange discourse, in which the activity of working on the body as a project toward a projected normativity is deemed to be productive and to have its returns – more sex, longer life, and other rewards that are culturally constituted and in a high circulation across marketing information as well as contemporary liberal discourses of health. Here, the turn to digital technology is thereby sponsored as the necessary response to the question of how to be a human body today.

# CHAPTER 5

# Identity, Internet, and Globalization

## 1 INTRODUCTION

In Chapter 3 of this book, I discussed one of the common buzzwords used in relation to what we loosely refer to as the digital age: interactivity, as one of the forms through which users engage cocreatively with texts as a particular disposition of contemporary media use. In this chapter, I would like to unpack another term that is coterminous with digital media and digitization (but not necessarily the same thing) and has often been discussed in relation to shifts in identity: globalization. Globalization has a number of different meanings, many of which I address below. In short, it has come to stand for the vast movement of information across the globe that has developed alongside increased migration and mobility (Urry, 2007). It also refers to a number of cultural changes that occur in relation to the global spread of corporate neoliberalism as a mode of exchange, commodification, and valuation, subsequent to the fall of Soviet Bloc and the power of its anticapitalist discourse. Paul James (2006) notes that globalization can best be understood as "the extension of social practices across world-space where the notion of "world-space" is itself defined in the historically variable terms in which it has been practiced and understood" (p. 42), thereby pointing to the ways in which globalization is not a specific, revolutionary condition or event, but a layered, uneven process that does not conceptually shirk off or eradicate older models of nationhood, locality, or regionalism. Globalization has often been articulated through Marshall McLuhan's (1962, p. 31) notion of the global village – in which all participants on the planet can engage with each other in the form of a local community as if members of the globe know and research each other as face-to-face locals. While this, of course, is today both nostalgic and mythical, it does remain that new digital technologies have operated to integrate parts of the world into "global networks of instrumentality" as an "array of virtual communities" (Castells, 2000, pp. 21–22), bringing together sites of difference and increasing not only the capacity for networks of peers and kin that crisscross the geographic space of the globe to talk together, but also – importantly – to

*Digital Identities.*
http://dx.doi.org/10.1016/B978-0-12-420083-8.00005-5

permit different practices, ideas, uses, and concepts of space and time, as well as formations or intelligibilities of identity to be critically exposed to each other. This has the potential to create discomfort, but also to create new possibilities for doing identity in other ways.

In following James' articulation of globalization as processual, it is important to differentiate the phases of globalization that occurred in different historical epochs, while understanding that earlier phases frame how later phases have unfolded and, simultaneously, how we understand earlier forms of globalization in the context of later concepts. These phases, as identified by Terry Flew (2013), include an early modern phase from the fourteenth to the eighteenth centuries which saw the emergence of the modern nation state, territorial expansion, empires of territory, and colonialism linked to trade; a modern phase from the early nineteenth century to the end of World War II, which was marked by foreign trade and international investment, substantial international movement of people and migration, and the consolidation of colonial empires; and a contemporary phase since 1945 which is framed by the settlement of a global system of states, decolonization of non-European regions, and an intensification of economic globalization in all its forms, including trade, investment, and production (p. 20). We can add to this the vast increase in communication on a global scale, from the internationalization of simplified international calls on the telephone to international sharing of television with both recorded and, later, live broadcasts, and ultimately the Internet. Contrasting these differing frameworks of globalization with each other opens up the need to think about globalization as one of the competing formations through which information about the world is made available. This affects the ways subjects participate in identity projects in relation to others (such as through the conceptual "nearness" of places that were formerly seen as markedly different – which is not to say that there is a leveling out, a universal peace, or an embrace of concepts of sameness across the globe by any means). Exposure to otherness here is the key to how subjectivity and selfhood are altered in the context of globalization. However, this is not limited to the capacity to access information about prior forms of otherness, since it also includes how we locate ourselves in globalized terms in the contexts of prescribed and abstract relations and ways of perceiving global space and global time.

Identity is not formed through practices of citing discursively given concepts of subjectivity, selfhood, and identification alone. Rather, identity is performative always in relation to others, sometimes by markers of difference (e.g., by thinking of oneself in ethnic terms in contrast with

other ethnicities, occasionally in ways which overemphasize the difference of everyday practices), and sometimes by myths of sameness (e.g.,
by approaching nonheterosexuality as a particular stereotype that crosses
all cultural, ethnic, and national boundaries, ignoring the vast distinctions
between ways of doing nonheterosexual identity in different parts of the
globe). Such similarities and differences occur across the globe (Woodward, 2002, p. 1) and, today, those similarities and differences are articulated
and made knowable through engagements that occur in the globalizing
technologies of digital, networked media and communication. This may be
achieved through the perceived reduction in spatial distance between parts
of the globe and the online production of what we can refer to as global
time, that is a perception of time that is much less marked by the local and the
nearby and instead constituted in the 24-h accessibility of information,
entertainment, communication, and engagement online. Media of the
twentieth century were very much about playing with boundaries in ways
which trouble, critique, or confront them, and this has arguably played a
substantial role in the production of new ways of thinking about identity,
subjectivity, and selfhood as more fluid, changeable, and open to experimentation (Creed, 2003, pp. 11–12). That is not to say, however, that in light
of globalization and the networking of digital media there is, suddenly, a
global identity that flattens out all differences (Eagleton, 2005, p. 85). Indeed, it has been argued that identities come to be constituted today just as
much by the local, the regional, and the global in ways which can produce
internal conflicts and negativity as well as highly positive, complex, and
fruitful selves (Messerschmidt, 2008, p. 106).

There are two elements of the interactive environment that we can say
have implications for how we understand identity formation in the context of performativity and digital media. The first relates to the different
frameworks of distance, closeness, and relationality that make new kinds of
identity configuration accessible in networked diaspora. The second relates
to the ways in which digital and interactive network distribution changes
figurations of space and time and thereby the ways in which we can locate ourselves within histories, spatialities, places, and senses of the global.
In the case of the latter, space is transformed by the capabilities of speed,
where to build, articulate, and perform an identity in New Zealand as one
marked by distance from, say, the former source of colonial governance in
London is altered by the shifts in perception of space such that this distance
no longer has the same kinds of meanings. While other forms of mobility and movement make possible this shift (e.g., technologies of transport,

the techniques and strategies of international tourism, international policy frameworks that permit international work visas, or even the governance of climate change responsiveness that posits a globe over localized environments in concepts of place and responsibility), it is the development of an array of communication technologies from the telegraph, to the telephone, to internationally networked news and media services to, most recently, the Internet that allows us to perceive ourselves within new ways of "doing" belonging.

In close relation to the critical engagement with the concepts of space and distance that emerge with digital technologies are shifts in the perception of time. For example, perceptions of space are altered by the speedy time in which we can send and receive an email – a substantial contrast from the only recently residual communication form of the paper letter that both required physical movement to take the written word from one part of the globe to another, but also facilitated a culture of reflective engagement with the text in the writing of a response. The somewhat different cultural practices of email foster different ways of performing identity. This is pertinent given that a written response articulates an identity and this is itself framed by the practices of email as a time-instant mode of receipt and responsiveness. While this mode of interactive communication in global time is important, in this chapter I am more interested in thinking about the emergence of a global time in terms of the ways in which we access textual, audio, and visual information and, particularly, how this has facilitated shifts in the perception of "clock" time that, itself, is both localized and yet conceived as standardized in relation to other time zones. In recent years, a sense of global time has come about in part through the 24-hour news cycle, in which the breaking of major news stories has more than just global political impact but literally "keeps people awake" across the globe, as if media time occurs outside of any concept of standard day–night sleep patterns. It has also emerged through the deeply ingrained audience desire to control entertainment-viewing patterns of television series outside of the demands, codes, and practices of broadcast scheduling. This is particularly notable in the case of television series – as well as music – which engender strong identifications through the richness of their narratives, thematic material, and (promoted) fan cultures. How global time produces new ways of thinking about identity in the context of accessing televisual material from other parts of the globe is a significant emergence within the age of digital media, and one which causes ongoing consternation given that this movement of media material occurs in substantial conflict with national and international copyright regimes.

I would like to address next some of the ways in which the concepts and arguments around globalization – as both a driver of digital communication and an effect of the culture of digitization – inflect how we can think about identity, particularly in terms of the extent to which global thinking overcomes, reinforces, or operates parallel to national identities and nationalistic identifications. I will then work through some of the issues related to the ways in which global communication "makes available" particular kinds of encounters with otherness that can be both transformative and discomforting. Regardless of their effect, such encounters refigure how identity can be understood in relational terms on a global scale. Global time and space must be engaged with in order to understand the context in which such encounters occur, and I will attend to these before a brief, conclusive discussion of alternative globalizations, identity, and ethics as an example of some of the ways in which there can be an opening up of possibilities and potentialities for doing relational identity differently through digital media and communication.

## 2  THE CONCEPT OF GLOBALIZATION

As with most buzzword concepts that have consistent use in common parlance leading to simplistic presumptions of understanding, globalization is a very complex concept, with numerous conflicting, but nevertheless potentially productive, definitions. Broadly speaking, it is important to start with the point that globalization is constituted in culture and is, itself, constitutive of political, economic, and social changes. In this sense it is what Ien Ang (2011) has, following Raymond Williams, labeled a "structure of feeling" in which the world is conceived as globally complex, noting that this sensibility is pervasive in the twenty-first century and drives both positive and negative developments and changes (p. 779). In this way, globalization is always a multiple but uneven process, and is most certainly neither a flattening out of difference nor a universalization of identity. For many writers, globalization refers to a time-space compression of the world, producing an intensification of information and knowledge that centers on the world as globe, rather than as a globe made up of many differences across many locales (Barker, 1999, p. 34). Naturally, and not at all surprisingly, the process that makes globalization possible is, according to these writers, built on the production and circulation by media of images, concepts, texts, and thoughts from some parts of the world to other parts of the world. In the so-called Information Age of digital connectivity, that globalization then is understood as an awareness of the rapid movements of money, images, people, and information around the globe. John Urry (2007) argues that this produces a sense of complexity, in that order becomes contingent in the context of such rapidity, although it is not necessarily always replaced by chaos either (p. 27), rather, it is more complex than that. For some writers, this rapidity is also a kind of warfare, both physical and symbolic, stemming from the demands for capital that always move beyond national boundaries within what is sometimes seen as a push toward an "aggressive global society" (Carver, 1998, p. 18) in contrast with a more peaceful separateness of spheres that include sites not marked by commodification.

Globalization is, within this perspective, understood, on the one hand, to produce new and sometimes highly productive or positively transformative relationships that are actively focused by communication between the local and the global (Woodward, 2002, p. 55) and, on the other, a systemic interchange of capital, commodified information, and population that produces insecurity to enough specific parts of the globe to be of considerable ethical concern (Poynting, Noble, Tabar, & Collins, 2004, p. 82). Such framing of globalization's communication/capital elements when, balanced in the negative, rightly point to the ways in which the United States of the 1990s and 2000s operated through globalization as a formation-seeking "global empire" (Jensen, 2004, p. 124). Concepts of internationalization and relationality that use an idea of empire include Michael Hardt and Antonio Negri's (2000) perception of new, postmodern forms of sovereign imperiality and global order that produce new logics and ways of thinking in globalizational terms. Paul James (2006) has remarked that while empires have traditionally been understood through models of Roman, British, and the Ottoman Empires, the notion of an empire today is not necessarily about territorial control and influence from the United States over the rest of the world, but a particular form of power that includes a globalized mediatizing of image, thought, idea, and social life (pp. 42–43). Empire, in the case of globalization, is therefore not necessarily political control or direct influence, but the dissemination of discourses of thinking about relations, including identity, that occur through the seemingly harmless distribution of entertainment media. John Hartley (1998), for example, centers a definition of globalization on thinking about a constitutive textual system of contemporary popular media that is operationalized by power and functions at times in contrast with the democratic public sphere (p. 10). This is not, of course, to suggest that globalization is only about the global flows of cultural discourse in a west-to-east framework, as Barker (1999, p. 38) has put it. In a broader context, the movement of popular media across the globe with increasing ease through digital, networked globalizing technologies, and in a broader media matrix with North American popular culture distributed through more traditional film and television, is often understood as working in tandem with the closely related expansion of transnational capital. For example, this can be seen alongside military intervention in the Middle East to articulate globalization as problematic and dangerous, in spite of the positive or hopeful communicative potential of digital networking that produces a culture of the global marked by heterogeneity, diversity, mixture, and plurality (Appadurai, 2004).

In contrast with these more political critiques that, taken together, articulate globalization through concepts of reducing distance and the capacity to escape the discourses that tend to make global capitalism a conceptual absolute alongside a global movement of persons that produces a healthy diversity on a broadly global scale, other ways of defining globalization as a cultural and conceptual refiguring of local, regional, national, and global relationalities include thinking about the ways in which the conditions of globalization are located directly on the body. Lauren Berlant (2007) suggests for example, that the catchphrase term "globesity" links the global practice of Westernization of traditionally non-Western regions of the world with health concerns around fitness and bodies, whereby globalization is written on the body through the uneven distribution of privilege and poverty, of agency and control, and of development and underdevelopment (p. 758). For Mark Poster (2001), the body is, itself, rewritten through the conditions of globalization as both a global capitalism/imperialism and a new way of doing community, drawing together technologies of the human and technologies of the machine. Within a corporeal understanding of globalization as a structure of feeling, then, it is more than just a mode of communication, a transnational capitalist enterprise, and a formation that acts upon people to change concepts of space, time, and speed to produce new mappings of the world in shorter distances (Sharma, 2011, p. 439). Rather, it is indelibly tied up with new cartographies of identity that bring subjectivity and technologies of communication together in ways which neither produce cyborgian identities nor simply see digital communication as a tool for furthering liberal–humanist projects on a global scale, but instead rewrite the perception of identity as framed in relationalities beyond Enlightenment perspectives of individuals.

## 2.1  Beyond Local/Global Distinctions

Much writing on globalization has struggled with the ways in which new communication technologies of the digital network, the movement of information, popular culture, the politicoeconomic projects of neoliberal and transnational capital, and the increased mobility of migration and movement have all come to have an effect on the relationship between the local and the global. At one level, of course, globalization as a conceptual framework for locating selves and producing identities in relation to others across the world helps to counterpoint, critique, and – at various times – undo the role of national identity as a wholly problematic coordinate of subjectivity and selfhood that has, for two centuries, actively served nationalism (Anderson, 1983). Both the idea of the nation and the globe are forms of narrative – while the narrative of nations, nationhood, and nationality as identity have been perceived as totalized, the symbolic force of nations and national progress have increasingly been in retreat in the latter half of the twentieth century and early twenty-first century (David & Munoz-Basols, 2011, p. vxii). The state centrism which discursively governs the thinking of relationality among human beings has only recently become subject to competition on cosmopolitan, polycentric, and diasporic terms, as well as other frameworks that uncouple citizen/subject from a territorially based state (McNevin, 2007, pp. 658–659; Poster, 2001, p. 3). This has altered the efficacy with which national identifications are formed. Nationality is one, among several, normative coordinates of identity in which one performs a particular nationality according to accepted and recognizable norms (e.g., national pride or affective support of sports players during the Olympic Games) or even extreme versions of those norms (antiimmigrant attitudes or racist violence). The extent to which this coordinate is deemed to be a requirement for a normative self is now in question, to some extent in favor of global identities that are forged partly through concepts of globalization and partly through the capacities to make bonds of relationality in international contexts, sustained through digital networking, videoconferencing, social networks, and other interactive engagement.

At the same time, it is important not to labor under an assumption that the global and the national are "two mutually exclusive entities," as these formations occur "at multiple, mutually entwined scales" whether territorial or social in form (Ang, 2011, p. 783). The genealogical force of the nation state in the public imaginary remains strong (Butler & Spivak, 2007, p. 76), both in spite of, and as a result of, increased nomadism, migration, movement, and travel whereby bodies cross borders in swelling mobility

(Ang, 1993, p. 33). What emerges from the reactionary perspective on glo-balization and the enhanced nationalism that peaks and wanes in peculiar moments of public discourse and corporeal interaction is a sensibility in which digital media are framed as a kind of safe globalization that exposes figures identified by nationality to other cultural forms and other nations without the physical encounter of the other in one's imagined home space of the nation (Cover, 2014b). Popular culture, diasporic film, digital com-munication, and online tourism are positioned as globalizational, that is, ap-pealing, educative, and combative of ignorance, but this does not mean that global discourse comes to replace the nation, only that it (1) competes with the nation by adding an additional layer of constitutive discourse on top of it, and (2) puts in question but does not broadly eradicate the appeal of national identity as a coordinate of contemporary selfhood. In other words, there is substantial risk in celebrating the idea that nationalism has been overcome by a cosmopolitan force that weaves across mobility and digital communication. Rather, the situation is, as I discuss further below in the context of global discourse, global space, and global time, far more complex.

While it may be the case that a national/global dichotomy is not only false but involves interstices that permit both to coexist as frameworks through which identity relationality is constituted, produced, and enacted, the local/global distinction is another that is put into question in different ways. Local is not always the same as national and never has been – local at-titudes, concepts, rivalries, identifications, nostalgia, and community forma-tions have traditionally been positioned as capable of being at odds with the national; likewise regional identifications that put into question the mono-liths of national and global affiliation complexifies the local. Discourses of globalization create new relationships between the concepts of the local and the global in ways which network the two (Woodward, 2002, p. 55), although the two concepts remain discursively mutually constituting with the particularity of the local often marked by access to the global, whether that is global consumerism and marketing or accessibility of globalized in-formation through mobile devices (Barker, 1999, pp. 41–42). While broad-cast televisual media altered the balance between local communities and global affiliations or sensibilities (Cooper, 2002, p. 135), and while digital media consolidate that new arrangement by providing a conceptual and technological framework that links up different sites, towns, and cities in a space of flows in nodes and hubs (Castells, 2000, p. 445), the notion of the local remains both meaningful yet subordinated by virtue of the ways in which it puts into question the formerly self-evidence ideas of economic agency and self-determination (Gibson-Graham, 2003, p. 50). Responses to this uncertainty include the emergence of journalistic style labels such as glocalization to account for the ways in which both local and global forces interact with each other to form particular ways of thinking about space and selfhood, although anxieties over the extent to which the global influences the local remain in force in ways which have an effect on how we think about identity (Perera, 2007, p. 5). While popular culture, media, and digital communication bring transnational and global information into the site of the local, it remains that the ways in which such material, experiences, commodities, and concepts are interpreted, understood, or have their meanings productively activated occur only through the lens of the local and the regional, both of which may become reframed through a nostalgic romanticization of home as the mythical source of all identity (Woodward, 2002, pp. 49–50). Thus, when an identity framework emerges and circulates around the globe as a particular way of thinking about selfhood, that information is tailored and nuanced through the experiences a subject has gained in the local environment of place.

## 2.2 Global Identities

While place, space, the local, the regional, and the national inform knowledge that can be identified as the global, it is indeed the case that there are identity formations that can be attributed to the global and can cross the globe in waves of communication, experience, mobility, migration, diasporic knowledge, and marketing. This is not, of course, to suggest that a global identity emerges in such a way that produces a flattening out of "the very differences on which any identity depends" as Eagleton (2005, p. 85) has put it. There are, of course, universalizing forces (Radhakrishnan, 1996, p. xxvii) that circulate through globalization and networked media exchange and digital communication. These are not, however, wholly produced through the imperialism that guarantees ways of thinking about self will be hegemonic in all places and all sites (Barker, 1999, p. 43). Rather, a Westernized identity formation of liberalism circulates in a formation that, as I have discussed in Chapter 2, is broadly a juxtaposed and interwoven conceptualization of Enlightenment liberal humanism of fixed, categorized, and rationally discernible identity and a postmodern fluidity that articulates identity as always available to the fluidity of agency, self-creation, and consumer recommodification.

One element of the globalizing force of Westernized identity frameworks is the resultant formation of diversity as the only conceptual means by which local selves and global difference can be thought. This framework is the default model by which multiculturalism is expressed as a means of conditional integration and social cohesion rather than a performance of un-conditional welcome to others, whether permanent or temporary migrants residing in the country. More than population cohesiveness and integration, multiculturalism and appeals to diversity retain a core, liberal–humanist ele-ment of assimilation which, as Greg Noble (2011) has pointed out, is a logic that "has not been supplanted but operates as a larger frame" for under-standing relationality between peoples in cultural and multicultural terms (p. 836). Indeed, the tolerance-based condition of multiculturalism can be said to be built primarily on assimilation: that is, those who arrive and settle in one part of the globe (within a nationalist identity framework) are tolerated on condition that they assimilate into the imagined core national identity and the local ritual practices of identity. While doing so, they may retain certain cultural practices usually related to the consumption of food, the performance of festivals, and other traditions that are effectively residues of older cultural forms in their countries of origin. This is what Ghassan Hage (2000) noted as a "white multiculturalism" in which safe cultural practices such as food, restaurants, and festivals are tolerated while the core Western (usually Anglo-Celtic) culture remains unaffected. Diversity is thus resignified as a tool of neoliberalism by invoking an assumed contribution to business productivity and as a resource for a knowledge-based economy (e.g., Commonwealth of Australia, 2003, pp. 8–9). A framework for multi-culturalism that conditions, and makes conditional, tolerance of others op-erates by assuming the fixity of the population as an ongoing entity through the myth that without migration its composition remains absolutely the same over time and generations. It thus reifies a Westernized framework of identity that is built on categorization (Foucault & Bouchard, 1977, pp. 232–233), albeit one that accounts for hybridity, fluid movement between categories, and a slightly more nuanced notion of agency. Such categorization and framing in liberal multiculturalism's version of diversity can be understood to be as much an effect of globalization as a form of power and communicative potential as that which facilitates it.

Globalization's capacity to reframe identity also occurs through neolib-eralism, and the critique of neoliberalism is a major aspect of contempo-rary reactions to globalization. Within a neoliberalism that makes market forces the dominant mechanism for conceptualization of relationality, self, and place in the world, it is the citizen as a global consumer which be-comes standard, and not the commodities consumed which are tailored for individual local, national, and regional sites (Bloom, 1990, p. 15). We bear witness to this not only in the consumption of physical goods that are transported around the world but, poignantly, in the consumption of information accessed through digital networking. For example, the use of a search engine can result in the tailoring of globally accessible information for local and national audiences – at times depending on the national IP address, at other times on the geolocational site from which the user accessed the search. While, on the one hand, this may seem like a convenience (a search for a particular type of food will, when in Waikiki, produce a list of local restaurants that reduce a user's time spent refining a search), on the other, this posits marketing as the most substantial outcome of the search, whereby a user's search for global information about an international cuisine will result in the localized marketing of a commodity. The user, then, is called upon to identify oneself through both the global as a site of identity sameness and difference, and the local, as a site through which one can perform a particular attribute of identity through making a purchase. This is an element of what Gayatri Spivak (1999) identified as the "lazy cruelty of moral imperialism" in which the West, in the guise of liberal globalization, does "deals with local entrepreneurs" (p. 415). Global capitalism here triumphantly subsumes differences in identity, not in order to establish a harmonious humanity but for the more insidious purpose of articulating a normativization of consumption (Korten, 1999, p. 62) as the means by which identity is produced in both local and global terms. While liberal–humanist identity frameworks will, regularly, sideline notions of class demarcations in favor of categorizations of ethnic, gender, sexual, and other identities that can be understood in the context of rights discourses and consumerist self-management, global neoliberal consumerism restores class in order to constitute an identity framework of a global high class; for example, CEOs of corporations, leading industrialists and entrepreneurs, venture capitalists, and senior executives all have substantial privileges and identities expressed through nonlocalized mobilities (Hall, Massy, & Rustin, 2013, p. 12). In contrast, a global poor retain a more localized set of identities, even if that locality is not a place of origin but a site of temporary refuge while waiting resettlement. Class, then, returns at the globalized ends of capitalist neoliberalism in ways which, for some, very heavily inflect identity. In this context, globalization can be understood not as a singular thing, nor a particular historical phase of the world, but as a form of power that includes – but most certainly also exceeds – neoliberal commodification of texts, meanings, information, identities, and subjects. While there is much to bemoan about this element of globalization, the conditions of globalization are neither wholly positive nor negative, and popular journalistic attempts to lament globalization fail to see how the access to new discourses opens possibilities for critical engagement and changes in attitude toward others including those subjects of radical alterity; how local/global struggles over time and space create new ways of being in the context of communication; and how ethical relationalities are made available, although never guaranteed, through global positioning and global communication.

## 3  GLOBAL DISCURSIVITY

Globalization has nuanced relationships with the local, including sometimes a nostalgia for a preglobal romanticization of the myth of place. However, the flow of consumer commodities and capital, and the production of new classes of global elite and global poor produce new ways of doing identity that are articulated through global information and global flows of popular culture. It is therefore important for us to think through what it might mean to be exposed to global discourses. These might be said to include information from across the globe that is accessed through online searches, Wikipedia entries on the histories of places that are distant from our places of origin and conceptually different from our pedagogies of authorized national histories, or visual exposure to the differences of everyday life for the markedly vulnerable on continents different from our own. Wendy Brown (2009) has pertinently asked whether globalizational information works to undo a "Western civilizational identity" grounded in notions of liberalism, whereby "Westerners might begin to think differently about themselves and their imagined global opposites" (p. 13). That is, will exposure to difference – or to that which is not filtered through popular culture and Hollywood representations of difference – on a global scale help to reframe relationality in order to produce identity differently and, perhaps, more ethically? In a similar vein, Barbara Creed (2003) has noted that globalization is tied up with the concept of a global self who is "able to easily communicate around the world and experience life from the viewpoint of others" (pp. 11–12). At one level, this might be seen to be a slightly Utopian perspective in contrast with some of the earlier concerns around neoliberal expansionism that rewrite all identity within conceptualizations of Western capital's valuation and commodification of subjectivity. At another level, however, the capacity to undertake critique of the self and the relationalities that produce particular kinds of selves might be thought to be opened through exposure, including forms of exposure that trouble our normative self-perceptions. The Internet, in that sense, has had the capacity to be a primary tool for powerful social change by making possible that exposure in ways which are not necessarily filtered through the normative lenses of authority or through the sanitized frameworks of tourism. Digital media's capabilities of producing communication with a "global reach" (Castells, 2000, pp. 355–357) and facilitating the broad representation of multiple discourses frameworks, cultures, and means of understanding (Liu, 2002, p. 67) can thus be argued to be a tool through which new identities are produced in the encounter with knowledge of those who are radically different in crosscultural communicative terms.

In some ways, this is to represent the capacities of the Internet for exposure to radically different others as a means for overcoming ignorance. Ignorance of global contexts in sites away from one's local area is an important element of identity and attitude, whereby an unwillingness to know is often deemed in liberal–humanist discourses as a lack that is the result of a failure of curiosity about those subjects and selves from different parts of the globe. For Ien Ang (2011), ignorance is the opposite of cultural intelligence, which involves "a mode of analysis which does not reduce the complexity of particular realities to some underlying simplicity, but proceeds by acknowledging that complexity is inherent and open-ended" (p. 780). For example, a failure by an adult subject in the West to have basic knowledge of the industrial and postindustrial everyday setting in China – and to rely only on stereotypes of China and Chineseness derived from older television and trashy films – is coded as ignorance of the global diversity of everyday life broadly. Likewise, a failure to see the broad distinctions between different parts of Asia or to lump all persons from all parts of Asia under one stereotype is effectively ignorance. So too is, for example, making the assumption that all persons living in the Middle East are strict Muslims or, much worse, to assume and articulate the idea that the attitude of all persons in the Middle East is one of violence toward the West. Here, the lack of exposure to otherness is seen as a focus on the local, the realm of the predigital, and to be outside the network of globalized humanity – an older style of normativity that disavows the need to understand others in a crosscultural context. Normative frameworks, as Butler (2009) indicates, can mandate ignorance about a subject (p. 143), meaning that ignorance becomes not a trait of a person, a claim to their being uneducated or undereducated or without knowledge or wisdom, but a cultural product whereby the capacity to see the humanness, precarity, "and vulnerability of the other is suspended."

Ignorance is not a "lack of knowledge," although we often speak of ignorance in this way, assuming that a person who might be labeled ignorant has simply not read up on a topic, or encountered and learned some important piece of information or routine way of living. Ignorance, rather, is something that is "actively produced and maintained" by cultural forces, power arrangements, and disciplinary techniques (Gilson, 2011, p. 309). Likewise cultural intelligence for Ang (2011) is not something that can be "reduced to an individual capability" but is a broad cultural orientation to knowledge and understanding which involves a practical engagement with complexity (pp. 789–790). Ignorance, in this more nuanced context, might not be the failure to have sought out information about China, Chinese persons, or Chinese history, but the failure to have built an identity which compels one to understand the importance of doing so in order to live a more livable life.

## 3.1 Visuality and Discomfort

One way we can understand how globalizational perceptions of digital media engagement bring people together is through the notion of exposure. New media technologies which rely on cable, satellite, and international digital networks actively work with a sense of relational curiosity, not only allowing media texts, sounds, and images to be distributed across the world (Barker, 1999, p. 51) but enabling them to be enthusiastically consumed through interest, inquisitiveness, and pleasure. Although there are of course a number of ethical concerns related to how we might perceive the consumption of otherness as a commodity – whether that be differences through geographic location or through class demarcations, both cases explaining the popularity of television documentaries in both national and international terms – it remains that contemporary identities in their globalizational form are built on a curiosity of the other that helps to define not only the relationship of difference but the qualities of similitude, consolidating both sets of identities. This occurs through a network formation in which people actively embrace knowledge of otherness and thereby also embrace what can sometimes be a "dramatic reorganization of power relationships" (Castells, 2000, pp. 501–502). While tourism, including global travel for pleasure and sightseeing, has been one form through which that inquisitiveness of otherness has been expressed since the end of the Second World War (Urry, 2007, p. 4), such tourism is typically hived off from the everyday, and becomes a carnivalesque experience of difference from subjectivity. Where we see genuine change is in media consumption and engagement in digital communication, whereby exposure to that otherness becomes part of everyday interaction, filtering across pedagogies, normative articulations of identity, face-to-face conversations and casual browsing of one's social-networking profile. To be an "armchair traveler" in a television culture (Barker, 1999, p. 7) was to move from embodied, corporeal tourism to incorporate an element of exposure to otherness into the everyday. To have images, sounds, and texts of global otherness and difference flowing through digital media on an everyday basis, shifts the global into the everyday of local identity, demanding persistent attention to otherness, that is never stopping at just the screen but moving into everyday practices of verbal, physical, and corporeal communication. For example, we may actively choose to participate in cultural production from areas distant from our traditional, normative flows of consumption such as the 2010s' phenomenon of K-pop from South Korea. This exposure changes how we perform identity.

This change occurs not simply by consuming and engaging with foreign media products that inform us and thereby shift us from ignorance to knowingness about the other, rather, significantly, this change is demanded and ethical responsiveness promoted through the kinds of discomfort that visual exposure to otherness can bring. The connection between globalization through digital interaction and engagement and ethics is an important one, and I would like to discuss this in the remainder of this section before moving on to thinking about how global time and space are implicated in the refiguring of selfhood by making discourses available differentially. Following work on ethics by Judith Butler (2004, 2009), Anna Szorenyi (2009) has pointed out some of the ways in which the images of otherness that are built on stereotypes and familiarity do very little to evoke an ethical response, whereas images that prompt an emotive or affective response, including images of war, death, or that otherwise make the viewer uneasy or uncomfortable (including being uncomfortable about one's own comfort) have enormous capacity to invoke an ethical responsiveness of care, welcome, hospitality, or nonviolence (pp. 95–96). This was certainly the case in the postwar era when images of the Jewish holocaust were made public (Zizek, 2002, p. 51); it was the case when the images of United States soldiers abusing prisoners of war at Abu Ghraib were circulated both online and on television news (Butler, 2009, p. 11); and it has more recently been the case in Australia where the circulation of images of the realities refugees experience have been instrumental in changing not only how refugees are perceived by some people, but in changing how one perceives oneself in the context of the figure of the refugee as other (Cover, 2013). Whereas in an older era in which global images did not circulate as freely and it was unusual to be exposed to that otherness perhaps the trope of distance was an element in the framing of refugees as not being one's problem, the discomfort of bearing witness to the lives marked by otherness makes it less easy today to disconnect the subject position of the privileged viewer from an ethical engagement with suffering. The image of suffering "throws into question and literally makes *visible* the taken-for-granted comfort of a perspective in which the center is home and suffering is elsewhere" (Szorenyi, 2009, pp. 104–105). This serves to change how one's identity is performed: no longer is an identity stabilized with no knowledge of otherness; today in the exposure to that discomfort through visuality – the recognition of suffering – the capacity to critique one's own comfort, place, and privilege is invoked in ways which can, effectively, produce an ethical response of care.

## 3.2  Global Exposure, Attitude, and Ethics

In some ways, this is about how attitude to others can be opened through both visual and conceptual exposure to othernesses via digital communication and media, particularly in terms of the capacity of today's networked communication to provide well-defined images without the filtering and sanitization of broadcast television that is required to suit the local and the national (e.g., in contemporary news reports). Attitude is an important element of performative identity in that, even when private and not disclosed, it is a means by which identity is articulated and stabilized, lending the illusion that an attitude, for example, to a racialized other, is part of a core identity. Attitude, as a habitual mode of regard toward an object of thought, is typically discussed within the field of psychology. While the idea of attitude is both problematic and undertheorized from a cultural perspective, it is a term which is invoked regularly in discourse around difference, particularly the ways in which tensions over difference emerge in the context of globalization and globally accessible information. From the perspective of understanding difference and alterity on a globalized scale *via* exposures that occur through digital communication and media, then, the concept of attitude frames debates, policy initiatives, public discussions, surveys, interviews, and the ways in which stories of otherness are related. Attitude can be fixed, adopted, changed, or reoriented, but its role as a mechanism that governs and deploys power relations through particular ways of performing and articulating must be addressed in the context of understanding not only how attitude makes inequitable or unethical relations persist, but how it – sometimes unexpectedly – shifts some of the ways in which ethical relationships with others are produced in the context of ethnic, racial, migrant, or religious difference.

Judith Butler (2004, 2009, 2012) has made a case for an ethics of nonviolence grounded in a new approach to vulnerability and precarity as social condition. This provides some useful ways to approach and understand how an exposure to otherness via digital encounters with alterity can, in some cases, produce an ethical perspective based on the key concept of recognition. Butler argues that an ethics of nonviolence can be formed through an understanding that all humans are vulnerable in our exposure to language and each other's faces. By perceiving the commonality of vulnerability for ourselves and for the other whom we encounter, following Levinas, we are compelled to engage in relationality through responsibility and responsiveness to one another. What she thus articulates is a means by which the human subject is conceived as predicated on a primary vulnerability through dependence upon others, meaning that all our identities are built on relationality. This is marked by the fact that we are vulnerable to the violence of others and yet are always from the very beginning of our lives dependent on others for physical support. Rereading Levinas, Butler proposes an ethical position through the notion that one has a responsibility to others that emerges in an act of encounter and recognition of the other. This ethics is not, for either Levinas or Butler, a simple injunction to behave in a particular way. Rather, it produces a quandary, a requirement persistently to question one's actions and a situation that can reconstitute the subject anew in the encounter with the other. What the encounter with the face of the other describes is a "struggle over the claim of nonviolence without any judgment about how the struggle finally ends" (Butler, 2007, p. 187). The encounter, then, does not resolve the ethical problems raised in that encounter, but opens the possibility for subjects to apprehend and witness the vulnerability of others on a global scale by understanding it in terms of their own vulnerability, thereby initiating a struggle one must undertake with one's own violence (p. 181). It is therefore, as Angela McRobbie (2006) puts it, a discourse capable of "intervening to challenge, interrupt and minimize aggressive retaliation" (p. 82). The possibilities of violent responses, which might include exclusion, hatred, racism, mocking, or other forms of bullying, points to the fact that while vulnerability is a universal condition of human life on a global scale (we are all vulnerable bodies to begin with), the extent of vulnerability and precarity is not evenly distributed. An ethical response begins with understanding that point, and that comes through exposure to global communication, discomforting images, and other experiences that may occur through digital exposure which undo ignorance.

In formulation by Butler (2000), it is at a moment of fundamental vulnerability that recognition becomes possible and self-conscious: a form of recognition that establishes relationships that are reciprocally for the other or given over to the other. It is not a collapse of the self into that of the other, but a communicative process through which one understands oneself to be reflected in the other and *vice versa*; not a literal moment of seeing and being seen but a communicative form by which one is transformed through engagement (p. 272). Such a discourse of intervention comes to the aid of the political (McRobbie, 2004, pp. 505–506) through a concentration on the scene of the encounter between selfhood and the other. Such an encounter should not, however, be understood as a real encounter between subject and the other. An encounter or act of bearing witness to the conditions of vulnerability of the other does not in itself produce an ethical relationship. Rather, this opens up the possibility of a shift away from liberal individualist perceptions of identity politics and attitude change (Murphy, 2011, p. 587), to an intervention built on the notion of an ethical relationship between people who are, or appear to be, wildly different or distinct.

Can this engagement occur in an online capacity, and will that open the possibility of a transformation that is ethical? The Internet as the communication tool *par excellence* of globalization facilitates exposure to broad othernesses that can work to undo negative or violent attitudes and unethical responses to subjects of difference from other parts of the globe. However, more than just exposure is required. For Ang (2011), the undoing of stereotypes, negative attitudes, and ignorance itself requires an orientation toward attitudes of cultural intelligence – beyond simply knowing about others. It requires an attitude that seeks to complexify, which is:

> … to denounce everything that seems reductionist or essentialist; to reject all binary oppositions in favour of the blurring of boundaries; to replace unitary identities with multiplicities; to be suspicious of notions of coherence and homogeneity to pluralize everything which used to be talked about in the singular (e.g. truth, culture, reality and of course complexity itself) (p. 785).

This is not to suggest that an ethical subject seeks out complexity for its own sake but that one engages with the broad diversity of information, discourses, ways of thinking, and ways of being in order to transition toward an attitude of hospitality and openness to the other and thereby toward an ethics that foregrounds nonviolence which, as always, disavows not only physical violence and killing but includes the disavowal of violent language, reductionist speech, stereotyping, and exclusion from participation in social and financial belonging.

However, the question of what prevents an overwhelmingly ethical responsiveness, that is, an adoption of an attitude of welcome and acceptance as opposed to violence or othering, remains. Butler (2009) provides a way of understanding why an ethical position is commonly and popularly disavowed in *Frames of War*. For Butler, interpretative frames are those that socially and politically constitute formations which "allocate recognition differentially" (p. 6), producing some subjects as recognizable and others as more difficult to recognize (pp. 5–6). That is, for the internationalized other to be recognized as human and therefore worthy of participating peacefully in a globalized sociality without violence, that subject must be framed as recognizable. For example, the Afghani Muslim can only be responded to with welcome and nonviolence if the frames of interpretation that permit that person to be recognized as worthy of being regarded human are enabled. Instead, in many media and political frames, Afghani Muslim people are cast as so radically other as to be unacceptable within globalized, community (currently) led, Western ideologies of liberal–humanist subjectivity. For Butler, such frames are the operations of power through which we understand or fail to understand the lives of others as vulnerable, injurable, or losable (p. 1). That is, our capacity to understand and recognize the other as a life is "dependent on norms that facilitate that recognition" (pp. 3–4). Frames set the conditions for reactions to particular scenes, visualities, texts, images, or knowledge (p. 11), and this can include the ways in which attitude is constitutively performed by particular subjects in relation to particular scenes, sites, or personages. That is, frames presuppose certain "decisions or practices that leave substantial losses outside the frame" (p. 75). Such decisions, practices, or, in the case of the argument here, attitudes, are the performative articulation of subjects which are made intelligible, reasonable, coherent, and recognizable in accord with discourses which govern those frames. In this way, framing makes it possible for an attitude to be not a fleeting, easily shifting view or opinion or, indeed, a subjectively chosen rational commitment (Rushing & Austin, 2008, p. 251), but a habit of deep attachment that, if disrupted, can be the undoing and remaking of a subject or point to the instability and processual nature of subjectivity. By corollary, the undoing and/or awareness of the instability and processual nature of subjectivity can be one of the ways in which an attitude, as its performance, shifts in line with the critique or undoing of the frames which make such an attitude seem reasonable and sensible. And that undoing can occur, as I have been arguing, through exposure to global images across digital networks. Exposure to the discomforting global images of otherness invoke not merely a simple act of reflection or recognition of the self but encounters that bring about a disturbance in selfhood or what Cathy Caruth (1995) refers to as an "event's essential incomprehensibility, the force of its *affront to understanding*" (p. 154). Such an affront to what seems knowable in the local experience of the everyday destabilizes identity, opening the possibility for self-critique.

One of the possible ways in which to understand Butler's concept of frames is as power formations which, in a media-saturated culture, govern how certain communicative activities make some discourses available and others broadly unavailable. Print, broadcast, and online media are not the only means by which discourses are produced, rendered, and disseminated as ways of thinking or understanding a topic or personage. The capacity to find new or alternative discourses through which the perception of globally dispersed otherness becomes knowable are culturally produced, yet it is the frame which makes a particular way of thinking and speaking on the figure of the refugee sensible, logical, and taken for granted, such that alternative discourses encountered are not adopted as they appear insensible, illogical, or excessive. This is a particularly pertinent point in a culture in which, broadly speaking, an array of discourses are available, at least through online searches, and yet are not necessarily taken up. In attempting to apprehend the precariousness, and enhancing the possibility of recognition of the other, our task is more than simply replacing existing frames with new ones, even though, as Butler (2009) points out, that is an important part of the project of alternative media (p. 12). Rather, the critical task is to show how frames, which are never wholesale or monolithic, can break with themselves such that "a taken-for-granted reality is called into question, exposing the orchestrating designs of the authority who sought to control the frame" (p. 12). That is, the frames which decide which lives can be recognized as lives circulate in order to establish hegemony, but in that circulation they risk their own undoing and the undoing of their bounds, thus figuring the collapsibility of the norm.

By understanding the performative nature of attitudes, it is possible to see attitude as an expression or articulation occurring in accord with the available discourses that lend the illusion of a fixed subject behind that attitude but which, in fact, constitute the subject and thereby fulfill the demand in contemporary culture for identity self-coherence. Attitudes, then, are expressed in particular ways not only in terms of the available discourses by which the subject seeks to be intelligible, but by the frames that govern the pathways through which those attitudes themselves become not only recognizable but align with the intelligibility of the self. For Butler (2003), an ethics built on mutual recognition is one that involves subjective change, which means a disruption or shift in the performativity that constitutes retrospectively the illusion of a fixed subject. As she has argued, the call for recognition or the scene in which we recognize another "is to solicit a becoming, to instigate a transformation, to petition the future always in relation to the other. It is also to stake one's own being, and one's own persistence in one's own being, in the struggle for recognition" (p. 31). A change of attitude, then, can be the performative expression and, simultaneously, the indicator of an alteration or a disturbance in subjectivity, and this occurs through the realization that one is not what one thought one was.

## 4  GLOBAL TIME, FLUCTUATING SPACE

I will return to some of the questions related to space in the context of globalization later in this section and then again in the context of digital mobility and ubiquitous connectivity in Chapter 6. However, for thinking through the relationship between interactivity and identity it is important to think about globalization and global space in relation to time and temporality, by virtue of the fact that the great revolutionary elements in the introduction of digital connectivity for identity and relationality are the speed of communication (such as in sending an email in contrast with a letter, to use a simple example) and the capacity to self-manage communication access (e.g., by choosing when to download a media text, rather than waiting for it to be broadcast at a particular hour in accord with a localized broadcast schedule). These together factor into how identity is performatively articulated and the ways in which the discourses making identities intelligible are made available in forms that are both instant and manipulable (rather than requiring what might be thought of as a stabilizing period of time until a sought-after text, discourse, concept, or idea can be accessed). Although for Foucault (1986), writing in the 1960s, the history of the twentieth century could be understood to be related to anxieties over space more so than time, which he argued was only "one of the various distributive operations that are possible for the elements that are spread out in space" (p. 23), it can be reasoned that – in a digital communication framework – time plays an extensively determinative role over the changes in how we do and perform identity in relation to others across space in a postnational conceptualization of media and communication.

Space and proximity are, in many ways, determined through time, by virtue of the ways in which travel time or communicative time measures distance. Space changes with the instantaneity of communication, such that the interactive engagement one has with peers on the other side of the globe – for example, in sending a photograph or seeing each other's faces – is instantaneous online, whereas it is only in the very recent past that a photograph would need to have been sent as a physical print to update our friends and families on how we look, and *vice versa*. In temporal terms, then, the engagement we have with others is more immediate, and in some ways can be said to do what Jameson (1985) felt was necessary for the performance of identity without schizophrenia, which is to unify the past, present, and future. That is, the spatialization of temporal moments of identity importance is adjusted such that the capacity for one subject's friend in a distant part of the globe to view old and new images, to see and relate to the image of a subject eating a meal so far away today, or to describe that meal or, better, to eat together through the framework of shared communicative space, changes how time occurs such that the performativity of one's selfhood in relation to distant others has an immediacy that undoes the past–present–future framework of subjectivity and the separation of these when it is in relation to distant friends.

At another level, however, temporality relates closely to conceptualizations of identity as psychic, lived, and social experiences, and these change within perspectives related to the everyday uses of communication technology. For John Urry (2007), following Lefebvre, lived time is separated increasingly from any concept of nature and replaced by clocks and other measuring instruments separate from natural and social space: "Time becomes a resource, differentiated off from social space, consumed, deployed and exhausted" under the domination of clock time (p. 98). Clock time is the product of one phase of globalization (industrial capitalism), produced in relation to the timetabling necessary for large-scale national and international transport systems such as trains and, later, air travel (Castells, 2000, p. 463). The relationship between communication, technology, and time affects our sense of temporality, particularly in the ways in which we relate to ourselves, our bodies, and others in global frameworks (Cooper, 2002, p. 120) and the means by which we regulate ourselves through patterns of bodily use that produce identities in relation to work, careers, entertainment choices, leisure, health, and play (Munt, 2002, p. 21). In the realm of interactive media, however, clock time is, on the one hand, separated from the time zone as we engage interactively with media, breaking news, social communication, Facebook updates, etc., from across the globe thereby flattening out the zones into a generally diverse experience of time that is increasingly disconnected from the patterns of sunrise and sunset. On the other hand, the presence of the time zone becomes more marked and users of interactive media become more aware of their location within time zones, particularly during acts of planning out videoconferences, group discussions, meeting deadlines across the globe, and social engagement with dispersed friends and family. This dual framing of locationality in terms of temporality – both the flattening and the marking of time zones – effectively rearranges the ways in which identity is performed, since although identity is formed in the citation of the signifier, category, name, or intelligibility, it is performed for and in relation to others (the other), and that includes others who are contextualized through competing or different temporal configurations (variations of clock time which may include diverse work/life balance practices or differing temporalities of labor).

In the interactive environment of a no-time/marked-time framework of relational others, the performance of selfhood is directed in ways which both do not need to account solely for the timing in one's own zone (e.g., how we might perform as a public individual during the day and a private subject at night) but now also account for the performances that occur toward many in the daylight and nighttime of many locations and zones. And, of course, how and where one is located in relation to other time zones can affect such performances – for example, to be the one member of a group located in New Zealand while others are in the United States and Europe can inculcate performances of marginality and social exclusion for obvious reasons of contactability during particular times. So while human interactivity passes, as Sally Munt (2002) notes, "through two forms of cognition before it can be conceived: space and time" (p. 3), time in the biopolitical production of selfhood that combined global networks, the compulsion to communicate globally across those networks, and the locationality of the body (Sharma, 2011, p. 440) produces new, more complex ways of performing selfhood that, in a performativity framework, are always toward the culturally required need for coherence, intelligibility, and recognizability for social participation and belonging. When concepts of temporality shift ever further away from natural time in order to engage interactively in global online networks, the time frame at stake is reframed.

## 4.1  Global Information Availabilities – Refiguring Time

Globalization as a mode of digital media use makes available information on demand, as I have discussed in earlier sections. This immediacy of identity resources – aside from the sheer ubiquity of information available, some of which may come in barely controllable floods of overwhelming confusion for some subjects – can be understood through the temporal relationships with information about how we make use of and access older media, such as traditional television broadcasts and music. Netflix and Spotify are two examples of sites that allow alternative distribution, although the very fact that users developed capabilities for the sharing of visual and audio texts long before mechanisms for capitalizing on this practice existed indicates a deep-seated desire to refigure the temporal controls of distribution by making available information from across the globe that would traditionally have been distributed through controlled temporal releases, such as television through broadcast schedules and music through CD releases. This convergence of the old and new (Jenkins, 2008), which is inseparable from anxieties over copyright and control of information (Lessig, 2008), has substantial implications for the ways in which we perceive identity and selfhood in the context of time as it emerges in a digital era in a triangular relationship with digital communication. At the level of creative production, the dependence on the concepts of flow and broadcast are in question. Media theorist Graeme Turner (2001) suggests that the liveness of television through broadcast does indeed contrast with the production imperatives implied by television program genre and format. This implies that the ways in which particular television genres communicate, such as the long narrative arc we began to experience as a common television format with the rise of new rich text TV narratives in the late-1990s (Kaveney, 2001, p. 12), are no longer fully reliant on broadcast television, nor do they necessarily retain a practical fit with broadcast technology and cultural patterns of reception. What is required is that we look to new frameworks through which media processes occur in terms of the ways in which new digital technologies emerge in culture, dynamically transform various cultural practices of entertainment and information access, and are utilized variously in unforeseen and often innovative means by users that serve diverse forms and means of gratification and pleasure, thus actively locating the site of gratification outside the time of the local and, instead, in global time.

I would like to address this through the important example of new digital forms of television program distribution that arose somewhat before the Spotify, Netflix, and other legitimate paid-for systems of distribution.

These earlier forms of digital distribution are important emergences, particularly in terms of the ways in which the desire to control broadcast and release schedules in global time come about alongside changes in employment and familial composition, and how these more broadly affect a temporality of the everyday that preferences alternative forms of television distribution such as Internet file sharing and downloads. This is not, of course, something that occurs merely at the user end of a media process, for the new television narratives and formats that were developing in the 1990s and early 2000s actively blurred the episodic series and the ongoing serial forms, aided and abetted a shift away from the traditions of television broadcast scheduling, and fostered and worked in a matrix formation with a broader cultural desire for new viewing patterns and for what we can think of as the interactive acquisition of television texts in ways not previously available with a fixed broadcast schedule (Cover, 2005a). I would argue that television itself has not been superseded, for it is certainly not the case that a general reduction in viewing can be discerned and the television screen itself has not yet given way to other alternatives – it remains a fixture in the everyday space of the shared and private locations within the contemporary home. Rather, the increased tailoring, personalization, and new forms of acquisition and engagement with television programs as text can be understood as differentiated from industrial "localized" and "zoned" clock times in ways which accommodate the newer cultural desires or demands that drive technological innovation. I am arguing here that broadcast schedules can and should be decentralized in our thinking about global media flows in light of a growing range of forms and practices of television viewing and acquisition that are constituted in various social, cultural, personal, leisure, and employment arrangements – by no means individual choices, but performatively involved in producing individual viewer behavior.

McKenzie Wark (1994; 1997) often used the phrase: "We no longer have routes, we have aerials," to point to the ways in which media inflects our sense of identity in contrast with much older models of familial subjectivities and identities built on association with the local and the nearby. In taking onboard Paul Virilio's concept of the vector to indicate the ways in which information travels – linking previously disparate geographic points and changing our conception of the world – Wark usefully points out the significance to cultural identity of broadcast media in late twentieth century Western culture. However, the usefulness of the aerial as a metaphor is not necessarily relevant in a globalized culture of networked digitality and identities built on new forms of digital media dissemination. At the crucial temporal moments at which new ways of engaging with media and communication in terms of global time were becoming obvious, commentator Brian Courtis (2003) wrote, we "watch television quite differently today than we did in the past." He pointed to a generational difference in the practice of television viewing, distinguishing between the dominant baby boomer scheduling that operates in the temporal everyday of his own generation, and patterns, rituals, and styles of viewing or media engagement he felt belonged more rightly to subsequent generations:

> My grown son watches considerably less TV, using it to surf for music videos, motoring programs, catch yet another Simpsons repeat, or a news bulletin, self-scheduling it much as he would his computer. His viewing is grazing; mine, alas, is still an addiction (Courtis, 2003).

This mapping of the changing patterns of television spectatorship works to locate viewing as potentially outside the temporality governed by the television broadcast schedule, which is a framing of media accessibility ruled by the decisions of others, both through precedence and familiarity and the deliberate risks taken in deciding what program belongs "when." It also links the idea of consumption of media in local/national time to the figure of an older generation, while the active engagement with media in global time is related to a newer generational population group. Unwittingly foreshadowing media engagement practices that would be truly visible globally a decade later, Courtis likened the more recent practices of viewing to the ways in which one uses a computer: a shift from the dominance of the aerial to a more complex, multiple, point-to-point, narrowcast ideal of the network. For Castells (1997), the concept of the network is constitutive of the contemporary media spectator as a node in an unstable, shifting, and expanding network rather than as a recipient on a broadcast vector provides a more productive way to understand shifting contemporary viewing patterns (pp. 320–321). The changing conception of television spectatorship takes place, then, in a dynamic relationship between the older form of broadcast scheduling and new digital/globalized forms such as the Internet as an audiovisual, file transfer system emerging in its use partly as a means to disseminate, use, and reutilize visual texts and particularly to gain some level of interactive control over the time, scheduling, and distribution of audiovisual releases. Viewers can best be seen as "located" variously, independently, and often self-consciously within an array of media dissemination possibilities rather than as a fixed-point-to-fixed-point recipient in a broadcast regime.

Theorization of television, television narrative, and television series has nonetheless remained firmly hooked on the concept of flow as outlined in Raymond Williams' important, but now dated, study of television as a cultural form. For Williams (1975), writing in an era in which the dissemination of both real-time and recorded television was in terms of a structured broadcast schedule, the experience of television is one located within a dialectic between flow and segmentation, ordered by the dictates of broadcast stations and their control of the broadcast schedule. As he put it:

> In all developed broadcasting systems the characteristic organisation, and therefore the characteristic experience, is one of sequence or flow. This phenomenon, of planned flow, is then perhaps the defining characteristic of broadcasting, simultaneously as technology and cultural form (Williams, 1975, p. 86).

What arises, culturally, to counter the dominance of planned flow is not further segmentation, fragmentation, or dispersal, but concepts of interactivity, customization, and networking as forms by which users seek to wrest some level of control over the text. While interactivity generally implies a technology requiring input from a user such that a text or series of texts work effectively (Green, 2002, p. xx), it also provides a set of concepts which allow us to see a media text – and indeed the history of mediated communication – not as something which is transmitted and received either passively or interpretatively, but as that which is engaged with by an audience member who seeks to maximize personalization, customization, and gratification from the text (Cover, 2004c). The increased use of electronic games as a media entertainment, the appeal of the Internet and interactive CD-ROM media, and the steps toward gestural interactive television provide some evidence of a cultural demand for such participatory engagement in media texts, and in ways which allow the user to utilize media forms in line with his or her own patterns of everyday temporality. As Robert Latham (2002) has suggested in his study of a younger generation's patterns of labor and consumption, a digital generation is seen as breaking free from a one-way centralized media form and provide evidence of "an emerging ethos of interactivity among young people who have been raised with computer technology" (p. 190)

In serving the personalization of media engagement that occurs through a narrowcast framework that envisions and creates niche audiences in favor of the broad, noninteractive audience of broadcast standardization (Smith-Shomade, 2004, p. 78), new formations of accessing television media on one's own terms or in one's own time is part of what Alan Liu (2002) identified as the contemporary habitus of the information environment (p. 75). We might say, then, that this habitus not only reorganizes the times in which we access, but reorganizes how we effectively think of ourselves in the context of time. More than just shifting the programs viewed into new moments of time that are outside the demands and controls of the schedule, this is about seeing oneself located not only in the global space of a global-ized media-saturated environment but as located in a global time in which all communication is radically freed from the needs of the local practices of scheduling which, themselves, bear a certain relationship to the natural and the physical routines of the locale – day and night, patterns of (healthy) sleep, and standard expectations around times of eating, resting, and engag-ing in family-based viewing practices.

Access to media texts as products or commodities – TV series, music, news, information, and the labor of viewing advertising – that occurs outside real-time broadcast, television scheduling, standardized or pro-grammed distribution, or through nationally legitimated aerial systems, continues to be understood in some discourses as an aberration, an excess, or a supplement. That is to say, rather than reading media spectatorship and media aesthetics through concepts of the network, diverse utilization, and emergent cultural technologies, the motif of broadcast flow continues to be presented as the norm and while the viewer is now predominantly and often understood as an interpreter of meaning and signification, she or he is still sometimes considered to be without a desire for interactive engagement with the televisual text. However, the conception of televi-sion as spectatorial now requires an acknowledgment that both the lived experience of television viewing and the production of television are in-creasingly disconnected from the priorities of broadcast flow and seg-mentation, and operate instead through a proliferation of user-controlled methods and concepts of access and engagement that are outside autho-rized clock time and, instead, are located (and locate ourselves) within global time as a time that has – temporarily – broken away from the neo-liberal demands for consumption of communication as commodity. It is being recuperated and subsumed within systems of capital, of course, but not without contestation. In other words, the kinds of global time that have been produced through the digital network accessibility of texts and practices of sharing have been more difficult to capture and commodify than earlier frameworks of time dominated by the clock and the schedule in local and national terms.

## 4.2 TV Time, Scheduling, and Agency of Choice

The historical significance of terrestrial broadcast in shaping the cultural everyday is found predominantly in the ways in which television scheduling has worked to constitute a particular sense of time. Time is, of course, purely subjective: multiple and conflicting conceptions of time condition any social or media formation. As Paul Virilio (1991) once remarked, "time is lived – physiologically, sociologically and politically – to the extent that it is interrupted" (p. 82) This is a useful way for thinking about time spent with older media forms as opposed to emergent technologies. The TV schedule is produced in and for cultural familiarity and recognition, generated within a particular standardized perception of clock time which, for Castells (1997), is "characteristic of industrialism, for both capitalism and statism, was/is characterized by the discipline of human behavior to a predetermined schedule creating scarcity of experience out of institutionalized measurement" (p. 125).

The television schedule is a form of media temporality that simultaneously disciplines, and is a disciple to, the conventions of Western "human time," taking place through standardized patterns of working, sleeping, eating, and familial life. The rise of new, networked, digital, and recorded media forms, however, has worked to change the ways in which "media time" operates. These changes emerge in a dynamic relationship with contemporary modifications in the temporal structure of labor such as in the growth of flexitime (Cooper, 2002, p. 9) or the expansive casualization of employment (Latham, 2002, p. 167); the growth of a consumer society and changes in consumer practices such as 24-hour and 7-day-a-week shopping; shifts in social and entertainment practices such as late nights at nightclubs and, indeed more recently, the "dayclub"; and the rise of a technological and digitized society in which forms of communication produce a sense of nowness whereby information is present and patience is (sometimes) unnecessary.

At the same time, diverse familial and living arrangements play a role in the cultural matrix that shifts viewing and entertainment patterns and produces a desire for alternatives to broadcast scheduling: increasingly, people are living alone in large urban centers. The image of the family sitting together around the television set, or slightly prior to that the radio, was certainly a formative social concept for the better part of the twentieth century. As Lesley Johnson (1988, pp. 84, 89) points out, the advertising for the broadcast radio medium and the aesthetics of the radio set itself worked connotatively to center the broadcast "box" within the home of the normative, nuclear family and programming centered particularly on the appeal of a type of temporality that was driven by family life:

> Listeners were spoken of as members of a family unit with two sets of needs: those dictated by the rhythm of family life and those dictated by the particular position occupied in the family. The family was portrayed as having specific rituals that wireless was said to serve (p. 90).

However, today it is possible to say that the television and radio as centerpieces of family leisure activity are a residue in the sense that they contribute to the everyday culture of everyday family life but are not necessarily essential to the dominant cultural structure of that everyday experience which is built on the multiplicity of screens, from personal mobiles to tablets, to both individual and shared computers. This, of course, can be thought of as an extension of the generational splits that were witness from the 1990s in the standard architectural arrangements of the contemporary home, whereby children and young adults are relegated to a separate part of the house away from the leisure spaces of their parents (Davis, 1997), with a separate television for separate choices of television products. The increased number of personal media devices atomizes that shared experience both in, and beyond, generational terms.

In addition to the ways in which changes in employment and familial relations bring the concept of a broadcast schedule and its internal temporality into question, a particular set of discourses around consumer demand and accurate scheduling have been invoked, particularly in relation to television narratives with significant fan followings but which do not acquire a large share of the ratings. Long-narrative television programs, often requiring an audience input of concentrated time to engage with the narrative viewed from geographically dispersed locations have been important examples during the 1990s. Greater cable and satellite access, and a subsequent motif in television series structure and viewing practices have in part sponsored an expansion in viewing patterns, such that audiences of a series can be categorized along the lines given by Reeves, Rodgers, and Epstein (1996): casual viewers (stumbling on and watching an episode), devoted viewers (viewing every episode), or avid fans (forming a community who utilize the series or are cocreative through fan activities). To put this in terms of time schedules, the casual viewer is the subject of a television flow of programs, the devoted viewer makes viewing the program a set segment of scheduling a particular event, and the avid fan utilizes the show in an extraschedule capacity for self-definition and contributes to a wider artworld community centered on the program. For both devoted viewers and avid fans, program–scheduling accuracy is vital if the program is to be engaged with predominantly through broadcast means. Annette Hill and Ian Calcutt (2002) have remarked on the ways in which scheduling of the exceedingly popular cult television series *Buffy the Vampire Slayer* in the late 1990s and early 2000s in the United Kingdom terrestrial broadcasts was "erratic." Among the resultant problems identified by fans and devoted viewers was the fact that scheduling anomalies interrupted complex story arcs and frustrated fan expectations of seeing their favorite show at regular times. Jenkins (1992a) has pointed out that responses from the major broadcasters to expressions of fans' desires often assume fans to be unrepresentative of general public sentiment and therefore an unreliable basis for programming decisions (p. 279). Regardless of the extent to which devoted and avid viewers comprise the broadcast audience, there is enough early evidence to suggest that the problems encountered in attempting to follow a complex narrative do indeed contribute to viewers seeking alternative methods of accessing a televisual text, that is, shifting viewers' engagement with the show from local, scheduled time to one that occurs within the global time of the download (often illegally, or today through Netflix and other paid-for download services) or through the more legal, but more costly and time–controlled wait for and viewing of DVDs (Cover, 2005b). Devoted viewers and avid fans might not comprise the greater portion of the contemporary viewing and ratings audience, but the practices that emerge in response to the inefficacy of broadcast scheduling, within a contemporary environment in which time has moved into a greater timelessness through flux, away from the everyday routines of the normative, national, and local, and toward the diverse and sometimes unhealthy practices of global time, have themselves become normative practices for viewing among broader audiences. Avid fans, as is often the case, lead the way for innovative cultural emergences and textual engagement adopted subsequently by a broader population – much as the figure of the male computer geek was the marginal figure outside dominant masculine practices and now a thing of the past within the cultural framework of the ubiquity of the computer. The television viewer identified within global time is standardized as the ideal viewer, but not necessarily for the programmers and broadcasters who cannot yet commodify the product for "new time."

## 4.3  TV, Global Time, Speed, and Identity

Many writers on emergent communications technologies have discussed time in conjunction with the concept of speed, from both positive and negative perspectives. For example, Paul Virilio (1995) in his *Art of the Motor* views speed – our ability to engage with information more quickly – as a form of colonization of time and space. This colonization, however, for Virilio is not something that effectively speeds our bodies and subjectivities or works to transform them in the sort of velocity and rapidity that, say, the Italian futurists celebrated (Cooper, 2002, p. 71). Rather, he sees the contemporary speed and acceleration of information systems as formative of a state of inertia, immobilizing us physically at workstations or media terminals. This might appear at first instance a useful way to consider new viewing practices occurring in online contexts, given that an increased speed of access to television – say, the next five episodes of the series *Breaking Bad* available through peer-to-peer file transfer across the Internet – would lead to another two or so hours sitting and watching. However, such a condemnation works to install a false and one-dimensional physical activity versus media entertainment dichotomy. Rather than a leveling out of the contemporary experience of information and entertainment, the possibilities for viewing and choosing to view are made more proliferate by the speed at which televisual texts can be accessed outside the broadcasting schedule.

Broadcast scheduling did more than attempt to fix viewing and entertainment leisure to a particular schema of temporality. It was segmented (Cubitt, 1991, p. 31), and not merely in the hourly changes in programs or the temporal nodal points at which program genres shift, nor the hour intended audiences change from children to adults, nor at which news is made available as a kind of "breach" or "slide" from the supposedly entertaining to the allegedly serious, nor the interruptions to a text by broadcast advertisements. A television program's narrative itself is, through broadcast, constituted in segmentation as a fluxing form of flow and interruption (Bernardi, 1998, pp. 9–10). However, television narratives from the 1990s onward, such as *The X-Files, Buffy, Babylon 5, 24, Lost, Dexter, Breaking Bad,* and the *Walking Dead* – among an increasingly broad range today – operate very much beyond the hourly segmentation as dictated by scheduling traditions. For Esther Saxey (2001), the long-season or multiyear narrative arc is endemic to recent television viewing and interpretive practice, and has a peculiar relationship with the concept of closure as it is enjoyed by various genres articulated in the novel, the play, or the film (p. 193). Such narrative extensions that defy episodic closure, and are noted for bringing about increasingly confused and long "previously on ..." teaser sections, are a feature of a number of contemporary television series. Rhonda Wilcox and David Lavery (2002) propose that recent "quality television" as it is characterized

by these lengthy narratives can provide greater depth and tackle more pro-
vocative and complex characterizations than its rival medium film, largely
because of the greater amount of time available in a multiple-episode season and a multiyear television series (p. xxv). Saxey (2001) suggests that
the televisual narrative arc is a particular structure that differs from film by
being driven by the style of broadcast made available through the television
as a medium: viewers watch at home on a weekly basis and look forward to
them (p. 195). While this is a useful point, one might remark that while the
narrative arc operates in a weekly format, it is undoubtedly also a response
to the increasing diversification of viewing practices (across localized options of broadcast and DVD, and globalized options of streaming and download) that are facilitated and encoded within global time.

It is important, then, to consider also how these series are being distributed through mediums that facilitate speed of access to (1) the entire series
itself and (2) between episodes that facilitate viewers choosing their own
patterns of engagement that are outside the "weekly-ness" of the schedule:
the transfer of episodes *via* Internet peer-to-peer file-sharing protocols enhances the speed of availability and access to episodes. Speed is figurative
here as a means by which television access is transformed in two ways. First,
the speed by which broadband Internet access allows digital files to shift
from computer to computer makes downloading a television series in a
digitized format feasible (an hour or two of download time for an entire
22-episode season of a television show in HD quality, compared with several days on a 56k modem as was more often the case until the mid-2000s).
The speed of access between episodes is similarly important in the transformation of televisual distribution – a weekly wait between episodes is not
necessarily desirable. While undoubtedly many viewers derive pleasure from
the weekly wait for the next episode, others whose personal scheduling
may operate under a different temporal logos (whether through flexible or
changeable work hours, or other social and recreational activities) may find
greater benefit in accessing the program not through its weekly broadcast
schedule but prefer to watch several episodes over a weekend. Embracing
the rapidity and connectedness of long-narrative arcs, many viewers will
wait until, say, an entire season of *Breaking Bad* is available through file sharing and attempt viewing over 24 hours rather than through the broadcast
weekly format. Importantly, in the context of identity formation, this exposes the viewer to a substantially focused capacity to engage with representations of identity in a series over, say, a single weekend (perhaps the most
genuine form of media immersion as an everyday cultural practice), as well

as the ability to critique what might have been designed in the tradition of the episodic and the weekly from the perspective of the fast paced (resulting in a more reflective engagement with knowledge of identity formation and performativity). Second, speed of access to television episodes that bypass syndication and distribution delays establish a scenario in which it is more expedient to utilize the Internet and DVDs than to wait the significant delays before the program is broadcast outside the United States. Factors such as ratings periods that differ seasonally between the northern and southern hemispheres, as well as various prioritizations of local content, can necessitate a delay of series broadcast for several months. Indeed, less popular series may be delayed by several years, or not broadcast at all. Devoted and avid viewers wishing to engage on website discussion boards, or to avoid "spoilers" through accidental revelations of plotlines, require faster access to the series overall, and these are frequently now facilitated by (sometimes illegal but popular) peer-to-peer file sharing. Among the numerous and diverse examples of viewers who require speedy access from potentially remote locations are global fan communities centered around different television narratives or genres. As Jenkins (1992b) has pointed out, fans in this context constitute an alternative social community that is unbounded from geographic location, with persons interested in a product or show often scattered and unavailable to meet face to face (pp. 213–214). Utilizing the World Wide Web for discussion boards has maintained a sense of fan community through communication across vast geographic spaces, and has produced significant activity in the sociality of a television text. Participation in such discussion forums is predicated on being up to date with the television series, particularly as the narrative disseminated through previous episodes is reread through later ones, and as character identity, development, and transformation remain a major aspect of fan and avid viewer debate and discourse (Zweerink & Gatson, 2002; Hill & Calcutt, 2002). This has certainly led to a culture in which downloading recent releases overcomes the scheduling differences between local stations and national networks. Likewise, this produces new ways of engaging with identity, as it further breaches the capacity of identity to be dominated by norms driven through the local (i.e., local broadcast) or the national (i.e., national censorship regimes that had previously had the capacity to stop a text at the literal border).

What does global time, then, tell us about how identities are differentially constituted in a contemporary framework of globalized digital accessibility? Within Butler's approach to identity as performative, as illusional, involving the citation of discursively given signifiers, categories of identity, formations of subjecthood, and stereotypes of performances, it is important to bear in mind that at no stage is it argued that a concept of identity is encountered in discourse and then immediately recognized, taken on, and articulated as that subject's sense of self. Rather, for Butler (1997), a subject is positioned into a subjectivity or identity which is sedimented "over time" (p. 33). This involves not a disjuncture in which, for example, a subject encounters within a media text a notion of national identity, recognizes himself in it, and comes to take that on and perform it in nationalist theatrics as a facet or attribute of selfhood; instead it takes a repeated and ongoing play of that identity for a subject to be reconstituted as a national subject, with the impossibility of repetition always betraying the linearity or fixity of that subjectivity (Butler, 1991, p. 18). When we factor in exposure to digital communications that occur in global time, the relationship between a sense of local time for a local space is dissolved in favor of a redistribution of forms of selfhood that can occur outside regularity, pacing, and other facets of the localized "clock." Performing one's identity in global time, then, breaches the kinds of relationships that are built and stabilized within the local time of the local space, drawing identity out into a fragmentation across not only spaces of the globe but time zones, ways of thinking about time, and timings that can clash with the local. The accessibility of discourses drawn from identity-rich television series – as one example of new media's making available of traditional forms of media in alternative ways – produces the possibilities for identity fragmentation through the nonpaced, high-speed access of the text, disbanding the pace necessary to stabilize an identity "over time" while, simultaneously, spreading the points of identification out across the globe.

## 4.4  The Reassertion of the (Non)Global Place

Although there is a dissolution of space that occurs with the introduction of global time as an everyday component of selfhood produced in line with globalizing digital communication, local place and space are not removed from the picture of identity altogether but are actively reasserted by older, more traditional frames of communicating in yet another push-and-pull struggle that characterizes the postmodernity of contemporary media and communication regimes and practices. In a seminal work for understanding the cultural perceptions of communication and media technologies, Joshua Meyrowitz (1997) notes that the specialness of place is transformed by electronic communication as a result of the ways in which it dissociates physical place and social space (p. 49). That is, because communication and interactive engagement with others can occur in spaces that are vastly separate (such as through a phone call, or through the parasocial relationships of broadcast media in which audience members are positioned to gain a sense of familiarity with unknown celebrities as if they are nearby neighbors), the sense of space between vast geographic and global frameworks is affectively compressed. Likewise, for Castells (2000), the transnational organization of information through concepts of both physical and conceptual networks operates to shift the ways in which subjects position themselves in terms relational to space, place, and distance. In this context, the performative enactment of identity through the citation of discursively given and interactively engaged intelligibilities of identity occur within an interaction with media and information technologies that actively "makes available" identities of difference, identities that were formerly place specific but are now broadly shared − often visually − and concepts of identity that are more fluid by virtue of the capacity for subjects either to be mobile, or to engage with information from across the globe as if they are mobile across places.

The compression of space and time is a feature of twenty-first century media and communication technologies in line with the globalization of economic activities, and this particular aspect of globalization has produced not only new ways of thinking about our location in global time and new ways of accessing information at greater speeds across space, but a transformation of spatiality altogether. In some of the earlier formations of the global network, such as that characterized by Web 1.0 concepts of online identity "play" separated radically from the offline world of corporeal bodies − a model that is no longer very meaningful − online space has been thought of as heterotopic. Heterotopias are conceptual spaces of difference, each with their own geographies, genealogies, and forms of disciplinary technologies of power, functioning separate from, but in relation to, the spaces around them (Munt, 2002, p. 16). For Foucault (1986), heterotopic spaces are not Utopias, which have no real placeness about them at all. Rather, heterotopias have a placeness that is connected with all the spaces surrounding them and yet are also simultaneously unreal, much as the mirror has place in the room but reflects a subject in ways which are unreal yet familiar (p. 24). All spaces − conceptual, physical, geographic, and heterotopic − are developed through adaptations and ideas that may have an affect but are constituted by preexisting cultural desires and demands. They do not develop if there has not been "in the play and strategy of human relations something which tended in that direction" (Foucault, 1993, p. 169). Importantly, however, heterotopias can be spaces for subjects whose identities are expressed by difference from the norm along a distributional curve of normativities (Foucault, 1986, p. 25). In that sense, we can view the conceptual space of the digital network as a space in which a subject can performatively articulate difference in ways that permit alterity alongside some nodes, but not necessarily in all other conceptual spaces. The difference between the local and the global can return in this context, structuring the subject of digital media as an identity that is fragmented between multiple possibilities. I will return to this important situation of the fragmented self in chapters six and eight.

In a slightly different context, we might consider how certain forces, factors, and interests attempt to restore space in nonglobal contexts in order to further the mission of neoliberal globalization. I would like to return momentarily to the important questions I raised earlier about global time as a framework in which subjects, positioned as consumers, actively seek out and gain access to traditional television series in new ways that defeat the local schedule and work outside the norms and traditional television episodic viewing. Although there is a clear movement toward the dissolution of local time for the consumption of entertainment media that is driven by a broad cultural desire or demand for interactive control over viewing, this compressed time as an effect of globalization is increasingly countered by programmatic blocking of those who have come to be referred to as "geododgers" (Grubb, 2015). Those television and film mediastreaming services such as Netflix and Hulu have sectionalized global space into traditional regions by preventing users from particular sites, countries, and regions from accessing on-demand media streams. In typical push-and-pull struggle cultures that emerge regularly in regard to the different forces acting for control over textual ownership and interactive engagement, users have developed geododging arrangements through the use of tools that trickthe service into believing one's computer in a restricted location (such as Australia) is in a nonrestricted site (such as the United States). Virtual private networks (VPNs) provided by third parties are among the most common form of disguising one's geographic location. In pushbacks against geododgers, streaming services have developed better ways to handle VPN-streamed data, reducing access (Martin, 2015; Grubb, 2015).

Three things happen to global space as a result of this struggle over digital interactivity and textual accessibility. First, such companies, seeking to capitalize on the broad cultural desire for streaming entertainment media in global time relocalize time for some spaces, sites, and countries – and not others – thereby making global time the province of certain subjects.

Second, a particular formation of global space becomes carved up into geographic regions, typically mirroring world marketing regionalisms that, for a time, governed the distribution of, and access to, region-locked DVDs (Cover, 2005b). Third, it fosters the fragmentation of both global space and global time – as compressed instances of globalization – by introducing multiple topias and heterotopias. These include those spaces through which data flow illegally (torrent downloading), semilegally (VPN-accessed streaming services), and legally (streaming accessed without VPNs). While the actual flows of data are, of course, more complex than simply occurring across three different planes of digital/global space, subjects are actively positioned and new categories of identity are made available and applied in accord with these different planes: for example, the figure of the geododger, the so-called Internet cheat, and the standardized user of paid-for streaming services as a new kind of digital consumer. Disciplinary regimes that activate nation state legal systems and rely on new forms of digital surveillance are productive in the inculcation of these new identities that are complexified by being at once both performative within local and global spaces. This is not to suggest, of course, that these particular coordinates of identity are meaningful to subjects, nor that the kinds of positioning of subjects in the context of differential regimes of time and space necessarily undo the powerful newness of encounters with otherness. Such encounters do not only occur in the realm of downloadable entertainment media, but in the broader context of a global digital network that is utilized in the everyday for manifold purposes. It is to the ethical implications of the latter, rather than the legal/criminal issues that dominate discussions of global streaming and geoblocking, to which I would like to turn in the final section of this chapter.

## 5  GLOBAL COMMUNICATION, ETHICS, AND THE IMPORTANCE OF SOUND AND LISTENING

In light of the above constructions for thinking about the manifold relationships between identity, access to visualities of otherness, discomfort, ignorance, and attitude, and a Butlerian approach to ethics, it remains to be asked what specific role digital interactivity as a global media formation might play in the production of ethical identities. In thinking about globalization as a logic that extends particular kinds of power over space and time and, particularly, neoliberalism's framework for the production of commodified identities within a market sensibility, Paul James (2006) makes the important point that there may be alternatives to thinking about globalization as a negative force that produces narrow subjectivities. I have already pointed out that the exposure to otherness might be one scenario in which globalization's bringing together of media and communication from different parts of the world can produce more ethical, less violent ways of perceiving subjects beyond traditional national bounds and racial, class, or other violence. For James (2006), however, there is a little more to it:

> ... what we need to do is find ways of building spaces that refigure relations outside those dominant layers of ... abstract empires of capital and liberal freedom. Building those spaces means relating to people within and across integral communities and connecting to persons in other places. It means working towards positive forms of globalisation, where extended relationships take the form of meaningful, long-term, obligatory and mutually-engaged partnerships (p. 45).

We can take from this the idea that the kinds of exposure to otherness through global, digital media I describe above can be useful, important, and present valuable opportunities for producing ethical selves in relationality with others, but that there may be more productive opportunities to think beyond just receipt, exposure, consumption, and access. One of those opportunities might be to think, then, not only about how ethical responsiveness to the other might be conditioned by responding with a change in attitude, but in how listening to the other (or to the needs, desires, and aspirations of the other) can occur in a digital media and globally networked context.

The very notion of listening is not often discussed in the context of digital communication, which continues to be perceptually dominated by ideas of textuality (the written word) and visuality (the benefits of real-time and recorded video distribution). Even in moments of digital communication which involve sound, such as a Skype conversation, it is the newness of the visual component that garners attention while the audio component is kept separate, perhaps on the whole because the idea of an oral conversation in real time across the globe is not, subsequent to several decades of the telephone, substantially novel, innovative, or revolutionary. Yet digital communication is very much about the sharing of sound – whether that is the audio that accompanies a video on YouTube, the verbal interactive conversation, or the automated sounds that alert, beep, and bother a digital connection – that is, bringing the sounds, verbal expressions, utterances, and voices of those from potentially distant places into the realm of the everyday, the private space of the domestic, the public space *via* a mobile device, as part of an exchange in a workplace, or as a commodity in a consumer purchase across international markets.

In her work on J.L. Austin's performativity, Cindy Patton (1999) points to the ways in which sound has often been made absent from understandings of performative utterances that convey both meaning and have an effect, doing what they enunciate. For Patton, however, sound can be understood as a necessary component of performativity:

> The emphasis on codes-in-speech mistakes as normative a situation which must be the exceptional case of sound: the case in which a sound is produced in a witnessed real time, and in which the witness acts as if the moment of production is equivalent to the sounds being produced (p. 473).

That is, then, sound itself can be performative, producing new arrangements much as particular words can declare a change in relationships (e.g., the pronouncement of marriage). This is to think about sound as being more than the bodily, corporeal accompaniment to speech, but to consider speech as one of many instances of sound (p. 474). However, sound is also the conveyer of particular forms of inequality and inequity in speaking, and this can occur in both recorded and real-time sound:

> Even in their absence, we make judgements about the producers of sound. We think we can hear race, and certainly gender. This is why the woman's "No!" is so universally disregarded, or the African American's statement of assent must be accompanied by rituals of deference (Patton, 1999, p. 473).

Sound, in global communication terms, carries particular connotations, much as the image of the war-ravaged Sudanese village, the appeal of the eyes of the refugee child, or the figure of the subservient prisoner in a war camp in Iraq are connotative. It is also subject to stereotypes that operate globally and, just as importantly, is used to build those stereotypes; for example, the sounds that accompany a tourism advertisement to visit Australia, such as a didgeridoo or the sounds of the untamed bush combined with images of the outback desert, bear little resemblance to the actual experience of tourism in Australian cities but produce a particular kind of identity for Australia and, by corollary, Australians. Sound is global, but how it is used is marked by difference, commodification, codes of communication, movement, and flows of information, recognizability, and discipline.

If we take these important points about sound and its role in digital communication through global networks to the level of metaphor, we can begin to ask not what it means to create, make, or share sound across the network as part of who we are as subjects, but also what it means to listen to others, and to listen to the other as part of who we are as subjects. This is not necessarily to listen to sounds, but to listen to the kinds of statements, situations, positions, and lives – both lived and unlivable – others make and have. Tanja Dreher (2009) has made some valuable contributions to furthering the politics of recognition as a framework through which to expand an understanding of responsibility, responsiveness, and ethics. Echoing Butler, Dreher makes the point that "distribution is in fact derivation of recognition and material inequalities are actually founded in institutionalized patterns of unequal cultural valuation" (p. 454), which leads to the call for listening to the other, not because it opens a conceptual space for the other to speak, "but rather foregrounds interaction, exchange and interdependence" (p. 450). To put this in terms of digitality, it is important not to assume that the persistent expansion of digital networks allow equitable access and participation by creating spaces in which subjugated others "from distant places" can be given a voice, space in which to write a blog, an opportunity to contribute to YouTube commentary, and so on. Rather, it obliges a cultural practice of listening as a pathway toward recognition and responsive ethics. This is to listen to the other not from familiar and available discourses, but to listen critically: to hear the context of what is said, the purpose, the background, to allow what is said to change cultural values, hierarchies of valuableness of subjects, and to break open institutional limitations in what can be heard and how it is heard.

Making these points is not necessarily about producing an obligation to listen in a particular way or prescribing an imperative on how one listens, nor even demanding that individuals as individuals make an effort to hear the lives and stories of others. Rather, it is to point to one potentiality that comes not from the increased capabilities of the Internet to distribute voices in both recorded and real-time scenarios, but as a phenomenon which changes perceptions of the globe, global space, and global time and therefore changes how we perceive our own location as participants (always as speakers and always as listeners) in a globe of many people.

# CHAPTER 6

# Mobile Telephony, Mobility, and Networked Subjectivity

## 1 INTRODUCTION

While much use of digital communication occurs within Web 2.0 frameworks characterized by interactivity, participatory cocreativity with texts, and the active sharing of self-information, self-image, and self-identity in online, networked contexts, there is a continued movement toward the über-connectivity of Web 3.0. The concept of Web 3.0 is particularly dominated by the interconnection of devices not traditionally thought of as part of the Internet, as well as the flexibility, willing surveillance, digital recording, and control-from-distance that produces new ways of thinking about ourselves and our identities in relation to the media, communication, and assistive tools we use as both capital and consumer commodities. This aspect of Web 3.0 has sometimes been referred to as the "Internet of Things," and is hailed as a radically disruptive new shift in communication technologies. For example, in a news report on recent developments, Stephen Cauchi (2011) draws on the increasingly common example of Internet-connected intelligent socks as an example of intelligent futures – socks which, through radio frequency identification (RFID) and other connectivity chips and transmitters/receivers, can find each other. As with the just as common example of the Internet-connected refrigerator that can order and thus replenish food stocks without human intervention, Web 3.0 is about the connectivity between people, subjects, bodies, and things within the domestic realm; part of a broader obsession with labor-saving technologies that will supposedly increase the amount of middle-class leisure time (or, for some, make greater time available for unwanted external labor) by routinizing the private household.

We might, however, extend this example of connectivity around the figure of the socks by bearing in mind that socks do not only belong in the sock drawer but are worn outside of the house, traveling wherever one's feet go. This is where the real mobility of Web 3.0 connectivity is at play – socks which not only can identify each other in order to more quickly make a pair, but socks which can be geolocated in the nondomestic space

*Digital Identities.*
http://dx.doi.org/10.1016/B978-0-12-420083-8.00006-7

of the public, that is, the sites of walking such as across the city or on public transport, basically anywhere radio signals can reach. These are socks which are mobile not only because they travel with our legs, but because they are connected like mobile phone devices to a networked connectivity. Indeed, it may be questioned whether this reduces a subject's sense of individual ownership over a pair of socks, potentially increasing the discursive and symbolic connectivity with others who wear similar socks. That is, these may be socks which know when their cousins are nearby, socks which can tell on us to other items of clothing, socks which know when our jacket should be worn, socks which will berate us for having not quite walked enough. We can be connected with our socks beyond the residue of foot odor and the holes we make in them, and our socks can effectively connect us with other subjects, other things, other devices, and other discourses as we travel about in public space with them. Importantly, there are three additional factors: (1) these are socks with which we can gain a sense of assemblage – the socks are part of that which constitutes us as subjects in relation to other subjects; (2) they are socks which enable types of mobility from being devices that connect us, travel with us, enable new connectivities, and, no doubt, enable kinds of social mobility through the conspicuous consumption of showing off our flashy, tech-heavy socks; (3) they are socks which, through mobility, connect the public and the private, the outer space and the realm of the domestic more thoroughly while complexifying the dichotomous distinction between the public and the private. Socks are a somewhat absurd, albeit very real, example, but if we think of the technologies of communicative mobility such as the mobile phone, the smartphone, the wifi-enabled laptop computer, the netbook, and the tablet, then we must be prepared to think about the ways in which subjectivity is made more relational through the capacity (if not always the reality, for devices fail) to be connected to others at all times, to be able to access information without needing to return to one's domestic homespace or office computer, to be able to seek help, advice, connection, affection without needing to find a landline, and to be able to engage with the full range of our favorite entertainment and informational media very quickly.

Web 3.0 cloud storage and the cloud sensibility of always being able to access information facilitates movement and mobility, makes it possible to move about in space more widely and more easily, and to develop new, more flexible ways of engaging with space, work, information, communication, familial life, kinship, friendship, and care. Mobile media is simultaneously radical and inherently grounded in pre-existing developments of technologies. From the radical perspective, we might pay attention to Joshua Meyrowitz' (1997) point, echoing an older television advertisement, that home is made by virtue of being in a place with a telephone (p. 50). Now, of course, mobile telephony has meant that home is simply one site or location in which telephonic communication occurs, and the device that takes communication outside of the home, breaching the domestic/public distinction built on the home/work landline and the public site payphone, is just as much a device of domesticity. Untethering communication from the home is, in that sense, a significant movement away from norms that developed over several generations and across much of the twentieth century. More disruptive still is the capacity for information-seeking and sharing in new sites and frameworks of mobility with the development of the smartphone, wifi-connected devices, and the ability to be online through mobile connectivity, releasing the performative acts of online reading, writing, downloading, and uploading from the desktop and the desk, from the corporeal frame of seatedness, from the two-handedness of standardized qwerty keyboards and mice, and from the stillness brought by the demand that one remain motionless in order to be online.

Interconnected communication tools that are part of the general shift toward the connectivity of all technological devices include those that are tools which bring computing power, digital storage, and other forms of communication into the realm of mobility. Mobility, here, is characterized by connectivity but it is not only the capacity to access cloud information and entertainment. Rather, the portability of mobile information leads to the contemporary era of über-connectivity that, in turn, facilitates new kinds of networking. There is a path between portability and relationality in historical terms, beginning of course with the portability of the book as a technology of information that can be carried about (subsequent to the printing press) that results in the paperback as a form of book designed specifically for even greater mobility – and initially typically sold in sites of mobility such as the railway station. The ebook, allowing greater portability of a number of books is a further development in a linear pattern of technologies that enable the mobility of information and entertainment and that, thereby, facilitate the mobility of subjects.

Although the Sony Walkman is one of the dominant communication technologies of the 1980s and 1990s traditionally highlighted in cultural study discourses as an exemplary device of mobile entertainment that revolutionized how we understand media, ritual practices of listening, and the space of public and private, it was the proliferation of the iPod (Berry, 2006) in the mid-2000s that truly changed practices of engagement with media. The iPod enabled people to listen, at will, to any sample audio (and later video) from one's personal collection (often an entire archive) while engaged in the activities of being mobile, walking, traveling by public transport, and generally moving about away from the domestic sphere of the private or the semipublic space inhabited by the jukebox. Building on pre-existing perspectives on mobility and actively sought in order to fulfill the cultural demand for mobility, the iPod saw a substantial shift in how media ritual in mobile contexts occurred, as it initially gave access to music and later video, forms of information which are among the many mediated forms of discourses that can have profound significance for the stabilization or destabilization of subjectivities and which are able to contribute to the citational draw of performativities. In giving access to such texts in ways which were as portable as the book, but accessible without the need for the focused concentration required by the book, the iPod made available particular kinds of mediated discourses to be utilized for performativities in public spaces. This is in addition, of course, to the various shifts in listening practices such a device enables, with the capacity to move very quickly from song to song and track to track and the capability to search through lists of names, categories, genres, etc. rather than rely on the physical cataloging of a record or CD. In this way it is now possible to listen and engage in very personalized, private ways (with headphones) without the collaborative engagement with any other subject. In some ways, then, the iPod is an isolating device that separates a subject from the audible world in a public space. At the same time, because engagement with media implies a connectivity with authors, producers, singers, and others – even across temporalities facilitated by the practices of recording – it does not represent isolation but rather represents new, different, and sometimes more appealing ways of engaging, interpreting, and interacting.

While, at the time of writing, iPods are still used and remain common as a result of their high storage capacity, the proliferation of the iPhone and Android smartphone has brought together a technology of storage and archiving with a technology of connectivity, expanding the mobile phone's capabilities of voice communication into the diverse, varied, and customizable forms of digital networked communication. For Lelia Green (2008), this is part of a more general shift from the computer to the mobile device as the device of choice for connectivity that builds explicitly on the experience of the iPod (p. 6). Indeed, we might argue that it is no surprise that the mobile device quickly became the most popular technology through which to undertake connectivity online and thereby to serve as a performative self in an online capacity, as it has been connected with entertainment (access to music) rather than information.

The increasing accessibility of online spaces, sites, and communicative forms through mobile devices is changing how, when, where, and in what contexts users engage with a digital media environment. A proliferation of new research on mobile cultures indicates the close connection between youth, identity, and mobile/portable technologies, although it also points to a number of distinctions in the capacity and form of access along gendered, racial, ethnic, and socioeconomic demarcations (Goggin, 2013). Mobile and dating applications such as Grindr used by gay men for sexual meetings form a certain kind of community disconnected from older models that relied on spaces such as bars, clubs, ghettos, or sex-on-premises venues, or alternatively on communities of friendship networks, potentially enabling communities of sexual difference to operate *via technological networks* without necessarily being built on space (Raj, 2011). Mobile phone–based contact for sexual and nonsexual meetings, in this instance, has shifted how subjects of a minority community are to be understood in terms of isolation, geography, and forms of belonging whereby access to a network of community peers does not occur from private space to private space but in a broadening range of sites and contexts that include digital/mobile access in and from public spaces. Access from mobile to mobile and space to space may lead to physical face-to-face encounters between subjects, but that does not mean these are encounters which *begin* from solitude – accessed by a mobile network, engaged corporeally in a sexual encounter, and returning to an aloneness – as older stereotypes would have it. Rather, this is about an opening up of different kinds of connectedness, a literal "queering" of connectivity that changes not only how subjects act in relation to each other *as subjects*, but what connectivity through communications technology means. In this case, it may mean a dissolution of traditional community built on place and locale to which one must travel as a concept of "center" to a decentralized place-to-place mobile connectivity that does not require a center.

Grindr is a useful example, made all the more important by the more recent rise of Tinder, an application which similarly facilitates sexual meetings and is used predominantly by heterosexual men and women, demonstrating the proliferation of new ways of doing connectivity and relationality, and therefore new ways of doing identity (as subjects and as sexual subjects). While the use of mobile devices for connective engagement is not always or only about sexual expression and sexual self-hood, thinking about technology as a tool of and for sexual identity and sexual relationality is very useful as it provides conceptual pathways for thinking about how media and communication technologies fit within contemporary everyday identity. In this chapter I demonstrate some points about mobile connectivity and identity through, at first, consideration of sexual identity and the minority LGBT community, not only because these provide interesting examples, but because this provides an opportunity to move beyond the idea that *first* there is technology and *second* it is utilized for sexuality. Sexual expression as a major part of everyday, normative identity is wholly tied up with communication technologies, including the use of mobile devices, smartphones, tablets, and other connective technologies that are also used in nondomestic spaces outside the home and the workplace.

I begin by thinking through Manuel Castells' network morphology, as a constitutive factor in the performativity of identities that are always social and relational, from the perspective of mobility and mobile devices that facilitate an always-connectedness of subjects moving through private and public space. What it means to be connected changes how we think about relationalities with others, because it upsets and adjusts some of the more traditional frameworks of community, categorization, and similitude, whereby the policing of community is no longer that which can be understood to occur through dichotomies of insider/outsider or belonging and nonbelonging, but through flows of relationality that produce diverse kinds of networked proximities between subjects within a networked community. I demonstrate how this works within an understanding of mobile connectivities by using an example of early adopters of mobile telephony – the LGBT community. Russell T. Davies' television series *Queer as Folk* from the late 1990s and early 2000s presents an account of the ways in which a Manchester (UK) queer community made heavy use of mobile phones in order to produce new concepts of networked forms of belonging. The metaphor of the phone as that which facilitates access between different subjects as nodes and hubs in a network of relationalities is powerful, and foregrounds some of the recent developments in mainstream social settings in which always-connectedness allows new ways of doing relational community not previously available to us conceptually. Finally, I address three important factors of mobile subjectivity that emerge in a contemporary morphology of the mobile network of relationality in discussing the always-connected sock metaphor: these are the different approaches to subjectivity that can be found in thinking about mobile cultures as assemblages, through mobility conceptualization, and through the ways in which mobility disrupts received understandings of public and private, thereby presenting new signposts for the conceptualization and constitution of identity as performative in relation to others.

## 2  MOBILE DEVICES, ACCESSIBILITY, AND UBIQUITOUS CONNECTIVITY

One of the most effective and useful ways of understanding the interface and relationality between belonging and identification as constituted through mobile communications technologies is in line with Manuel Castells' (2000) network morphology that characterizes contemporary sociality across political, economic, labor, and technological environments. Typical communications formations that are more obviously interstitial and networked, such as the Internet, electronic trading, and social networking, are unsurprisingly more regularly invoked in giving contemporary examples of Castells' framework. The network represented by the *mobility* of the mobile phone is pertinent here. Rather than place, the network of mobile relationality is articulated through a structural logic of "nodes and hubs" (p. 443). As Albert-László Barabási (2011) has explained, "[i]n a social network the nodes are the individuals and the links correspond to relationships – who is talking to whom, who is communicating with whom on a regular basis" (p. 1). In any digital network, then, subjects are seen to be not only actors who initiate and engage in communication, but as certain *kinds* of subjects who are constituted *by the network*. We can add to Barabási's articulation of nodal subjects the figure of the hub, which can be a subject, organization, device, or other interconnected thing that attracts the flows of relationality between different nodes that are part of network formation. In a network formation:

> … we can remove a significant fraction of the nodes without breaking it apart. What's going on here? By randomly removing the nodes, in a scale-free network we are typically removing small nodes, because there are so many of them. The probability of removing a hub is very low, as there are only a few hubs. Yet, removing a small node just means the network becomes slightly smaller. It shrinks, but doesn't fall apart. In fact, we can remove 98% of the nodes in a large scale-free network, and the remaining 2% will stay together and continue to communicate. There is a built-in robustness to this network because of the hubs – but there's also a price to pay. What if we remove the biggest hub, the next biggest hub, and so on. In this case the network breaks into pieces very quickly. Scale-free networks have this amazing property of robustness to random failures, but they are also very fragile. If we know what the system looks like we can destroy it very easily (Barabási, 2011, p. 11).

In this, the network of relationalities between subjects can be understood very neatly through metaphors of nodes and hubs whereby access to mobile technologies creates greater capacity for connections that enable relational, affective, friendship, and kinship flows more effectively through increased accessibility to one another and to the informational settings and discourses that are cited in performativity. Mobility increases the perceptive complexity of connection between subjects beyond that of the landline phone or the desktop computer, both of which maintain a connection with place, domesticity, workplace, private space, location, and access. Mobile phones, smartphones, tablets, and other devices that connect cellular and wifi networks, however, do not always articulate location in a real-time voice connection. Relationality, as formative of the networks of identification between subjects, provides the constitutive framework for making performativity intelligible and, in a mobile era, that relationality occurs in an increasing complexity of interaction (Castells, 2000, pp. 70–71) witnessed in the multiplicity of communicatory engagements across a mobile network.

Network formations and their technological frameworks are, for Castells (2000), part of the material foundation of contemporary society that govern, shape, and guide, without determining the processes of collective and individual subjectivity. Among the elements of this formation is the contemporary networking logic in which the

> … morphology of the network seems to be well adapted to increasing complexity of interaction and to unpredictable patterns of development arising from the creative power of such interaction. … this networking logic is needed to structure the unstructured while preserving flexibility (Castells, 2000, pp. 70–71).

Contemporary relationships, friendships, communities, and kinships therefore operate within a networking logic that is built on a notion of flexibility in order that the links be resilient and able to cope with changing circumstances, movements, and shifts. The networking of technological information and communication tools respond to the identity-based cultural desire or demand for more complex and flexible forms of identity, including sexual identities that work within a queer theoretical framework of fluidity, complexity, historicity, and temporality beyond the strictures of essentialist notions of sexual selves. Within a networking logic of flexibility:

> Not only processes are reversible, but organizations and institutions can be modified, and even fundamentally altered, by rearranging their components. What is

*distinctive to the configuration of the new technological paradigm is its ability to reconfigure, a decisive feature in a society characterized by constant change and organization fluidity (Castells, 2000, p. 71).*

The flexibility of the space of flows through a network serves as the material layer of contemporary communicative exchanges through micro-electronics, computing processes, broadcasts, and particularly telecommunications (p. 442), but they also result in a context in which relationality is constituted by "nodes and hubs" (p. 443). It operates to reshape the space of flows – and thus relationalities – by providing it with a new structural logic, rather than an overly celebrationist free flow of exchange:

*The space of flows is not placeless, although its structural logic is. It is based on an electronic network, but this network links up specific places, with well-defined social, cultural, physical, and functional characteristics. Some places are exchangers, communication hubs playing a role of coordination for the smooth interaction of all the elements integrated into the network. Other places are the nodes of the network; that is, the location of strategically important functions that build a series of locality-based activities and organizations around a key function in the network. Both nodes and hubs are hierarchically organized according to their relative weight in the network. But this hierarchy may change depending upon the evolution of activities processed through the network. Indeed, in some instances, some places may be switched off the network, their disconnection resulting in instant decline, and thus in economic, social and physical deterioration. The characteristics of nodes are dependent upon the type of functions performed by a given network (Castells, 2000, p. 443).*

The contemporary sociality of the mobile phone can be understood through this concept of a network morphology that structures relational and identity without necessarily freeing it altogether from structuration As a device of communications portability and one which refigures space into a frame that is organized by the mobility of information, mobile phones are figurative of the technological novelty by which identity and subjecthood are constituted. For Meyrowitz (1997), electronic media destroy the "specialness of place and time" (p. 49) and the telephone as specifically advertised as establishing home "wherever there's a telephone" prevents any domestic or public place from being "informationally special" (p. 50). The mobile phone, however, does this even more so as there is no longer any specific connection with place as that which is overcome, rather there is a network of space, of identity, of socialization, and of new hierarchies that produce the constitutive frames of normativities in potentially new ways.

## 3  REPRESENTING EARLY ADOPTERS: FROM COMMUNITY TO NETWORK

One of the ways in which we can trace the significance of mobile phones and mobile networks of connectivity in the everyday lives and thus in the constitution of performative identity of contemporary subjects is in looking at representations of the early adoption of mobile devices. LGBT communities are arguably among the earliest adopters of mobile telephony in the late 1990s and early 2000s, before the mass proliferation of mobile phones, smartphones, and tablet devices. This, in part, has been due to a number of lifestyle factors, such as the mobile experience of clubbing as a common LGBT leisure activity requiring increased ready-connectivity across multiple sites in order to engage in social activities, the broader array of sexual liaison occurring at the time outside the domestic sphere, the arguably greater likelihood of unsettled domestic mobility (Collins, 2005), and the use of mobile technology as an item of conspicuous consumption. Such intended consumption may be seen in the targeted marketing by mobile telephone companies of mobile devices and accounts specifically of the LGBT community in the 1990s, often via specific advertising within large festivals such as Mardi Gras in Sydney and Midsumma in Melbourne as well as in the use of celebrity drag performers, for a time, as the face of one of the major mobile telephone providers in Australia.

Technologies of communication have been a quiet yet pivotal element in the representation of the relationship between minority nonheteronormative identity and queer community formations, and thus play a constitutive role in the historical and specific performativities of queer identities. For example, in his 1993 film *Totally Fucked Up*, Gregg Araki's community of queer and alternative youth are built in part around their use of the landline telephone as a mechanism through which community is bound. Isolation, as a central trope in Araki's narrative and one that has been heavily associated in film and television as a causal factor in queer youth suicide (Cover, 2012a), is produced here through an inability to access community as a young gay teenager. In the final scene of the film, Andy (James Duval) poisons himself because he has been rejected by a boyfriend – he has found all his friends' phones are engaged when he attempts to discuss the rejection and find solace, and subsequently commits suicide alone. A temporary if painful disappointment and a breach of immediate access to one's community or peer network form the background causal reasons for his suicide. The inability to contact his peers is catalytic, and the suicide can be read as the result of the breakdown of the coherence of his identity

(Caputo, 1993, pp. 239–240), which we would understand to be dependent on sociality and relationality rather than a liberal individualism. Indeed, we might argue that the very need for social engagement in order to foster the *resilience* necessary to cope with contemporary experiences of loss drives the need for the mobile phone in contemporary communities of marginality first, because mobile telephony increases the efficiency of communication and therefore the efficiency of relationships, friendships, social groups, peer networks, and kinship. This is perhaps particularly significant when these aspects of life emerge in forms that are different from the traditional supportive environment of the twentieth century's nuclear family.

The mobile telephone has also been a marker of queer/LGBT identity since the mid-1990s, with the early adoption of the communication device operating at the interfaces of communication, community belonging, affirmative essentialism, neoliberal and conspicuous consumption, pride motifs, and nondomesticity (including nonrelationship sexual encounters) in queer representation. Sexual identity is constituted and made intelligible in the available discourses of sexuality, but how that intelligibility is operationalized centers on the available and appealing communicative methods. If identity is performed through a range of social relationalities, these include ways of relating that are wholly dependent on networked communication and communication forms that respond to increasing mobility and remote access (to information, to one another). That is to say, in terms of the performativity of identity, complexity, flexibility, and mobility are interrelated. Although the development of the mobile phone's cultural uses in queer contexts unfold historically over time, its outcome is exemplified by the queer mobile–dating application Grindr which, as Senthorun Raj (2011) has indicated, provides a site for sexual identity intelligibilities as well as for the contestation of identity norms. As a formation which puts dispersed persons in contact with each other – whether that be for dating, relationship-seeking, or casual sexual encounters (Cover, 2010) – mobile telephony becomes emblematic of a form of community belonging that is no longer centered on the spatiality of LGBT ghettoization, nor on the clarity of identity norms of difference offset against normative heterosexuality. Rather, this form of community belonging is performed, articulated, and related through a network logic of identity and relationality.

One site through which we see substantial early adoption and a fleshed out account of the centrality of mobile telephone technologies to the formation of contemporary queer communities and identities is in Russell T. Davies' *Queer as Folk* (UK 1999–2000) which, as I will argue, directly ties queer identity not to a community formation in the framework of Benedict Anderson's imagined communities, but to a mobile network morphology in the context of Manuel Castells' network society. *Queer as Folk* provides a useful example – not only because it presents an account that links mobility of network accessibility to particular ways of performing and stabilizing identity through relationalities beyond models of community and membership of categories, but because Davies' series presents an account of *media representing new media*, which matters significantly for how we perceive the relationships between self-hood, culture, and digital media technologies. Indeed, too little scholarly work has been done on this relationship and, although I will address it in a small way in this chapter, it would be valuable to the field to develop a more nuanced and worked out account of the ways in which media represent media as a formation that authorizes particular ways of perceiving the role of new technologies.

## 3.1  Beyond Community: Networks of Belonging

*Queer as Folk* has been noted for being the first television drama in which almost all the main characters were gay or lesbian, and in which the narrative operated without an overt focus on nonheterosexuality as an issue (Davis, 2007, pp. 7, 14). Interest in its narrative has been around the fact that while it is not ostensibly queer in the queer-theoretical sense of interrogating gender and sexual identities (although it can be read through queer theory), it is queer in the sense of its confrontational approach, disavowing the figure of the conservative, nonsexualized conformist, and coupled representation of nonheterosexuality in favor of sexually active, ideologically complex characters (Creed, 2003, p. 141). It has also been noted for the ways in which it explores ideological tensions within the expression of sexual orientation and cultural anxieties over the distinction between sexual pleasure and community or familial responsibility (Billingham, 2003, p. 155), critiques of the relationship between space and identity (Skeggs, Moran, Tyrer, & Binnie, 2004), and for the innovative ways in which it presents nonheterosexual characters as active, multifaceted, and complex in their intersections with space, history, shame, pride, gender, and sexuality. As Sally Munt (2000) suggests, the characters are distinctive in that they demonstrate a moving forward in television representation of queerness – they are not "stuck in an ur-moment of being gay [rather] they are busy *doing* gay – the confession/conversion moment has been superseded" (p. 534).

The central premise of the narrative focuses on the communicative relationships between three primary characters in the context of mobility, identity, and belonging. Central to the relationships is Stuart Jones (Aidan Gillen) who is about to turn 30 years old, is highly popular in the queer community of Manchester, and is an inner urban–dwelling successful advertising executive, both confident and sexually voracious. His closest friend is Vince Tyler (Craig Kelly), who is also turning 30, is shy, sexually unsuccessful, and a working-class shop assistant from a precarious social and financial background. Nathan Maloney (Charlie Hunnam), is aged 15, his social confidence and precociousness hides an apprehensiveness grounded in his unfamiliarity with the LGBT scene and the codes of conduct and behavior necessary for self-representation, recognizability, stable identity, and belonging – he spends much of the series developing the means for belonging within the community. All characters, in addition to several other friends, lovers, and family members, are portrayed across the series' broader narrative through questions over the means of belonging. This critical question plays out through a number of ongoing plot lines, including: Stuart and Vince's nonrelationship which is beyond friendship but not quite lovers and explores ways in which to maintain a relationality that is neither sexual nor romantic prior to them both turning 30; Vince's relationship with the Australian Cameron Roberts (Peter O'Brien) and Cameron's jealousies which tacitly disrupt the *status quo* among all characters; and Nathan's growing engagement with the Manchester queer community and his successful combating of homophobia in his school environment. Important, however, is the way in which the narratives all play out questions of belonging through the series' *symbolic* use of presmartphone late-1990s mobile telephony, demonstrating the ways in which the LGBT community served as a site of early adoption of mobile technologies for the purposes of moving beyond traditional community.

*Queer as Folk* depicts the use of mobile telephone technology not merely as an item of queer conspicuous consumption and fashionable gadgetry (although the narrative also includes an element of consumerism and the visibility of class demarcations and affluence) but as the mechanism by which identities are formed in relation to one another. The mobile phone figures across all episodes. For example, when Vince visits a straight pub for a work function he enters the space on the phone to Stuart, reporting back to him in anthropological terms (although the mobile is figurative here of a safety net in which the two have even set up a key word – twilight – for urgent rescue). Comic scenes of missed calls, uncertain receives in mixed up call-waiting scenarios, phone calls and phone messages that interrupt events, and self-calls used to remove characters from scenes and sites in which they are uncomfortable all point to the mobility of subjects within space and to the mobility of identity as that which is always "in process" across the series.

Several writers have investigated the British *Queer as Folk* for its invocation of queer community as constituted in space, particularly public queer space. Certainly the Canal Street queer social district of Manchester has been noted for its representation in *Queer as Folk* as both a location which defines community and pegs it to a locale, and as an imagined city, a heterotopia (Billingham, 2003, p. 119). For example, a number of writers present *Queer as Folk*'s site for the construction of queer identity through Anderson's framework of an imagined community that is produced by the differentiation of both identity and territory from other, broader communities and figures this space as having a deep, horizontal form of comradeship and belonging as both ideal and functional of community (Anderson, 1983). For Beverly Skeggs et al. (2004), drawing specifically on Anderson, a reading of *Queer as Folk* introduces the dialogical means by which space and community are collaboratively constructed:

> ... in Queer as Folk, the Village is not only safe but is also represented as a space of escape: Vince from work; Nathan from school homophobia, father homophobia and prying mother; Stuart from homophobic family; and Donna from school sexism and abusive home. There are three scenes of Nathan and Donna running away, leaving suburbia to enter the free and queer space of the Village. This escape becomes a claim on space, or territorialisation through sexuality—one way by which gay men have been able historically to instantiate their sexual identity. Territorialisation is made apparent through the character of Nathan as he becomes more and more confident about his occupation and inhabitation of the space called the Village (p. 1846).

However, one of the important departures I would like to make here – particularly around the performativity of the character Nathan's identity as produced in his relationality to queer community, queer characters, and queer space – works somewhat differently from an account that centralizes community within Anderson's framework. Instead, I look less at space as constitutive and more at the devices of networking and mobility that permit movement in space while maintaining forms of connectivity and connected relationally with one's community peers.

For Anderson (1983), community identity is a cultural artifact, the product of a complex system of historical forces (p. 4). Communities are figures on the model of the village as a group of subjects, identifying with each other because they have an oppositional identification with the community's other – the outside or the rival community, another village. Such a cultural community is always *imagined* into existence because the members will never meet *all* their fellow members yet "the image of their communion" is present, supposedly, in the minds of each member (p. 6). A national community, for example, is *imagined* because "regardless of the actual inequality and exploitation that may prevail in each, the nation is always conceived as a deep, horizontal comradeship" (p. 7). In Anderson's thesis, a community is therefore not awakened to a self-understanding or a discovery of its previously hidden existence, but invented (p. 6). This is not to say that a community is thus a fabrication or a false consciousness but that it is a created artifact. Anthony Cohen (1985) provides an important insight into how such a community is imagined into being by showing that in generating a community consciousness its structures and institutions are subordinate to its symbols (p. 76). The symbols, identities, and ways of being in community are traditionally performed in ways that are required to conform to particular norms and standards, including symbolic standards of similitude. All of these operate to bind the community and police its borders, and can be deployed in the Foucauldian sense of surveillance and self-surveillance of the community's supposed members. The signifiers which make an identifiable community possible do so on the basis of a cultural assertion of opposition, for they are fixed in the citation of similarity versus difference, whereby a community is produced as a kind of conceptual space in which all those internal are members, some subjects of uncertainty sit at the periphery, and then there are outsiders – the force of an insider/outsider dichotomy results in policing and surveillance. A networked community, however, is something quite different, and it is to this that contemporary technologies, concepts, and frameworks of networked mobility lead us in contemporary regimes of performativity. A networked community is one that is built on formations that center on proximities to particular norms within relational and communicative flows between different subjects in that network. This is a more complex, multivariant way of doing relationality beyond similar/different and insider/outsider dichotomies. Both the concept and the reality of the mobile device facilitate this ever-increasing complexity in relational identity.

Mobiles in *Queer as Folk* both operate within space and construct forms of spatiality in ways different from traditional communities. Here, however, it is a particular framework for queer space. Space has been a significant dimension for the construction of identity in recent critical theory, particularly drawing on Foucauldian concepts of subjectivity investigated from a genealogical perspective (Munt, 2007, p. 184). Mobile telephony allows queerness to be at once part of the ghetto of Canal Street clubs and bars, as a utopic or indeed heterotopic imaginary space (Billingham, 2003,

p. 119), and the wider social sphere. That is, queerness is found in the domestic space inhabited by and defining the corporeality of the three mothers in the series, the nonelite space of the supermarket which Vince moves in for his daily work, Stuart's advertising executive, creative, less surveiled workspace of mobility in which he works from funerals, bars, clubs, and queer sexual sites such as toilets via mobile telephony as much as from the office, and the straight bars and pubs which are explored by Vince in his workplace sociality. As a result of mobile phones and a morphic mobility, queerness cannot be contained in the Irigarayan sepulcher (Irigaray, 1985, pp. 143–144). Of course, queerness has never been fully contained in demarcated spaces: queerness itself starts off within the heteronormative family home, marks it, and returns more recently to dominate the representations of the normative domestic space through queer neoliberal coupledom (Cover, 2012b). However, less domesticated queer sexuality also occurs in the suburbs and other spaces routinely demarcated as straight, as facilitated by mobile telephony *via* sex-meeting applications such as Grindr (Raj, 2011). Mobile telephony as a network formation, has always been central to shifts in the intersection between queerness and space, even if the result is not necessarily liberatory but is implicated in a push away from community toward private domestic coupledom. While identity is very often foregrounded on a claim to be premised on the need for a physical space of one's own (Santos & Buzinde, 2007, p. 328), the representation of mobiles and hence mobility in *Queer as Folk* allows movement beyond the space of community, not as a means of establishing a networked "third space" (Soukup, 2006, pp. 422–423) but as a reconfiguration of the relationship between queerness and space itself into one marked by flows, accesses, affiliations, points, hubs, returns, and flexibilities.

This perspective on the contemporary modes by which identity is manufactured usefully applies to the conjunction between queer identity and queer community. Indeed, it demonstrates a contemporary mode of community that operates beyond Anderson's imagined community and naturalizes affective ties and identifications through manufacturing categories of identity and subjecthood. A mobile network morphology manufactures forms of identity and relationality, but it does so in ways that highlight the multiplicity of affiliations that can be mapped across relational *proximities* and *access*. In making such an application, we can see that belonging to community is active, rather than an assumed factor produced primarily by the self-articulation of being part of a category. That is, being a member of the queer community in *Queer as Folk* is processual and does not depend solely on an articulation or self-identification as queer. This is to differentiate, then, between identity that is produced through an articulation of similitude or membership of a category and the more complex elements of relationality understood through social participation and belonging. As Agamben (1995), drawing on Badiou, has pointed out, "inclusion always exceeds membership" (p. 25). The gap between self-perception of membership of a (marginal) category or identity of personhood and the capacity to belong or be included within the (marginal) community as the geographic or conceptual space of acceptance, overcoming isolation and refuge, is then a site of aspiration, necessary to the production of stable selves but always unevenly distributed (Appadurai, 2004). Aspiration here can be figured through the recognition of the self in relation to similitude with others. Subjects draw aspirations, then, in the context of seeing the lives, achievements, and goals of others. In the context of the representation of nonnormative sexual identity in *Queer as Folk*, then, what I am suggesting is that aspiration to belong is something which is not only processual but is articulated within and through the process of networking – a formula for the performativity of the young queer subject that is represented in the series through the metaphor of the mobile phone network.

In the series, Stuart is the figure of identification for Nathan, both sexually and in terms of coherent modes of performativity. In the first episode, Stuart mimics a *Titanic* posture on a rooftop, surveying Manchester, to announce himself "King of the World." In a network morphology reading, this is not necessarily the king of sovereign power but power in the microversion, it is to declare himself a pivotal node in a network of determinations, knowledge, gossip, and desire. Nathan, in the final scenes of the second series in which the fictional futures of each of the characters is captured on screen, is stated to have become "King of the World" and thereby not only to have usurped Stuart's position (traveling in the United States, Stuart is now absent from Manchester and the site of the network) but to have produced himself in Stuart's image. However, rather than looking at the performativity of Nathan as a direct replication of Stuart, an analysis grounded in a mobile network morphology calls on us to consider how his performative identity is located within the network. Nathan was not really desiring Stuart, or desiring to *be* Stuart – rather he desired the capacity to belong within the logic of the network at a point close to those pivotal hubs. While Nathan may not necessarily have understood this, it is his mother who comes to understand that the group is actually a network and, while out clubbing with Vince's mother, points this out to Stuart:

*Janice: Just keeping tabs on my son, that's all. If you're going out clubbing, Nathan's going out clubbing – His Master's Voice. ... Time was, Nathan thought you were boy-friend material. Now you're better than that – you're god.*

God, but again not in the sense of creator or sovereign – rather as being situated at the omniscient intersection of knowledge and life as a pivotal hub in the network which, to Nathan, represents perfection, community, communality, and intelligible subjectivity. God is not central in the logic of the network, neither is space nor territory nor identity. While in this net-work logic, decentralization is the network's primary characteristic, various points of substance – the nodes and the hubs – operate to govern, organize, receive, manage, and mechanize the multiplicities of flows (Castells, 2000, p. 385). To be king of the world is not to dominate or to possess the sovereign power to decide, but to be able to have unfettered access to the network, its knowledge, and its connectivity.

Indeed, Nathan's relationship with mobile technology demonstrates this movement toward becoming a nodal point in the network, shifting from his use of the semimobile cordless phone in the third episode of the first season, to his access and accessibility within a mobile network. Nathan is disappointed when Stuart hasn't appeared at his birthday party (his mother joking that he might appear by "satellite link," underlining the mobility of the central character of the mobile network). When Stuart does arrive, Nathan says to him casually: "You're late. Get me a present? You can get me a mobile phone if you want." Stuart, preoccupied with other issues includ-ing his intended departure from Manchester and an argument with Vince, ignores him at this point, leaving to find Vince, and repair the damage his actions have done to the network's affective flows. When Alexander hears that Stuart is leaving to move to London – aware that this will disrupt the network – it is he who calls Nathan to tell him that there is a drama, with the entire network brought together by mobile phone technology. But once Vince has convinced Stuart not to leave for London but, in fact, to go off traveling in the broader spatiality and mobility of the world, Stuart pulls out his mobile phone. He throws it over his shoulder to the approaching Na-than saying "Happy Birthday." The gift is not the gift of an electronic con-sumer device or a tool for access, but of having a certain position as a node within the network. Stuart indicates that after their travels he will return, insisting Nathan look after the city, the space (of flows), and the network. Vince tells him: "It's all yours now. Just stick with your friends and you'll be fine." That is, he tells him to remember the flows of relationality within the network and all will be well. Nathan is granted a place in the network, no longer precarious, having access within the metaphor of the process of mobility and the mobile phone. His identity is constituted in relationality with others, and it is the symbolic acquisition of the mobile phone that produces a sense of acceptance and, most importantly, self–acceptance within the network as proximate.

## 3.2  Exclusions and Disruptions: Proving the Robustness of the Mobile Network

During several episodes of the first season of *Queer as Folk*, Stuart and Vince spectacularly fall out when Cameron, a potential love interest for Vince, disrupts the network of relationships. The use of the mobile phone is central both to Vince's attention toward Cameron – as sponsored by Stuart, by Vince's mother, and by other characters – as well as the breaking of the network and Stuart's removal from it and his restoration to it in renewed affiliation. During Vince's first date with Cameron, Vince and Stuart are on their mobile phones with multiple calls waiting. Stuart has his colleague passing on a message to Martin Brookes, the client he is drinking with that night, while his sister complains about being stood up by him. Vince is chasing up Stuart to have someone look after Nathan who is out alone, and the calls move in multiple directions with Stuart's colleague attempting to get to Stuart through Vince, assuming they are in the same physical space. Cameron becomes frustrated: "Look, I hope you don't mind, but could you put it down just for a minute?" After a comic scene of the colleague and the sister talking to both Stuart and Vince and attempting to figure out who and where the client Martin Brookes is, Cameron intervenes with "Wait a minute, I know Martin Brookes, let me have a word." He takes Vince's phone, walks outside, and throws it into the water. Vince exclaims "Oy, that's my phone!" Cameron then kisses him and leaves, saying "Call me." "What with?" Vince calls after him. The act of throwing the mobile phone into the water begins the process of Cameron teasing Vince from out of his community network and out of the social spaces of queer life that he has stated he so dislikes in favor of coupled domesticity – an ongoing contemporary tension in queer representation (Cover, 2010).

The separation, however, is not complete. In the next episode (episode 6 of season 1), Stuart's secretary hand–delivers to Vince, at his workplace, a new mobile phone as a gift from Stuart, apparently claimed on insurance. The phone is ringing at the moment she hands it to him, even though Cameron is present, saying goodbye after a night together. Stuart's opening line is that the two of them have to go out, emblematic of the struggle between coupled domesticity with Cameron and belonging within the network of the queer community. Indeed, where Cameron is queer by virtue of LGBT membership, identity, and sexual orientation, Stuart and the network are the queered sites of social participation, care, and belonging, and Vince is caught in a struggle that plays out through the possession, representation, and use of mobile telephones. As Cameron seeks to dominate further in Vince's life he develops mechanisms to disrupt the flow of connectivity and relationality between Stuart and Vince, indeed by asking Vince to cut him off. He is beset by jealousies of the connectiveness between Stuart and Vince but can only understand that flow in the normative terms of romantic coupledom or sexual desire:

> Cameron: He's just waiting. He's been waiting so long he thinks he's happy. Being with you every day of his life is as close as he's going to get.
> Stuart: Close to what?
> Cameron: To the day you finally turn around and fuck him. And don't tell me you didn't know that. Leave him alone if you're any sort of a friend. Because there's no such thing as Vince. He doesn't exist on his own, you don't let him.

Cameron's demand that Stuart "leave him alone" is a demand that Stuart withdraw access and accessibility of the flow between the two identity nodes of Stuart and Vince. Yet he does not allow Vince a network, rather he seeks surreptitiously to push away the remaining characters, whether Vince's mother Hazel or young Nathan. Yet it is Nathan who facilitates the reconnection, having found that Stuart's self-identity is performatively disrupted by the disconnection. The reconnection with Stuart occurs most securely in episode 8 of season 1, once Vince becomes aware of Cameron's dominating attempt to prevent him from participating in the network. On a mobile call between the two of them, Vince complains of a noise in the door hinge of his new car and states that he will take it to his mother's gay lodger and close friend Bernie (within the network). Cameron says he doesn't trust Bernie: "I paid for the bloody thing, I'll take charge of it." Vince tests him by asking him to name all of the Doctor Who actors, an act which Stuart had done for him earlier that day. Cameron fails this test of the extent to which there is networked proximity through shared taste dismally: "What the hell does it matter?" Realizing that he must return to the flow of the network and overcome the blockage that is Cameron, for Vince the mobile phone becomes a metaphor of the network at its most explicit. Vince stands tall, stating "Sorry, what? It's breaking up. We're breaking up" and hangs up the phone, locking the keys to the Mini inside it in a refusal of accessibility, the locking off that particular node from his networked flow. The metaphor of the mobile call "breaking up" as an end to a brief relationship points powerfully to the networked logic of his affiliation with the other characters, an affiliation in which there is uncertainty, flexibility, and multiplicity of *types* of relationships.

Following Castells (2000), we might argue then that mobile telephony does not produce the weak ties of brief sexual engagement, acquaintanceship, spatial neighbourliness, or even social networking (so regularly accused of representing friendship in its weakest form and definition), but strong ties in the sense that access to a mobile number and the capacity to screen it is a marked distinction from online networks (p. 389). To be *within* the mobile network means to have access and connectivity. Identity here is produced and elaborated in terms of a network logic where nodes and flows of relationality are "resonant with meaning through its connections with selected others" (Livingstone, 2008, p. 403), and provide the discursive and relational resources that make (queer) subjects intelligible, coherent, and recognizable to one another. Here, relationality plays out through mobility and the mobile network. When Nathan decides surreptitiously to encourage Vince to reconnect, it is because he realizes not only that Vince's identity is performatively constituted through the network in which Stuart is a nodal point in proximity as beyond-family, beyond-friend, beyond-lover, but because Nathan's own identity is premised on the stability of proximity to the two men in the network. His own node requires this. Nathan, as facilitator, becomes the connective point between the two characters, inserted permanently into the network. Thus, when Vince calls Stuart to reconnect, it is on their two mobile phones. Stuart does not immediately answer it, and says nothing, but afterward in a longing for a restoration of networked normativity, they are both depicted staring at their individual mobile phones. It becomes clear, here, that mobile telephony is not only the increasingly used everyday form of communication, but is pivotal in the interrelationships between people, in the key moments of connection and confrontation that characterize the contemporary (and sometimes queer) network formation of belonging that supersedes the figuration of belonging through community and similitude of identity.

The example I have been discussing here is a fictional account of the production of identities in the context of mobile networks facilitated by earlier forms of technology that predate the smartphone and the tablet as devices of über-connectivity, and demonstrates how mobile networks may facilitate the relational constitution of identity within a marginal community framework. More recently, the expansion and proliferation of both devices and numbers of users has seen this model mainstreamed such that the manifold forms of connection a subject might build through friendships, peers, kinship, families, work colleagues, and others result in, for each of us, a series of networks in which our own positionality may differ in terms of proximities to others as nodal points and also proximities to those who serve as important hubs within our networks. It is thus significant that these devices allow connectivity across not only space but time through the increased capacity to remain connected – for example, to be persistently capable of both transmitting and receiving information, updates, and knowledge that sustain connectivities across Twitter feeds (as one application of mobile connectivity among many others). A subject's performativity is produced through the citation of discursively given intelligibilities of identity, and those intelligibilities, coherences, and disruptions now come across the mobile network at a ferocious speed. The result of this is that at one level there is more information capable of disrupting the stability of identity, giving rise to new coordinates of identity that allow us to have persistently renewed sensibilities of who we are. At the same time, however, the fact that this information flows to us – no matter where we are – through networks of mobility and networks of relationality allows a particular framework for the maintenance of identity through the stability of the network. It is important to bear in mind that the very basis of a network is that a node can be removed without the network itself falling apart, with flows able to find alternative pathways. As such, in the context of the communities and relationships that define us, there is likewise an added stability that results from the efficiency of the network in stark contrast to the potential disruptions of persistent information overload.

## 4 MOBILE ASSEMBLAGES, MOBILITIES, AND THE PUBLIC/PRIVATE DISTINCTION

While the framework of understanding identity, in the context of networks as the successor to community as the principal formation of communicative and associative relationality, has been described above in the context of televisual representations of LGBT minority subjects as early adopters, this approach to understanding identity through spatial relations remains intact as we move into the digital realms of Web 2.0's networking of sociality and Web 3.0's über-connectivity of nonplace-located storage, programming, and the Internet of things. Here it is important to question what it means to be connected to others communicatively while mobile. Connectivity through ready access that is beyond Castells' network morphology has had a substantial impact on how the performativity of identity is done, not only by changing how relationalities occur, but by ensuring those relationalities are available through communication ubiquitously across time. That is, a subject is reframed as a mobile subject by virtue of being able to connect with and communicate with others, to seek information, not merely at any place when being mobile but in terms of *saving* time or, at least, no longer having to factor in time to *get to the site of a communication device* (such as a landline or a desktop computer). A subject can be accessing the subjects of one's relational community that, in effect, constitute and give meaning to that subject's identity, without necessarily being anchored to place and, instead, drifting through and across multiple temporal zones, "existing, intersecting and unsettling one another" (Willson, 2012, p. 326) by virtue of constant connectivity without delay. Meyrowitz (1997) notes that electronic media, referring predominantly to the television, radio, telephone, and the introduction of portable music in the form of car stereos and the Sony Walkman tape player, "destroy the specialness of place and time" (p. 49). However, there are three ways available to help us make sense of what it means for identity performativity when the specialness of place and time are no longer the constitutive factors of self-hood: the relationship between subjects and mobiles as assemblage, the mobility of information and the mobility of subjects in terms of both corporeal movement and social movement, and the refiguration of public and private. I now address these three in order.

## 4.1 Mobile Assemblages

In what ways can we understand the subject as *mobile* in the context of digital mobile technologies of constant connectivity? For Gerard Goggin (2009), relationality in the context of mobile media consumption can be understood as an assemblage, whereby mobile communications have played a role in the active reconfiguration and destabilization of some social relations and media practices. Assemblage here refers to the organization and stabilization of certain new kinds of social relations (p. 153). Goggin argues that while most forms of telecommunication, particularly landline telephony, have been constituted within national communications and media systems, the mobile phone is very much a telecommunication device of the urban environment. Unlike the globalizational and globalizing technologies of networked access to information and entertainment discussed in the Chapter 5, mobile telephony has a functionality in the city resulting from the technical limitations of range, the cellular arrangement of transmission and reception, and the ways in which the radio spectrum use is organized (p. 161). Indeed, we could take Goggin's point of the urban nature of mobiles a step further into the context of its position as a form of assemblage to think not only about how mobile connectivity might produce new relationalities, but how it might embed and sustain more nascent and pre-existing forms of urbanized subjectivity. Cities are, of course, sites of globalization and globalization's effect. Indeed, they have been characterized by Zygmunt Bauman (2011) as the dustbins of globalization (p. 428) whereby they are understood to be the site for the convergence of radically new relationalities produced by mobility and migration. Rather than engaging with the context of ethical relationalities, they are the space where problem relationalities are left to fester. This role in globalization means that they perform certain arrangements and configurations of the local in the context of local/global tensions and synergies. The mobile phone is figurative of this arrangement, whereby it serves to mediate (1) the facilitation of local real-time and recorded communication and relationality; (2) access to globalized information and broadly diverse discourses through functionality as a smartphone Internet device; and (3) the coordination of the subject *as* a corporeal body in the context of urban locationality.

Similar to Goggin's framing of mobiles as technologies of assemblage, Elizabeth Grosz (1995) has pointed to the ways in which the body's reconceptualization within spatiotemporal locations of the contemporary city can be seen as an assemblage (p. 84). As noted in Chapter 4, the body–city linkage provides a parallel capacity to theorize the relationship between communication technologies and identity. For Grosz, the city comes to mean the complex, interactive setting that links together diverse social activities and processes, architecture, geography, and the public: it is a setting for the organization of power relations and, not unrelatedly, flows of information within a built environment that is both semipermanent and persistently changing. In this way, bodies and cities are mutually defining and relational, with the urban configuration providing an order and organization that actively links otherwise unrelated bodies (pp. 103–104). If we factor in the mobile telephone as a technology of corporeality – always in hand or as what John Urry (2007) describes as a prosthetic, always physically coterminous with the body and thereby always connected to a sense of corporeal subjectivity (p. 176) – we can understand the mobile network serving as an additional layer of assemblage in the city, providing a new stratum of routes, connectivities, relationalities, but not in a way that is radically different or disconnected from the city's pre-existing routes and connections. Rather, the mobile network is highly connected and integrated, operating on the model of the urban environment as an assemblage of bodies, place, and space. Here, then, the mobile network both facilitates new perceptions of subjectivities built on relationality and becomes part of them. It is not just embedded in everyday domestic and public activities, but is actively involved in the ways in which the corporeal subject is materialized into particular kinds of bodies that do particular kinds of things (i.e., they engage with each other in particular ways with particular gestures). Georg Simmel (2002), in his 1903 essay, The Metropolis and Mental Life, found the city to be the site of objective, impersonal, and instrumental relations lacking connectivity and deep emotional investment. However, not only is the city a site of corporeal and informational flows, the mobile phone – as a technology of assemblage which brings together the local, the global, the corporeal, and the informational while cementing the network of strong ties – points to the evolution of the city not as impersonal and instrumental but as a space in which deep relational engagement occurs. Much like the city, the mobile phone thus participates in the materialization of particular kinds of identities that may, on the surface, appear disconnected but that, instead, have intense forms of regular, always available connectivity. This connectedness between relational subjects, then, can be understood not in contrast with the impersonal nature of cities but as fruition of the city "process."

## 4.2  Sociality and the Mobility Turn

The "mobility turn" in the social sciences has produced important literature that provides a slightly different angle on the conceptualization of identities in the context of mobile communication and digital media technologies and which builds upon but differs from the above argument for mobiles as technologies of assemblage in the body–city compact. According to Urry (2007), there are a number of different senses of the use of the terms "mobile" and "mobility," including, first, to mean that which moves or is capable of movement – objects and things of portability, including but not limited to the mobile phone as device (p. 7). Second, it refers to the notion of a *mob*, being a rabble or unruly crowd. This kind of crowd is understood as disorderly "precisely because it is mobile, not fully fixed within boundaries and therefore needs to be tracked and socially-regulated" (p. 8). In this context, Urry finds an increasing public perception of the contemporary world as one more and more beset by dangerous multitudes requiring additional governance. Third, mobility is used in contemporary discourse in the context of upward and downward (vertical) social mobility, whereby a subject's status shifts in contrast with that of the subject's parents' position (p. 8). Fourth, mobility is used to refer to longer term formations of migration as well as both temporary and semipermanent geographical movement (p. 8). Finally, mobility refers to the perception and examination of transport, the transporting of people and information, the communication of messages and images, and the convergence of these different factors (pp. 8–9). The mobility turn, then, revolutionizes how social science and sociology are undertaken, requiring a wholesale revision of how social connectivities are rendered and how they have been historically examined (p. 44).

Urry points to the ways in which the iPod has helped to reorganize the sounds of the city (p. 77). This occurs in ways which, as a mobile device, the iPod, among other devices of portable sound, makes it possible for subjects to customize their exposure to the audible world, thereby controlling the discursivity and sign systems encountered that lend their availability to the citation of performative selfhood. The contemporary formation of the subject is one framed by the commodification of mobility and the growth of technologies and lifestyles that, on the one hand, facilitate movement in public space but, on the other, make it possible to engage with subjectivity separate from the sounds, voices, visuals, and ideas of the public/private. I will come back to the ways in which this effectively breaks down or complexifies some elements of the public/private distinction, although it can be said at this point that recent transformations in accessible and mobile technologies reorganize the sites, places, temporalities, and spatial arrangements that – even in the act of walking in the city – produce new subjectivities potentially different from those of earlier technologies of communication. The interconnection between mobility in terms of movement and mobility in terms of accessible communication, information, and media is an important one that operates across the standards, patterns, and stereotypes of performative self-hood such that it at once opens new ways of being and, simultaneously, reduces the capacity to encounter new, unfamiliar, mundane, or other elements of a population-built environment.

There are other forms of mobility relevant to thinking about the contemporary conditions of mobile network cultures beyond those of the bodies, technologies, and regimes that facilitate their movement in space. Thomas Faist (2013) has noted that there is substantial potential in bringing together different forms of mobility for analysis. These, in Faist's conceptualization, include spatial mobility as well as the upward shift in class, education, affluence, and status commonly referred to in policy analysis as social mobility. This is significant in helping us come to an understanding of the corporeal and relational place of subjects in the context of making relational identities traditional on the margins as forging, solidifying, and maintaining connectivities that produce community and resilience. Social mobility is the shift in social status of groups, communities, cultures, and populations measured by education, affluence, health status, literacy rates, employment types, and/or education (Borgatta & Montgomery, 2000, p. 2711). Regularly discussed in generational terms, social mobility frames the aspiration to belong to a superior class or socioeconomic demarcation than one's forebears, often articulated through the ways in which childhood education, location, and financial choices are deliberately structured in order to produce intergenerational progress (Lareau, 2003). Environmental structuring can depend on the capacity for spatial mobility, resulting in the common assumption that migrants move countries and join particular Western, industrialized populations (in residency or citizenship) in order to produce a "better life" for one's children. However, it should always be borne in mind that there are a number of disjunctures in terms of who is authorized to aspire to mobility when both the spatial and social forms of mobility do not work in tandem according to contemporary assumptions. Problematic here, of course, is the fact that within neoliberal regimes, it is the very technologies of social connectivity that come to serve as conspicuous consumer commodities, utilized for social mobility in economic terms and as signifiers of social space. These, then, serve to reduce the capacity to aspire for others who cannot access such technological services of connectivity in economic terms.

## 4.3 Mobility across the Public/Private

The public/private binary is a significant ideological node, a point in a set of beliefs and practices governing the ways in which we think, for example, about communication, self-articulation, representation, and privacy. The aim here is not to undo the public/private dichotomy altogether, but to suggest that there are alternative cultural factors which come into play in how we might understand the public/private division as it underpins the ethical questions surrounding surveillance, invasions of privacy, crossing of thresholds, and the making of identities in the context of mobilities that move through twentieth century spheres of domestic and spatial engagement. One that is worth mentioning, because it reflects the increasing complexity of public/private brought about by mobile technologies of connectivity, can be found in a critique on the semiotics of privacy by theorist Susan Gal (2002). Here, the distinction between public and private is not only correlative, thus never providing stable "spheres of activity, or even types of interaction" (p. 80), but can also be articulated as a "fractal distinction." By this, Gal means that the public/private is a pattern that occurs repeatedly *within* each of the two terms and multiplies within those divisions also (p. 81). As Gal puts it:

> Whatever the local, historically specific content of the dichotomy, the distinction between public and private can be reproduced repeatedly by projecting it onto narrower contexts or broader ones. Or, it can be projected onto different social 'objects' – activities, identities, institutions, spaces and interactions – that can be further categorized into private and public parts. Then, through recursivity (and recalibration), each of these parts can be recategorized again, by the same public/private distinction. It is crucial that such calibrations are always relative positions and not properties laminated on the persons, objects, or spaces concerned (p. 81).

This analysis of the distinction suggests that rather than accepting the distinction as wholly collapsed and given that attempting to use ethical approaches to determine what behaviors, attitudes, expressions, or rituals of identity articulation should or should not belong in the public sphere leaves the distinction intact, we should look to new, productive possibilities for understanding how identity is constituted in relation to place, home, and sociality.

Such fractal understandings of public/private are witnessed in some of the shifts seen in recent interactive applications – Facebook, Livejournal, and other sites – which allow users to render their contributions private or restricted to only a set of chosen users (Hodkinson & Lincoln, 2008, p. 32), thereby overcoming some of the emergent cultural issues related to younger persons' use of online media. At one level, then, any play by a person with a public/private sensibility by, for example, uploading a privately owned and personally meaningful digital image taken in a public space, occurs not in the context of a free-for-all dissolution of privacy, but in a more complex, finely tuned, individualized, and customizable framework for being a subject as a particular kind of *private subject*. However, privacy restriction affordances have not, on the whole, produced a broad culture of what we might think of as nuanced privacy. Rather, whole groups of people – sometimes for reasons of taste, politics, or their own personal take on the meaning of privacy – embrace nonrestrictive digital media sites (such as Twitter and Tumblr) for the regular uploading of images taken on mobile devices. Nevertheless, the complexity of contemporary fractal arrangements of public/private continue to produce certain kinds of performativities with regard to privacy, including the articulation of the self in terms of unwanted exposure.

This sense of vulnerability has come to be a part of contemporary characterizations of privacy, for example, in danah boyd's (2008b) definition:

> ... privacy is not simply about the state of an inanimate object or set of bytes; it is about the sense of vulnerability that an individual experiences when negotiating data. Both Usenet and Facebook users felt exposed and/or invaded by the architectural shifts without having a good way of articulating why the feature made them feel 'icky' (p. 14).

The broad shifts in the meaning of privacy, and the embrace of its complexity, obliqueness, and the fractal nature of public/private distinctions occur in order to account for the more complex frameworks that come from having communication devices which are not limited to the domestic and the personal but which move with the body, in hand, from private space to public space, and from different spaces of the private, utilized in ways which dissolve the distinction of performative sensibilities of private selves and public selves. This is not, of course, to suggest that subjects no longer identify themselves through private and public articulations – the naked self, for example, remains broadly as private as it always has, with a handful of exceptions that occur within specific contexts or frames, such as streaking (Cover, 2003). Nor is it to argue that subjectivities are not articulated any longer through secrets, including secret attitudes, secret experiences, secret perceptions of the self. Rather, it points to the fact that the very sense of space as constitutive of subjectivity is no longer as clearly demarcated as public and private, and that activities that were once deemed private articulations or expressions (the phone call or viewing pornography) are not necessarily kept from public spaces (the noisy Skype call on a tablet or the sharing of pornography by friends on a train).

## 5  CONCLUSIONS: PERFORMATIVITY, IDENTITY, AND THE MOBILE NETWORK

Expanding on and complexifying the flows between different nodes and hubs in the network, Barabási (2011) demonstrates that these streams of communication cannot be understood as equal, evenly distributed, constant in speed, or attracted broadly in a sharing capacity. Rather, some nodes and hubs attract greater flows, but not because they are more attractive, rather as the result of what he refers to as "fitness":

> Fitness is the node's ability to attract links. It's not the likelihood of finding a Web page, but rather once you've found a Web page, it's the probability that you will connect to it. It's not the chance of running into a person. But once you've met the

*person, will you want to see him or her again? Thus, fitness is the ability to attract links after these random encounters. To model the impact of fitness, we assign a parameter for each node which represents its ability to compete for links. You can build it into preferential attachment, because now the likelihood that you will connect to a certain node is the product of the fitness and the number of links. The number of links is there because it tells us how easy it is to find the node. If a node is very highly connected, it is easy to bump into it. But the fitness tells me the likelihood that I will actually link to it, once I find it (Barabási, 2011, pp. 9–10).*

From the perspective of a subjectivity removed from the fixed community of place and, instead, built on relationalities and relationships of communicativeness and ethical encounter, it is possible to see that it is not a matter of similitude and difference, of closeness or distance, but relates to a host of other qualities that make that relationship a relationship. Important, here, is that in the conceptualization of a mobile network where the nodes and hubs are not fixed places but are subjects and subject-like devices, encounters *may* follow certain patterns of normative attraction and attractiveness, but for any one communicative flow, these patterns are built on an array of fitness determined differentially.

Bearing in mind that such technologies also produce new ways of placing ourselves under surveillance, it is important to acknowledge that identity is not formed merely through relationalities that stabilize across a network in contrast with the persistent disruption to identity that comes with increased flow of information and discourse. Rather, the fact of being connectively available requires that we are under increased surveillance, and that is something that we embrace to some extent willingly as a kind of payment for the benefits of relational mobility. Geotagging, being able to be found, announcing online without realizing when we enter a particular shop or restaurant and, by corollary, tweeting information that might once have been thought to be private (e.g., what we have eaten), becomes simultaneously an aspect of how we are constituted and how we articulate identity in a contemporary era.

## CHAPTER 7

# Online Selves: Digital Addiction

Moral panics around compulsive and addictive use of digital media have emerged every few years since the mid-1990s, building on older discourses around obsessive television viewing (and the social problem of the identifiable figure of the couch potato). Increasingly, public sphere issues reporting focuses on the imagination of Internet and gaming addiction, as well as crossing into various newer platforms of digital communication, most recently addiction to mobile devices. The release of Kimberly Young's pop psychology text *Caught in the Net: How to Recognize the Signs of Internet Addiction — and a Winning Strategy for Recovery* in 1998 caused a considerable media flurry about overuse of the Internet and a number of public confessions of Internet addiction. Popular and news media representations of digital addiction draw significantly on media releases regarding academic research which, for the most part, is conducted in certain narrow formations within the fields of psychology, information technology, and educational pedagogy departments. Several writers have supported or extended Young's initial work, although others have used psychodynamic research methods to suggest that there is nothing specifically addictive about digital gaming as an activity (Egli & Meyers, 1984). Some behaviorist research has sought to show a link between Internet or video-gaming addiction and problems of self-esteem or multiply addictive personalities (Greenberg, Lewis, & Dodd, 1999). And still others have outrightly refuted the concept of digital addiction or the value in drawing parallels between chemical drugs and substantial time spent online. Nevertheless, the idea of an addictiveness produced through individual exposure to digital, online, and mobile communication persists in moral panic reporting and anti-Internet opinion writing that evokes a prenetwork and presmartphone nostalgia for certain kinds of behaviors and cultural forms. This discourse of digital addiction has, then, had the effect of producing a new kind of self: an identity characteristic and set of concomitant behaviors and attributes that can be referred to as the "digital addict."

In 2005 a South Korean couple were arrested after their child, aged 4 months, died after being left alone at home while they left to play *World of Warcraft* at an Internet café (Moses, 2009). An example such as this is, of

*Digital Identities.*
http://dx.doi.org/10.1016/B978-0-12-420083-8.00007-9

course, contrary to panic claims that online activity and obsessive or addictive online behavior isolates subjects or makes heavy users hermits incapable of engaging with others in face-to-face settings (e.g., Technology, 2009), instead pointing to the important fact that gaming and other online entertainment are social activities that are, indeed, sometimes conducted in highly social public spaces and settings. However, the formation of moral panic results often in policy responses that seek to target and remove – rather than investigate – the situation of a scandal or incident (Cover, 2015). This is why responses to the South Korean incident resulted in a prime minister's initiative to provide free software designed to limit the amount of time spent online. Estimating that South Korea had two million web addicts, it planned software designed either to shut down connectivity after a predetermined time (set by a parent, guardian, or user) or another designed to make "games harder as time goes by so that the player becomes bored" (South Korea Takes up Arms Against Web Addiction, 2010). Digital addiction stories such as this likewise produce public community responses such as Digital Detox Week (run by the group Adbusters) and the challenge sponsored by the *Huffington Post* called Unplug and Recharge, both of which have been described as necessary responses to those who have begun using wireless connectivity to get a fix of digital time in settings away from the more traditional desktop computer (Pryor, 2010). Stories of parents attempting to gain police intervention by calling 911 to help stop a teenaged son playing computer games all night have emerged, including in one case from Boston where police were needed to persuade a 14-year-old boy to obey his mother and spend less time playing digital games (Mum Calls 911, 2009). At other times, more strenuous measures are adopted such as in China where rehabilitation bootcamps were operating in the late 2010s designed to cure Internet addiction – in some cases with punishments so harsh that teenaged participants have been beaten to death (Senshan, 2009). Also in China, it has been reported that psychologists and mental health hospitals have used electric shock therapy "to cure youths of Internet addiction," with obvious public questions over whether or not there is any scientific evidence of the value of such severe methods (China Halts Shock Therapy, 2009). Similar camps and rehabilitation centers have appeared in other parts of the world, including a residential treatment center for Internet addiction located in Seattle in the United States (2009). In such cases, digital addiction is reported as a "threat" to young people or to populations more broadly, either articulating it as an individual pathology or reporting very high figures of so-called Internet addiction as a social problem. In both cases, however, it amounts to a particular kind of labeling or articulation of *time spent using digital media*. This is a culturally produced activity for which, following LaRose, Kim, and Peng (2011, p. 74), we need always to work actively to ensure that uses of digital connectivity that are time consuming, habitual, regular, or engaged are not necessarily problematic behaviors. Due to the nature of digital connectivity when viewed through some more conservative prisms that dictate how people should best relate, there is a tendency to see digital connectivity as generally problematic, particularly producing risks to the self, to the young, and to society more broadly – that is, moral panic discourse.

Thinking about online time as being time that one is at risk of becoming addicted involves problematic concepts which label digital media use as addictive and, more problematically, label those who spend large amounts of time engaged in on-screen activities, gaming, socializing online, or reading on-screen rather than on paper under the identity category banner of "digital addicts." This concept operates across governance policy, moral panic, community intervention and the interpellation of subjects who begin to see themselves as digital addicts. This is a case in which we witness the emergence of a new identity category or label and concomitant identity attributes as a direct result of widespread responses to the uptake of newer digital technologies and tools. The identity label emerges at the intersection of a range of discourses – the conditions necessary to produce the very *idea* of the digital addict as a subject more than just a behavior – and these discourses include the ways in which digital media are perceived as somehow like a drug or as a dark, murky, dangerous, and risky world, as well as through stereotypes, particularly of youth, of avid gamers, and of those whose social activities occur online or are face-to-face but enhanced by digital, mobile, and on-screen engagement. The murkiness of the online world is often articulated through associating a small number of tragic examples of outcomes of digital media use with the fact that a large number of younger persons (available to be categorized as being at risk of all sorts of terrible outcomes) are perceived as being heavy users. Unpacking these discourses by investigating their historical and conceptual development is an important aspect in studying online identity and in making sense of the ways in which such subjectivities as the digital addict are produced. While to many users (whether light or heavy, professional or excessive users) the very idea of the digital addict is an absurd one, it has clearly been taken up against many of the realities of Internet use that include simply the fact that time spent communicating online is increasing not as a threat or a risk to reality but in the same way takeup of the radio, television, and telephone had occurred (likewise without harmful side-effects). As Nicola Johnson (2009) has cogently pointed out, heavy use is not an addiction, nor is it addictive; rather the discourse of computer addiction suggests that "as twenty-first century participants, [we] are dependent on technologies because they make our lives easier and we prefer to use them rather than not" (p. 4).

Whether digital games or Internet use can, indeed, *cause* addiction remains a moot point from the perspective of media and cultural theory, partly because it replicates media effects and a technologically determinist understanding of the relationship between behavior and new media, and partly because it represents the individual utilization of both digital games and Internet as level and homogenic. However, one aspect at play here is the insistence that online, mobile, and gaming platform use is an engagement with a kind of popular "low culture" in opposition to "high art." The distinction between high culture and popular culture emerged in the latter half of the nineteenth century as part of a series of classifications that produces a social boundary between different kinds of activities, texts, artforms and, ultimately, classes (Storey, 2003, pp. 32, 33). The dichotomy, of course, is mythical in that there is no logical boundary between different kinds of cultural practices, productions, textual/communication forms, and art, only an arbitrary set of distinctions that, at times, is built on taste and determined by those who have the social and cultural capital to produce and circulate opinions on appropriate and inappropriate cultural forms. Here, digital addiction is productively activated as a way of explaining the heavy use of online and mobile communication and gaming media by virtue not of a particular kind of behavior but in the context of its distinction from what, in elite terms, is labeled, understood, and spoken about as proper behavior, particularly for young people. For example, no one today would speak of a heavy, avid reader of novels as a literature addict. Nor, today, would there be a panic if it were revealed that a large number of schoolchildren were actively spending a great deal of after-school time reading the poetry of Wordsworth (presumably as a homework assignment, and regardless of whether it is read on printed paper or on an electronic book reader device). Young men and women who play football for many hours every weekend are not considered sports addicts. Residual and archaic activities that consume time might be considered eccentric affectations (e.g., knitting), but no ardent knitter is considered an addict with the same kind of scorn, parental concern, psychiatric investigation, policy prevention, or urgent techniques of intervention is devoted to the identity figure of the digital addict and the figure of youth who is, today, seen to be persistently on the verge of addiction to on-screen activities.

Part of this results from the still-nascent nature of digital communication, media, and gaming activities within the broader framework of contemporary culture. To say this is to refer to culture not only as the textual and artistic output of a society (high art, low culture, popular culture, or mass culture in terms of actual texts that can be read and viewed) but as the whole lived experience of those of us who engage regularly and at great devotion of time in the use of digital communication. For Williams (1976), culture is understood as a complete way of life for an identifiable group of people (pp. 80, 81), although it is not static and unchanging, despite the common claims to, say, British culture or working class culture or ethnic culture; rather it is always a process (Williams, 1981, p. 10). Structures of feeling is a concept used to understand the ways in which a culture is operating at a particular historical moment, which includes common perceptions and values articulated in politics, art, media, textuality, and forms of communication. Within the structures of feeling of a particular society is Williams' articulation of "dominant, residual and emergent" elements that operate as stresses and tensions in the context of culture as a persistent process of change. What is dominant in a culture is that which occurs through hegemonic processes. Contemporary late capitalism, neoliberalism, an ethic of work and − importantly for this study − cosmopolitan white-collar consumer masculinity can be considered elements of the dominant. The emergent refers to new meanings, values, practices, and relationships that are continually being created, not as an isolated process for they emerge from within culture but may be oppositional to that which is dominant or hegemonic even though they are often incorporated into it as the most direct means by which dominance maintains itself against the visibility of alternative and oppositional elements (Williams, 1977, p. 124). Here, it is not simply digital communication, gaming, or the Internet that is emergent but the uses, practices, attitudes, and ideas that emerge in ways which include very large amounts of time spent engaging with screens, interactive communication and play, and the production of online digital content. These emerge from within culture (not alien to it), but sit somewhat at odds from the dominant perspectives of cultural expectations on younger persons to develop and maintain patterns of the use of time in line with the norms established for older communication forms and media (e.g., from the landline telephone to television and books). Digital media and gaming are only available as targets for panics around addictive behavior *because* they are emergent, not because there is anything inherently addictive about the technologies or practices, nor because those who spend long hours in these pursuits are in any way addicted.

This is not to suggest that there are not problematic compulsive or obsessive behaviors in relation to online use ("Net addicts," 2009) – there are with any activities, for example from those who feel compelled to clean themselves obsessively in a way which interferes with normative everyday social and labor engagement to those who feel they can only function after knitting for several hours to those who jog or run far more than their bodies can safely handle. The repetitive activity of some kinds of digital media use, such as gaming, in addition to the possibilities that, for some, the production of adrenalin through gaming helps one to feel valuable in oneself – running and jogging can do this too (Elliott, 2014) – are factors that can produce the *idea* of digital addiction (Walters, 2009). However, the one real difference between claiming that there are millions of digital addicts and that a very small number of people demonstrate genuinely compulsive behaviors is that, for the latter, the technology and that activity are not in themselves causal of addictive behaviors in the way that a drug that chemically enhances mood (such as a cigarette) is genuinely addictive. It is important to bear in mind that the American Psychiatric Association's 2013 release of the codification of disorders in *The Diagnostic and Statistical Manual of Mental Disorders, Fifth Edition* (DSM-5) did not include Internet addiction despite calls for its inclusion. Rather, it created in this update a new category for behavioral addictions and listed gambling as its only disorder. It was decided that Internet addiction be listed in the appendix to the DSM-5 in order to encourage further study without preempting research findings by describing it as an official addiction (Fairburn, Lane, Mataix-Cols, Tian, Grant, & Von Deneen, 2013). Problematic overall, of course, is that digital addiction is produced as a concept based on a myth that normal behavior involves limited time engaging interactively or via a computer screen, and that therefore those who do spend a great deal of time (because it is enjoyable or productive) are identifiable as – and have the identity of – digital addicts.

To some extent, public discourse writing on digital addiction articulates addictiveness through broad statistical uptake of new media technologies, often relating the concept of addiction to ubiquity. Much of this in recent years has been associated with the uptake of mobile phones and smartphones and the extent to which they are used for web-based activities such as social networking; often these are given in the number of hours an average person reports use of the device for these purposes (Wray, 2008) or the numbers of members of a specific population – typically a national population – who have begun using social networking in a given period (Moses, 2012), or focus on the assumed pitfalls of substantial market penetration of smartphones and wireless connectivity (Galvin, 2012). At other times, it relates to Internet use in general and the idea that all online activity is somehow likely to lead to a loss of productivity for industry and the labor force generally and/or problems managing work/life balance (Lucas & Schneiders, 2013). Most articulations of digital addiction, however, focus on the figure of the individual addict as an at-risk younger person, spinning the narrative outward to argue that all young people, and therefore the future of humanity, are at substantial risk of becoming mindless addicts of digital communication. This is not, of course, wholly uncontested in public discourse as, at other times, the very idea of the digital addict has been caricatured or mocked in the press, indicating the ways in which the conservative articulation of a problematic digital media user is out of step with broader community understandings of the ways in which technology enhances sociality, the manner in which they are used excessively but not necessarily problematically, and the potential of networked digital com-munication for healthy entertainment, productive engagement, work, and relationships.

I am arguing here that digital media forms are by no means addictive in and of themselves, and that the representation of digital cultural products as addictive relates to understandings that attempt to *install* digital media within arguments that support an artificial divide between the real and the virtual, or the natural and the technological. The assertion that new media are addictive is produced in such a way that the conceptual and imagina-tive spaces of both games and various Internet documents and activities are given as unknown, dangerous, unsafe, or menacing with strong similarity to the discursive representation of chemical drugs. Such a connection be-tween digital relationality and drugs is obviously tending toward the absurd, despite the one slightly comic scenario of the "i-dose" phenomenon in which a downloadable audio file was marketed in 2010 as a digital form of methamphetamine, cocaine, crack, and heroin, whereby users were duped into paying as much as USD $2000 on the false premise that listening to the file would provide a drug-like high (Hearn, 2010b). While there is no doubt that there are some social problems associated with spending exces-sive time online or in compulsive use of digital gaming (whether solo, with others physically present, or in online gaming), problematic behavior online has more to do with excessive sociality than with viewing, understanding, or relating digital communication, games, and media to the mythical über-addictive drug. As John Grohol (2000) neatly puts it: "Socializing with a friend, reading a book, work, and watching television are [also] all activities which people enjoy but sometimes take to an extreme" (p. 140). It is the *specificity* of digital worlds as they are imagined in popular culture, news media, and certain strands of academic egopsychology discourses that provides digital environments with a set of significations making them, on the one hand, somehow less than real (virtual) and, on the other, hyperreal negative environments which are understood to be addictive in and of themselves.

I want to discuss, first, the processes and politics of *producing* a new identity figure in the form of the supposed digital addict as a new coordinate of performativity that is imposed through discursive deployment of frames of expertise and normativity and that, through surveillance and moral panic, interpellates some heavy users to see themselves as being addicted selves. I would then like to consider some of the ways in which digital addiction has been represented in academic and media discourses, and particularly in the pop psychology of online addiction guru Kimberly Young (1997, 1998, 2003). I will follow with an examination of the rhetoric of digital-gaming addiction that collapses the question of frequency of use with addiction, violence, play, competitiveness, tension, and questions of the loss of the self. Finally, drawing on an interview given by Jacques Derrida on drug addiction I show how the meaning of talk and debate *about* addiction works to represent *all* digital (as opposed to traditional) communication, games, and Internet as purely simulacral, unreal, and unnatural, thereby locating them together in an unproductive and undertheorized real/virtual dichotomy. I am particularly interested in dealing together with two representations of digital addiction (Internet and digital gaming) which are most often separated in both academic and popular discourses of new media use, neither because the concepts and rhetoric supporting these representations are easily collapsed, nor because they amount to the same thing, but because they both work in similar ways to establish digital and interactive media as forming virtual worlds that are equated with the conceptual unreality of physical drug use.

## 1 THE DICTION OF ADDICTION

According to Anne Federwisch (1997), the first identification of the phenomenon of "cyber addiction" was made by New York psychiatrist Ivan Goldberg who identified groups of people abandoning family obligations to stare at the computer screen. While Goldberg's statement was a spoof on contemporary North American culture's fascination with addictive behaviors (Federwisch, 1997), the idea of Internet and digital-gaming addictions soon became a field of debate at a number of levels – including academic research, popular cultural production, judicial institutions, and news media. Goldberg's joke has been transformed into a number of discursive formations that weave together the digital and the behavioral. What the identification of digital addiction does, effectively, is apply a set of connotations under the drug-related signifier "addict" to a new set of behaviors, usually having no special or direct relationship with drugs (whether legal or illicit) or alcohol. Sex addiction, gambling addiction, workaholism, addictions to serial monogamy, addictions to violence or physical exercise, and compulsive eating have all been identified under the singular signifier addiction, and usually in such a way that reduces a set of *frequent* and/or *unusually excessive* activities to a single form and cause, relegating the object that is utilized compulsively to a danger, an unknown or a moral concern. The use of new media forms, particularly aspects of Internet use and digital games have likewise been subject to this identification in what appears to be a continued "netting" of behaviors under this one signifier.

Chemical drug addiction is often associated with moral disorder, a physical failing, a social failing, a bodily disease the symptom of which is substance abuse, (the view adopted by Alcoholics Anonymous who evoke the figure of the forever recovering alcoholic) or as an infectious disease that must be contained or monitored for fear of spreading addiction from one body to another (Lart, 1998, p. 61). It is variously one or several of these concepts that are used in the rhetoric of digital addiction to produce the figure of the frequent Internet user or game player as *an addict*. Often this is seen simultaneously as a psychological disorder and in the terms of a model in which addiction is determined by that to which one is addicted – digital media in this case (e.g., Holliday, 2000, p. 10).

While I do not have the necessary disciplinary expertise to engage fully with a neurological scientific account, I would like here to give a brief description of drug dependence in the physical context (what was formerly referred to typically as physical drug addiction) in order to demonstrate some of the ways in which it differs from both popular cultural representations of drug abuse and from the discourses of addiction as applied to nondrug activity such as gaming and mobile phone and Internet use. The body's drug receptors are molecules present at the cellular level to which a drug combines and mediates its effect. Certain physical drugs (both natural and chemically produced) alter the ability of nerve cells to fire and produce various body chemicals associated with pleasure. Different drugs are understood to react with different receptors, for example, specific opiate receptors in the case of opioid drugs. Drugs are eventually metabolized by the body, broken down by enzymes in the liver or bloodstream, and flushed from the body through urine or sweat. Although biological accounts of addiction to most chemical drugs agree that biologic, psychosocial, and cultural variables need to be taken into account, prolonged use of drugs is predominantly understood to alter permanently the system of receptors such that persistent use is necessary for receptor function (Zweben & Payte, 1990). This account is merely one particular narrative or language of addiction and, from the perspective of cultural theory, none of this is to suggest that what constitutes a drug is necessarily clear or final, nor that biological responses to drug-like substances are universal or necessarily will ever be fully mapped. That is, there is a substantial difference between externally sponsored addiction through the drug that comes into the body and fosters the production of dopamine, and behaviors which are enjoyable, productive, and/or habit-forming and which demand or result in large amounts of time devotion to those behaviors (e.g., playing games and interacting socially online or through mobile devices).

Much of the problem with the application of drug rhetoric to digital media is that it fails either to take into account the more nuanced neurobiological narratives around the permanent and physical alteration of the body's receptors, or to query how the very notion of drug *can* be applied to digital media. Young, whose widely distributed and frequently cited study *Caught in the Net* (1998) is a popular example of moral panic writing, utilizes the pop rhetoric of chemical drug addiction and, indeed, modeled her clinical framework for Internet addiction on examples of dependency on psychoactive substances without criticizing the distinction between an injection or infusion of chemicals and the activity of engaging with others online (Griffiths, 1998, p. 68). Her writing is filled with comparisons reductively suggesting that Internet addiction is not different from "alcoholism, chemical dependency, or addictions like gambling and overeating" (Young, 1998, p. 7). Young explains an apparent frequent use of the Internet by undergraduate students in her study as the result of a higher legal drinking age (21 in parts of the United States), suggesting that the Internet becomes a "substitute drug of choice: no ID required and no closing hour" (Young, 2003). She refers to Internet addiction as an epidemic (Young, 1998, p. 5), much as the moral panics around drug use among youth invoke concepts of spread, contamination, and conformity. She also suggests that Internet users experience various "mood states derived from such on-line stimulation [ranging] from reduced loneliness, improved self-esteem, and euphoria" (Young, 1997). Importantly, Young does recognize that this is the application of addiction rhetoric to a nondrug dependence phenomenon. However, rather than establishing too close a set of parallels between the Internet as "drug" and drugs themselves, she works through a notion of addictive behavior, drawing on previous writings which have looked for commonalities between chemical drug dependence and habits such as compulsive gambling, chronic overeating, sexual compulsion, and obsessive television viewing. For Young (1998), it is the feeling experienced that is addictive rather than the digital media itself (p. 17). However, in relying on a pedestrian account of technological determinism, her claim locates itself in an idea that exposure itself to the Internet is the root *cause* of the addiction, much as two or three shots of heroin or a couple of days of smoking are understood to bring on physical drug dependence: "Most Internet addicts, you'll recall, get hooked within months of first venturing on-line" (p. 97). The terminology used in her theorization and subsequent recovery program also works to solidify a comparison between the digital and the chemical drug: hooked, denial, relapse, triggers (Young, 1998, 2003).

The application of drug rhetoric to nonchemical behaviors and activities works to constrain a complex set of behaviors, patterns, and analyses within a narrative of addiction that, on the one hand, suggests frequent or compulsive use is a weighted negative and, on the other, defines the artifact used as dangerous, negative, or, as with certain chemicals, the cause of addiction. In an interview on the cultural semiotics and connotations of drug use and dependence, Jacques Derrida (1995) referred to a "diction of addiction" notion as a set of significatory characteristics that are applied to drug users and effect connotations which bind the applicant within particularly fixed ideological and political valencies. I want to return to Derrida's diction of addiction at the end of this chapter, but it is important at this stage to note that the application of the addiction metaphor constrains behavior, performatively producing behavior in the form of the identity "digital addict" through establishing the digital world as an unnatural, unreal, dangerous substance.

## 2  THE YOUTHFUL ADDICT – A STEREOTYPE

In Australia in 2010, a research team from the Psychological Medicine Department of a Sydney hospital surveyed almost 2000 users of digital games aged above 13 years and found that 8% appeared to have an addiction problem. For the researchers indicators of a digital addiction problem included "if gamers admitted playing longer than they had planned, or were playing games despite knowing "one should not do it," arguing that respondents who were "male, young and single" were more likely to have lost control playing games such as *World of Warcraft* (Pullar-Strecker, 2010). In the same month, indicating a peak in panic reporting on Internet and gaming addiction, a London hospital announced an intensive inpatient program directed to teenagers to help them reduce the amount of time spent in front of a computer screen, with a spokesperson stating that the service "will address the underlying causes of this addiction to transform screenagers back into teenagers" ("London Hospital," 2010). The articulation here not simply of addiction online as an identity attribute but as a category of self-hood and identity – the "screenager" – is significant. In this framing, both youth in transition from childhood to adulthood and the figure of the addict as suffering from an endemic disease that stems from within while simultaneously being produced through the use of digital communication is important. The picture of the teenager to which the program seeks to return these youth is, of course, a figure grounded in nostalgia for a teen who is seen to be sociable, active, fit, and engaged in a face-to-face community – ignoring that playing online games and communicating through digital and visual technologies is, indeed, being sociable, active, fit, and engaged in community, only that this is a community that is articulated relationally through online communication (and, naturally, may well be a subset of a peer network or community that also is engaged face-to-face at other times). The idea that the screenager is a figure who performs addiction in a way which is deemed nonnormative, pathological, and in need of intervention from psychiatric medicine in hospital settings actively stereotypes along generational lines. It operates alongside very outdated stereotypes of gamers as being young, teenaged, and male spending time in the basement playing games alone, the result of an inherent lack of social skills or confidence (Campbell, 2009). Yet, in cases of digital addiction, this stereotype is always combined with a generational discourse of youth. For cultural theorist Mark Davis (1997), generations of a population that are determined by categories of age range are overdetermined through the deployment of an artificial distinction that categorizes particular traits and attributes for an identity group articulated by age (pp. 1–20). Indeed, generations and the discourse of youth have often been used as a policy-led excuse for biopolitical governance and increased surveillance, ostensibly to protect such youth from themselves.

Earlier than these moral panic accounts of digital addiction, Rob Latham (2002) usefully drew on the mutual concepts of vampirism and consumption to argue that contemporary young adults were being figured as subjects who were both voracious consumers (of culture and technology) and actively consumed (commodified, used, and exhausted by such cultural and technological engagement). Latham stated that digital communication technologies in this context represented "a convergence of commodifying logics, in which subversive technology and resistant youth are mutually recuperated and exploited" (p. 194). Here, we see the figure of the digitally addicted youth who is, on the one hand, out of control in the use of digital media and gaming by virtue of being a youth and, on the other, articulated as being at risk to an addictive nature of the technology itself through a technologically determinist sensibility in which digital communication and gaming are represented as dark, shady, and dangerous activities capable of corrupting young persons and young minds. For example, British commentator Janet Street-Porter (2010) proclaimed Facebook to be a "toxic addiction" in an opinion piece in the *Daily Mail*, arguing that the murder of a 17-year-old girl by a serial sex offender who contacted her on Facebook using a fake identity is preventable if only teenagers, described as "[i]nnocent, normal kids," were able to control themselves and spend less time engaging in this dangerous online space of social networking. For Street-Porter: "Going online to chat is like taking crack. It's so addictive, you soon find yourself constantly tweeting, texting, messaging, emailing. Mostly harmless bilge, but for vulnerable teenagers it's a drug that can end in death." In writing that uses the kind of rhetoric designed to generate widespread panic, Street-Porter views the Internet as "a jungle online" and the problem "too late to do anything about," labeling those who use social networking as among the millions of fans, associating the behavior with some very old representations of hedonistic group behavior and loss of control among, for example, fans of the Beatles in the 1960s – a claim to youth using online technologies not as rational beings with agency but trapped in a drug-addled mindlessness. In her framework, this situation is not entirely of young people's making, but a social problem in which exposure to digital technologies puts young people at risk *because* they are vulnerable and at risk.

Such discourses effectively deploy a stereotype of youth as both addictive and corruptible, producing a particular kind of identity. All stereotypes serve to link an identity category – usually a minority representation or characterization of a group deemed nonnormative but sometimes threatening – with a set of behaviors, attitudes, desires, and norms (Rosello, 1998). Easily recognized because they are built on repetition and difficult to eradicate, stereotypes work as a "package" or "byte" of information (not necessarily accurate or truthful) about an identity or identity group. In that sense, stereotypes are consensual, communicative, and operate at a collective level within ongoing social processes (Karasawa, Asai, & Tanabe, 2007, p. 516) and are thereby implicated in the ways in which younger persons' identities are performed toward collectivity, coherence, and belonging. In the case of digitally addicted youth, a particular identity is conferred on younger persons who are actively using digital media. Younger users are being read as not just heavy or sometimes even obsessive users of digital communication technologies, but are being actively hailed to adopt and recognize themselves as digital addicts, forever at risk from the digital world and, at the same time, producing an enhanced addictive engagement with digital media in order to fulfill that identity category's requirements for coherence and intelligibility. This identity leads to examples of younger persons self-articulating their need for help and intervention to overcome their addiction. Part of this emerges from the *culture of confession* related to problematic behavior, in which we are culturally compelled to speak about any behavior, attribute, attitude, desire, dream, fantasy, dysfunction, or nonnormativity in public and private as part of the articulation and telling of the self (Plummer, 1995, p. 4). In the case of digital addiction, this is a response to the call to find a behavior that is deemed problematic such as digital addiction, to identify with the problem, and to draw parallels. This requires people to adopt the identity category of digital addict as it is presented by "experts" and then go on to speak about that problem within a framework either of adopting the identity as nonnormative but acceptable to oneself (in a claim to agency) or adopting the identity as nonnormative but seeking help to overcome it, while – like the alcoholic – always being able to claim and call upon the identity as something from which one is persistently recovering and always at risk of relapsing into that identity category and its associated behaviors.

This confessional behavior operates as a form of performative articulation of particular kinds of digital self-hood and includes those who have confessed to journalists that they are digital addicts, such as Alexander from the United States discussed in an article in *The Age* newspaper from Melbourne (Australia). The article states:

> Alexander is a tall, quiet young man who always got good grades and hopes to become a biologist. He started playing World of Warcraft, a hugely popular online multiplayer role playing game, about a year ago, and got sucked right in. "At first it was a couple of hours a day," he said. "By midway through the first semester, I was playing 16 or 17 hours a day. School wasn't an interest," he said. "It was an easy way to socialise and meet people." It was also an easy way to flunk out. Alexander

*dropped out in the second semester and went to a traditional substance abuse program, which was not a good fit. He graduated from a 10-week outdoors-based program in southern Utah, but felt he still had little control over his gaming. So he sought out a specialised program and arrived in Fall City in July. He thinks it was a good choice. "I don't think I'll go back to* World of Warcraft *any time soon," Alexander said (Net Addicts Get Clean with Hard Labour, 2009).*

Here we have a number of intersecting – as well as conflicting – discourses of addiction, identity, normativity, and technology at play. At one level, the article articulates the problem for individual younger persons, such as students at school and university deemed to be particularly at risk. Alexander confesses the interruption to study that gaming presented. At another level, however, he actively reveals the social, rather than isolating, nature of using digital media and gaming for relationality with others. However, by presenting himself for treatment he not only suggests himself as a person expressing what he sees as nonnormative behavior (*too much* time spent online) but also as an addict with the identity figured by the category "addict." The fact that he will, subsequent to treatment, avoid playing *World of Warcraft* establishes an identity performativity context in which he confesses to being permanently at risk of becoming addicted again should he engage with the game. At yet another level, however, Alexander's confession points not only to the discourse of addiction but to an underlying uncertainty over addiction, by framing his digital media use as potentially a formation of procrastination which has sometimes been articulated as a result of the distractive nature of hyperlinked web surfing (Knight, 2013). As a student, he found that his study was boring and he began engaging socially using *World of Warcraft* to meet others. Should he have articulated this as going to a bar regularly or attending parties more often than he thought healthy, he would have been no different from the vast majority of older teenagers and tertiary-level students on a worldwide scale. Of course, digital sociality and physical, corporeal, and localized sociality are regularly distinguished in popular media accounts of problematic computer and mobile use, with the latter typically related to being an impersonal interaction and therefore problematic (Pfarr, 2011). Here, digital media and digital gaming are assigned responsibility for being a problematic site through which to procrastinate, and the confession simultaneously articulates Alexander's identity as one of risk, vulnerability, permanent addiction, loss of agency, and incapacity for normative (read: conservative, proper) everyday studious living. At the same time, the potential alternative discourses that point not to addiction but to heavy sociality and relational engagement persist alongside the confession, effectively pointing to the fact that younger persons are typically *positioned* for greater social activity that may, temporarily and without any pathology, interrupt more serious obligations. That is not about addiction – it is about being young.

## 3 ONLINE ADDICTION

Young's research has argued that 5–10% of Internet users (at the time of writing approximately 5 million Internet users) are addicted. Having utilized user responses she articulates a particular narrative of online addiction, but in methodological terms her estimate of addiction rates have little legitimacy, and her concern that 97% of her respondents spent more time on the Internet than they might have liked tells us little about overall estimates of addiction. Young's study has been criticized for its reliance on a self-selected sample replying to advertisements posted on Usenet groups and internationally distributed newspapers (e.g., Griffiths, 1998; Grohol, 2000, p. 139) and might be further criticized for her attempt to use such a sample to estimate rates of Internet addiction among a much broader demographic. However, it is her production of the normative and its location in the real that has much broader implications for the idea of digital addiction. Likewise, it is important that her premise relies on the assumption of a total separation between online and offline which no longer makes any sense in an era of the ubiquity of digital access in Western social and technological settings in terms of connected devices. Today, one does not log in to the Internet as such, as if it is a particular (and dangerous) pastime separate from other activities in everyday life and sociality.

However, Young sees the space of digital communication, digital textuality, and interactive performance as a highly separated realm that, unlike reality is a world of make believe (1998, p. 21) which has dangerous consequences for one's personal identity and behavior. By enforcing a strict distinction between real life and virtual life behavior, she validates the real over the digital, while presenting only a nostalgic and predigital picture of real life. Her concern is that in spending time online, inhibitions are broken down and people will type "words you wouldn't dream of saying in your real life" (p. 21). She claims that heavy Internet users neglect their real lives: "other family members and friends of Internet addicts lament the addict's total loss of interest in once-treasured hobbies, movies, parties, visiting friends, talking over dinner" (p. 7). Rather than examining the ways in which the availability of online communication might afford opportunities for new social and personal arrangements and interests, or might indeed be viewed not through a technological determinist approach that understands the Internet as foisted on users rather than as produced through various cultural demands for new forms of interactive communication, she bemoans the ways in which it distracts from the real:

> Mary Lou is neglecting her husband and four kids, Bob's children can't get through to him, and Jennifer disappeared so far into the black hole of cyberspace that her mother worries that she won't get back. ... Brenda and Bob are withdrawing from those around them to hang out with their friends on the Internet, much as alcoholics prefer the company of fellow drinkers who will support them in their addictive behavior (pp. 16–17).

The validation of the real as normative over digital communication shuts down the possibility of addressing the ways in which online communication is sociality itself and how arrangements for conducting communication, friendships, learning, information access, entertainment, and leisure activities might indeed be highly diverse and productive. Instead, she works to establish the *physical* and *local* as the real, while viewing the social space of the Internet as the virtualor the pseudo – a lesser form of communication experience that is addictive by virtue of its virtuality. In public discourse about productivity in the workplace and work/life balance, email is bemoaned as unproductive interruptions with the sometimes valid response that a more interactive phone call or face-to-face chat would be more efficient; however, we should not thereby assume that all online communicative activity such as email or Skype is unproductive, problematic, antisocial, unsociable, or less than real.

For Young, it is not only the predication of a virtual world that is problematic, but the amount of *time* spent engaging with it, communicating through it, or utilizing it for some purpose. She separates the experience of the Internet from other experiences in which time is wasted or lost or flies: talking on the telephone, evenings out with friends. For her, time spent online is the major criteria to indicate addiction: as she puts it, "In my survey *97 percent* of all respondents reported that they found themselves spending longer periods of time-on-line that they intended" (Young, 1998, p. 36). Television and radio are not treated to the same concerns around interactivity because they are not viewed as an ingress into a virtual or cyber world. I would suggest that they in fact do invoke imaginary spaces, a point Joshua Meyrowitz (1997) makes in invoking the conceptual difference between physical place and communicative social space utilized through television and telephone. These are exempt from claims of addictiveness, then, not because they differ substantially – they are all media and communication forms of varying levels of interactivity – but because television and radio are structured around scheduling and time.

There are three further methodological or conceptual problems in Young's work that contribute to a reductive view of the Internet as addictive. The first of these is that she collapses all Internet usage into one form or into several related activities that center on one form and one use. Young relates the chat room as the hub of the Internet:

> … the path that leads to obsessive involvement with the Internet community usually leads directly to the center of chat rooms and interactive games. Once you get there, you rapidly immerse yourself in this community despite its limitations, its pitfalls, and its addictive nature that pulls you away from your actual life and the people and predicaments you should be facing (Young, 1998, pp. 114, 115).

Even in the late 1990s of Web 1.0, such views were highly outdated: email and browsing were already dominant activities becoming more ubiquitous than the characterization of online engagement through Relay Chat. The multiplicity of sites, uses, forms of information and activities – indeed, the very multiple structure of *the* Internet as a combination of Usenet newsgroups, email use, chat use, websites, and interactive games – is ignored.

Second, rather than viewing the *use* of digital media as diverse, Young works through a severe and strict technological determinist method – the blame for Internet addiction lies in the dynamic between the addictive potential in all users and the presence or existence of the Internet. For Young (1998), repressed and buried emotions are brought out in accessing the Internet, and she is particularly interested in the ways in which playing violent games draws out repressed childhood resentments of being ignored, causing subsequent violence to be expressed in real life (p. 73). The Internet here is understood as an invention that will have significant effects on human behavior, not as emerging within and through culture and being accessed as a result of particular cultural demands and desires, as a culturalist model would have it (Williams, 1990). In Young's discourse, the Internet is alien to culture, and comes to destroy the civilizing processes that are already in place.

This leads to a third point: the ways in which Young presents particular social arrangements not only as normative but as desirable. In favoring her conception of real life over the mythical "virtual," she predicates not only physical and geographically local relationships over communication, entertainment, and information seeking in digital forms, but celebrates the suburban and conservative family as a social unit to be hermetically sealed off from alternative friendships, relationships, and communicative practices that occur through digital means and across distances. She is concerned with what access to the Internet *does* to people, like Jeanne,

> ... *a 34-year-old wife and homemaker from South Carolina. By appearances, Jeanne had a perfect life; an attentive husband, a nice house, two healthy toddlers, a few good friends through her church (Young, 1998, p. 18).*

After use of the Internet, Jeanne "began sharing her most personal thoughts and intimate details of her life" with online friends (not her husband or real-life friends) and soon began an online rendezvous with another man, exchanging erotic messages as cybersex. "Through the Internet, she had formed a bond so close that she tossed aside a 15-year marriage" (Young, 1998, pp. 18–20). Rather than examining the ways in which a marriage-interrupting bond formed through online communication might not be dissimilar from those formed in other social experiences, the statement here is that access and frequent use of the Internet destroyed the normative family which is given here as the "perfect life." Likewise, players of interactive games are seen to be ignoring their real families who "are in the next room singing and laughing with holiday merriment" (p. 89), and Young bewails the fact that families "hardly ever eat together" (pp. 113, 114). Although all sweeping gestures to a conservative articulation of home life, these obscure the possibility of viewing the Internet as emerging culturally alongside broad sociocultural changes, including variations in the perception of family, friendship, and ways in which leisure time is legitimated. Instead, it is presented as an alien substance facilitating the breakdown of lived culture *per se*.

## 4  GAMING ADDICTION AND NEW TEMPORALITIES

While a markedly different media form from the Internet, digital gaming is likewise subject to accusations that it is inherently addictive, which works to locate the activity of gaming as a dangerous yet virtual substance separated from the cultural. Digital games, computer games, arcade games – all have been subject to various ideological positions on their social valency, the promotion of violence, and ideas around the loss of self in the notion of the collapse between self-identity and game character identity (e.g., Slater, Henry, Swaim, & Anderson, 2003; Funk, Buchman, Jenks, & Bechtoldt, 2003). Indeed, many of the arguments in public discourse which attempt to assert that digital games are the *cause* of violence often cite or at least imply an idea of addiction to digital gaming as a significant factor working to desensitize players to violence (Plusquellec, 2000). Academic research into digital gaming and addiction has often pointed to digital gaming as an addictive activity (Wolf, 2001, p. 4), although this view is also frequently denounced as overly reductive. Nevertheless, a certain wariness at denouncing gaming as addictive is discernible, frequently by making the point that although there is nothing addictive in games themselves, they are subject to excessive use leading to personal isolation from social activities (e.g., Plusquellec, 2000). As with the frequent collapse of Internet and online communicative and media forms into a single phenomenon, digital-gaming activities tend to be relegated to just one form, usually under the heading "video games." There is of course an array of different gaming genres, from action adventure, god games, first-person shooters, fantasy (Berger, 2002, pp. 12, 13) and significantly diverse forms of utilization of gaming, from solo play on a computer or gaming platform such as PlayStation 2 or X-Box, as well as online gaming (Humphreys, 2003). This collapse of gaming serves the accusation of addiction by allowing critics to ignore the vast array of uses, types, and pleasures that inspire ongoing game play in diverse ways.

Digital gaming is a markedly different category of digital media and entertainment from most online use (with the exception of online games), although one marked similarity, which I will discuss in more detail in the next section, relates to the ways in which both gaming and the Internet are seen to establish a separate, dichotomous, and virtual imaginary space in opposition to real-life activities and real play. Nevertheless, gaming in the popular imaginary is often seen to be diametrically opposite to the Internet, particularly in celebrationist accounts of online interactivity. For Lister, Dovey, Giddings, Grant, and Kelly (2003), a dichotomy between computer-mediated communication (CMC) forms and video games is supported by several of the following binaries: creative content versus mindless entertainment; adult users versus youth consumers; fluid identity versus hypermasculinity; sociality versus commodified space; tool versus toy. More importantly, where the Internet is sometimes seen as positively immersive, gaming immersion is rewritten as addiction (Lister et al., 2003, p. 263). What also appears to differentiate the video-game addict from other digital addicts produced within popular culture is the differing weighting given to the concept of the addict as a social menace. While online Internet addicts are produced within a discourse of liberal egopsychology and popular neurosis, the addicted gamer is seen as a low-class, protoviolent, addicted, and dangerous kid (Beavis, 1998), learning to express repressed anger and aggression (Young, 1998, p. 73), sociopathically isolated (Thompson, 2002, p. 28), and potentially capable of perpetrating extremely violent behavior such as a high school shootout (King & Borland, 2003, p. 175). Unlike writers such as Young who lump games and online use together and read all digital immersion as addiction, there is clearly a strand in popular discourse that seeks to celebrate one over the other, marking *only* digital games as addictive. Two reasons are significant: the greater association of gaming with youth culture, and the interactive goal-seeking form that constitutes much of game play.

Although it is certainly true that younger persons, children, and teenagers, make up a significant proportion of the known game player demographic (Latham, 2002, p. 47; Buchanan, 2004, p. 143), it is also the case that games have now for some time been a highly popular lifestyle choice among adults (Newman, 2002), particularly since the marketing of Sony's PlayStation 2 and Microsoft's X-Box consoles. Nevertheless, the nexus between youth, gaming, and addiction continues to be posited in popular discourse, alarmist moral panics around game culture, and some academic writing. Popular concerns that children are now playing digital games rather than with physicaltoys such as building blocks or footballs are made often by opinion makers and politicians (Hudson, 2004). Some public discourse continues to reaffirm the older framework of separating the value of reading literature from digital gaming as activities appropriate for children. Chris Bantick's *Why Computer Games Should Worry Parents* (2004) suggested three problems with younger persons playing computer games: (1) games usurp the creativity involved in playing with Lego building blocks, (2) games along with DVDs distract from reading, and (3) games are compulsive and addictive. What is striking yet representative about this particular piece is that it continues an artificial high/popular culture division, and locates the alleged addictiveness of games within an anxiety over interactive, participatory, and immersive formats that are understood to compete with the conceptual representation of high art that is embodied in the noninteractive print book. Compulsive reading, then, is exempt from calls of addiction – though there may well be grounds for the application of addiction rhetoric to some readers – because it bears no resemblance or association with the less legitimate form of new media arts.

There remains at play, then, a logic which suggests that frequent use of games and digital media is addictive *because* they are used by youth. This is part of what Davis (1997) identifies as cultural generationalism in the West that denounces the practices, behaviors, concerns, ideas, and pastimes of youth and children while nostalgically venerating those of the recent past. Certainly, Bantick's (2004) concern that Lego has been displaced in favor of digital games and online entertainment is rooted in a celebration of the popular toys of a baby boomer generation over those used by people currently under 30. At the same time, it is fed by a concern around the toys of the real world over those available in digital formats. Bantick expresses a concern that it may lead to an "addiction to electronic stimuli at the expense of the physical." With this set of connections between youth and digital media, and given the already packaged discursive linkage of youth and drugs (Redhead, 1997, pp. 58, 59; Murji, 1998, p. 78), associating youth and digital cultures in the rhetoric of drug addiction and risk finds a moral basis in a set of panics around the protection of children and younger persons.

A further way in which the signifiers of addiction and digital gaming are frequently conflated in alarmist responses to game culture is through the amorphous and undecidable nature of games as text and/or play. This is to continue the misreading of immersion or interactivity as addiction, but it is a perception that is legitimated by the subsequent goal seeking and anticipation that constitute this form of digital interactive entertainment. Games are a form of digital media that work across the interface between narrative and play or, in Henry Jenkins and Kurt Squire's (2002) terms, a hybrid of text and interactive play (p. 65). Play, as Huizinga (1949) pointed out in his *Homo Ludens*, is virtually always conditioned by tension through goal seeking (pp. 10, 11). As he elaborates:

> There is always the question: "will it come off?" This condition is fulfilled even when we are playing patience, doing jig-saw puzzles, acrostics, crosswords, diabolo, etc. Tension and uncertainty as to the outcome increase enormously when the antithetical element becomes really agonistic in the play of groups. The passion to win sometimes threatens to obliterate the levity proper to a game (p. 47).

His mobilization of the concept of passion is highly significant here: many of the fears invoked around violence and games and around digital-gaming addiction have to do more with a passion for the game, for game play, and for achieving a success in the outcome of meeting a goal. Such goal seeking across many games requires *familiarity* with the game, its environment, and its internal narrative structures; it requires training and practice; it requires dedication – whatever the personal or social value in game play, it remains that in the discourses of moral panics passion is rewritten as addiction, supported by the witness of a player's time and dedication.

Familiarity, temporal engagement, and pedagogical learning of skills necessary to play a game – whether alone or as part of online, multiplayer-gaming sociality involves a particularly *necessary* set of traits for digital game play, in which various physical and mental skills are required. The introduction of the joystick in the 1980s into the home computer game-playing environment was met with initial negative reactions by some over the difficulty of its use – not because it was inherently difficult but because it took some time to gain familiarity with it. Other interface devices such as the mouse also require time to gain familiarity; indeed, switching computers can cause some delay in efficient use of interface devices if they have been programmed differently or are set to have different reaction speeds, for example between a mouse and the cursor. The gaming environment itself takes time: there are instructions either on screen or in print form to be read, the various goals of more complex games need to be learned, a god game such as *Civilization III* requires time to learn strategies for success – often by trial and error. This itself, along with some forms of sociality, is both the passion and pleasure of game play for many players. No doubt, for some lifestyles, certain particularly difficult games must be shunned for the amount of time that may be required to become familiar with the internal narrative operations of the game, for example, the goals, narratives, play maneuvers, and possibilities of older games such as *Tetris* or *Space Invaders* are far more apparent on first playing than those of, say, *Buffy the Vampire Slayer: Chaos Bleeds*. A sporting game, such as *Stacey Jones Rugby League*, will be more easily learned by those familiar with the rules of rugby than by novices to the sport that the game replicates and represents. Whatever the personal or social value in game play, it remains that in the discourses of moral panic, passion is rewritten as addiction, supported by the witness of a player's time and dedication. It is of course ironic to note that a passion for career, a sporting activity, or even legitimate politics is seen as healthy, whereas passion for that which is in digital form is represented as dangerous or addictive, a reaction to the continued novelty of games as opposed to other, more essentially physical or localized activities.

Simultaneously, the question of time emerges as something in game play that is measured differently from those more traditional forms of media activity and engagement, and causes a certain amount of anxiety among those suggesting game play is addictive or overly immersive. Time, as we have long known, is purely subjective, and multiple conceptions of time exist for any social or media formation. As Paul Virilio (1991) has remarked, "time is lived – physiologically, sociologically and politically – to the extent that it is interrupted" (p. 82). This is a useful way to think about time spent with older media forms as opposed to digital games. Television as a concomitant set of media texts and a form of media flow is temporally segmented (Cubitt, 1991). Its schedule is produced and familiar, generated within what

Manuel Castells (1997) refers to as "clock time" which "characteristic of industrialism, for both capitalism and statism, was/is characterized by the discipline of human behavior to a predetermined schedule creating scarcity of experience out of institutionalized measurement" (p. 125). The television schedule is media time that both disciplines and is disciple to the conventions of Western human time as they arise through patterns and standards of work, sleep, dinner, family arrangements, and so on. The rise of new, networked, digital, and recorded media forms, however, has worked to change the ways in which media time operates. These changes are not determined by media form or alterations in media programming but emerge simultaneously with changes in the temporal structure of labor such as in the growth of flexitime (Cooper, 2002); the growth of a consumer society and changes in consumer practices such as 24-hour and 7-days-a-week shopping in the rise of a consumer society; and the rise of a network society in which digital forms of communication produce a nowness in which information and communication are present and patience is (sometimes) unnecessary.

There is nothing inherent about television, radio, or print that prevents, alters, or produces different uses of time: television can be watched for an entire day, whether stationary on one channel or zapped endlessly for hours. A book can be read with few breaks throughout the night. And like digital games, they invoke a particular imaginary space where time operates in different cycles – the temporality of a television narrative is generally not working at the same speed as the clock time of the viewer; the narrative of an epic novel can span generations but be read in a matter of days or hours. Likewise a digital game such as a god game can narrate interactively the events of a thousand years but be played in 5 hours. I would suggest that these invoked and imaginary spaces can be related in the same way that Joshua Meyrowitz (1997) separates and differentiates the conceptual physical place from the communicative social space imagined through television and telephone use. The difference in temporality, then, is not that one entices or immerses the reader/player to a greater or lesser extent, but because television is structured around scheduling and time, a standard print work of fiction is likewise visibly structured by chapters and an ending – both in the sense of the narrative ending (Kermode, 1967) and the physicality of the book produced in its limitation of pages. Indeed, in the case of the television program, the clock on the VCR beneath or above the set seems to indicate clearly how long you've been accessing that virtual and imaginary world, and how long you can expect a particular program to continue. Because (1) the interactive nature of most games relies on human input, user familiarity, and user training, (2) the random generation of events, situations, and configurations that emerge through the program and the CPU, and (3) the frequent lack of clarity over, for example, the number of levels in which a player might be engaged in a first-person shooter, game time is unknowable, unforeseeable, external to Castell's clock time and beyond measurement according to our contemporary social criteria of time use.

Where the television is thus thoroughly marked by cycles of clock time, gaming is marked by unstructured time, and this causes anxiety for those who would in conservative terms see time as responsibly measured (by work, family). It may be this fact that leads some people to look to the analogy with drugs and drug rhetoric, as well as the concept that lengthy periods of play are an indication of addiction. Playing an action adventure game such as *Myst* or an online game such as *EverQuest* between 2.30 p.m. and 7.30 p.m. might have been difficult or impossible given some traditional twentieth century labor, familial, and temporal arrangements. However, in emerging social formations in which activities such as labor are frequently disconnected from standards based on measured time, it is possible to choose to play at such times. This, however, is subsequently read by alarmists as addiction as if a compulsion toward game play has distracted from those traditional activities rather than viewing the game player as exercising a choice to play at those times. Indeed, under new conditions of contract and casual labor, such temporal flexibility is imposed: if gaming is an increasingly dominant entertainment form among those in their teens or the late-30s – loosely constructed as "Generation X" – then they are a group who are more likely to be long-term unemployed (Davis, 1997) and a group who have experienced a growth in casual, flexible, and shift-based employment over permanent salaried positions with their standard operating 8-h day beginning at 9 in the morning (Hardt & Negri, 2000). They are also a group who have more amorphous family living arrangements including single-parent and blended families (Colebatch, 2002), leading to schedules that are less easily engendered by and through cycles of child feeding, family meals, or Sunday outings. However, rather than examining the ways in which various alterations to social arrangements or their general diversity can be represented and understood in the context of digital game use, alarmists of game addiction look only to the differences in time and to the extent to which games are played (as opposed to watching television or reading print).

## 5  DIGITAL/REAL AND THE DISCOURSE OF THE ADDICT

It follows within the diction of addiction that there is an addiction of the self or the body or the personality or some other facet of performative selfhood *to* something. While drugs are seen to be an ingested physical supplement (a pill, a powder, a liquid) penetrating the body through the hypodermic or otherwise consumed, it is what drugs represent – effect – that is considered virtual, unreal, without reality, or outside reason. Addiction is generally given in terms of an addiction *to* the unreal, something that is lesser than that which is categorized as natural, righteous, appropriate, beneficial. In the rhetoric of digital addiction, both game play and online Internet experience is given as the unreal or the virtual not because of something that takes it outside physicality and normal behavior, nor because they are technologies which are relatively new, but because the narrative, communicative, articulable worlds that are evoked interactively have no *physical* substance – they are represented as a substance of unreality. Both the real and the virtual, as a number of writers have pointed out, are conceived simultaneously, such that both are represented as pure, self-sufficient, and separate. Both technology celebrationists and Luddites view the virtual scape of video games, Internet usage, and other virtual reality (VR)-related technologies as the realm of order and a new world, posthuman, postculture. As Elizabeth Grosz (2001) puts it:

> *Whereas many see in VR the ability to aspire to God-like status, to create, live in, and control worlds, to have a power of simulation that surpasses or bypasses the uncontrollable messiness of the real, others (sometimes even the same writers) revile and fear VR's transformation of relations of sociality and community, physicality and corporeality, location and emplacement, sexuality, personal intimacy, and shared work space – the loss of immediacy, of physical presence. ... Unashamed apologists of cybertechnologies and nostalgic Luddites yearning for days gone by see VR as a powerful force of liberation and a form of ever-encroaching fascistic control, respectively (p. 77).*

It is significant that an era of digital ubiquity has arisen in the decade and a half since this quotation was written, taking us beyond notions of being introduced to the digital from within a nondigital and nonnetworked real life. The binary of real and virtual was always mythical, but it reemerges specifically *in order to* assert a notion of online addiction. The salient point here is that whether those who celebrate or denounce new media forms from *within* a binary concept of real/virtual, all see a transformative potential for the real and the real self (whatever that might yet come to mean) in the encounter with the virtual, such that repetitive, frequent, passionate, and even obsessive encounter*ing* of digital media sparks an anxiety that equates the virtual with the unreal drug. Digital media and games are understood as addictive not because they are compulsively used, but because as unreal they are like drugs, and thereby become subjected to a discourse of drug addiction.

For Derrida (1995), we reject the drug addict because:

> ... he cuts himself off from the world, in exile from reality, far from objective reality and the real life of the city and the community; ... drugs, it is said, make one lose any sense of true reality. In the end, it is always, I think, under this charge that the interdiction is declared. We do not object to the drug user's pleasure per se, but to a pleasure taken in an experience without truth (pp. 235–236).

Although I am arguing here that the connection between drug addiction and digital addiction is more than a metaphorical comparison – for *both* are rooted in a perception of what it is that constitutes real – a simple insertion of the signifiers "game" or "Internet" or "digital" or "online" in place of drugs in the above quote indicates neatly the ways in which digital addicts are produced in contemporary culture. Because they are not within the knowledge of objective reality, digital communication and interactive entertainments are seen as a pleasure experienced without truth. The digital world is seen, then, as a paradox that makes it foreign to the representation of the real – it is both ordered and chaotic. In the rhetoric of digital addiction, digital media are seen as chaotic, neither structured around time nor centralized; categories are mixed, crossbred, hybridized, and blurred (Gaillot, 1998, p. 44). Indeed, Young's (1998) connotative terminology for online media bespeaks a messiness in its unreality, it is "make believe" (p. 21), it will "lure" the user into a "world without limits [that is] multidimensional" (p. 23), it asks for time to "trudge through the garbage swirling in the whirlpool of info glut" (p. 38). At the same time, digital forms are viewed as being too structured – a sealed world, such as the narrative space of an interactive game that no matter how complex, has a structure that is overdetermined and simplistic (Newman, 2002), a set of rules that one can imagine breaking but are impossible to defy (Humphreys, 2003, p. 84; Beavis, 1998), and lacks the genuinely random pleasure of real life play and communication.

The fact that the work of Young and others on digital addiction is driven by the ideological position that digital texts and communication possess less value than physical artifacts and relationships conducted in face-to-face capacities point to the fact that addiction is located in the digital viewed as a negative space, negative spaces being addictive by nature in her view. But for Young and for the diction of drug addiction, the object of addiction is neither that which is consumed nor that which influences. Rather, both drugs and the digital are seen to pervade the mythical naturalness or *nature* of the user. As Derrida (1995) puts it:

> By the grace of the technical or artificial, and ever-*interiorizing* violence of an injection, inhalation, or ingestion, by taking into my self, inside myself a foreign body, or indeed a nutriment, I will provoke a state of productive receptivity (pp. 240–241).

For Young (1998), digital addiction is seen to "penetrate" like an "epidemic" (p. 5), a foreign and (to her, at least) unknowable or unreasonable substance that comes to infiltrate her ideal of the natural body. The factor that comes into play here relates to the fear of digital forms, not because of a cultural fear of new technologies or Luddism, but the result of the available politics of new media forms. As John Downing (2003) has pointed out, it is possible to typify mainstream media as focused on hegemonic integration and alternative media "with their frequent focus on challenging the structures of power" (p. 626). If the familiarity of the ideologically hegemonic brings it into the real – the production of our everyday realities – then that which challenges it is relegated not only to a place of fear and danger, but to a virtuality which is exacerbated in the contemporary cultural imaginary by its frequent digital form and its accessibility through the screen, keyboard, joystick, and other accoutrements of cybervirtuality. Alternative media and alternative, structure-challenging politics thus become associated with the digital world, and relegated to a space on the other side of the artificial real/virtual binary. The terminology of escapism into digital media and communication – escape from the real – is also dominant in addiction studies and panics about digital addiction (Binaisa, 2002, p. 45; Reid, 1998, p. 29). What occurs in a deconstructive understanding of digital addiction, then, is that one takes inside the real body or identity the virtual in order to escape the real.

Thinking about digital addiction becomes productive for thinking about the relationships between digital media and sociality if it begins with breaking down the artificial, outdated, and problematic distinction between the real and the virtual that is so pervasive throughout both celebrationist and alarmist discourses of new media. Grosz (2001), among other writers, points out that what the world of the digital does best is "reveal that the world in which we live, the real world, has always been a space of virtuality" (p. 78). It is thus to look at how a sociality that is built today on a broad addiction to digital connectivity and interactivity comes to inflect how we think about and represent addiction otherwise. Simon Cooper (2002) links the idea of addiction to communication technologies as an addiction to sociality (pp. 3, 4), thereby drawing back from the artificial separation of real space and digital space. It is only in rejecting this distinction and looking to how the concepts of the virtual teach us what might constitute real that we can move beyond the reductive arguments as to whether or not digital media are addictive and consider the more important issues not only as to how or why they might be compulsive for some users or players or how they might produce the self-confessed and declarative figure of the digital addict, but what it means that this form of compulsion emerges at this time in contemporary culture.

# CHAPTER 8

# Digital Surveillance, Archives, and Google Earth: Identities in/of the Digital World

This book began with a discussion of selfies and continued by presenting an approach to personalized self-production of identities in the context of social networking using complex theories of identity performativity that understand selves to be articulated in accord with available forms, discourses, and intelligibilities drawn from culture, ritual, and practice, including online practices. We have worked through a number of frameworks in the intervening chapters that attend specifically to the relationality that is fostered by digital communication environments, and that both consolidate traditional identities and open new ways for thinking and doing identity as performative. For example, in Chapter 1 we considered how the processes of social networking provide opportunities for identity performances that can be both coherent and yet dissolved through complex online relationalities. Similarly, in discussing the environment of mobility that is afforded by new devices such as smartphones and tablets, the subject and, indeed, the processes of subjectivity come to be spread across a space in ways which simultaneously extend the subject and also reduce the effect of place and location as aspects that are incorporated into the intelligible performativity of selfhood. Whether in social networking, digital interactivity with textuality, devices used to produce corporealities that are understood as projects or in environments of globalized discourses of subjectivity, identity rears itself as large, despite being in the context of an Internet that increasingly is so ubiquitous it disappears into the background. That is, while we make use of digital communication technologies for the creative production of identity, the practices have become so normative in the affluent West that it is no longer practical to distinguish between a corporeal real and an online virtual environment for the performativity of selfhood.

While I have been discussing some of the ways in which identity operates as a large-scale cultural project across media and communication in ways that, we might say, make us seem larger than ourselves, I would like to conclude this book by opening some questions as to how we might

*Digital Identities.*
http://dx.doi.org/10.1016/B978-0-12-420083-8.00008-0

understand the contemporary human subject as small in the context of digitality. This is to think about our digital selfhood not only as performative in a way that both conforms to contemporary discourses of normativization and simultaneously gives a sense of agency over the digital relationalities through which that performance occurs, but also in the context of the world as itself, a digital project that is given sense through discourses made available through online tools. Here, I am thinking about sites such as Google Earth that make a geolocational mapping of the world in which we can self-locate as well as explore accessible, but also serve to produce a particular way of thinking about the world that reorients us from the face-to-face to the God's-eye view of a world from above – a trait of contemporary affluent societies found in skyscraper towers and the airplane – to the figure of the satellite which is no longer a background node in telephony and broadcast media but the standpoint through which we are given a sense of place in the context of the Earth.

At the same time, Google Earth itself serves as emblematic of the intersection of this reorientation of the body and space with two other important elements that change how our identities are produced in the context of world spaces: surveillance and the archive. In the case of the first, the meaning of surveillance has changed substantially over the past century, moving from one which figures us as personally surveilled and, following the work of Foucault (1977) work in *Discipline and Punish*, as taking on the project of self-surveillance in order to ensure our own normativity in terms of disciplinary societies. Surveillance shifts in a postdigital era to one in which we are made small in the surveillance of our communicative, financial and relational activities through our accessibility within the "big data" of contemporary data collection regimes. Here, we are regularly invited to plot our identities in the context of represented distributions and ranges of normativities that produce us as surveilled subjects who are able to make sense of "who we are" in the context of large-scale information. Again, digital technologies play a central role not only in the acquisition of such data and the ways in which it is disseminated publicly, but also in the discourses and frameworks that make such data relevant to ourselves as a nodal point governing self-performativity. In this respect, the activity of searching out where we fit on a range of norms and in proximity to a given norm, and negotiating the extent of that proximity in ways that allow us to respond to the cultural requirement for coherent and recognizable selves, is an activity that appears to have a certain agency, although, again, it is both governed by cultural demands and made easier and more normative itself by the cultural technologies of digitality.

In the case of the third term in this conjunction, the figure of the archive, it is important to understand precisely the ways in which digital technologies operate a form of surveillance that produces an intelligibility of the world through a particular viewpoint on place (presenting the world from above) and people (presenting the world as large populations in which we are invited to find ways of producing and managing our own belonging). It is also important in the context of time (making the world and ourselves searchable by the persistent fixing of particular frameworks of understanding the past). Digital media make available an archive, but not only in the sense of a personal past that is produced, sometimes unwittingly, in a timeline on Facebook, as discussed in Chapter 1. Rather, I am referring to the broad, composite repository of information that includes Google Earth (Munster, 2008, p. 405), but also an array of other information that one can key into through search engines – a semipublic archive of the entire world, albeit one that works through narrow frames and inequitably distributed accessibilities to the archive and the tools needed to utilize it and the discourses and digital literacies necessary to engage with it. In the sense of the archive, then, the subject is coded both small and omniscient in the context of time through digital media's capacity to archive. Here the subject is writ small within the archive of the entire world. Simultaneously they have access to the capacity to change archiving practices, while in the past domestic and private articles such as photographs and letters would ordinarily remain within families and not official archives (unless one was famous enough to warrant it), however today they can thereby unwittingly be a contributor to that which is subjective largeness or largesse within the archive.

Finally, in the context of digital surveillance the subject is made both that which can be focused upon and pinpointed through disciplinary investigations into the digital fingerprints and footprints one leaves in the metadata of online engagement and, simultaneously, through the surveillance that places subjects within investigations into normativity coded today as "big data." This refers to data sets which often include financial, online search, commercial, genomic, and other statistical information, whereby digital capabilities of archiving, surveillance, and global flows have enabled the collation of such information into sets that are so large, that traditional methods of analysis, storage, and discourses of informatics have needed to give way to new approaches. While the notion of the subject as just one statistical number among many is a twentieth century and often reactionary view in relation to the collection of large-scale government data about populations, Big data take this a step further whereby the information about subjects is on the one hand integral to the data set and, on the other, produces a frame of understanding subjectivity as immaterial and miniscule. What is essential to big data, however, is the practice of surveillance as a contemporary norm in which data about human and nonhuman activity is collected without necessarily having purpose, in contrast to government demographics, for example, that are used in town planning and education spending. Here, big data surveil, record, and archive subjectivities in ways that make the activity of surveillance disappear into the background of ordinary sociality – an expectation rather than a privacy invasion.

In this conclusive chapter, I would like to show how the three areas of surveillance, the archiving of everything, and the visual remapping of the Earth conjoin in ways which contribute to new forms for the constitution of subjectivity and identity in a digital era, and cross through a number of important questions for contemporary sociality, related to ethics and cohabitation, surveillance and privacy, and the production of normativities that provide frameworks for coherent performativities of selfhood. I will move through surveillance, archives, and Google Earth step by step in order to open some of the new, interesting ways in which we can think about subjectivity in digital contexts, particularly thinking about how some of the important questions about digital identities that are produced in these contexts might open up how we think about, experience, enact, and ensure ethical relationalities. I would like to conclude the chapter and the book by coming back to some of the questions with which we began, particularly in relation to the ways in which digital media actively invite subjects to engage in self-production online, only here I would like to question the efficacy of any concept of agency in the context of digital social norms. This is not, of course, to provide a final answer to what it is that might constitute digital identities, but to consider some of the possibilities for new questions around what identity itself might be, and what identities or manners for performing selfhood might be opened up and made available in the future.

## 1  DIGITAL SURVEILLANCE AND CONTEMPORARY IDENTITY

Surveillance – and particularly digital surveillance – is often treated as a concept of substantial alarm and sometimes moral panic. An entire discourse of what might referred to as "accusatory reaction" in regard to the idea of data collection about a person's communication, relationships, finances, or other details emerges in this context, with a view that surveillance practices will be used to actively suppress or coerce members of the public toward some hidden governmental agenda. This is not, of course, the reality of surveillance, which in contemporary biopower arrangements of discipline and governmentality does not seek to coerce or suppress and is not necessarily an activity emergent from government and security administration alone. Rather, surveillance is today designed to instrumentalize information, to incite productive activity, to create thresholds of allowable and nonallowable social crimes (Foucault, 2009, pp. 22, 23), consumption, or self-commodification, and is as much a tool of capital as it is of governmentality in the sense of the administration of states, territories, and populations. That is, in everyday discourse we tend to persist with the idea of surveillance as a deliberate tool of sovereign oppression, however the mechanism of power of surveillance applies to the body and what the body does in a disciplinary framework (Foucault, 2004, p. 35) and in a biopolitical framework of data collection. The latter here operates as a redeployment of surveillance away from the body to large-scale "biosociological processes characteristic of human masses" through "complex systems of coordination and centralization" (pp. 249, 250) that are arguably made more available and more effective through the digitization of processes of communication and archiving, by making use of the ease by which digital communication can be recorded, stored, and maintained, both at the level of content and the metadata level of details around time, place, location, and intended recipients, among other aspects. Surveillance in this framework is not of individuals, who become somewhat meaningless in the collection of data as a purposeful exercise, and instead is surveillance of whole populations.

In a digital framework, surveillance today is very much centered on the bringing together of questions of technology and questions of the bodies of subjects as biological citizens (Zylinska, 2010, p. 160), whereby surveillance is both about the broad biopolitical populations, but digital media make available the capacity for simultaneous narrowing in on bodies through aspects of self-surveillance. However, when it comes to the individualized body, surveillance operates a little more carefully as a technology of power, because it intersects questions of privacy (Woo, 2006, pp. 951, 952), whereby the notions of private bodies, private space and private data remain connected with individuals, but only when the performance of individuality is heightened. During times in which one experiences the self as member of a group or a population or in some other framework of relationality – all of which are automatically heightened in online forms of communication – questions of surveillance become less meaningful. However, as David Savat (2013), following Deleuze, has noted, new forms of digital observation tie in with the notion that databases, through the exteriorization of knowledge, reflect a general shift in which the production of knowledge is connected with the production of truths of the self (p. 27). In relation to this important point, then, surveillance and digital observation of both large groups and whole populations for a range of purposes disappear into the background of everyday use of digital communication, such that the production of selves is naturalized through processes of surveillance which, themselves, come to seem natural, normative, endemic, and inescapable – mere background in the context of the many wilful activities one engages in through being situated in a ubiquitous digital media environment.

The contemporary regime of surveillance that operates across institutional discipline and biopolitical demographization of populations and large-scale groups in a big data framework is one which has two immediate social effects in relation to identity and digitality. The first is that our digital activities provide enough information for corporations to catalog taste, test it against norms, consider it in terms of demographics of financial capabilities, and serve subjects niche marketing (Chaput, 2009, p. 98). Online marketing is one example where tailored advertisements have a particular power to attract interest precisely because they appear to be personalized for the user, despite the fact that there has been no actual human intervention in producing such marketing content; instead they are the product only of powerful computing algorithms. Such niche marketing simultaneously invites subjects to try out new commodities of identity – and thereby new identities themselves – because they are likely to be appropriate choices for that subject and also to confirm and reinforce one's own identity through purchasing according to existing tastes. At the same time, such digital surveillance operates to most effectively encourage self-monitoring and self-surveillance. In that context, while surveillance is sometimes treated as a negative or fearful event that invades privacy, it has a level of ubiquity that enables it to be seen as the normative activity, such that for a subject to achieve coherence of performativity, one responds by surveilling the self in order to ensure the most acceptable self is put forward for digital surveillance.

This kind of self-reflexivity and self-monitoring is both invited and yet compulsory, whereby to be a subject and to have an identity in a digital era is also to be required to account for oneself both to the self and to others (Buckingham, 2008, p. 10). In the context of self-surveillance, many scholars and public commentators have been surprised at the extent to which younger persons are seen to reveal information about themselves online, whether through actively posting information, filling out surveys, or ignoring warnings about surveillance (Tufekci, 2008, p. 20). From the perspective of contemporary digital identities, however, this is not in any way surprising. Rather, it points to the fact that a coherent identity is one which embraces surveillance because surveillance is a key ingredient of performativity. Subjects must self-surveil to determine the coherence of identity category and identity behavior, but digital media expands that role by automating some aspects of that process (Andrejevic, 2002, p. 234). In that context, digital media serve the dual function of gathering data about the subject for the subject and, in doing so in ways which help produce intelligible subjectivities, also gather data for others. In several ways, then digital identity is very much about being given over not only to the discourses of identity that precede us, but to the process of social and economic flow that relate to and are beyond us.

danah boyd (2014) has pointed to substantial evidence that younger persons live with, but respond to, surveillance of online activities in varied ways. While some people have a more nonchalant attitude to questions of privacy, others take active means to protect themselves from being observed when they themselves are not online, such as by deleting and reloading a Facebook account for use only when actively awake and engaged with a machine (pp. 70–73). Responses to privacy, of course, depend on the available discourses through which surveillance and observation is counterpointed to privacy and/or secrecy, both of which have become more complex in recent years, more subject to both alarmist and blasé accounts, and which are more – not less – tied up with questions of identity in online settings. In Chapter 6, I drew on the work of Susan Gal (2002) to point to the fractal and complex form which the public/private distinction takes, pointing out that it may no longer have substantial relevance to today's subjects and users of digital communication. One of the important corollaries of this is that questions of privacy become more pointed at particular times under which one feels surveillance. This is certainly the case when public debates about data retention emerge in news and media discourses and when a parent might, for example, demand to look at a child's social-networking content or friends list. By way of analogy, this is not dissimilar from the awareness of one's private parts of the body when under the deliberate and usually well-meaning surveillance of a medical practitioner. Surveillance, in that context, is a felt experience and privacy becomes in those piqued moments an attitude toward the self and others to which one can be deeply attached. However, one of the key points here is that in an era of digital ubiquity, the experience of surveillance is far less obvious, and is not undergone in the same way on an everyday basis as the parental observation of one's digital activities or the medical officer's observations of one's body. Rather, it extends through time and space and practice, across hidden activities from the radiofrequency-identifiable chips that are carried in our wallets in identity cards (Gane, 2007, p. 350) to the background downloading of software updates on a computer. Surveillance is, today, naturalized and comes to be felt as natural as breathing, which is only ever remarked upon when one becomes corporeally aware of breathing or when breathing is interrupted. By disappearing into the background of everyday activities of digital communication and digital being, our identities are more readily marked by surveillance and produced in the context of observation than we are otherwise aware.

## 2 ARCHIVING THE WORLD

Subjectivity is, from some perspectives, produced through the bringing together of memory, archive, and surveillance which, for Anne Brewster (2005, p. 399) is implicated in the production of the body as that which is constituted in the knowledge that come before it, whether social, institutional, or individual formations of memory. In this section, I would like to consider how one of the products of past and contemporary surveillance, the archive, is reproduced through the vast and powerful digital storage capabilities of the Internet in ways which participate in and, to some extent, refigure the constitution of contemporary subjectivities. Archives themselves operate as that which draws attention to the "pastness of the past" (Kouvaros, 2009, p. 401) but in very real ways that have an impact through the making available and unavailable of particular frames of being and particular discursive knowledge and sensibilities of the normative self, archives produce limits and forms of memory, reactivation, and expressibility (Mills, 1997, p. 56). In other words, when we argue that performativity is governed by processes in which subjects cite, take onboard and articulate in a drive toward coherence a set of behaviors, attributes, categories, names, and signifiers that are given discursively, it is the archive that is made available digitally that has to be accounted for in this context. Not only does the archive of information, material, and prior surveillance serve as one particular repository for discourse, it is also a site that governs the subsequent production of knowledge by providing frameworks for the knowability of what is included in knowledge and what is not. The formation of digital capabilities allowing for processes of archiving, the production of new and sometimes alternative archives and for the access to archives of information in ways markedly different from the hidden, difficult, effort-laden, or voluntary form of retrieving archives only in specific geographic locations, such as the state library, further centralizes the figure of the archive in our everyday experience of performativity. The archive, in this sense, upholds fixity and norms of identity over time.

At the same time, however, the archive is also a kind of documentation that operates as an intervention. According to Arjun Appadurai (2003), it does not merely precede but is a step toward different forms of change, imagination, alternative memory, "a tool for the refinement of desire" (pp. 24, 25). For Appadurai, archives are implicated in kinds of cultural change through which we sometimes consider the capacities for marginalized groups and minority communities to formulate, record, and disseminate knowledge that is excluded from the mainstream. However, as an intervention, the archive is also typically related to how we think about the kinds of changes that are brought about by digitization of media and the ubiquitous access to information more broadly. That is, the archive in its contemporary digital use has both conservative (conservational) and revolutionary (culturally transformative) potential (Halberstam, 2011, p. 86). Where the Internet was understood and regularly labeled the "information superhighway" in order to indicate some of the ways in which media flow at greater and greater speeds in a digital, networked era (Burnett & Marshall, 2003, p. 206), it is the first term "information" that is truly important, in the sense that the digital capacity to archive and share information generally is that which produces broad cultural change as an intervention, thereby figuring for us a way of conceiving how identities are produced distinctly in a digital era and through the capabilities of digital media to make available not merely discourse but an archive. The practices of performing identity change and develop, because the practices of disseminating information change and develop, and one of those changes is the making available of information both as an archive and, in a very real sense, also hiding the fact that the digital repository of information found online is an archive, risking always the complexification of discourse by making what once might have been thought of as the chronologically old, the record, the database, and the outdated sit alongside the new, the novel, the current, and the dominant.

The notion of the archive in its digital media use is, of course, both social and personal. Subjects are actively compelled to create their own archive of information that is not necessarily collectable for any specific reason other than it is a particular way of performing and articulating one's sense of identity. This is the formation of archiving practices that operates in the nexus of personal archives and surveilled databases (Smith & Watson, 2014, pp. 72–74). Online entries, social-networking updates, the storage of photographs, are not different from the kinds of collectivities kept as part of a post–nineteenth century culture of information storage, all symbolic of "past identity within boxes or cupboards" (Hodkinson & Lincoln, 2008, p. 36). Such a "will to archive" (Featherstone, 2006, p. 595) is not, then, merely a particular cultural practice that might be described as a hobby or a self-reflective private endeavor but, today, disappears into the everyday activities of using digital applications such as email that maintains permanency of correspondence. The practice disappears into the background of digital activities such that it therefore becomes normative and endemic of identity practices, since performativity is never voluntarist and conscious but involuntary and routinized, operating within a sensibility of natural behaviors. This is not, of course, to suggest that archiving is not sometimes depicted as a risk activity, such as utilizing cloud storage to preserve one's documents as a way of preventing risk, but also coded within discourses of suspicion as to the motivation of the companies providing cloud storage server space. Rather, it is to point to the fact that the glut of information about individuals online is supplemented by deliberate if unseen practices of maintaining records, at least partly because there is so much information, that the act of a digital spring clean is too large an endeavor for the average digital identity.

## 2.1 Theorizing the Digital Archive

The concept of the archive is generally figured in the context of the modern state as the site of repository through which memories related to national identity and nationalistic belonging are constructed. Archives in that sense are an element in the "apparatus of social rule and regulation" via the accumulation and organization of information (Featherstone, 2006, p. 591). Through the archive, for Mike Featherstone, the individual subject of the Enlightenment and modern European era was formed as a category of site of knowledge "through the accumulated case records (the file) which documented individual life histories within a particular institutional nexus such as a school, prison, hospital or more generally through governmental welfare or security agencies" (pp. 591, 592). Here, the archive constructs the subject within the coupling between national and subjectivity, producing each individual as a national subject (citizen or otherwise) through the crossreferencing of different elements of information about that subject's finances, life decisions, educational achievements, medical health, compliance with law, and other elements.

The archive of the nineteenth and twentieth centuries, while persisting into the twenty-first, is not necessarily as consequential or as empowered in the construction of the subject today, in part by the irrelevance of the classificatory systems that may no longer have a contemporary value in defining and subjectivizing a person (Featherstone, 2006, p. 593), but also in the context of the growth of neoliberalist desires to catalog information more relevant for direct marketing through the surveillance and production of an image of the subject as a consumer with specific tastes and attributes that extend into tastes for particular kinds of purchases. Here, digital media's tools of data collection and surveillance are deployed to produce a particular kind of digital identity, one not necessarily easily categorizable, but produced in an individualized complex of tastes to form the intelligible requirements for that subject to persist performatively in recognition and intelligibility. This is to point, in part, to the multiplicity of the archive as tools of surveillance that, on the one hand, operates in conjunction with the nation state through public-motivated but highly protected information gathering on subjects that is completed efficiently through digital tools (taxation records, immigration and border crossings, health and education). These tools operate in disciplinary ways to produce particular kinds of conformable identities and concomitant actions (Foucault, 2008, p. 138) that serve the sociality of the nation. On the other hand, digital-archiving practices produce the subject through fostering particular biopolitical norms. These are not norms of social engagement but norms unto the individual alone, such that the habits, behaviors, costs, commodifications, expenses, and finances serve as the basis for the production of the individualized consumer who must recognize himself or herself in that depiction that is presented through cookie-derived advertisements on a social-networking page, search engine suggestions, advertisements, and the array of financial records, statements, invoices, correlated recommendations on eBay, and so on.

Here, then, the production of a particular kind of archive in a digital context is the product of the languages of digitality. As Butler (2012) notes, language "does not only record, preserve, and transmit, though on occasion it does all those things. Language also invariably works upon the material it records, preserves and transmits" (p. 182). Thus while digital discourses convey names and categories that serve as both memory and archive (Düttmann, 2000, p. 74), the language of digitization operates to transform the archive from that which served the nation and national identity to that which serves the individualization of the individual as a relationally produced singularity governed by performative practices rather than categorization, location, nationality, and citizenship. In that the archive becomes not only protected against the threats that might be expected of a Medieval book repository in a monastery, such as fire and flood, it also begins to operate as mobile and thus separated from both tangible form and presence (Urry, 2007, p. 162). At the same time, however, it begins to preserve the utterances of identity performance in ways which operate as a surveillance across time, the past, and the lifecycle of subjects, producing the capacity for the production of enyclopedias of the self.

## 2.2 The Vulnerability of the Archive

At another level, however, archiving serves not only the nation and contemporary marketing by producing subjects via cultures of surveillance but, through digital recordkeeping, simultaneously serves the production of a particular kind of humanity by acting as a repository of all human knowledge, an archiving of the world. Here, the depiction of the metaphor of postapócalyptic worlds is instructive. The contemporary obsession in film and television with the representation of postapocalyptic worlds is, ultimately, about the fantasy of the loss of civilization where that civilization is the interconnected relationality that makes survival and livable lives possible. That is, it is an expression of anxiety over the social, cultural, economic, and civilizational effects and the impact on identity and subjectivity that would be wrought by a substantial, sudden, and unexpected drop in population numbers along with the loss of the accumulated knowledge of the world that is archived across human memory, print, and digital archives. In that sense, the digital archive that is the Internet is also the subject of deeply held fears of the passing of a particular frame of civilization that is built on information and its accessibility. This has implications for the instability that is relational identity itself. Identity and civilization are represented as simultaneously inseparable but always at risk of being made separate by the loss of the latter and the continuation of the former; the loss of the latter is representable through the idea of the loss of past human knowledge, its repositories, access to its digital records, and the destruction of archive as both object and concept.

Civilization here can be understood to mean both the force of law and the formation of civil society in which relationality between subjects within the population is managed by both formal and informal frameworks of sociality. Foucault (2008) pointed to the concept of civil society as that field of reference through which governance technologies of power manage populations in ways distinct from, but absolutely interwoven with, the dominance of neoliberal economic processes, markets, production, consumption, and exchange (p. 295). Civil society is inseparable from the dominant form of selfhood in neoliberal conditions, which is *Homo oeconomicus* or economic man – the figure of selfhood in which the subject is responsible for managing his or her own risk and finance as an "entrepreneur of the self" (p. 226) whereby "economic behavior is the grid of intelligibility one will adopt on the behavior of a new individual" (Foucault, 2008, p. 252). Civil society operates within this framework but for the purpose of ensuring that governmentality is not split between a branch of governing economically and a branch of governing juridically – biopolitical governmentality operating within and on behalf of neoliberalism establishes civil society as a frame of reference. Civil society, or just "society" is the framework through which the workable bond of subjects as *Homo oeconomicus* is constituted. The state and civilization or civil society are often conflated, although in a Foucauldian perspective they are not necessarily the same, if interconnected – rather, the state can operate without civility to exclude certain population and care for others (Butler, 2012, pp. 143, 144). For Foucault, civilizational governance emerges historically, in a modified form, from the pastoral care of the Medieval church (Petterson, 2012, pp. 90, 91) to produce disciplinary institutions and, later, biopolitical and security forms of governance that look after groups and populations; in doing so, such postpastoral governance technologies produce a spontaneous bond of individual subjects. Here, "there is no explicit contract, no voluntary union, no renunciation of rights, and no delegation of natural rights to someone else; in short, there is no constitution of sovereignty by a sort of pact of subjection. In fact, if civil society actually carries out a synthesis, it will quite simply be through a summation of individual satisfactions within the social bond itself" (Foucault, 2008, p. 300). It operates, then, as the matrix of political and social power that permits the neoliberal economic technologies of power to flourish without dissent. At the same time, civil society provides a constitutive force for the social relationalities between subjects within a population grouping beyond the purely economic. While neoliberal societies require subjects to produce themselves as entrepreneurs of the self by managing their own risk, the economies of ethical care, assistance, and participation that are neoliberalism's excess and inherent to human subjectivity are the product of civil society and the concern of technologies of governance that have given over the economic to the market but retained the pastoral, the disciplinary, and the law as the means by which relationality is regulated across multitudes.

Within civilizational formations, an archive of information is therefore both pastoral in providing care of the lifeforce of populations through the sharing of material necessary for ongoing and intergenerational livability, and monumental in providing the sign and symbol of civilization. The digital archive, here, constructs both together, providing the capacity for subjects to seek out the information necessary for maintenance of livability, whether that be biological basics such as health information or social elements such as relationality with one's forebears, histories, documentations, finance. Both are, of course, intertwined (Agamben, 1995). Yet because the archive of shared information is so essential to the ongoingness of civilization as a formation of human subjectivity, from the running of electricity, to the agricultural production of food, to the education of the species for the next generations of livability, the archive and therefore civilization and the production of identity are vulnerable to loss, a loss that would establish unlivability. Indeed, the figuration of the digital archive as somehow more vulnerable to global catastrophe than, say, books and papers has been well represented in film and television depictions of postapocalyptic worlds, whereby the lack of digitality and bare basics of survival are what govern, for example, the kinds of human identity possible in series such as *The Walking Dead* (2010–) or *Survivors* (1975–1977, remade 2008–2009) in which digital technologies of communication and archiving are wholly absent. In that context, the subject constituted in relation with the archive – whether the individualized self archive, the collation of information produced for the state, or the collection of shared information that represents a variant of Enlightenment civilizational practice – is a subject that is produced through the simultaneous attachment to the archive and its ever-present potential for loss. This is a deep, passionate attachment necessary for subjectivity and subjectivation (Allen, 2006, p. 200), which is simultaneously an attachment to civilization, to the archive and the selfhood that is produced at the conjunction of both in the context of the world and the Earth as an ongoing, yet highly vulnerable, endeavor.

The conjunction of the archive and surveillance thus produces a repository and an activity of recording which is at once losable and grievable but, nevertheless, central to the contemporary production of identities in the context of digitization. This is not only at the level of the individual record as described in Chapter 1 on social networking, but is also significant in terms of the past and present categories, continuities, and formations of knowledge through which subjectivity is produced. If performativity is always a citation that is made sensible in the terms of knowledge that precedes us, then today it is the digital archive that comes to constitute not only the categories, names, signifiers, and forms of specific identity characteristics and attributes, but also the necessary intelligibilities through which identity coherence is recognized and judged. The digital archive serves as the point of reference for both spectatorship and ongoing (self-)surveillance of subjectivity, so integral to identity today that it becomes that of which we fear loss. At the same time, as the repository of personalized memory in an era of information overload and the glut of personal, community, population, and global recordkeeping, the archive becomes the representation of the self, both in terms of that which is the individualized subject and that which is simultaneously the representation of what it means to be human in contemporary terms.

## 3  ARCHIVING AND SURVEILLING THE EARTH

In previous chapters, I have noted some of the development of new approaches to thinking about the relationship between bodies, identities, and spaces that occur alongside digitization and networking of everyday communicative and relational lives. One element of that relates to the everyday practice of using digital maps based on geolocational technologies (the pinpointing of the self on the map through our mobile devices to present us with a relatively accurate "you are here") and satellite imagery which places us within a visual terrain seen from above. The fact that one can view one's location – or any location on the Earth – from above without the effort of climbing a hill or a tower or the cost of chartering a flight, enters the everyday experience of digital media in a way which makes another of those little reorientations of how we do identity in a network, digital culture. Importantly, however, the capacity to see from above is also linked with discourses of surveillance: the notion of the private back garden of the private home that is obscured from public surveillance by the use of fences and walls is, in the later twentieth century, put in question by often fictionalized accounts of spy satellites that are usually represented as doing a great deal more in real time than is accessible to us in any realistic technological setting today. Nevertheless, the ability to look down upon terrain, place, towns, suburbs, commercial, and industrial districts, and oceans from a god's-eye perspective in addition to the capacity the online tool provides for giving street view angles, provides a form of noninvasive surveillance of the landscapes – both known and unknown – through which we derive at least some element of subjectivity and incorporate, whether through knowingness or foreignness of the image, into the coordinates of intelligible performativity.

At the same time, Google Earth's satellite imagery provides an archiving of the Earth, a screen-cap (region by region) at particular points in time, enabling deployment of archive in a way that opens up the capacity to experience nostalgia differently. For example, the highly accessible imagery enables a user to explore the homes at which he or she has previously lived, the changing landscape of a rear garden as seen from the affectively omniscient view from above, the changing or eroding façade of a house from the street view provided in multiple angles, shots, and zoom-ins. Nostalgia and memory are indelibly tied up with the performativity of selfhood, in part because individual past memory is typically resignified or recognized in the context of the articulation of identity in the present, but also because our performativities of selfhood are not built merely on discourses and categorizations given to us socially and made accessible in communication, but on our own self-interpretations of personal, group, and social experiences of the past that are reworked to fit into a presentation of the coherent self (Cover & Prosser, 2013). This rerememebering of the past through personal archives of photographs and memorabilia is a normative formation of selfhood in contemporary everyday life, and this includes nostalgia around places one has been and places one has lived (Probyn, 1996). However, Google Earth facilitates particular kinds of nostalgic experiences in providing a new angle of viewing from the god's eye perspective the places about which we are nostalgic, simultaneously re-exciting those elements in our performative complexities but simultaneously disrupting our identities by providing us with new angles that were not part of our everyday in the past. Obviously this would not necessarily be the case for future generations should they have ongoing access to a god's eye view of their habitat from an early age; future generations who have grown with the digitization of the representable Earth will find that it is normative, and therefore naturalized and therefore unremarkable. In the sense of that which disappears into the natural background, this representation becomes more, and not less, constitutive of contemporary regimes of identity and the performativities of selfhood.

## 3.1 Viewing Ourselves from Above

Google Earth and Google Maps present depictions of our everyday world space, our cities, towns, roads, forests, buildings, roofs, and oceans from the god-like perspective of/from above. While skyscrapers and airflight have given rise to the many occasions on which the average subject can view the world from this above view perspective, it is the sharing of satellite imagery through near-seamless interwoven tapestries of terrain, overlaid by maps and utilized with geolocational direction-finding and mapping applications (as well as consumer advice in terms of nearby spaces in which to eat, shop, buy accommodation, or otherwise purchase commodities) that has integrated the god's-eye view into the everyday experience of contemporary digital subjectivity. Maps that give a drawn representation of the built environment, coastlines, and roadways from the god's-eye perspective present discontinuities by marking spaces in separation to each other, images of territory, and fixing of space to territorial bounds (Roy, 2006, p. 1). This has provided a node through which twentieth century identity is made sensible, whereby national and state boundaries operate to define, name, and give citizenship as one among several coordinates of identity experienced by the vast majority most of the time. Google Earth here transforms this perspective by disestablishing the link between space and national/state boundaries, presenting subjects with a perspective of the world that is divided not into territories but marked by the seams at which different satellite images have been pulled together, allowing us to experience flying across many different spaces without boundary, honing in on spaces that were once territories, at will.

At the same time, however, the representation of the world comes to be experienced in the context of realistic images from above whereby human subjects are positioned ever more so as masters of the space, a space which we surveil (not in real time) at our own will, whenever we engage in locational activities whether for entertainment or practical direction finding and information seeking. In this context, the experience of digital identity in the act of using Google Earth and Google Maps is one that is produced via a notion of subjectivity, that is not one of being surveilled but of actively positioning oneself in the vantage point for surveillance. All subjects surveil and self-surveil as part of disciplinary and biopolitical processes of engaging in sociality, however here the god's-eye view of such satellite-derived images allow us to take that participation in surveillance to a different level (literally) by articulating our selves through performativities of viewing terrain from above that enacts subjectivity as a kind of über-spectator.

## 3.2 The Faceless Earth, Cohabitation, and Ethics

Munster (2008) has made the point that there is something alarming about the absence of people in Google Earth's imagery from above, and we can extend that to include the eradication of faces and bodies, subsequent to many humorous incidents of embarrassing corporeal representations on Google Maps' street view. In this respect, Munster finds the use of Google Earth in flying from location to location as emphasizing an unexpected solitary experience:

> There are buildings, tanks, trees, and monuments represented in the data sets but never any sense of cohabitation of the environment with others. This distinguishes Google Earth, again, from other online environments such as blogs, social software networking and tools, as well as gaming, where the presence of and relation to others (albeit sometimes homogenised and somewhat forced) assume primary status. The [Google Earth] environment is one in which there are many individual users in full flight but no dimension of the social within its visual space (p. 399).

Indeed, there is something both disconcerting and destabilizing about the notion of representation of the world which marks our subjectivity and provides a frame for a relationality that is depicted as empty, without community or sociality. While it would be interesting to extend Munster's analysis in the context of the corporate and neoliberal drives to represent subjects as individualized consumers in an Earth without social community, the point that is important here to an understanding of contemporary digital identities is that, in a world of populations and crowds, Google Earth and its mapping tools provides an alternative heterotopic space of a subjectivity that is articulated in terms of an aloneness, an overemphasized solitary individuality, as if radically separated from others, as if not obliged toward the care of others and the mutual receipt of the care of the other toward oneself. This non-Utopian spatial representation serves as a node of intelligible subjectivity through which performances are seen to be coherent and recognizable, articulated in, for example, the movement of only the individualized body in a direction from one place to another in an exercise of geolocational mapping. (Of course, Google Maps does account for other subjects in cities and locations where traffic data are accounted for in a directional search, although this too is represented without sociality but aggregates traffic as if driverless and without relationalities of car to body, driver to driver, subject to subject.) Terrain, whether natural or built, is all that a subject has here in order to articulate selfhood in relationality.

The lack of other subjects in this representation of the Earth presents ethical issues in which the individual is given primacy not only over relationality with other bodies as the formation of subjective and social life, but also in terms of the subject produced in disregard for others and otherness by representing the world as uninhabited and in which the individual Google Earth user is sovereign, the inheritor of this heterotopic empty space. Judith Butler has recently expanded on her ethics of nonviolence by foregrounding the notion of cohabitation. For Butler (2011), cohabitation begins by acknowledging the heterogeneity of the Earth's population "as an irreversible condition of social and political life itself" (p. 83). Such heterogeneity can include the diverse ways in which persons from across the world represent themselves online or elsewhere, in ways that may never be recognizable but call for recognition of a right to cohabit the Earth. Cohabitation means that

> ... we not only live with those we never chose, and to whom we may feel no social sense of belonging, but we are also obligated to preserve those lives and the plurality of which they form a part. In this sense, concrete political norms and ethical prescriptions emerge from the unchosen character of these modes of cohabitation. To cohabit the earth is prior to any possible community or nation or neighborhood. We might choose where to live, and who to live by, but we cannot choose with whom to cohabit the earth (p. 84).

Butler is not suggesting here that we cohabit the Earth and therefore must live in peace in a way that locates those we do not wish to live with in places other than here. Rather, this is to argue that the primacy of the nation, the sovereign border, and by extension the definition of a particular population or space cannot be built on the idea that the other can be asked not to inhabit the world (our world, our space) without eradication of that other. In that Google Earth represents a relationship between the digital identity of the subject and the digital identity of Earth as one of an individual in uninhabited space, we find ourselves framed by a lack of ethics of cohabitation, where the regard for the otherness of the other as one who shares the Earth with us is made redundant. The implications for ethical and nonviolent relationality are untold in this very new way of experiencing the world, its cities, and its built terrain depopulated.

To extend this from the view-from-above realm of the depopulated planet of Google Earth to the street view of Google Maps, we might consider the ethical concerns of the space in which the body can indeed be represented, but in which the face is obscured or erased. The face is significant to relational identity, for it is through the notion of the face that subjects are ethically obliged to perform their identities in ways which are nonviolent to others – the basis of a social contract of a world, whether online or in the space of corporeal movement, that is a world cohabited, a world of population. Faces and other information understood to risk compromising individual and corporate privacy was systematically obscured, blurred, or deleted from Google's Street View image archive as concerns were raised ("Privacy concerns over Google," 2007), regularly in terms of discourses of risk and surveillance that understood such technologies to empower the archiver over the archived. There are, of course, also spaces of actual disembodiment and facelessness made available through Google's Street View applications including, for example, images of Japan's town of Namie, which is empty of its 21,000 residents since the nuclear accidents subsequent to the 2011 earthquake and tsunami, but captured in its decimated state by Google's Street View vehicles and their imaging technologies ("Google street view offers rare glimpse," 2013). In this context, the desire to archive significant and rare moments in a time of a depopulated space has important value not only for the nostalgia of those who had once resided there but also social value in terms of a unique or rare phenomenon of the contemporary ghost town. This space where there are, indeed, no actual faces is of course the exception that draws attention away from the rule – that the contemporary form of representing space online does so in ways which erases identity by obscuring the face.

It is the face here that opens further questions as to how we proceed ethically as subjects who perform our identities in relation to others in ways governed by the face, which of course includes not only the face-to-face encounter one might have in the street, but the representation of the still or moving image of bodies with faces as well as the communicative forms of representing our own faces online as selfies, as discussed in the introduction to this book, or the use of technological tools such as Skype for face-to-face digital videoconferencing across large spaces. The face, then, is significant to how we perceive identities, even in an era of ubiquitous digitality. As understood through philosophic approaches to ethics that are derived from the work of Emmanuel Levinas (1969) and utilized by Butler (2004, 2011), Derrida (1999), and others, nonviolent ethical relations can be the form that relationality between the subject and the other takes, and this is understood through the notion or metaphor of the encounter in which subjects come face to face. In certain readings of Levinas, it is the face that is the site by which ethics is sought and obliged. As Bob Plant (2011) has put it:

> According to Levinas, the "face" is poorly understood as an object possessing certain attributes. Of course, in one sense, the face is an "assemblage of a nose, a forehead, eyes, etc." But what ultimately interests Levinas is how, through its active dimension of facing, the face of a concrete Other affects and challenges my complacent being-here. Through the face, the Other "is the most naked" (even "nakedness itself"), and as such, the face that faces me is the paradigmatic expression of vulnerability. This, roughly speaking, is why Levinas maintains that "access" to the Other is "straightaway ethical" (p. 57).

Similarly, for Nuyen, the face of the other is the primordial expression of the obligation not to enact violence against that other. Since the subject is already premised and possible through the otherness of the other, the obligation to be responsible for the other is already there before motivation, but always encountered in the face (Nuyen, 2000, p. 414). If the face-to-face encounter of concrete subjects is the site by which ethics is enacted, then the question remains as to what occurs when the call for recognition of the other is no longer characterized in terms of the primary tool of representing space online as one which is faceless when depicting space as standing upright, and depopulated when viewed from the gods' perspective from above.

## 4 CONCLUSIONS: DIGITAL IDENTITIES

In Chapter 2, I made a number of points in relation to Foucault's work in *Security, Territory, Population* (2007) and *Birth of Biopolitics* (2008) around the ways in which institutionally based disciplinary regimes of individualized surveillance and normalization both dovetail with and give way to broader biopolitical technologies of power that make whole populations and large numbers the object of surveillance. Through the large-scale surveillance of biopolitics, subjects are no longer categorized in identity terms of normal and abnormal but are invited to actively plot themselves on curves of normativities that are produced through the big data frameworks of knowledge, in which norms may form a central point in a distributional variance, and normativity is not about coherent identity performance but is produced through proximity to the norm. This opens the field for identity performativity by allowing for greater variance to be captured in a normative array, while not foreclosing on the nonnorm but accounting for the complex gray areas that comprise any large-scale articulation of norms. Such a biopolitical framework of subjecthood is in service to capital, predominantly through the ways in which it sets normative standards for *Homo oeconomicus* (Foucault, 2008, p. 226) in which the subject becomes the entrepreneur of the self, active on one's own commodification and in the production of proximity to a norm through practices of consumption.

This is the central element in the relationship between identity and digital media and communication as a ubiquitous element of contemporary everyday life that has become so significant in the affluent West as to make it meaningless to think about identity outside of digitality. That said, the kinds of highly complex identity projects of digital performativity that

I have been discussing in this book, from social networking to interactive engagement with textualities that redefines authorship of the self to body projects through digital means to refigurations of place, are expanded and tempered by the contemporary conjunction of digital surveillance, archiving and the archive of the world that is Google Earth. These together establish norms – normative places to be, absences of people in ethical terms from the representation of the world as place and space, curves of normativities through big data network-accessible information produced through participation in cultures of surveillance – and these norms are constraints. At the same time, the invitation to participate in these projects is one that masquerades as agency but is not necessarily agential. That is, the performativity of identity may be made more complex and variable with broader capacities for a subject to be a coherent self. In spite of a greater range of identity categories and blurred areas, all in the aid of producing subjects as coherent consumers, the fact of coherence remains in that subjects are not invited to play with identity but to build an identity in the context of the available discourses that always precede the self. What is central in the new world of surveillance-archive-Earth is the fact that the discourses that make certain identities recognizable and intelligible are more broadly available than ever before, and the means of responding to the call or hail of identity coherence are made more widely available through the technologies by which one can articulate one's identity, not as the digital separate from some kind of real, but regardless of where one is and in terms of what one is doing always a digital identity.

For all that has been said here and in earlier chapters about digital media's capacity to produce subjects in relationality, it is important to remember that through the activities of surveillance, that is the production of the digital archive as a marketing tool and a record of consumption and the individualizing and solitary-making depiction of the world in Google Earth, the subject of digital communication is one who is emphatically individualized. This is not to suggest that there is no relationality, for all performativity is in the context of the social discourses and significations that both precede and surround us. Rather, it is to say that the contemporary subject of digital media may be one who is engaged forcefully in interactive behavior, innovative creativity, sharing, and participation, but the basic requirement to participate is to be a subject who conforms vehemently to an individualized stylization of performativity. This opens up a number of problems for ethics in that, while we regularly celebrate digital communication as a site of relational interactivity, an overemphasis on individualization reduces the capacity to recognize the vulnerability of the other and thereby obscures the social and ethical obligation toward that other. Perhaps this is why cyberbullying, racism, sexism, and homophobia are rampant features of the contemporary experience of relating online: it is not that the screen serves merely to anonymize users who then go on to feel they can articulate attitudes that negatively demean those of minority, marginal, or subjugated identities. Rather, it is the broader framework through which performativity of selfhood is produced as an individual consumer rather than a social subject which positions users to forget the social obligation of nonviolent behavior and language in digital communication and self-articulation. This need not be understood as fixed through time, but it does emerge as the contemporary problem of sociality in a digital context and one which needs urgently addressing.

Throughout this book, I have been making the point that it no longer makes any sense to think about our digital experience and our digital selves in terms of a separation between real in the physical and corporeal sense and virtual in the online, communicative, mediated, and sometimes anonymous sense. Neither the concept of the real nor the virtual has any value for us today, nor should either side or aspect – if they are to be frames of understanding identity – be celebrated or bemoaned. Rather, the ubiquity of digital media, communicative forms, practices, and technologies in our everyday lives results in it being constitutional of our subjectivities, selfhood, and identity. How we perform identity in the affluent West is not, therefore, in any way separable from the experience of digital communication, regardless of where our mobile device or connective computer might be located at this present moment. While this has resulted in both continuities of forms of identity that remain governed in past fixities, it has also produced ruptures in how identity is performed; not through an idea of virtuality or identity fluidity, as such, but through the complexification of subjectivity and selfhood that results from the practices of recording, interacting, creating, engaging, globalizing, mobilizing, and archiving our selves. How the shifts and turns in what constitutes normative subjectivity move in the future is, likewise, unknowable, although in light of some of the above points, it can only be hoped that this will involve new, ethical ways in which to cohabit our spaces, our socialities, and our worlds that produce a genuine sociality.

# REFERENCES

Agamben, G. (1995). *Homo sacer: Sovereign power and bare life* (D. Heller-Roazen, Trans.). Stanford, CA: Stanford University Press.

Ahmed, S. (2011). Problematic proximities: or why critiques of gay imperialism matter. *Feminist Legal Studies, 19*(2), 119–132.

Allen, A. (2006). Dependency, subordination, and recognition: on Judith Butler's theory of subjection. *Continental Philosophy Review, 38*(3–4), 199–222.

Allor, M. (1995). Relocating the site of the audience. In O. Boyd-Barrett, & C. Newbold (Eds.), *Approaches to media: A reader* (pp. 543–553). London: Arnold.

Althusser, L. (1971). *Lenin and philosophy and other essays* (B. Brewster, Trans.). London: NLB.

American Psychiatric Association. (2013). *Diagnostic and statistical manual of mental disorders* (5th ed.). Arlington, VA: American Psychiatric Publishing.

Anderson, B. (1983). *Imagined communities: Reflections on the origins and spread of nationalism.* London: Verso.

Andrejevic, M. (2002). The work of being watched: interactive media and the exploitation of self-disclosure. *Critical Studies in Media Communication, 19*(2), 230–248.

Andrejevic, M. (2011). Social network exploitation. In Z. Papacharissi (Ed.), *A networked self: Identity, community, and culture on social network sites* (pp. 82–101). London: Routledge.

Ang, I. (1991). *Desperately seeking the audience.* London: Routledge.

Ang, I. (1993). Migrations of Chineseness: Ethnicity in the postmodern world. In D. Bennett (Ed.), *Cultural studies: Pluralism and theory* (pp. 32–44). Melbourne: University of Melbourne.

Ang, I. (2011). Navigating complexity: from cultural critique to cultural intelligence. *Continuum: Journal of Media & Cultural Studies, 25*(6), 779–794.

Appadurai, A. (2003). Archive and aspiration. In J. Brouwer, & A. Mulder (Eds.), *Information is alive* (pp. 14–25). Rotterdam: V2_Publishing and NAI Publishers.

Appadurai, A. (2004). The capacity to aspire: Culture and the terms of recognition. In V. Rao, & M. Walton (Eds.), *Culture and public action* (pp. 59–84). Stanford, CA: Stanford University Press.

Attwood, F. (2006). Sexed Up: theorizing the sexualization of culture. *Sexualities, 9*(1), 77–94.

Baker, J. (September 2, 2011). Generation V buff but not so pretty after dark. *Sydney Morning Herald.* Retrieved from http://www.smh.com.au/it-pro/.

Banks, J., & Humphreys, S. (2008). The labour of user co-creators: emergent social network markets? *Convergence: The International Journal of Research into New Media Technologies, 14*(4), 401–418.

Bantick, C. (January 15, 2004). Why computer games should worry parents. *The Age.* Retrieved from http://www.theage.com/au/articles/2004/01/14/1073877896185.html.

Barabási, A.-L. (2011). Introduction and keynote. In Z. Papacharissi (Ed.), *A networked self: Identity, community, and culture on social network sites* (pp. 1–14). London: Routledge.

Barker, C. (1999). *Television, globalization and cultural identities.* Buckingham: Open University Press.

Barthes, R. (1975). *The pleasure of the text* (R. Miller, Trans.). New York: Hill & Wang.

Barthes, R. (1977). *Image/music/text* (S. Heath, Trans.). New York: Hill & Wang.

Baumann, Z. (2003). *Liquid love: On the fragility of human bonds.* London: Polity Press.

Bauman, Z. (2011). Migration and identities in the globalized world. *Philosophy and Social Criticism, 37*(4), 425–435.

Baym, N. K., Zhang, Y. B., Kunkel, A., Ledbetter, A., & Lin, M. (2007). Relational quality and media use in interpersonal relationships. *New Media & Society, 9*(5), 735–752.

*Digital Identities.*
http://dx.doi.org/10.1016/B978-0-12-420083-8.00009-2

Beavis, C. (1998). Computer games: Youth culture, resistant readers and consuming passions. Paper presented at Research in Education: Does it Count – Australian Association for Research in Education Annual Conference, Adelaide, Australia, 29 November–3 December.

Beck, U. (1992). *Risk society: Towards a new modernity*. London: Sage.

Bell, V. (1999). Performativity and belonging. *Theory, Culture & Society*, *16*(2), 1–10.

Benford, S., Bowers, J., Fahlén, L. E., Greenhalgh, C., & Snowdon, D. (1997). Embodiments, avatars, clones and agents for multi-user, multi-sensory virtual worlds. *Multimedia Systems*, *5*(2), 93–104.

Benjamin, W., & Arndt, H. (Ed.), (1992). *Illuminations* (H. Zohn, Trans.). London: Fontana.

Benn, S. I. (1982). Individuality, autonomy and community. In E. Kamenka (Ed.), *Community as a social ideal* (pp. 43–62). London: Edward Arnold.

Bennett, T. (1983). Texts, readers, reading formations. *Literature and History*, *9*(2), 214–227.

Berger, A. A. (2002). *Video games: A popular culture phenomenon*. New Brunswick, NJ: Transaction Publishers.

Berlant, L. (2007). Slow death (sovereignty, obesity, lateral agency). *Critical Inquiry*, *33*(4), 754–780.

Bernardi, D. L. (1998). *Star Trek and history: Raceing toward a white future*. New Brunswick, NJ: Rutgers University Press.

Berry, R. (2006). Will the iPod kill the radio star? Profiling podcasting as radio. *Convergence: The International Journal of Research into New Media Technologies*, *12*(2), 143–162.

Billingham, P. (2003). *Sensing the city through television*. Bristol, CT: Intellect.

Binaisa, M. (2002). All clicked out. In L. King (Ed.), *Game on: The history and culture of videogames* (pp. 44–45). New York: Universe Publishing.

Biriotti, M., & Miller, N. (1993). *What is an author?* Manchester: Manchester University Press.

Blaine, L. (August 14, 2013). How selfies are ruining your relationships. *Time*. Retrieved from http://newsfeed.time.com/2013/08/14/how-selfies-are-ruining-your-relationships/.

Blood, R. W., & Pirkis, J. (2001). Suicide and the media: part III Theoretical issues. *Crisis*, *22*(4), 163–169.

Bloom, C. (1990). MacDonald's man meets Reader's Digest. In G. Day (Ed.), *Readings in popular culture: Trivial pursuits?* (pp. 13–17). New York: St. Martin's Press.

Bordewijk, J. L., & van Kaam, B. (1986). Towards a new classification of tele-information services. *InterMedia*, *14*(1), 16–21.

Borgatta, E. F., & Montgomery, R. J. V. (2000). *Encyclopedia of sociology*. New York: Macmillan Reference.

Bourdieu, P. (1990). *The logic of practice*. Oxford: Polity.

Boyce, T. (2007). The media and obesity. *Obesity Reviews*, *8*(Suppl. 1), 201–205.

boyd, d. (2008a). Why youth (heart) social network sites: The role of networked publics in teenage social life. In D. Buckingham (Ed.), *Youth, identity, and digital media* (pp. 119–142). Cambridge, MA: MIT Press.

boyd, d. (2008b). Facebook's privacy trainwreck: exposure, invasion, and social convergence. *Convergence: The International Journal of Research into New Media Technologies*, *14*(1), 13–20.

boyd, d. (2014). *It's complicated: The social lives of networked teens*. New Haven, CT: Yale University Press.

Brabazon, T. (2007). *The University of Google: Education in the (post) information age*. Aldershot, UK: Ashgate.

Brewster, A. (2005). The poetics of memory. *Continuum: Journal of Media & Cultural Studies*, *19*(3), 397–402.

Brooker, W., & Jermyn, D. (2003). Conclusion: Overflow and audience. In W. Brooker, & D. Jermyn (Eds.), *The audience studies reader* (pp. 332–335). London: Routledge.

Brown, W. (2009). Introduction. In T. Asad, W. Brown, J. Butler, & S. Mahmood (Eds.), *Is critique secular? Blesphemy, injury and free speech* (pp. 7–19). Berkeley, CA: The Townsend Center for the Humanities & University of California Press.

Bruns, A. (2008). *Blogs, Wikipedia, Second Life, and beyond. From production to produsage.* New York: Peter Lang.

Buchanan, I. (2007). Deleuze and the internet. *Australian Humanities Review, 43*(December). Available from http://www.australianhumanitiesreview.org/archive/Issue-December-2007/Buchanan.html.

Buchanan, K. (2004). Video games: Ritual or rebellion? In L. Goode, & N. Zuberi (Eds.), *Media studies in Aotearoa/New Zealand* (pp. 135–145). Auckland: Pearson.

Buchbinder, D. (1997). *Performance anxieties: Re-producing masculinity.* St. Leonards, NSW: Allen & Unwin.

Buckingham, D. (2008). Introducing identity. In D. Buckingham (Ed.), *Youth, identity, and digital media* (pp. 1–24). Cambridge, MA: MIT Press.

Buckingham, D. (Ed.). (2008). *Youth, identity, and digital media.* Cambridge, MA: MIT Press.

Buffardi, L. E., & Campbell, K. W. (2008). Narcissism and social networking web sites. *Personality and Social Psychology Bulletin, 34*(10), 1303–1314.

Burnett, R., & Marshall, P. D. (2003). *Web Theory: An Introduction.* London: Routledge.

Burgess, J., & Green, J. (2009). *YouTube: Online video and participatory culture.* Cambridge: Polity.

Butler, J., & Athanasiou, A. (2013). *Dispossession: The performative in the political.* Cambridge: Polity.

Butler, J., & Spivak, G. C. (2007). *Who sings the nation-state? Language, politics, belonging.* London: Seagull Books.

Butler, J. (1990). *Gender trouble: Feminism and the subversion of identity.* London: Routledge.

Butler, J. (1991). Imitation and gender insubordination. In D. Fuss (Ed.), *Inside/Out: Lesbian theories, gay theories* (pp. 13–31). London: Routledge.

Butler, J. (1993). *Bodies that matter: On the discursive limits of 'sex'.* London: Routledge.

Butler, J. (1995). Collected and fractured: Response to Identities. In K. A. Appiah, & H. L. Gates, Jr. (Eds.), *Identities* (pp. 439–447). Chicago, IL: University of Chicago Press.

Butler, J. (1997). *The psychic life of power: Theories in subjection.* Stanford, CA: Stanford University Press.

Butler, J. (1999). Revisiting bodies and pleasures. *Theory, Culture & Society, 16*(2), 11–20.

Butler, J. (2000). Longing for recognition. *Studies in Gender and Sexuality, 1*(3), 271–290.

Butler, J. (2003). Violence, mourning, politics. *Studies in Gender and Sexuality, 4*(1), 9–37.

Butler, J. (2004). *Precarious life.* London: Verso.

Butler, J. (2005). *Giving an account of oneself.* New York: Fordham University Press.

Butler, J. (2007). Reply from Judith Butler to Mills and Jenkins. *Differences: A Journal of Feminist Cultural Studies, 18*(2), 180–195.

Butler, J. (2009). *Frames of war: When is life grievable?* London: Verso.

Butler, J. (2011). Is Judaism Zionism? In E. Mendieta, & J. VanAntwerpen (Eds.), *The power of religion in the public sphere* (pp. 70–91). New York: Columbia University Press.

Butler, J. (2012). *Parting ways: Jewishness and the critique of Zionism.* New York: Columbia University Press.

Campbell, G. (September 24, 2009). Girls play games, too, explains pro gamer 'Jinx'. *The Age.* Retrieved from http://www.theage.com.au/digital-life/games/.

Campbell, J., & Harbord, J. (1999). Playing it again: citation, reiteration or circularity? *Theory, Culture & Society, 16*(2), 229–239.

Caputo, J. D. (1993). *Against ethics: Contributions to a poetics of obligation with constant reference to deconstruction.* Bloomington, IN: Indiana University Press.

Carey, J. (1988). *Communication as culture: Essays on media and society.* London: Routledge.

Carter, R. (January 23, 2015). Internet will 'disappear', Google boss Eric Schmidt tells Davos. *Brisbane Times.* Retrieved from http://www.brisbanetimes.com.au/digital-life/digital-life-news/.

Caruth, C. (1995). Recapturing the past. In C. Caruth (Ed.), *Trauma: Explorations in memory* (pp. 151–157). Baltimore, MD: Johns Hopkins University Press.

Carver, T. (1998). *The postmodern Marx*. Manchester: Manchester University Press.

Castells, M. (1997). *The Information Age: Economy, society and culture. Volume II: The power of identity*. Oxford: Blackwell.

Castells, M. (2000). *The rise of the network society* (2nd ed.). Oxford: Blackwell.

Cauchi, S. (June 19, 2011). Prepare for the 'internet of things', where socks stay connected. *The Age*. Retrieved from http://www.theage.com.au/technology/technology-news/.

Chaput, C. (2009). Regimes of truth, disciplined bodies, secured populations: an overview of Michel Foucault. *Science Fiction Film and Television, 2*(1), 91–104.

China Halts Shock Therapy for Internet Addicts. (July 14, 2009). *The Age*. Retrieved from http://www.theage.com.au/digital-life/digital-life-news/.

Clough, P. T. (2008). The affective turn: political economy, biomedia and bodies. *Theory, Culture & Society, 25*(1), 1–22.

Cochrane, N. (August 27, 2002). How you see it, how you don't. *The Age*. Retrieved from http://www.theage.com.au/articles/2002/08/24/1030052995857.html/.

Cohen, A. P. (1985). *The symbolic construction of community*. London: Ellis Horwood & Tavistock Publications.

Colebatch, T. (August 22, 2002). More and more it is a case of till divorce do us part. *The Age*. Retrieved from http://www.theage.com.au/articles/2002/08/22/1029114163415.html.

Collins, D. (2005). Identity, mobility and urban place-making: exploring gay life in Manila. *Gender & Society, 19*(2), 180–198.

Commonwealth of Australia (2003). *Multicultural Australia: United in diversity. Updating the 1999 New Agenda for Multicultural Australia: Strategic Direction for 2003–2006*. Canberra: Commonwealth of Australia.

Cooper, S. (2002). *Technoculture and critical theory: In the service of the machine?* London: Routledge.

Courtis, B. (July 27, 2003). Square-eyed by the box of magic. *The Age*. Retrieved from http://www.theage.com.au/articles/2003/07/26/1059084255981.html.

Cover, R. (2003). The naked subject: nudity, context and sexualisation in contemporary culture. *Body & Society, 9*(3), 53–72.

Cover, R. (2004a). From Butler to Buffy: notes towards a strategy for identity analysis in contemporary television narrative. *Reconstruction: Studies in Contemporary Culture, 4*(2). Retrieved from http://reconstruction.eserver.org/Issues/042/cover.htm.

Cover, R. (2004b). Bodies, movements and desires: lesbian/gay subjectivity and the stereotype. *Continuum: Journal of Media & Cultural Studies, 18*(1), 81–98.

Cover, R. (2004c). Interactivity: reconceiving the audience in the struggle for textual 'control'. *Australian Journal of Communication, 31*(1), 107–120.

Cover, R. (2005a). Changing channels: scheduling, temporality, new technologies (and the future of 'television' in media studies). *Australian Journal of Communication, 32*(2), 9–24.

Cover, R. (2005b). DVD time: temporality, interactivity and the new TV culture of digital video. *Media International Australia, 117*(November), 137–148.

Cover, R. (2006). Audience inter/active: interactive media, narrative control and reconceiving audience history. *New Media & Society, 8*(1), 213–232.

Cover, R. (2010). Object(ives) of desire: romantic coupledom versus promiscuity, subjectivity and sexual identity. *Continuum: Journal of Media & Cultural Studies, 24*(2), 251–263.

Cover, R. (2012a). *Queer youth suicide, culture and identity: unliveable lives?* London: Ashgate.

Cover, R. (2012b). Performing and undoing identity online: social networking, identity theories and the incompatibility of online profiles and friendship regimes. *Convergence: The International Journal of Research into New media Technologies, 18*(2), 177–193.

Cover, R. (2013). Undoing attitudes: ethical change in the Go Back to Where You Came From documentary. *Continuum: Journal of Media & Cultural Studies, 27*(3), 408–420.

Cover, R. (2014a). Separating work and play: privacy, anonymity and the politics of interactive pedagogy in deploying Facebook in learning and teaching. *Digital Culture & Education, 6*(1), 47–59http://www.digitalcultureandeducation.com/cms/wp-content/uploads/2014/05/cover.pdf.

Cover, R. (2014b). Mobility, belonging and bodies: understanding attitudes of anxiety towards temporary migrants in Australia. *Continuum: Journal of Media & Cultural Studies*.

Cover, R. (2015). *Vulnerability and exposure: Footballer scandals, masculine identity and ethics.* Crawley, WA: UWA Publishing.

Cover, R., & Prosser, R. (2013). Memorial accounts: queer young men, identity and contemporary coming out narratives online. *Australian Feminist Studies, 28*(5), 81–94.

Cranny-Francis, A. (1995). *The body in the text.* Melbourne: Melbourne University Press.

Creed, B. (2003). *Media matrix: Sexing the new reality.* St. Leonards, NSW: Allen & Unwin.

Cubitt, S. (1991). *Timeshift: On video culture.* London: Routledge.

Curran, J. (2002). *Media and power.* London: Routledge.

Dahlberg, L. (2001). Computer-mediated communication and the public sphere: a critical analysis. *Journal of Computer-Mediated Communication, 7*(1).

Dance Pad lets your feet do the typing. (March 2, 2006). *The Age.* Retrieved from http://www.theage.com.au/news/breaking/.

David, M., & Munoz-Basols, J. (2011). Introduction: Defining and re-defining diaspora: An unstable concept. In M. David, & J. Munoz-Basols (Eds.), *Defining and re-defining diaspora: From theory to reality* (pp. xi–xiiv). Oxford: Inter-Disciplinary Press.

Davis, G. (2007). *Queer as Folk: TV classics.* London: British Film Institute.

Davis, M. (1997). *Gangland: Cultural elites and the new generationalism.* St. Leonards, NSW: Allen & Unwin.

Derrida, J. (1978). *Writing and difference* (A. Bass, Trans.). Chicago, IL: University of Chicago Press.

Derrida, J. (1988). *Limited Inc.* (S. Weber, & J. Mehlmantrans, Trans.). Evanston, IL: Northwestern University Press.

Derrida, J. (1995). The rhetoric of drugs (M. Israel, Trans.). In E. Weber (Ed.), *Points… Interviews, 1974–1994* (P. Kamuf, et al., Trans.) (pp. 228–254). Stanford, CA: Stanford University Press.

Derrida, J. (1999). *Adieu to Emmanuel Levinas* (P. A. Brault, & M. Naas, Trans.). Stanford, CA: Stanford University Press.

Dery, M. (1992). Cyberculture. *South Atlantic Quarterly, 91*, 508–531.

Dery, M. (1993). Culture jamming: hacking, slashing and sniping in the empire of signs. *Open Magazine.* Revised edition (2010). Retrieved from http://markdery.com/?page_id=154.

Descartes, R. (1968). *Discourse on method and the meditation* (F. E. Sutcliffe, Trans.). Harmondsworth: Penguin.

Deleuze, G. (1988). *Foucault* (S. Hand, Trans.). Minneapolis, MN: University of Minnesota Press.

Deuze, M. (2006). Ethnic media, community media and participatory culture. *Journalism, 7*(3), 262–280.

Diaz, J. (April 16, 2008). Facebook's squirmy chapter: site's evolution blurs line between boss and employee. *The Boston Globe.* Retrieved from http://www.boston.com/bostonworks/news/articles/.

Donath, J., & boyd, d. (2004). Public displays of connection. *Technology Journal, 22*(4), 71–82.

Downes, E. J., & McMillan, S. J. (2000). Defining interactivity: a qualitative identification of key dimensions. *New Media & Society, 2*(2), 157–179.

Downing, J. D. H. (2003). Audiences and readers of alternative media: the absent lure of the virtually unknown. *Media, Culture & Society, 25*(5), 625–645.

Dreher, T. (2009). Listening across difference: media and multiculturalism beyond the politics of voice. *Continuum: Journal of Media & Cultural Studies, 23*(4), 445–458.

Dunning, E., & Waddington, I. (2003). Sport as a drug and drugs in sport: some exploratory comments. *International Review for the Sociology of Sport*, *38*(3), 351–368.

Durkheim, E. (1952). *Suicide: A study in sociology* (J. A. Spaulding, & G. Simpson, Trans.). London: Routledge & Kegan Paul.

Düttmann, A. G. (1997). The culture of polemic: Misrecognizing recognition. (N. Walker, Trans.). *Radical Philosophy*, *81*(Jan–Feb), 27–34.

Düttmann, A. G. (2000). *The gift of language: Memory and promise in Adorno, Benjamin, Heidegger, and Rosenzweig* (A. Lyons, Trans.). Syracuse, NY: Syracuse University Press.

Eagleton, T. (2005). *Holy terror*. Oxford: Oxford University Press.

Eco, U. (1979). *The role of the reader: Explorations in the semiotics of texts*. Bloomington, IN: Indiana University Press.

Egli, M. A., & Meyers, L. S. (1984). The role of video game playing in adolescent life: is there a reason to be concerned? *Bulletin of the Psychodynamic Society*, *22*(4), 309–312.

Elias, N. (1991). *The society of individuals*. Oxford: Basil Blackwell.

Elliott, T. (December 13, 2014). Running on empty: exercise fanatics running themselves into the ground. *The Age*. Retrieved from http://www.theage.com.au/good-weekend/.

Ellison, N. B., Steinfeld, C., & Lampe, C. (2007). The benefits of facebook 'friends': social capital and college students' use of online social network sites. *Journal of Computer-Mediated Communication*, *12*, 1143–1168.

Eribon, D. (2004). *Insult and the gay self* (M. Lucey, Trans.). Durham, NC: Duke University Press.

Erikson, E. H. (1968). *Identity: Youth and crisis*. New York: Norton.

Ess, C. (1994). The political computer: Hypertext, democracy, and Habermas. In G. P. Landow (Ed.), *Hyper/Text/Theory* (pp. 225–253). Baltimore, MD: Johns Hopkins University Press.

Fairburn, C., Lane, C., Mataix-Cols, D., Tian, J., Grant, J., & Von Deneen, K. (May 25, 2013). Internet addiction: five new mental disorders you could have under DSM-5. *The Conversation*. Retrieved from http://theconversation.com/.

Faist, T. (2013). The mobility turn: a new paradigm for the social sciences? *Ethnic and Racial Studies*, *36*(11), 1637–1646.

Featherstone, M. (2006). Archive. *Theory, Culture & Society*, *23*(2–3), 591–596.

Federwisch, A. (August 8, 1997). Internet Addiction? *Nurseweek*. Retrieved from http://www.nurseweek.com/features/97-8/iadct.html.

Filiciak, M. (2003). Hyperidentities: Postmodern identity patterns in massively multiplayer online role-playing games. In M. J. P. Wolf, & B. Perron (Eds.), *The video game theory reader* (pp. 87–101). New York: Routledge.

Fiske, J. (1989). *Understanding popular culture*. London: Unwin Hyman.

Flew, T. (2008). *New media: An introduction* (3rd ed.). Melbourne: Oxford University Press.

Flew, T. (2013). *Global creative industries*. Cambridge: Polity.

Foucault, M. (1977a). *Discipline and punish: The birth of the prison* (A. Sheridan, Trans.). London: Penguin.

Foucault, M. (1977b). *Language, counter-memory, practice: Selected essays and interviews*. In D. F. Bouchard, (Ed.), (D. F. Bouchard & S. Simon, Trans.). Ithaca, NY: Cornell University Press.

Foucault, M. (1986). *Of other spaces* (J. Misowiec, Trans.). *Diacritics*, *16*(1), 22–27.

Foucault, M. (1988). The ethics of the care of the self as a practice of freedom. In J. Bernauer, & D. Rasmussen (Eds.), *The final Foucault* (pp. 102–118). Cambridge: MIT Press.

Foucault, M. (1993). Space, power and knowledge. In S. During (Ed.), *The cultural studies reader* (pp. 161–169). London: Routledge.

Foucault, M. (1994). *Ethics, subjectivity and truth*. In P. Rabinow, (Ed.), (R. Hurley et al., Trans.). New York: New York Press.

Foucault, M. (2004). *Society must be defended: Lectures at the Collège de France, 1975–76* (M. Bertani, & A. Fontana (Eds.), D. Macey, Trans.). London: Penguin.

Foucault, M. (2007). *Security, territory, population: Lectures at the Collège de France, 1977–78*. In M. Senellart (Ed.) (G. Burchell, Trans.). Hampshire: Palgrave Macmillan.

Foucault, M. (2008). *The birth of biopolitics: Lectures at the Collège de France, 1978–79*. In M. Senellart, (Ed.) (G. Burchell, Trans.). Hampshire: Palgrave Macmillan.

Foucault, M. (2008). Alternatives to the prison: dissemination or decline of social control (C. Venn, Trans.). *Theory, Culture & Society, 26*(6), 12–24.

Funk, J. B., Buchman, D. D., Jenks, J., & Bechtoldt, H. (2003). Playing violent video games, desensitization, and moral evaluation in children. *Journal of Applied Developmental Psychology, 24*(4), 413–436.

Gabriel, F. (2014). Sexting, selfies and self-harm: young people, social media and the performance of self-development. *Media International Australia, 151*, 104–112.

Gaillot, M. (1998). *Multiple meaning: Techno. An artistic and political laboratory of the present*. Paris: Èditions Dis Voir.

Gal, S. (2002). A semiotics of the public/private distinction. *Differences: A Journal of Feminist Cultural Studies, 13*(1), 77–94.

Galvin, N. (October 21, 2012). Just hook it into our veins. *The Age*. Retrieved from http://www.theage.com.au/digital-life/digital-life-news/.

Gane, N. (2007). Ubiquitous surveillance: interview with Katherine Hayles. *Theory, Culture & Society, 24*(7–8), 349–358.

Garnham, N. (1995). The media and the public sphere. In O. Boyd-Barrett, & C. Newbold (Eds.), *Approaches to media: A reader* (pp. 245–251). London: Arnold.

Gauntlett, D. (1998). Ten things wrong with the 'Effects Model'. In R. Dickinson, R. Harindranath, & O. Linné (Eds.), *Approaches to audiences – A reader* (pp. 120–130). London: Arnold.

Gibson, W. (1984). *Neuromancer*. New York: Ace Books.

Gibson-Graham, J. K. (2003). An ethics of the local. *Rethinking Marxism, 15*(1), 49–74.

Giddens, A. (1991). *Modernity and self-identity*. Cambridge: Polity.

Gilson, E. (2011). Vulnerability, ignorance, and oppression. *Hypatia, 26*(2), 308–332.

Giroux, H. A. (1999). Cultural studies as public pedagogy: making the pedagogical more political. *Encyclopaedia of Philosophy of Education*. Retrieved from http://www.vusst.hr/ENCYCLOPAEDIA/main.htm.

Giroux, H. A. (2004). Education after Abu Ghraib: revisiting Adorno's politics of education. *Cultural Studies, 18*(6), 779–815.

Glik, D., Prelip, M., Myerson, A., & Eikers, K. (2008). Fetal alcohol syndrome prevention using community-based narrowcasting campaigns. *Health Promotion Practice, 9*(10), 93–103.

Goffman, E. (1959). *The presentation of self in everyday life*. Garden City, NY: Doubleday.

Goggin, G. (2009). Assembling mobile culture: the case of mobiles. *Journal of Cultural Economy, 2*(1–2), 151–167.

Goggin, G. (2013). Youth cultures and mobiles. *Mobile Media & Communication, 1*(1), 83–88.

Google StreetView offers rare glimpse into eerie ghost town (March 28, 2013). *The Age. The Age*. Retrieved from http://www.theage.com.au/digital-life/digital-life-news/.

Green, L. (2002). *Communication, technology and society*. St. Leonards, NSW: Allen & Unwin.

Green, L. (2008). Is it meaningless to talk about 'the Internet'? *Australian Journal of Communication, 35*(3), 1–14.

Greenberg, J. L., Lewis, S. E., & Dodd, D. K. (1999). Overlapping addictions and self-esteem among college men and women. *Addictive Behaviors, 24*(4), 565–571.

Griffiths, M. (1998). Internet addiction: Does it really exist? In J. Gackenbach (Ed.), *Psychology and the internet: Intrapersonal, interpersonal, and transpersonal implications* (pp. 61–75). San Diego, CA: Academic Press.

Grodal, T. (2003). Stories for eye, ear, and muscles: Video games, media, and embodied experiences. In M. J. P. Wolf, & B. Perron (Eds.), *The video game theory reader* (pp. 129–155). New York: Routledge.

Grohol, J. M. (2000). Review: caught in the net. *Addiction, 95*(1), 139–140.

Grosz, E. (1994). *Volatile bodies: Toward a corporeal feminism.* St. Leonards, NSW: Allen & Unwin.

Grosz, E. (1995). *Space, time and perversion: The politics of bodies.* London: Routledge.

Grosz, E. (2001). *Architecture from the outside: Essays on virtual and real space.* Cambridge, MA: MIT Press.

Grubb, B. (January 11, 2014). Las Vegas consumer electronics show unveils heaps of gadgets. *The Age.* Retrieved from http:// www.theage.com.au/technology/technology-news/.

Grubb, B. (January 4, 2015). Is Netflix declaring war on geo-dodgers? *The Age.* Retrieved from http://www.theage.com.au/digital-life/digital-life-news/.

Hage, G. (2000). *White nation: Fantasies of white supremacy in a multicultural society.* London: Routledge.

Halberstam, J. (2011). *The queer art of failure.* Durham, NC: Duke University Press.

Hall, D. E. (2004). *Subjectivity.* London: Routledge.

Hall, S. (1980). Cultural studies: two paradigms. *Media, Culture and Society, 2,* 57–72.

Hall, S. (1993). Encoding/decoding. In S. During (Ed.), *The cultural studies reader* (pp. 90–103). London: Routledge.

Hall, S., Massey, D., & Rustin, M. (Eds.). (2013). After neoliberalism? The Kilburn manifesto. *Soundings: A Journal of Politics and Culture.* Retrieved from http://www.lwbooks.co.uk/journals/soundings/pdfs/manifestoframingstatement.pdf.

Halavais, A. (2009). *Search Engine Society.* Cambridge: Polity.

Happer, C. (January 28, 2013). Google Glass: augmenting minds or helping us sleepwalk? *The Conversation.* Retrieved from http://theconversation.edu.au/.

Haraway, D. (1991). *Simians, cyborgs and women: The reinvention of nature.* London: Routledge.

Hardt, M., & Negri, A. (2000). *Empire.* Cambridge, MA: Harvard University Press.

Hartley, J. (1998). 'When your child grows up too fast': juvenation and the boundaries of the social in the news media. *Continuum: Journal of Media & Cultural Studies, 12*(1), 9–30.

Hearn, L. (May 5, 2010a). The terrors of twittering: growing up in an unexploded data mine-field. *The Age.* Retrieved from www.theage.com.au/technology/technology-news/.

Hearn, L. (August 13, 2010b). A dose of i-dose. *Sydney Morning Herald.* Retrieved from http://www.smh.com.au/technology/technology-news/.

Hill, A., & Calcutt, I. (2002) Vampire hunters: the scheduling and reception of *Buffy the Vampire Slayer* and *Angel* in the UK. *Intensities: The Journal of Cult Media, 1.* http://www.cult-media.com/issue1/Ahill.htm.

Hoadley, C. M., Xu, H., Lee, J. J., & Rosson, M. B. (2010). Privacy as information access and illusory control: the case of the Facebook news feed privacy outcry. *Electronic Commerce Research and Applications, 9*(1), 50–60.

Hodkinson, P. (2007). Interactive online journals and individualization. *New Media & Society, 9*(4), 625–650.

Hodkinson, P., & Lincoln, S. (2008). Online journals as virtual bedrooms? Young people, identity and personal space. *Young: Nordic Journal of Youth Research, 16*(1), 27–46.

Holliday, H. (2000). Hooked on the 'net'. *Psychology Today, 33*(4), 10.

Hudson, P. (February 1, 2004). Latham's book pledge. *The Age.* http://www.theage.com.au/articles/2004/01/31/1075340895376.html.

Huizinga, J. (1949). Homo ludens: *A study of the play-element in culture.* London: Routledge & Kegan Paul.

Humphreys, S. (2003). Online multi-user games. *Australian Journal of Communication, 30*(1), 79–91.

Irigaray, L. (1985). *Speculum of the other woman* (G. C. Gill, Trans.). Ithaca, NY: Cornell University Press.

James, P. (2006). Globalisation and empires of mutual accord. *Arena Magazine, 85,* 41–45.

Jameson, F. (1985). Postmodernism and consumer society. In H. Foster (Ed.), *Postmodern culture* (pp. 111–125). London: Pluto Press.

Jaworski, K. (2008). 'Elegantly wasted': the celebrity deaths of Michael Hutchence and Paula Yates'. *Continuum: Journal of Media and Cultural Studies, 22*(6), 777–791.

Jenkins, H., & Squire, K. (2002). The art of contested spaces. In L. King (Ed.), *Game on: The history and culture of videogames* (pp. 64–75). New York: Universe Publishing.

Jenkins, H. (1992a). *Textual poachers: Television fans and participatory culture*. London: Routledge.

Jenkins, H. (1992b). 'Strangers no more, we sing': Filking and the social construction of the science fiction fan community. In L. Lewis (Ed.), *The adoring audience* (pp. 208–236). New York: Routledge, Chapman and Hall.

Jenkins, H. (2003). Interactive audiences? The 'collective intelligence' of media fans. http://web.mit.edu/21fms/www/faculty/henry3/collective%20intelligence.html.

Jenkins, H. (2008). *Convergence culture. Where old and new media collide*. New York: NYU Press.

Jensen, R. (2004). *Citizens of the empire: The struggle to claim our humanity*. San Francisco, CA: City Lights.

Johnson, L. (1988). *The unseen voice: A cultural study of early Australian radio*. London: Routledge.

Johnson, N. F. (2009). *The multiplicities of internet addiction: The misrecognition of leisure and learning*. Aldershot, UK: Ashgate.

Karasawa, M., Asai, N., & Tanabe, Y. (2007). Stereotypes as shared beliefs: effects of group identity on dyadic conversations. *Group Processes & Intergroup Relations, 10*(4), 515–532.

Kaveney, R. (2001). 'She saved the world. A lot': An introduction to the themes and structures of Buffy and Angel. In R. Kaveney (Ed.), *Reading the vampire slayer: An unofficial critical companion to Buffy and Angel* (pp. 1–36). London: Tauris Parke.

Kennedy, H. (2006). Beyond anonymity, or future directions for internet identity research. *New Media & Society, 8*(6), 859–876.

Kermode, F. (1967). *The sense of an ending: Studies in the theory of fiction*. Oxford: Oxford University Press.

Kim, P., & Sawhney, H. (2002). A machine-like new medium – Theoretical examinations of interactive TV. *Media, Culture & Society, 24*(2), 217–233.

King, B., & Borland, J. (2003). *Dungeons and dreamers: The rise of computer game culture*. Emeryville, CA: McGraw-Hill/Osborne.

Kiousis, S. (2002). Interactivity: a concept explication. *New Media & Society, 4*(3), 355–383.

Knight, D. (April 26, 2013). How to not get things done. *The Age*. Retrieved from http://www.dailylife.com.au/news-and-views/.

Korten, D. C. (1999). *The post-corporate world: Life after capitalism*. San Francisco, CA: Berrett-Koehler Publishers.

Kouvaros, G. (2009). Images that remember us: Photography and memory in Austerlitz. In G. Fischer (Ed.), *W.G. Sebald: Expatriate Writing* (pp. 389–412). Amsterdam: Rodopi.

Kristeva, J. (1982). *Powers of horror: An essay on abjection* (L. S. Roudiez, Trans.). New York: Columbia University Press.

Kubrick, S., & Clarke, A. C. (1968). *2001: A space odyssey* [Motion picture]. Metro-Goldwyn-Mayer: United States.

Kwon, Y. J., & Kwon, K.-N. (2015). Consuming the objectified self: the quest for authentic self. *Asian Social Science, 11*(2), 301–312.

Lacan, J. (1977). *The four fundamental concepts of psycho-analysis* (A. Sheridan, Trans.). Harmondsworth, UK: Penguin.

Lahti, M. (2003). As we become machines: Corporealized pleasures in video games. In M. J. P. Wolf, & B. Perron (Eds.), *The video game theory reader* (pp. 157–170). New York: Routledge.

Lareau, A. (2003). *Unequal childhoods: Class, race, and family life*. Berkeley, CA: Berkeley University of California Press.

LaRose, R., Kim, J., & Peng, W. (2011). Social networking: Addictive, compulsive, problematic, or just another media habit? In Z. Papacharissi (Ed.), *A networked self: Identity, community, and culture on social network sites* (pp. 59–81). London: Routledge.

Lart, R. (1998). Medical power/knowledge: The treatment and control of drugs and drug users. In R. Coomber (Ed.), *The control of drugs and drug users: Reason or reaction* (pp. 49–68). Amsterdam: Harwood.

Latham, R. (2002). *Consuming youth: Vampires, cyborgs, and the culture of consumption*. Chicago, IL: University of Chicago Press.

Lazzarato, M. (2004). From capital-labour to capital-life (V. Fournier, A. Virtanen, & J. Vahamaki, Trans.). *Ephemera: Theory & Politics in Organization, 4*(3), 187–208.

Lazzarato, M. (2009). Neoliberalism in action: inequality, insecurity and the reconstitution of the social. *Theory, Culture & Society, 26*(6), 109–133.

Lessig, L. (2008). *Remix: Making art and commerce thrive in the hybrid economy*. London: Bloomsbury Academic.

Levinas, E. (1969). *Totality and infinity* (A. Lingis, Trans.). Pittsburg, PA: Duquesne University Press.

Lewis, J., & West, A. (2009). 'Friending': London-based undergraduates' experience of Facebook. *New Media & Society, 11*(7), 1209–1229.

Lingis, A. (1994). *Foreign bodies*. New York: Routledge.

Lister, M. (2013). Introduction. In M. Lister (Ed.), *The photographic image in digital culture* (2nd ed., pp. 1–21). London & New York: Routledge.

Lister, M., Dovey, J., Giddings, S., Grant, I., & Kelly, K. (2003). *New media: A critical introduction*. London: Routledge.

Liu, A. (2002). The future literary: Literature and the culture of information. In K. Newman, J. Clayton, & M. Hirsch (Eds.), *Time and the literary* (pp. 61–100). London: Routledge.

Liu, H. (2008). Social network profiles as taste performances. *Journal of Computer-Mediated Communication, 13*(1), 252–275.

Livingstone, S. (2008). Taking risk opportunities in youthful content creation: teenagers' use of social networking sites for intimacy, privacy and self-expression. *New Media & Society, 10*(3), 393–411.

Livingstone, S., & Brake, D. R. (2010). On the rapid rise of social networking sites: new findings and policy implications. *Children & Society, 24*(1), 75–83.

Locke, J., & Laslett, P. (Eds.). (1988). *Two treatises of government*. Cambridge: Cambridge University Press.

London Hospital to Treat Internet-Addicted Teens. (March 19, 2010). *Sydney Morning Herald*. Retrieved from http://www.smh.com.au/technology/technology-news/.

Lucas, C., & Schneiders, B. (June 1, 2013). Dark side of the digital revolution keeps work front and centre all day, all night. *The Age*. Retrieved from http://www.theage.com.au/digital-life/digital-life-news/.

Luders, M. (2008). Conceptualizing personal media. *New Media & Society, 10*(5), 683–702.

Lumby, C., Green, L., & Hartley, J. (2009). *Untangling the net: The scope of content caught by mandatory internet filtering*. Report. Retrieved from http://www.ecu.edu.au/__data/assets/pdf_file/0008/29474/Untangling_The_Net.pdf.

Martin, P. (January 7, 2015). Netflix, Apple, Adobe. How geoblocks rip you off. *The Age*. Retrieved from http://www.theage.com.au/comment/.

McCoy, T. S. (1993). *Voices of difference: Studies in critical philosophy and mass communication*. Cresskill, NJ: Hampton Press.

McDonald, K. (1999). *Struggles for subjectivity: Identity, action and youth experience*. Cambridge: Cambridge University Press.

McLuhan, M. (1962). *The Gutenberg galaxy: The making of typographic man*. Toronto: University of Toronto Press.

McMillan, S. (2002). A four-part model of cyber-interactivity: some cyber-places are more interactive than others. *New Media & Society, 4*(2), 271–291.

McMillan, S. J., & Morrison, M. (2006). Coming of age with the internet: a qualitative exploration of how the internet has become an integral part of young people's lives. *New Media & Society, 8*(1), 73–95.

McNevin, A. (2007). Irregular migrants, neoliberal geographies and spatial frontiers of 'the political'. *Review of International Studies, 33*(4), 655–674.

McQuail, D. (1997). *Audience analysis.* Thousand Oaks, CA: Sage Publications.

McRobbie, A. (2004). Feminism and the socialist tradition. Undone? A response to recent work by Judith Butler. *Cultural Studies, 18*(4), 503–522.

McRobbie, A. (2006). Vulnerability, violence and (cosmopolitan) ethics: Butler's Precarious Life. *The British Journal of Sociology, 57*(1), 69–86.

Meadows, M. (1994). At the cultural frontier. In J. Schultz (Ed.), *Not just another business: Journalists, citizens and the media* (pp. 131–147). Leichhardt, NSW: Pluto Press.

Mendelson, A. L., & Papacharissi, Z. (2011). Look at us: Collective narcissism in college student facebook photo galleries.' In Z. Papacharissi (Ed.), *A networked self: Identity, community, and culture on social network sites* (pp. 251–273). London: Routledge.

Messerschmidt, J. W. (2008). And now, the rest of the story: a commentary on Christine Beasley's 'Rethinking Hegemonic Masculinity in a Globalizing World'. *Men and Masculinities, 11*(1), 104–108.

Meyrowitz, J. (1997). The separation of social space from physical place. In T. O'Sullivan, & Y. Jewkes (Eds.), *The media studies reader* (pp. 45–52). London: Edward Arnold.

Mill, J. S., & Acton, H. B. (1972). *Utilitarianism, on liberty, and considerations on representative government.* London: J.M. Dent & Sons.

Miller, V. (2011). *Understanding digital culture.* London: Sage.

Mills, S. (1997). *Discourse.* London: Routledge.

Moores, S. (1993). *Interpreting audiences: The ethnography of media consumption.* London: Sage.

Moses, A. (August 27, 2009). World of Warcraft addicts to get in-game shrinks. *Sydney Morning Herald.* http://www.smh.com.au/digital-life/games/

Moses, A. (October 4, 2012). 'Necessary evil' Facebook a hard habit to break. *Sydney Morning Herald.* http://www.smh.com.au/technology/technology-news/

Mougayar, W. (1998). *Opening digital markets.* New York: McGraw Hill.

Mulvey, L. (1999). Visual pleasure and narrative cinema. In L. Braudy, & M. Cohen (Eds.), *Film theory and criticism: Introductory readings* (pp. 833–844). New York: Oxford University Press.

Mum calls 911 over son's video game habit. (December 23, 2009). *The Age.* Retrieved from http://www.theage.com.au/digital-life/games/.

Munster, A. (2008). Welcome to Google Earth. In A. Kroker, & M. Kroker (Eds.), *Critical Digital Studies: A Reader* (pp. 397–416). Toronto: University of Toronto Press.

Munster, A. (2009). Editorial: Web 2.0. *Fibreculture, 14.* Retrieved from http://journal.fibreculture.org/issue14/index.html.

Munt, S. (2000). Shame/pride dichotomies in *Queer as Folk. Textual Practice, 14*(3), 531–546.

Munt, S. (2002). Framing intelligibility, identity, and selfhood: a reconsideration of spatio-temporal models. *Reconstruction, 2*(3). http://www.reconstruction.ws/023/munt.htm.

Munt, S. (2007). *Queer attachments: The cultural politics of shame.* Aldershot, UK: Ashgate.

Murji, K. (1998). The agony and the ecstasy: Drugs, media and morality. In R. Coomber (Ed.), *The control of drugs and drug users: Reason or reaction* (pp. 69–85). Amsterdam: Harwood.

Murphy, A. V. (2011). Corporeal vulnerability and the new humanism. *Hypatia, 26*(3), 575–590.

Nakamura, L. (2008). *Digitizing race: Visual cultures of the internet.* Minneapolis, MN: University of Minnesota Press.

Net Addicts get Clean with Hard Labour, Psychotherapy and Baby Goats. (September 4, 2009). *The Age.* Retrieved from http://www.theage.com.au/digital-life/.

New Zealand Ministry of Health. (2000). *Suicide and the media: The reporting and portrayal of suicide in the media.* Retrieved from www.moh.govt.nz.

Newman, J. (2002). The myth of the ergodic videogame: some thoughts on player-character relationships in videogames. *Game Studies, 2*(1). http://www.gamestudies.org/0102/newman/

Nguyen, M. (September 7, 2002). Switched on TV. *The Age*. Retrieved from http://www. theage.com.au/.

Nuyen, A. T. (2000). Lévinas and the Ethics of Pity. *International Philosophical Quarterly, 40*(4), 411–421.

Nicholls, B. (2011). Hardt, Negri, and antagonism: media and communication studies in the context of empire. *Journal of Communication Inquiry, 20*(10), 1–6.

Noble, G. (2011). 'Bumping into alterity': transacting cultural complexities. *Continuum: Journal of Media & Cultural Studies, 25*(6), 827–840.

Olivarez-Giles, N. (February 23, 2012). Google to launch 'Terminator-style' smart glasses: report. *The Age*. Retrieved from http://www.theage.com.au/technology/technology-news/.

Papacharissi, Z. (2002). The virtual sphere: the internet as a public sphere. *New Media & Society, 4*(1), 9–27.

Papacharissi, Z. (2011). Conclusion: A networked self. In Z. Papacharissi (Ed.), *A networked self: identity, community, and culture on social network sites* (pp. 304–318). London: Routledge.

Patton, C. (1999). How to do things with sound. *Cultural Studies, 13*(3), 466–487.

Pearce, C. (2002). Story as play space: Narrative in games. In L. King (Ed.), *Game on: The history and culture of videogames* (pp. 112–119). New York: Universe Publishing.

Penley, C. (1997). *Nasa/Trek: Popular science and sex in America*. London: Verso.

Perera, S. (2007). 'Aussie luck': the border politics of citizenship post Cronulla Beach. *ACRAWSA e-Journal, 3*(1), 1–16.

Petterson, C. (2012). Colonial subjectification: Foucault, Christianity and governmentality. *Cultural Studies Review, 18*(2), 89–108.

Pfarr, J. (January 23, 2011). Flick Facebook and tune in to real life. *Sydney Morning Herald*. Retrieved from http://www.smh.com.au/federal-politics/.

Philo, G. (1993). Getting the message: Audience research in the Glasgow University Media Group. In J. Eldridge (Ed.), *Getting the message: News, truth and power* (pp. 254–270). London: Routledge.

Philo, G. (1995). The media in a class society. In G. Philo (Ed.), *Glasgow Media Group reader, Volume 2: Industry, economy, war and politics* (pp. 176–183). London: Routledge.

Pilnick, A. (2002). *Genetics and society: An introduction*. Buckingham: Open University Press.

Plant, B. (2011). Welcoming dogs: Levinas and 'the animal' question. *Philosophy and Social Criticism, 27*(1), 49–71.

Plummer, K. (1995). *Telling sexual stories: Power, change and social worlds*. London: Routledge.

Plusquellec, M. (2000). Do virtual worlds threaten children's and teenagers' mental health? *Archives de Pediatrie, 7*(2), 209–210.

Poster, M. (2001). Citizens, digital media and globalization. *Mots Pluriels, 18*, 1–11.

Poster, M. (2006). *Information please*. Durham, NC: Duke University Press.

Powers, W. (2005). The massless media. *The Atlantic Monthly*, January/February, 122–126.

Poynting, S., Noble, G., Tabar, P., & Collins, J. (2004). *Bin Laden in the suburbs: Criminalising the Arab other*. Sydney: Sydney Institute of Criminology.

Prada, J. M. (2009). 'Web 2.0' as a new context for artistic practices. *Fibreculture, 14*. http://journal.fibreculture.org/issue14/index.html.

Privacy Battle Looms for Google and Facebook. (March 25, 2010). *The Age*. Retrieved from http://www.theage.com.au/technology/technology-news/.

Privacy Concerns over Google 'candid camera' Feature. (September 13, 2007). *The Age*. Retrieved from http://www.theage.com.au/news/web/.

Probets, S. (n.d.). *Semantics of macromedia's flash (SWF) format and its relationship to SVG*. Retrieved from http://www.eprg.org/projects/SVG/flash2svg/swfformat.html.

Probyn, E. (1996). *Outside belongings*. New York: Routledge.

Pryor, L. (May 8, 2010). Extract your digits and escape the world wide web of addiction. *The Age*. Retrieved from http://www.theage.com.au/it-pro/.

Pullar-Strecker, T. (March 11, 2010). Nearly one in 10 gamers addicted: research. *Sydney Morning Herald*. Retrieved from http://www.smh.com.au/digital-life/games/.

Radhakrishnan, R. (1996). *Diasporic mediations: Between home and location*. Minneapolis, MN: University of Minnesota Press.

Rafaeli, S., & Sudweeks, F. (1997). Networked interactivity. *Journal of Computer Mediated Communication, 2*(4). http://www.ascusc.org/jcmc/vol2/issue4/rafaeli.sudweeks.html.

Raj, S. (2011). Grindring bodies: racial and affective economies of online queer desire. *Critical Race and Whiteness Studies, 7*(2), 1–12.

Redhead, S. (1997). *Subculture to clubcultures: An introduction to popular cultural studies*. Oxford: Blackwell.

Reeves, J. L., Rodgers, M. C., & Epstein, M. (1996). Rewriting popularity: The cult files. In D. Lavery, A. Hague, & M. Cartwright (Eds.), *Deny all knowledge: Reading the X-Files* (pp. 22–35). London: Faber and Faber.

Reid, E. (1998). The self and the internet: Variations on the illusion of one self. In J. Gackenbach (Ed.), *Psychology and the internet: Intrapersonal, interpersonal, and transpersonal implications* (pp. 29–41). San Diego, CA: Academic Press.

Revel, J. (2009). Identity, nature, life: three biopolitical deconstructions. *Theory, Culture & Society, 26*(6), 45–54.

Rey, C. (2002). *Macromedia flash MX: Training from the source*. Berkeley, CA: Macromedia Press.

Rheingold, H. (1993). *The virtual community: homesteading on the electronic frontier*. Reading, MA: Addison-Wesley.

Rojek, C. (2006). Sports celebrity and the civilizing process. *Sport in Society, 9*(4), 674–690.

Rosello, M. (1998). *Declining the stereotype: Ethnicity and representation in French cultures*. Hanover, NH: University Press of New England.

Roy, A. G. (2006). Imagining APNA Punjab in cyberspace. In S. Marshall, W. Taylor, & X. Yu (Eds.), *Encyclopedia of Developing Regional Communities with Information and Communication Technology* (pp. 405–411). Hershey, PA: Information Science Reference.

Rushing, S., & Austin, E. (2008). Conflict and community: Butler's *Precarious Life* and land use public hearings. *Administrative Theory & Praxis, 30*(2), 246–252.

Ruston, S. W. (2012). Calling ahead: Cinematic imaginations of mobile media's critical affordances. In N. Arcenaux, & A. Kavoori (Eds.), *The mobile media reader* (pp. 23–39). New York: Peter Lang.

Salih, S. (2002). *Judith Butler*. London: Routledge.

Santos, C. A., & Buzinde, C. (2007). Politics of identity and space: representational dynamics. *Journal of Travel Research, 45*, 322–332.

Savat, D. (2013). *Uncoding the digital: Technology, subjectivity and action in the control society*. Hampshire: Palgrave Macmillan.

Saxey, E. (2001). Staking a claim: The series and its slash fan-fiction. In R. Kaveney (Ed.), *Reading the vampire slayer: An unofficial critical companion to Buffy and Angel* (pp. 187–210). London: Tauris Parke.

Schultz, J. (1994). Universal suffrage? Technology and democracy. In L. Green, & R. Guinery (Eds.), *Framing technology: Society, choice and change* (pp. 105–116). Sydney: Allen & Unwin.

Senshan, D. (August 4, 2009). Net addict son 'beaten to death' at camp. *The Age*. http://www.theage.com.au/technology/

Shannon, C. E., & Weaver, W. (1949). *The mathematical theory of communication*. Urbana, IL: University of Illinois Press.

Sharma, S. (2011). The biopolitical economy of time. *Journal of Communication Inquiry, 35*(4), 439–444.

Shilling, C. (2003). *The body and social theory* (2nd revised ed.). London: Sage.

Simmel, G. (2002). The metropolis and mental life. In G. Bridge, & S. Watson (Eds.), *The Blackwell city reader* (pp. 11–19). Oxford: Wiley-Blackwell.

Simpson, G. (1952). Editor's introduction. In E. Durkheim (Ed.), *Suicide: A study in sociology* (pp. 13–32). London: Routledge, Kegan Paul.

Skeggs, B., Moran, L., Tyrer, P., & Binnie, J. (2004). *Queer as Folk:* producing the real of urban space. *Urban Studies, 41*(9), 1839–1856.

Slater, M. D., Henry, K. L., Swaim, R. C., & Anderson, L. L. (2003). Violent media content and aggressiveness in adolescents: a downward spiral model. *Communication Research, 30*(6), 713–736.

Smith, S., & Watson, J. (2014). Virtually me: A toolbox about online self-presentation. In A. Poletti, & J. Rak (Eds.), *Identity technologies: Constructing the self online* (pp. 70–95). Madison, WI: The University of Wisconsin Press.

Smith-Shomade, B. E. (2004). Narrowcasting in the new world information order: a space for the audience? *Television & New Media, 5*(1), 69–81.

Smythe, D. (1995). The audience commodity and its work. In O. Boyd-Barrett, & C. Newbold (Eds.), *Approaches to media: A reader* (pp. 222–228). London: Arnold.

Soukup, C. (2006). Computer-mediated communication as a virtual third place: building Oldenburg's great good places on the World Wide Web. *New Media & Society, 8*(3), 421–440.

South Korea Takes up Arms Against Web Addiction. (March 17, 2010). *Sydney Morning Herald.* Retrieved from http://www.smh.com.au/digital-life/games/.

Spivak, G. C. (1999). *A critique of postcolonial reason: Toward a history of the vanishing present.* Cambridge, MA: Harvard University Press.

St Louis, B. (2009). On the Necessity and the 'Impossibility' of Identities. *Cultural Studies, 23*(4), 559–582.

Storey, J. (2003). *Inventing popular culture: From folklore to globalization.* Oxford: Blackwell.

Street-Porter, J. (March 27, 2010). I believe Facebook is a toxic addiction. *Daily Mail.* Retrieved from http://www.dailymail.co.uk/femail/.

Szorenyi, A. (2009). Distanced suffering: photographed suffering and the construction of white in/vulnerability. *Social Semiotics, 19*(2), 93–109.

Technology hasn't Made us Hermits: Study. (November 5, 2009). *The Age.* Retrieved from http://www.theage.com.au/technology/technology-news/.

Thompson, C. (2002). Violence and the political life of videogames. In L. King (Ed.), *Game on: The history and culture of videogames* (pp. 22–31). New York: Universe Publishing.

Tiidenberg, K. (2014). Bringing sexy back: reclaiming the body aesthetic via self-shooting. *Cyberpsychology: Journal of Psychosocial Research on Cyberspace, 8*(1). http://cyberpsychology.eu/view.php?cisloclanku=2014021701&article=3.

Tong, S., Van Der Heide, B., Langwell, L., & Walther, J. B. (2008). Too much of a good thing? The relationship between number of friends and interpersonal impressions on facebook. *Journal of Computer-Mediated Communication, 13*(3), 531–549.

Tsukayama, H. (August 9, 2013). Google Glass gives independence to people with disabilities. *The Age.* Retrieved from www.theage.com.au/digital-life/digital-life-news/.

Tufekci, Z. (2008). Can you see me now? Audience and disclosure regulation in online social network sites. *Bulletin of Science, Technology & Society, 28*(1), 20–36.

Turkle, S. (1995). *Life on the screen: Identity in the age of the internet.* New York: Simon & Schuster.

Turkle, S. (1997). Multiple subjectivity and virtual community at the end of the Freudian century. *Sociological Inquiry, 67*(1), 72–84.

Turkle, S. (1999). Cyberspace and identity. *Contemporary Sociology, 28*(6), 643–648.

Turner, B. S. (2008). *The body and society: Explorations in social theory* (3rd ed.). London: Sage.

Turner, G. (1993). Media texts and messages. In S. Cunningham, & G. Turner (Eds.), *The media in Australia: Industries, texts, audiences* (pp. 205–266). St. Leonards, NSW: Allen & Unwin.

Turner, G. (2001). Genre, format and 'live' television. In G. Creeber (Ed.), *The television genre book* (pp. 6–7). London: British Film Institute.

Urry, J. (2007). *Mobilities*. Cambridge: Polity.

Virilio, P. (1991). *Lost dimension*. New York: Semiotext(e).

Virilio, P. (1995). *The art of the motor* (J. Rose, Trans.). Minneapolis, MN: University of Minnesota Press.

Vukov, T. (2003). Imagining communities through immigration policies: governmental regulation, media spectacles and the affective politics of national borders. *International Journal of Cultural Studies*, *6*(3), 335–353.

Walcott, D. D., Pratt, H. D., & Patel, D. R. (2003). Adolescents and eating disorders: gender, racial, ethnic, sociocultural, and socioeconomic issues. *Journal of Adolescent Research*, *18*(3), 223–243.

Walker, R. B. J. (1999). Foreword. In J. Edkins, N. Persam, & V. Pin-Fat (Eds.), *Sovereignty and subjectivity* (pp. ix–xiii). Boulder, CO: Rienner Publishers.

Walker, K., Krehbiel, M., & Knoyer, L. (2009). 'Hey you! Just stopping by to say hi!': communicating with friends and family on MySpace. *Marriage & Family Review*, *45*, 677–696.

Walters, C. (October 18, 2009). Teen net addicts at risk of mental health problems. *The Age*. Retrieved from http://www.theage.com.au/technology/technology-news/.

Walther, J. B., Carr, C. T., Choi, S., Seung, W., DeAndrea, D. C., Kim, J., Tong, S. T., & Van Der Heide, B. (2011). Interaction of interpersonal, peer, and media influence sources online: A research agenda for technology convergence. In Z. Papacharissi (Ed.), *A networked self: Identity, community, and culture on social network sites* (pp. 17–38). London: Routledge.

Walther, J. B., Van Der Heide, B., Kim, S., Westermanand, D., & Tong, S. (2008). The role of friends' appearance and behavior on evaluations of individuals on Facebook: are we known by the company we keep? *Human Communication Research*, *34*, 28–49.

Wark, M. (1994). *Virtual geography: Living with global media events*. Bloomington, IN: Indiana University Press.

Wark, M. (1997). *The virtual republic: Australia's culture wars of the 1990s*. St. Leonards, NSW: Allen & Unwin.

Webster, J. G. (1998). The audience. *Journal of Broadcasting & Electronic Media*, *42*(2), 190–207.

Who's That Girl? Facebook Entries Stir Jealousy. (August 14, 2009). *Sydney Morning Herald*. http://www.smh.com.au/digital-life/digital-life-news/.

Wilcox, R. V. & Lavery D. (Eds.) (2002). Introduction. In *Fighting the forces: What's at stake in Buffy the Vampire Slayer* (pp. xvii–xxix). Lanham, MD: Rowman & Littlefield.

Wiley, J. (1999). Nobody is doing it: cybersexuality. In J. Price, & M. Shildrick (Eds.), *Feminist theory and the body* (pp. 134–139). Edinburgh: Edinburgh University Press.

Williams, R. (1975). *Television: Technology and cultural form*. New York: Schocken.

Williams, R. (1976). *Keywords*. Glasgow: Fontana.

Williams, R. (1977). *Marxism and literature*. Oxford: Oxford University Press.

Williams, R. (1981). *Culture*. Glasgow: Fontana.

Williams, R. (1990). The technology and the society. In T. Bennett (Ed.), *Popular fiction: Technology, ideology, production, reading* (pp. 9–22). London: Routledge.

Williams, R. (1997). Mass and masses. In T. O'Sullivan, & Y. Jewkes (Eds.), *The media studies reader* (pp. 18–27). London: Arnold.

Willson, M. (2012). Book review: material becoming. *Cultural Studies Review*, *18*(2), 321–329.

Wolf, M. J. P. (2001). *The medium of the video game*. Austin, TX: University of Texas Press.

Woo, J. (2006). The right not to be identified: privacy and anonymity in the interactive media environment. *New Media & Society*, *8*(6), 949–967.

Woodward, K. (2002). *Understanding identity*. London: Arnold.

Wray, R. (November 20, 2008). Our digital addiction: 727 hours of surfing, 27 phoning and 972 texts. *The Guardian*. Retrieved from http://www.guardian.co.uk/technology/.

Young, I. M. (1990). *Throwing like a girl and other essays in feminist philosophy and social theory*. Bloomington, IN: Indiana University Press.

Young, K.S. (August 15, 1997). What makes the Internet addictive: Potential explanations for pathological Internet use. Paper Presented at the 105th Annual Conference of the American Psychological Association. http://netaddiction.com/articles/habitforming.htm.

Young, K. S. (1998). *Caught in the Net: How to recognize the signs of internet addiction – and a winning strategy for recovery*. New York: John Wiley & Sons.

Young, K. S. (2003). Surfing not studying: Dealing with internet addiction on campus. Retrieved from http://netaddiction.com/articles/surfing_not_studying.htm.

Zizek, S. (2002). *Welcome to the desert of the real! Five essays on September 11 and related dates*. London: Verso.

Zweben, J. E., & Payte, J. T. (1990). Methadone maintenance in the treatment of opioid dependence. *The Western Journal of Medicine*, 152(5), 588–599.

Zweerink, A., & Gatson, S. N. (2002). www.buffy.com: Cliques, boundaries and hierarchies in an internet community. In R.V., Wilcox & D., Lavery (Eds.). *Fighting the forces: What's at stake in Buffy the Vampire Slayer* (pp. 239–249). Lanham, MD: Rowman & Littlefield.

Zylinska, J. (2010). Playing god, playing Adam: the politics and ethics of enhancement. *Bioethical Inquiry*, 7(2), 149–161.

# SUBJECT INDEX

Made in the USA
Columbia, SC
23 August 2017